REACHING YOUR POTENTIAL

REACHING YOUR POTENTIAL

Tap into your inner strength and discover the power to succeed

NORMAN VINCENT PEALE

JAICO PUBLISHING HOUSE

Ahmedabad Bangalore Chennai
Delhi Hyderabad Kolkata Mumbai

Published by Jaico Publishing House
A-2 Jash Chambers, 7-A Sir Phirozshah Mehta Road
Fort, Mumbai - 400 001
jaicopub@jaicobooks.com
www.jaicobooks.com

Published in arrangement with
Peale Foundation, Inc.
c/o Berlandi Nussbaum & Reitzas LLP
527 Route 22, Suite 2, Pawling, NY 12564

To be sold only in India, Bangladesh, Bhutan,
Pakistan, Nepal, Sri Lanka and the Maldives.

REACHING YOUR POTENTIAL
ISBN 978-81-8495-916-1

First Jaico Impression: 2016
Third Jaico Impression: 2018

Printed by
Trinity Academy For Corporate Training Limited, Mumbai

CONTENTS

FOREWORD

These days there seems to be a lot of confusion about whether there are any permanent truths to hang on to. So much is changing, and in the course of my life I have certainly witnessed many profound changes in this world.

But I have discovered that some things do not change. Because of that, I can write this book based on enduring principles that I have built upon in my lifetime.

First, I have found that the spiritual help available through Jesus Christ is the same today as fifty years ago. If anything, the method of living I have called "Positive Thinking" has gained greater acceptance throughout the years.

Second, the simple formulas for applying this spiritual guidance to everyday life are the same today as when I started to preach the Gospel. As we worked on this book, I asked myself, would people in the 1990s, trying the same methods, achieve the same results as someone I told about in 1970? It was exciting to answer that question with a resounding yes, because everywhere I travel today I hear similar stories of powerful results in the lives of people from many walks of life.

Third, the hurts and needs of people stay the same. Our clothes may change, or the ways we earn a living, or our method of travel. (I used to go everywhere by train and thereby met many interesting people.) But the basic human problems of inferiority, loneliness, worry, fear, tension, and doubt never change. I suppose they have not changed much since the beginning of time.

So, you are holding the result of those three discoveries. These concepts work when you work them; they are timeless; people still have the same needs that provoked the development of these ideas. My positive prayer for you is that you will find something for your life.

If I could get across just one concept, it would be this: *You are someone special because you have divine potential within you just waiting to blossom.*

Once you start with that idea, nothing can hold you back, because you will start to see yourself as God does: a person of wonder and beauty. You will find the source of positive attitudes that lead to belief, faith, hope, anticipation, enthusiasm—in a word, LIFE.

By now, I'm sure you have deduced that the germination of the material for this book came to me as I performed my function as a minister of the Christian Gospel. These days, there seems to be uncertainty about what preachers should preach and whether the teachings of Jesus are valid today.

To me, Jesus is simply the greatest personality who ever lived. He has the greatest thoughts of any philosopher. He has the greatest wisdom of any counselor. He has the deepest insight of any psychiatrist. But most of all, He has the greatest love possible for every man, woman, or child who was ever born.

Perhaps He summed it up best when He described His purpose in coming to this earth and walking among men. He knew that many negative forces would press upon mankind. He called these forces "thieves" who set upon unsuspecting lambs:

"The thief does not come except to steal, and to kill, and to destroy: *I am come that they may have life and that they may have it more abundantly*" (*see* John 10:10).

Abundant life! What a wonderful concept. That life is open to you.

Norman Vincent Peale
Pawling, NY

ONE

A Positive Attitude Works Wonders

Any person who needs a change within himself, or within his life, can have this take place by changing his mind. This, however, cannot be superficial mental change; it must be in-depth. Such a change can be extremely effective.

Are you, perhaps, facing a hard situation? Are you involved in some unsatisfactory personal relationship? Is there some other kind of trouble in your life? We could hardly enumerate all the problems a human being has to deal with. But there is a great answer to them all, and it is this: They can all be changed and you can be changed—everything for the better—through the magic of a positive mental attitude.

Now, a positive mental attitude, a phrase coined by my dear friend W. Clement Stone, is not just some cheery, blithe point of view. A truly positive attitude faces all the cold, hard realities of a situation and sees them straight. It does not desire to evade them—because it knows it can handle them. A positive mental attitude is positive thinking in-depth. It is vertical thinking: it rises to God, comes back to you, back to God, back to you; the power passes along a vertical line and, lest you think this is some kind of psychological dissertation, there is a text from the Bible that supports it. Romans 12:2 says, "Be ye transformed by the renewing of your mind." That means if you don't like the way you are now, you can change yourself by making a fundamental change in your mind.

Let us imagine a difficult situation. There does not seem to be any hope in it, any possibility, any potential. Now, let's bring two men with different points of view up against it. One has a negative attitude and the other a positive attitude. The man with the negative attitude will immediately, of course, be appalled by it. He will see no chance of light in the darkness. It is all impossible. It's hopeless. There is no chance of doing anything with it. So naturally, a series of unhappy circumstances develops from it. What else could he expect? His negative outlook emphasizes every destructive aspect of the situation. He is an expert at that.

Now, on the other hand, a man with a positive attitude, facing precisely the same situation, asks himself some questions. He is no Pollyanna. He knows the score; he sees the difficulties. But he asks himself, *What is God trying to say to me through this tough situation? There is an answer here, and I mean to find it. I know that, with the help of God, I can handle this situation and turn it to happy results.* Consequently, from the situation flow bright and happy potentials.

Isn't it strange—or is it? What makes the difference? It is how you think about something. It is whether you bring to a situation (personal, business, social, or whatever it may be) the magic of a positive mental attitude.

I admire the industrialist Henry Kaiser. He was a great big man, physically, spiritually, and mentally. He came from humble beginnings, but he had been raised in a Christian home, with a positive Christian spirit, and he believed that with the help of God you could accomplish anything. He had a principle that anything you can conceive, you can achieve. It was said of him that he never knew when something couldn't be done, which is a remarkable virtue to have.

During World War II, this country had to have more ships and have them fast, and the shipbuilding companies couldn't produce enough. Their methods were too slow. Kaiser came forward and offered to build them. Now, he had never built a ship, but ships were needed, and he was an American, and he believed that God would help him do it. I was at the meeting where he told a whole ballroom full of leading industrialists how he was going to build what they called "liberty ships." Some men sitting near me made the most uncomplimentary remarks about Mr. Kaiser: "He's a fool. He knows nothing about ships. How can he build them?" But Kaiser did build them, because he didn't know he couldn't!

There are so many people around today saying that society is going to pieces and the country is going down the drain. Let us hope these people never become the majority in this country—or we will be through. Fortunately, we still have people who believe that, out of all the tumult of this hour, we will build a greater world than ever before. With a positive attitude, the minds of all people can be transformed so they will see things from the standpoint of new and more profound justice and brotherhood than ever before. And these things will come to pass. A positive mental attitude—it's a magical thing!

I was reading the sports pages of the newspaper one day. These I enjoy even more than the front pages, because you know that there are pretty decent people on the sports pages. If you read the sports pages, you can stand the front pages. Anyway, I was reading about a football player named Tom Dempsey, who was then playing for the New Orleans Saints. He had just single-handedly won a game over the New York Giants. He was twenty-two years old and considered by some the greatest field—goal kicker in the game. With unerring accuracy, he would boot the ball right over the crossbar. He was a genius with the foot–because he was also a genius with the mind.

His foot was motivated by a positive attitude, for Tom Dempsey, big fine husky chap that he is, was born with a right hand without fingers and a half-formed right foot. He had to wear an orthopedic kicking shoe that cost him two hundred dollars. But with that half foot, he made incredible kicks. One sportswriter asked him, "How do you do so well, being handicapped?"

"What's that you say?" he asked. "I don't know the word. I never thought of myself as being handicapped.

And, as for the word can't, it's not in my vocabulary."

Now, how about you? Your difficulty, little or big–is it bigger than you? Or are you bigger than it? "Be ye transformed by the renewing of your mind." Know that, with Jesus Christ, all things are possible, *all* things; and you will be the beneficiary of the magic of a positive mental attitude.

What is it that undergirds this positive attitude? It is nothing dreamy or Pollyannaish; it is a solid fact, a fact that should be brought again and again to the attention of us all. It is the fact of who you are. Who are you? You are a child of God. You are a being in time and eternity.

You have a physical body and this physical body is a marvelous instrument. We take it too much for granted. Only God could have thought of the physical body. Only God could have created it. Look what it can do. Take, for example, a hand. It may seem ordinary. But look at the various positions and motions you can make with your fingers and your hand. You can turn it down and you can raise it up; you can reach behind and sideways. Think of the angles, the joints, the engineering that goes into that one small member of your body known as a hand! And that isn't all there is about you. There is the heart and the central nervous system. There is the blood vessel system and the bone structure. And this wonderful body isn't the greatest thing about you, either.

There is in you that indescribable thing called God's power. It is a power over yourself, a power over situations, a power over circumstances. If you exercise this power, amazing things can be done. It is through the use of a positive mental attitude that you have such power. Now, you must be humble about it. It isn't *your* power. It is God living within you. This is why we constantly urge people to come into a closer relationship with Jesus Christ. Why? He releases power, whereby anyone can manage himself and make a contribution through this inner thing called spiritual power.

One of the first stories ever published in *Guideposts* magazine was by aviator Eddie Rickenbacker, who was a great American and a sincere Christian. He titled the article "I Believe in Prayer," and he told how, in his adventurous life, the power of prayer had enabled him to face death a dozen times, look it right in the eye, and live. He said this was one of the things that made him believe in a protective Providence and in life after death.

He related an experience he had while driving a racing car, many years ago, on a speedway. He had it going at the top of its power. He was leading the pack, driving skillfully. Suddenly he felt a faint tremor in the mechanism. Now, he knew that, if anything went wrong at that speed, it could mean disaster and possibly death. But instead of thinking disaster, he prayed in confidence and faith. He sent up the vertical thought to God. And suddenly, he said, he had one of the greatest experiences of his life. He knew exultantly that he had power over that machine, that he could bring it in even if it deteriorated—he could bring it in, driving it not by his hands but by his mind. Rickenbacker said that if he had told other drivers of this, they would have thought he was crazy. He knew that there is built into a human being an enormous power, if he will but use it.

I once went with Rickenbacker to a hospital to speak to airmen who had been sent back from the fighting front, many of them broken in body and in spirit. I'll never forget him standing there, as he spoke to those airmen about the power God had put in them. He told them they mustn't give in to depression or defeat in the face of any problem. He closed his speech in this manner: "Let me tell you guys something," he said. (They all had their eyes riveted on him.) "If you haven't had an experience of God in your life, you get yourself one mighty quick, because with that you will have power over all your problems."

"Well," you say, "Rickenbacker was an extraordinary person." That is right. But so are you, if you will allow yourself to be. The trouble is that many people write themselves off as ordinary. But God never made an ordinary human being. Maybe you think you never could have power like this. But you really can, if you believe you can.

I once made a speech to a chamber of commerce in a southern city, and it was recorded for a radio broadcast later on. When I went back to my hotel to get my bag, I heard a radio playing in the lobby, and I recognized my own voice. I saw there weren't many people in the lobby, so I sat down behind a pillar to listen to my own speech, just to see how it sounded. After listening for a little while, I decided to go upstairs to my room and get my bag.

Now, the girl running the elevator was leaning there, chewing gum. I got in the elevator, and presently she pulled herself together and got in to run it up for me. I asked her, "Did you listen to that speech on the radio there in the lobby?"

"Yeah," she answered, "I listened to it."

"What did you think of it?"

"Well," she replied, "that man sure does like to hear himself talk, doesn't he?"

"You don't know me, do you?" I asked. And she said no, she didn't, for which I was profoundly grateful!

God never made an ordinary human being.

Well, I got my bag and, on the way down, I talked with this elevator operator again. She said, "You know that speech by that man?"

"The one who likes to hear himself talk?"

"Yes, sir, that's the one." She continued, "You know, there was one little point that got to me. It was pretty good."

"What was that?" I asked.

"Well," she said, "you know what he said? He said, 'Everyone has something greater in him than he ever knew.'

"You think you've got that in you?"

"Yes, sir. I know I have, and someday I'm going to go places."

Well, that was the last I ever saw of her. But from the look in her eyes and that sense of latent power she expressed, I have no doubt that the positive mental attitude, if cultivated, can give her power over her problems.

God has planted this potential in you and me, and it will never rest until it is realized—until you get yourself "transformed by the renewing of your mind" through Christ. It is Christ who does it. The greatest thing that can happen to anyone is to accept Christ, to find Him, to have Him explode in your mind, to become identified with Him. He is not merely the head of a religious faith or someone whose picture is in stained-glass windows. He is a vital principle. And when this principle connects with a human being, a great: transformation takes place. There is romance in the way people's lives can be changed through Christ. A man is weak, defeated, sinful, confused, and everything suffers accordingly. All of a sudden, God comes into this man's mind and soul and works a transformation, a miracle, and the man is changed. He is no longer the same person. Everyone can become a changed person by the power of God and the magic of a positive mental attitude.

Some years ago, I was speaking in a church in New Jersey on a Sunday afternoon. Sitting in the pulpit before speaking, looking at the congregation, I noticed the face of a certain man. The minute my eye caught his eye, he smiled at me and I smiled at him. And I sat there thinking about him, for this man is a miracle of transformation. There was a time when he was really licked and had become a heavy drinker, for that was the only way he felt he could live with himself. Everything was at loose ends. He was mixed up, hopeless, and running low on money. It was one job after another and all that disorganized kind of living.

Well, one day he was slumped over a bar in Brooklyn, as he describes it, about half shot. There was a radio in the bar and it was tuned—get this—to one of my sermons. And he was listening. Now, thousands of people listen to sermons and nothing happens. But once in a while something does. So here he was slumped over a bar. And something was said in that sermon about the immense possibilities of a human being who would accept God into his life to reorganize him.

The next Sunday, this man came to Marble Collegiate Church, and he was there every Sunday thereafter for a long time. He became a member of the young adult group. His life was completely changed. But, he said, it was not in the church or in the group that the change occurred. He was changed in that bar when an idea penetrated his consciousness and exploded in his mind. The explosion was from the sudden belief that God could change him. He experienced then and there the magic of a positive mental attitude.

Now, however the change takes place, it is valid. If you live your days thinking on an elevated, positive level with God, everything, including yourself, will change. Problems that you couldn't handle before, you now will be able to handle. Situations that previously you couldn't endure, you now will be able to endure or even change. Accept this concept. Tell yourself, "I will live with the magic of a positive mental attitude through the help of the Lord Jesus Christ." You'll never be the same person again–you will be a new person.

TWO

BE YOURSELF!

If you travel the whole world over, in country after country, amid the teeming millions of this earth, you will never find a person quite like yourself. And that isn't the whole story. To the best of our knowledge, from the beginning of time, *there has never been anyone quite like you.*

Furthermore, a genetic scientist has said that if you had 300 *billion* brothers and sisters, none of them would be exactly like you. What a marvel and a wonder of creation you are! When you look at yourself in the mirror you can say, "I am unique. There has never been another person quite like me."

Now, if you stop at that, you are likely to build up egotism, which isn't the idea. This uniqueness of the individual lays a tremendous responsibility on you and on me. I should say to myself, "I am different; I have a job to do in this world. If I do not do it, it will never be done." And you, too, have a job to do in this world. If you do not do it, it will never be done. There is no one quite like you. And I repeat, this is the wonder and the marvel of divine creation.

It is a good thing God made man, rather than man making man, for God has a sense of the uniqueness of the individual. If man had made man, we would probably all have been standardized types from a vast assembly line, with no infinite variation, no profound difference. God's creation of man is another example of the vast respect He has for each human being.

God tell us, in 2 Corinthians 5:17, how to realize ourselves: "If any man be in Christ, he is a new creature: old things are passed away; behold, all things are become new."

Now, how do we realize this uniqueness? First, the only way to approximate the greatness implicit in human creation is to *be yourself.* One of the basic laws of human existence is this: *Find yourself, know yourself, be yourself.* If any generation of people needs to relearn this lesson, it is the American people today. Historically, we regard ourselves as the greatest nation of creative individuals in the history of mankind. This nation became great because it stimulated individuals who regarded themselves, under God, as uncrowned kings. But through the years this idea has been

> *If you try to imitate someone else, you become second-rate. All great thinkers are people who dare to be themselves.*

eroded. A social concept has developed that depreciates individualism. Why the two cannot walk together is difficult to understand. But now we have become a generation of imitators; no one must be different from anyone else.

It is a dangerous thing to be an imitator. Ralph Waldo Emerson, in his famous essay on self—reliance, says, "Imitation is suicide." This means, I believe, that if you try to be anyone other than yourself, you kill your own personality; you actually kill your own soul. I sometimes think we ought to bring a bill into Congress changing our national symbol from the eagle to the buffalo, because we are more like the buffaloes today than we are like the eagles. The eagle is a powerful bird. He flies alone. He rises up with authority into the sky. He is master of all he surveys. He is an individualist and was selected in the old days from among the rest of the birds to be our symbol. But the buffalo was never alone. He always ran in a herd with the rest of the buffaloes. And friends, I call to your attention that the buffaloes are gone from the open range, but the eagles are still here.

The lesson is clear: Any nation that becomes a nation of the herd ceases to produce great figures. If ever the idea comes to your mind, *Don't be different, because people will think I am peculiar,* remember what Emerson said: "Imitation is suicide." If you try to imitate someone else, you become second-rate. All great thinkers are people who dare to be themselves.

I read once about the American musician George Gershwin. Gershwin idolized the great Irving Berlin. He was a struggling composer, getting about thirty-five dollars a week in New York City's Tin Pan Alley, and Berlin noticed him. Berlin offered him a job as his musical secretary at three times thirty-five dollars a week. But he said, "George, I advise you not to take this job, because if you do, you will become a second-rate Irving Berlin. But if you say to yourself, 'I, George Gershwin, am unique, and I'll be nobody else but George Gershwin,' you can become immortal." And that was exactly what he did.

Years ago, I watched the life story of Willie Mays on television. He is one of the greatest athletes baseball ever produced. But he wasn't always like that. Willie Mays idolized Joe DiMaggio. He watched how DiMaggio stood, how he walked, how he swung the bat, how he ran; he tried his best to be another DiMaggio. Finally, some wise coach said to him, "Willie, you have great ability. Don't be like anybody else. Be yourself." And he became Willie Mays. If you were to name the greatest players in the history of baseball, no list would be complete without the name of this man who became himself.

Almighty God put a personality in you, different from any other He ever made. And He means for you to bring it out, to let it loose. Be yourself.

My wife and I were once invited to dinner by friends who live in a swanky Park Avenue apartment. It was quite a place, but even in such well-appointed homes things can go wrong. The cook became ill at the last minute and we had to be taken out for dinner. By this time it was about nine o'clock. The restaurant we entered was so dimly lit that you almost needed a flashlight to find your seat. Under the cover of darkness, I asked my wife, "What is this joint, anyway?"

In a quiet, exasperated whisper she replied, "Don't show your ignorance, Norman. This is a nightclub."

Well, I hadn't been in one before and I asked, "Do you suppose I can get a sermon illustration here?"

"I have my doubts." But she was wrong.

After a while, a woman came out to sing. She broke every rule I thought was necessary to be a nightclub singer. She was about fifty and looked it. She had no makeup on whatsoever that I could see. She was as homely as a—well, she was homely. Her hair had no style. She wore no jewelry. She had on a simple black dress that sort of hung on her. Pretty drab description, I admit it. But when she started to sing (and she wasn't the greatest singer I had ever heard, either) she let her personality flow out. She was different; she was herself. She made a contribution to me. She taught me once again that God puts a personality in each human being and if we let it be itself, truly itself, it is a wonderful thing.

You know what we need in this country? We need more nonconformists. I would like to start a campaign to produce the greatest generation of nonconformists we've ever had. You might ask, "What do you want with nonconformists? We've got nonconformists."

I want a nonconformist who will out non-conform the nonconformists. We have those who are nonconformist against the Puritan tradition. But these people are now old- fashioned and outdated. We need a new generation of young people, and older people, too, who will be their own fine, good, honest, dedicated selves, who will be so different from the common herd that everyone will look at them in astonishment.

Do you know what people will say? "We want to be like them."

The second thing to remember is this: By the grace of God you can do tremendous things. It makes no difference how little training, money, or status you have to begin with. The great question is what you do with what little you have. I remember one of my classmates from Ohio Wesleyan University who spoke to me one Sunday morning after I had preached a sermon. He said, "Norman, I'm glad to be here this morning. I've been studying you and I just want to say you've done pretty well with what little you have." Well, at the moment that disturbed me, but afterward I realized it was sort of a compliment. Anyone can bring wonderful things out of himself.

It makes no difference how unfavorable your situation, how many hazards you meet, what adversities you encounter; you can do tremendous things with yourself. I know a lady who is blind physically, but she is not blind spiritually. In her blindness she has become one of the greatest experts on Mexican cookery in the United States. She once had me to dinner in her home in San Francisco and served a fourteen-course dinner, every one a masterpiece, and all prepared by her. Yet, people come around and tell me how hard life is. I have even said that myself. Of course life is hard; it is made that way. It is supposed to be difficult. But the great message is that you can be a new creature through Jesus Christ, and no matter how many difficulties you must face, you can develop a wonderful life.

As I rode down Fifth Avenue, I happened to look up at the Empire State Building. This, in its day, was the greatest building in New York City and it still is a marvelous structure. My mind went back to a boy who lived far downtown in New York in devastating poverty. When his father died, friends of the family had to chip in to buy a cheap coffin. His mother worked ten hours a day in an umbrella factory and continued working far into the night at home. The boy was a loyal member of the Catholic Church. He joined a drama society in the church and got such a thrill out of acting that he decided to try public speaking. He did so well that at the age of thirty he was elected to the New York State Assembly. There they put him on the committee on forests; he had never seen a forest in his life. Then they put him on the committee on banking; he had never had a bank account up to that time. He was so discouraged trying to read the bills that came before him, which he couldn't understand, that he almost decided to quit.

I am talking about Alfred E. Smith, four times Governor of New York State, once Democratic candidate for President of the United States, the greatest authority of his time on New York State government. He was a solid citizen who believed in the American system of freedom under God. And he realized his dream of building the tallest building in the world, the Empire State Building. I once sat with him in that building and said, "Governor, you have had a great career. Tell me about it."

He smiled and replied, "My mother always believed in me. She said there was something in me that God would bring out if I allowed Him to do so."

The great American story is that any boy or girl, however humble his beginnings, no matter what his education or his race or his background, has built within him marvelous personal gifts. These gifts can be brought out if he works and realizes that God never made another human being exactly like him and that he can do anything he wants to do.

So, if you are not satisfied with your life right here and now, say to the Lord, "Lord, I thank You for making me different. Help me to be different. Help me to bring out of myself the great person that is within me." What God can make out of a person is astounding.

A man started coming to Marble Collegiate Church when I was still the minister there, and I had never seen a more mixed-up, defeated human being. But he kept coming and one day he found Someone there, that Someone who can change any individual. I repeat and underscore, *any* individual. And He changed this man. Here is a letter he wrote to me:

> Dear Dr. Peale,
>
> When we think of all the wonderful things that have happened to us since we started going to Marble Collegiate Church, it seems nothing but a miracle. When you realize that six years ago this month I was totally broke, thousands of dollars in debt, a complete physical washout, and had hardly a friend in the world because of my excessive drinking, you can see why I have to pinch myself sometimes to realize that my good fortune is not all a dream.
>
> As you well know, alcohol was not the only problem I had six years ago. It has been said that I was the most negative person anybody ever met. Filled with gripes and all sorts of irritations, I was the most supercritical, impatient, cocky individual you could imagine.
>
> Now, please don't think I have overcome all these things. I haven't. At times I become discouraged with my progress. I am one of those people who have to do a day-by-day job on myself, and this I do. Gradually, by trying to follow the teachings of Jesus, I am learning to control myself and be a little less critical. It is like being released from a prison. I never dreamed life could be so full and wonderful.

Do as this man did and you will say to yourself with gladness in your heart, "How good God is!" There is no one quite like you. Be that one person God made and walk ahead, with the light of God on your face, and experience joy; release happiness and power. "If any man be in Christ, he is a new creature: old things are passed away; behold, all things are become new."

In the long run, you determine what your life will be by your decisions. Your decisions, little and big—and you never know when a little one is a big one in its consequences—will add up to what you become.

THREE

HOW TO MAKE RIGHT DECISIONS

How do you get the wisdom to make right decisions? In James 1:5 we read, "If any of you lack wisdom, let him ask of God, that giveth to all men liberally." A person cannot make right decisions consistently, except by stepping up his wisdom and stepping down his stupidities. Dale Carnegie, who wrote the book *How to Win Friends and Influence People,* was a great friend of mine. He told me once that he thought he'd write a book entitled *Dumb Things I Have Done.* I told him the difference between him and me was that I'd have to write a whole series of books to encompass the subject.

In the long run, you determine what your life will be by your decisions. Your decisions, little and big—and you never know when a little one is a big one in its consequences—will add up to what you become. You can decide yourself into failure or into success, into mental turmoil or into mental peace, into unhappiness or into happiness. A man remarked to me, "Let's face it; life goes the way the ball bounces." I don't go for any such idea as that at all! There is a deeper reality. You and I can decide, to a large degree, which way the ball bounces. We can control the bouncing of the ball of life's circumstances and outcomes, as we learn the art of making right decisions.

And how do we learn it? I repeat: If any man lacks wisdom, let him ask of God (really ask, *believing*), because God is liberal, and it will be given him. Believe, really believe, that there is an answer for you, and that God will give you the wisdom to find that answer. People who have become great people are those who have discovered that God will guide in all the problems of their lives. They have discovered that they can know God's guidance. This is no theory. I have seen it work in practice so many times that I could summon hundreds of witnesses to corroborate it. Let me call up two:

Some years ago, I had a pleasant friendship with the founder of the Kraft Foods Company, Mr. J. L. Kraft. He was a dedicated Christian, a great Baptist layman. He really loved the Lord Jesus Christ, and he had a tremendously astute mind. He was a truly remarkable individual with a simple but wise faith. One time, I got to talking with him about his early days.

Like many Americans, in the great tradition that has been a wonder to the world, Mr. Kraft started at the bottom. All he had was an old wagon, a horse called Paddy, and an idea about cheese processing. With his horse and wagon, he peddled his own cheese. Then he got two or three helpers. He told me he was always on the brink of failure in those early days. He said, "I would go home at night not knowing where I was going to get the money to pay my employees or to buy the materials I needed. But I always talked to God about it. I told God what I needed and asked Him for the wisdom to build up this business, so that I could do a service for Him in the world. And," he said, "God always heard me. God built my business."

He soon noticed, he said, that if he thought he had to have an answer to a problem by, say, nine o'clock Thursday morning, God might not give him the answer on Monday, or on Tuesday, or on Wednesday. But, if he really did have to have it at nine o'clock on Thursday morning, he then had the answer. And, if he didn't get it at nine o'clock Thursday, he would find out later he didn't need to have it then. When he did need it, he got it.

Mr. Kraft held the principle that if you need wisdom and you ask for it, and believe that there is an answer, it will come. He was one of the strongest personalities I ever knew because of his absolute, unshakable conviction that there was an answer and that God would give it to him. "Things didn't always turn out right," he noted, looking back on his career. "That was because I never was able to get rid of quite all the error in me. But to the degree to which you live with God, to that degree does error drop out and truth remain."

I have seen this demonstrated in some remarkable ways. For example, one night in Chicago I boarded a plane to go to Minneapolis, which is not a long flight. When we were airborne, the attendant sat down beside me and said she had a problem she would like to discuss. I said, "It had better be a little problem, because before you know it we'll be in Minneapolis."

"Well," she said, "it's a big problem to me. It's this: I've been dating two young men. They both tell me they're in love with me and want to marry me. The problem is, I don't know which one to take." She told me about the two young men and how she felt about each one—or thought she did. "Which one would you say I'm in love with?" she asked.

"Now look, this is not exactly in my line. Why don't you write to Dear Abby?"

"Because I've got you right here, Dr. Peale, and this problem really bothers me."

"Well, you've asked me, so I'll tell you. I don't think you love either. I wouldn't marry either one."

"But," she exclaimed, "I've got to marry one of them! I'm twenty-two years old!"

"Oh," I said, "don't let being twenty-two bother you. I still have an eye for feminine beauty, and I think you'll find someone. If you don't, they're all blind."

"You think I'll find the right one?" she asked anxiously.

"If you go at it the right way," I replied.

"What is the right way?"

"First," I said, "you must have a clear idea of just what kind of man you want. Make it specific. Can you describe the man you want to marry?"

"I want him to be nice looking," she said.

"To equate with your own looks, he would have to be. What else?"

Her face grew serious. "I want him to be a good man, a clean, decent person. And I hope there will be a lot of fun in him. Also, I want him to be a man who believes in God."

"Sister, you're all right," I said. "You've got a head on your shoulders. Now, what you should do is take that picture and hold it up to God, and just believe that you and that man will be drawn together in God's good time. But let's face it," I added, "maybe the man God brings you won't be handsome. Remember, the homely ones often turn out a lot better than the glamour boys. So don't press the Lord on that good-looking business. Be willing to settle for the answer you get from Him."

"I never thought of praying about a thing like this."

"Well," I asked, "aren't we supposed to pray about important things? And what could be more important than your lifelong companion, who will also be the father of your children? Isn't that something big enough to pray about?"

> *Often, we think of Christianity primarily as giving morality, or as giving sustaining strength in sickness or trouble. . . . But it also makes people wise.*

Then I really went all out. I said, "Every day, as you stand at the top of the steps of your plane, I want you to visualize that sometime the perfect man for you will walk up those steps and right into your life!"

"Oh," she said, "do you think he will?"

"Why not? In any case, you'll meet him someplace." And she did! He didn't walk up the steps of her plane, however. She met him at a church party while spending the weekend with her parents. "You know, it's wonderful the way things work out," she wrote to me. "The minute I saw him, I knew he was the one. He didn't know it—then. But it wasn't long before I got through to him and he knew it, too."

Everyone has a problem. And there is an answer to that problem. There is an answer to yours. So believe in that answer. Confide your desires to God, but be willing to take what He gives you. Believe that He will give you wisdom.

Often, we think of Christianity primarily as giving morality, or as giving sustaining strength in sickness or trouble. And it does give moral strength; it does give comfort, and peace, and love. But it also makes people wise. The more you live it, the more you have in you the mind that was in Christ Jesus our Lord. And you develop perceptiveness, astuteness, understanding, so that you have the wisdom out of which come right decisions. We can be healed of stupidity; we can be healed of dishonesty; we can also be healed of ineptitude. The second thing is to bear in mind that you never arrive at a truly wise decision unless it is a right decision. A wrong decision cannot turn out right, because it is wrong. Only a decision based on ethical rightness can be a wise decision. You may use some clever formula and get a clever result for the time being, but it won't hold if it has error in it. So be sure your decision is basically right.

J. Arthur Rank, the great British producer of motion pictures, who was also a devout Christian, held, they say, that the first principle of a decision is to consider, Is it right or is it wrong? It was said that often when Mr. Rank was with his associates and they were considering some problem, though he might be surrounded by fifteen or twenty men in a room, he would go into what he called "the silences." He had a remarkable ability to isolate himself behind a barrier of silence, even in the midst of confusion. And, in these silences, he would ask himself these questions: *Is this decision we are about to make a right one or a wrong one? Is there anything wrong about it, however small? It doesn't make any difference whether the amount involved is six thousand pounds or sixpence. The decision won't turn out right unless it is right.*

There are a lot of people in this world having trouble with decisions they have made, because they made them knowing there was wrongness in them. Most people know when a thing is wrong and when it is right. They may contend that they don't know. They sometimes maintain that there is a big gray area between the two, and you can't always tell what is right and what is wrong. I deny that. Wrong is wrong! You can squeeze it, and try to get the black out of it, and make it gray, until it almost gets to the edge of white, but it never quite does get white. It still has too much gray in it, which means basically it has too much black in it. Right is right and wrong is wrong!

This country, incidentally, grew great by following this principle. When I went to school, we knew right from wrong, because we had people teaching us who knew, and we had a culture in this country that knew. That was before we had characters like the present-day publishers of pornographic literature and other such people who have undercut the American concept of ethical values. But anyone who really seeks the truth still knows what is right arid what is wrong. If he doesn't, then he'd better ask the Lord for wisdom, because when you admit an unethical factor into a decision, you get unethical and unfortunate results: The thing isn't soundly based and it won't hold up; it will let you down badly just when you can't afford it.

A friend asked if I would stop by and talk with him at his office. He said he wanted me to help him with a business decision. Knowing what business he was in and that I knew not the slightest thing about it, I remarked, "Bill, I don't know anything about your business. Why do you want me for a business decision?"

"You know about God's business, don't you?"

"A little," I replied.

"Well," he said, "this is God's business. Come on down. I'd come to you, but I've got a lot of papers and charts on this matter that I want you to see."

When I sat down with him in his office, and he started describing his problem, he used so many tabulations and diagrams that I was lost. I found myself mumbling at intervals, "Yes, I see. I see." Actually, all I saw was an isolated fact here and there. Then Bill produced a sheet of paper with a tentative solution outlined and a list of pros and cons lined up in two columns. "Please take a look at this," he said.

I read it through carefully but still had no grasp of the total problem. "Look, Bill," I said, "I know less than nothing about this technical problem. But one thing I can do is pray that you get the right insights and guidance."

"I'd like to go one better," he replied. "We'll pray together. But first let's have a few moments of mind-emptying. I know I'll never get the proper answer unless I first get all preconceived notions out of my mind. And two empty minds will be even better than one!" So we sat there trying to get our minds blank. Bill then prayed aloud: "Lord, our minds are emptied. Please fill them with truth about this situation. I don't want to make a mistake. Show me the right answer. Or show it to Norman, so he can showme.

We sat for another five minutes in silent prayer and reflection. Then suddenly, I remembered something I'd seen in one of the columns on that sheet of paper. I said, "Let me look at those columns again, Bill—those pros and cons." He showed them to me. I said, "Now, Bill, I don't know anything about it and it's all pretty involved, but this one point here bothers me. If you'll forgive my saying so, it looks a little shady." And I handed the sheet back to him, pointing to the item I meant.

Bill stared. "Well!" he exclaimed. "Here you are, knowing nothing about my business, yet when we emptied our minds and prayed, you put your finger on the very thing that has been troubling me the most! Now, surely you wouldn't spot it by your own intelligence alone." Which was certainly a fact, and I knew that better than he did! "This must be spiritual guidance," he added. "It just has to be. And it proves to me that this item has to be changed. Privately, I've been trying to convince myself it was not unethical and really no one's affair but mine. It would mean a little extra money for me, you see, if I let it stand. But I've been kidding myself. So out it comes. And now we've got a decision that is absolutely clean."

And, as the results later demonstrated, it did seem he'd had the benefit of more than his own wisdom, for the amended answer (minus the shady item) worked out beneficially for him and everyone concerned. God's guidance is always available.

Our lives today are the result of the decisions we have made over twenty years, thirty years, sixty years, as the case may be.

What is your life going to be five years from now? The decisions you make in the next five years will determine that. Remember, you can decide yourself into failure, confusion, or unhappiness, but he who humbly admits that he lacks wisdom can find it if he turns to God, who gives liberally. If you really ask Him, believing, God will fill you with perceptive understanding, reduce the error, and enhance the rightness, so that you will make right decision after right decision, and your life will be right. And when it's right, it's good and creative and joyous.

FOUR

GIVE THANKS—EVERY DAY

Thanksgiving is one of the most important, most creative capacities of the human mind. As we practice it, assiduously and constantly, we develop a deep joy in living, even though life is filled with all manner of suffering and difficulty.

The individual who learns to practice thanksgiving activates within himself, and around himself, continuous victories and blessings from God. If you practice thanksgiving, victory, and joy, satisfaction will be engendered in your life and will contribute to the happiness of all those who touch your life.

The idea of systematically practicing thanksgiving is hardly original with me. Actually it came to me from a man who regularly attended Marble Collegiate Church in the latter years of his life. His name was John Riley. At the time of his death, he was the oldest practicing physician in the state of New York. So long had he lived and practiced medicine that he had actually been, at one time, physician to President Grover Cleveland. He had also attended to President William Howard Taft on several occasions. And he was what you might call a character.

Sometimes, when we use the expression "he's a character," it carries a deprecatory connotation. To my notion, "a character" is an individual who is different—and Doctor Riley certainly was that. On his deathbed, he sent me a message. He said, "I'm dying, and I want you to send a message to Dr. Peale. Tell him to talk spiritually to the people, and I will be working for him on the other side." It touched me deeply that he would think of me as he went through the valley of the shadow of death, and his message was a source of encouragement.

One day, as he was chatting with me in my study, Dr. Riley had talked about this idea: If a person would each day deliberately practice thanksgiving, he would thereby activate new sources of energy and power within him. He stood up before me, straight and tall—a very alive and obviously healthy man, even in his nineties—and said, "Every day of my life, when I rise in the morning, I do my exercises and my deep breathing, and then I have a prayer and give thanks to God for my good body.

"The body," he continued, "is a wonderful instrument. Think of the skill that went into the making of its intricate, interrelated parts and functions! When it works well, it is a thing of beauty and a joy forever. And, one of the ways to make it work well is to affirm it as efficient.

"So," he said, "I start at my head and I run down through my whole body: I give thanks to God for my two eyes that

> *Do not be unmindful of the simple everyday blessings God showers upon you. The practice of the art of thanksgiving produces joy and satisfaction.*

bring the world into my awareness. I thank God for my good digestion. I thank God for my joints, that they work freely and without inhibition. I thank God for the temple of the soul, and for the effectiveness of its operation over these many years."

I stood looking at this man over ninety years of age, the picture of health, and had a new sense of respect for the physical body, temple of the soul, created by the good God.

The body is one of those things nearest to us that we tend to take for granted, or that we disregard to our hurt. It should be an object of thanksgiving.

Remember Psalm 103:2: "Bless the Lord, O my soul, and forget not all his benefits." Do not be unmindful of the simple everyday blessings God showers upon you. The practice of the art of thanksgiving produces joy and satisfaction. I'm afraid most of us are deficient in the practice of thanksgiving, except on rare occasions. I've observed, however, that the people who live the most joyously live in what you might call a constant attitude of gratitude. They are astonished and delighted and receive the blessings of life with a sense of wonder.

One such person I have known in my life was William L. Stidger. He was, in his time, one of the most distinctive and persuasive preachers in this country. He was a professor of theology and, as that usually implies, a great scholar; yet he also had, to a marked degree, that quality known as the human touch.

At one time, Bill Stidger had a nervous breakdown, during which he sat for months in abysmal gloom and mental darkness. I remember the description he gave me of this nervous breakdown. He said, "I cared nothing about anything. Everything was hopeless, everything was dark, everything was black—utter despondency.'*

And how do you think he emerged from this? By the practice of thanksgiving. One day, a friend told him that, with God's help, he could bring himself out of his despondency by practicing thanksgiving. And this friend suggested the manner in which he might go about it. "Think," he said, "of people who have greatly benefited you in your life, and ask yourself whether you have ever thanked them."

"I can think of many right away, but I do not recall having ever thanked one of them," Stidger said.

"Well," his friend suggested, "why don't you select one of them and write that person an affectionate letter of thanks?"

Stidger gave it some thought, and he remembered an old schoolteacher. Let us call her Miss Smith. He hadn't communicated with her in years, but he began to think about her. He remembered the gift she had of being able to inspire. It was she who had given him an appreciation of literature and made him love the great poets. (I never knew a man who could recite quite as much poetry—deeply meaningful poetry.) So he sat down and wrote her a letter, telling her that her influence had been a great blessing to him and that he had never forgotten her. He wrote that he wanted to thank her for what she had done for him.

He received, in reply, a letter written in the shaky handwriting of an aged lady. "Dear Willy," she wrote, addressing him by the nickname used in his boyhood. "When I read your letter, I was blinded with tears, for I remember you as a boy and, as I think of you now, I see you as a little fellow in my class. You have warmed my old heart." She continued, "I taught school for fifty years. Yours is the first letter of thanks I have ever received from a student, and I shall cherish it until I die."

This brought a ray of sunshine into Stidger's mind and encouraged him to try another letter of appreciation, and another, and another, until he had written five hundred such letters! In the years that followed, whenever depression began to seize him, he would take out his copies of the letters of thanks he had written to people, and the happiness he had experienced in writing them would well up in his heart once again.

This is a scientific procedure for anyone who wishes to develop joy and satisfaction in his life. "Bless the Lord, O my soul." Forget not all the benefits you have received from Him and from His children along life's way. If you're a bit down and discouraged right now, why not thank God, and then think of some human being to thank. Call that person on the phone, or send a telegram, or at least write a letter to express your thankfulness. Tell your wife how much you appreciate her, for example. She'll probably be so surprised she'll give you *two* slices of pie with your dinner.

Another way to practice thanksgiving is to remember what a wonderful country we live in, and give thanks for that. We need to be thankful for America. I really believe that if we Americans thanked God each day for what this country is, we would remember where its greatness came from and would learn how to keep it great.

The problem of preserving our country is acute. We do not realize how easily a civilization can decay. I have been to Byblos, at the eastern end of the Mediterranean Sea, where you can see, at a glance, the excavated traces of seven successive civilizations, due to the skill with which the excavations there have been performed: Egyptian, Phoenician, Persian, Greek, Roman, and others. All mighty civilizations. If, at the height of any of those civilizations, a preacher had stood in a pulpit and said, "This civilization can die," his listeners would have laughed at him. But they all did die, and their cities were covered over by dirt and sand, and now a few crumbling monuments are all that is left of them. This mighty civilization of ours likewise has within it the seeds of death. All human beings have within them the seeds of death. You have them. I have them. It is necessary to counteract these seeds of death with those of life. Our civilization can die, or our civilization can live.

Edward Gibbon, eighteenth—century author, in his classic *Decline and Fall of the Roman Empire,* cites several causes for the deterioration of Roman power. The prevalence of divorce and breakdown of the home was one. Building up vast armaments was another. Enormous taxes that drained all incentive from the worker was another. Spending vast sums of money for bread and circuses, to entertain the populace and blind them to the decay of their political institutions, was another. Do these things sound familiar? In our thankfulness for our wonderful country, we should remember that its civilization was given to us by God.

This nation was originally established on a definitely religious base. I have copied down, for example, the beginning of the Mayflower Compact. Now, the men and women who came to this continent in the *Mayflower* were tough-minded believers in God, and they didn't accommodate themselves to everyone else's beliefs so that everyone would be nice to everyone else. They had convictions and principles. Nowadays, we are so afraid we are going to offend someone's sensibilities that everything is getting reduced to the lowest common denominator—with emphasis on the word "lowest." Here is what those who prepared the Mayflower Compact wrote first: "In the name of God, amen." That is the way the whole business began. "In the name of God, amen." There are lots of people today who wouldn't do it that way. They would work up something like this: "In the name of philosophical interfaith harmony, in which we are all brothers and all avoid voicing opinions to which anyone might take exception..." and so forth.

The Mayflower Compact then declares:

> We whose names are under-written, the loyal subjects of our dread Sovereign Lord King James by the Grace of God of Great Britain, France, Ireland, King, Defender of the Faith...Having undertaken, for the glory of God and advancement of the Christian Faith {they never could say that today} and honor of our King and country, a voyage to plant the first colony in the northern parts of Virginia, do by these presents solemnly and mutually in the presence of God and one of another, covenant and combine ourselves together into a civil body politic...

Is that old-fashioned? Have we gotten beyond it? Well, that is the way America began; that is what made it great.

When they got around to the New England Confederation, they wrote: "But all came into this part of America with one and the same purpose to advance the Kingdom of our Lord Jesus Christ and to enjoy the liberties of the Gospel." How things have changed! For example, one of the most eminent divinity schools in the United States used to have on all its literature, and in its buildings, the motto *Christo et Ecclesia*—"for Christ and the Church." This phrase was later eliminated from the catalogs because it represented too narrow a point of view. Apparently, that divinity school doesn't go 100 percent for Jesus Christ. It practices accommodation.

Now, maybe the school could offer some justification. But weak, willy—nilly behavior of this kind can never produce, or maintain, a great nation. As the outward emphasis on God has decreased, so have ethics and morals come to a sad condition—so much so that a Chief Justice of the United States not long ago made a speech on how urgently we need to recover ethics and morals.

I was reading an editorial in the *Wall Street Journal,* a paper that runs some of the finest editorials I come across anywhere in American newspapers. This editorial gave quite an extensive treatment to the Chief Justice's speech on ethics and morals, the gist of which seemed to be that we no longer know what is moral or what is ethical. Consequently, legal associations and business associations develop codes of ethics for their own observance: "This is ethical; that is not ethical."

Where did we originally get our ethics? Right out of the Bible. But now we have come to a point where many people believe that the ethics of the Bible are narrow or old- fashioned. So, for new ethics, they look to professors who develop them out of their personal prejudices or viewpoints. I, for one, am not about to let any professor in the United States substitute his morals and ethics for those taught in the Bible.

Are we going to become so liberal that we abandon the ethical and moral principles on which this nation was established? Do we or don't we believe in the ethics and the morality of the Bible? If we do—we who are Christians—then we should be committed and dedicated, thanking God for the goodness He gave to us through His Son, Jesus Christ, and for the benefits that have accrued there from.

The Chief Justice went on to observe that the home no longer teaches religion. And now that religion is completely taken out of the educational process, who, he asked, is going to teach us ethics? Let us thank God that there are still people who are reaching out for God to bring Him back into our lives today.

In conclusion, I would like to quote from a statement by Carlos P. Romulo, the Philippine statesman who served long at the UN, playing an important part in its development—a great, solid thinker.

General Romulo, before returning home to the Philippines to become president of the University of the Philippines, wrote this moving farewell to America:

> I am going home, America—farewell.
>
> For 17 years, I have enjoyed your hospitality, visited every one of your 50 states. I can say I know you well.
>
> I admire and love America. It is my second home.
>
> What I have to say to you, now, in parting, is both a tribute and a warning: *Never forget, Americans, that yours is a spiritual country.*
>
> Yes, I know that you are a practical people. Like others, I have marveled at your factories, your skyscrapers, and your arsenals.
>
> But, underlying everything else is the fact that America began as a God-loving, God-fearing, Godworshiping people, knowing that there is a spark

> of the Divine in each one of us. It is this respect for the dignity of the human spirit which makes America invincible. May it always endure.
>
> And, so I say again, in parting, thank you, America, and farewell. May God keep you always—and may you always keep God.

Each day, let us bless the Lord and be mindful of all He has done for us, as individuals and as a nation. Let us keep God.

FIVE

THE MAGIC OF BELIEVING

The mail received by ministers is sometimes most extraordinary. People are likely to write to us about the most intimate concerns of their lives. The subject matter may cover the gamut of human experience: from drama to tragedy, with comedy in between. I once received the following letter from a Baptist minister in California:

> I came across an interesting story the other day—about a young man who liked to play the horses. At a local store, he came upon a book entitled *You Can Win* and, thinking it was a tip sheet, he purchased it. Imagine his surprise when he discovered at the racetrack that it was a book by Norman Vincent Peale on how to win in the game of life! He tells me he didn't have any winning horses that day, but it was the luckiest day he ever had—because through that book he came to know Jesus Christ as his Savior.

You see, you never know where—or how—the simple message of the Gospel is going to reach a person. That

> *Believing ... is hard. It requires mental discipline. It requires self-surrender. It requires giving your whole self to it.*

young man got it when his attention was diverted from horse racing to a book about the magic of believing. His betting on the horses did not pay off, but the magic of believing, if he continues to pursue it, will pay off in dividends beyond compare through all the days of his life. Indeed, whoever applies the magic of believing to his problems, and to his life, will have wonderful results.

There is a text in the New Testament bearing on this point: Mark 9:23. It is probably one of the greatest gems of truth you will find in the greatest Book of wisdom in the world: "If thou canst believe, all things are possible to him that believeth." Notice that you are offered something tremendous, but there's an *if. "If t*hou canst believe," then all things are possible. Believing—in the depth to which we are now directing our thought—is hard. It requires mental discipline. It requires self-surrender. It requires giving your whole self to it. It isn't something off the top, or the surface, of your mind. It certainly isn't the glib recital of a creed. But, if you can overcome your doubts and your negativisms and really, deeply believe, you will thereby enter into a life transformed, for "all things are possible to him that believeth." This is the magic of believing.

Belief is factual; it is truth. The term *magic* is synonymous with utter wonder. The magic of believing is a manifestation of one of the greatest powers in the universe, the power of thought. By our thoughts, we either create or destroy.

You can build up your life by thinking constructively. You can tear down your life by destructive thinking. What you are this day is the result of what you have been thinking for many years. We become what we think. If you would like to know what you will be, let us say, five years from now, you do not need any soothsayer or fortune-teller to give you the facts. I can give them to you right this minute. Five years from now, you will be precisely what you think over the next five years. You will be a bigger person, then, if you think big; you will be a smaller person if you think small. We do not bear in mind nearly enough the creative and the destructive power of thought. The Roman Marcus Aurelius wrote, "Our life is what our thoughts make it." Emerson said that a man is what he thinks about all day.

Now, thought isn't something that is ethereal. A thought is actually a thing. It has substance. A thought is also alive. "Cut a word," said Emerson, "and it will bleed." That is a picturesque way of saying that a thought is alive. Emerson doesn't mean that literal drops of blood are going to come out of the word. But he is saying that, if you take a word that is vital and put it with some other vital words to make a thought, it can cause life or deterioration, according to the manner in which you use it.

Suppose, for example, you are a negative thinker. You are full of negative thoughts from morning until night, and you voice them. What are you doing? Something dangerous: you are activating negatives in the world around you. There is a law that like attracts like. If you send out negative thoughts, you activate negative influences in the world through the operation of this law of attraction, and you draw back to yourself negative results. There is no other way it could be. On the other hand, if you send out positive thoughts—bright, resplendent thoughts of faith—you activate positive influences in the world around you, and you draw back to yourself positive results.

Let's suppose you think fear thoughts. These thoughts activate fearsome anxious tendencies in the life around you, and you draw back anxiety results to yourself. If, on the other hand, you remind yourself, "I am a child of God, and God is with me, so I need not be afraid," you will be sending out positive thoughts of courage and faith, and if you keep it up, you will draw back to yourself thoughts of courage and faith. We get what we think. The magic of believing brings back to us the great things a good God gives.

I was in Charlottesville, Virginia, sometime ago. In front of the hotel in Charlottesville is a marvelous statue of the famous Confederate General Stonewall Jackson, who was in some respects one of the greatest men this country produced. Once, when Stonewall Jackson was planning an audacious Civil War campaign in the Shenandoah Valley, a timorous general—one of his subordinate commanders—came to him the night before a scheduled forward push. He said, "General, I'm afraid. I'm afraid that this is an improper deployment of our troops. I'm afraid our strategy is not sound. I fear we're going to lose a lot of men."

The great Jackson put his hand on the shoulder of this commander and said, "General, never take counsel of your fears."

If you take counsel of your fears, your fears will reproduce themselves. If you harbor doubts about yourself and your ability, and think of yourself as inferior, you will get back failures and limitations. It is very serious, friends, how we so often defeat ourselves by our thoughts, when by the magic of believing, we could be winning victories.

Years ago, I read a statement by the late American psychiatrist Karl Menninger that fascinated me. A man who had heard me quote this statement in a sermon once presented me with a wooden plaque with the words inscribed on it, and I keep that plaque in my study. I've had people come in, look at it, and want to argue about it. And I've had others come in and be inspired by it. This is what the plaque says: "Attitudes are more important than facts." You will sometimes hear hardheaded businesspeople stressing the point that facts are facts. And some people have the notion that nothing is more important than facts. But it just isn't so. The most important thing is not the facts but your attitude toward the facts.

One man examines a situation and says, "Well, those are the facts. There's nothing you can do about it. The only thing you can do is accept the facts." That is his attitude toward the facts—so the facts defeat him. Another man looks at the situation and says, "Those are the facts, all right. But I never saw a set of facts yet to which there wasn't a solution. Some facts can be changed. And where there is one that can't be changed, maybe I can get around it, or under it, or over it. Or, maybe I can weave that fact into a new pattern and live with it and use it to my advantage." His attitude toward the facts brings the magic of believing into play, and he defeats the facts rather than letting the facts defeat him. "If thou canst believe...."If you can only believe, then nothing shall be impossible to you.

One time, when I was speaking at a business convention, I spoke along this line—which is a theme I often touch upon, because I think it points the way to living victoriously. After my speech, a man came up to me and said, rather wistfully, I thought, "I only wish I could believe all that you said about the power of believing."

"Well," I told him, "one way is to practice believing it. And I would suggest you study the passages on faith in the Bible. It's the Bible that tells us, 'All things are possible to him that believeth.' "

"Where is that?" he asked, and I told him he would find it in Mark 9:23. Then he protested, "But, you just don't know my problems. I've got a lot of trouble. Being a preacher, you wouldn't understand that."

"Say that again, my friend."

"I've got a lot of trouble," he repeated.

I assured him that I shared his feelings about trouble but said that, when I feel I am having a hard time, I often think of a line from an old spiritual: "Nobody knows the trouble I've seen. Glory Hallelujah!" Yes, we have trouble, but we also have God. So, Glory Hallelujah! With faith in God we can overcome the trouble.

I finally convinced him to give the magic of believing a try. And what do you think he did? Like many other executives, he was accustomed to having boxes on his desk for the mail, reports, and papers he must deal with. There was a box for incoming items, one for the outgoing mail, and a third labeled "Undecided." The "Undecided" box usually had more in it than the other two boxes put together. But now, he got a fourth box and put it alongside the other three. He put a label on it that said, "With God All Things Are Possible." When he found himself faced with a tough problem, he'd write a memo on it and throw the memo and any related papers into this fourth box. There he would leave the matter, believing that, when the problem had to have an answer, God would supply it. He would pray about the situation and surround it with the magic of believing. Some weeks later, he wrote, "It's wonderful, the results I get from this box." This may be a simple, primary-school way to do business. But it demonstrates that believing brings results.

A distinguished Canadian chemist wrote a book I have kept at my bedside for years. It is called *Let Go and Let God.* You wouldn't think a distinguished chemist would write a book on this subject, would you? But this one did.

He was the late Albert E. Cliffe. He was a food chemist, one of the greatest in Canada. He was also a religious man and conducted a large Bible class in Toronto. "As a chemist," he wrote, "I have faith in science, and I can prove it every day. The salt we use so commonly is made up of two deadly poisons; combined in a certain manner, they produce a commodity which is absolutely essential for every one of us. This is the magic of believing the laws of chemistry." He summed up his views on believing by saying he was no theologian and had no desire to study orthodox theology in any university. "I simply believe that God is my Father and that I am His son, and that my mind is a part of His Divine mind—and by this magic of believing I can be in tune with that tremendous mind of His at any time I choose. And, by so doing and by so believing, I can gain the answer to any problem which I have to face."

He goes on to say:

> What you get out of religion is entirely up to you. You can make your faith a super atomic dynamo, or you can make it a routine affair without progress. You can be healed right now, and your healing can start at any time, regardless of how serious your condition may appear to you, if you will let go your fears and give God His rightful place in your life.
>
> How can you afford to refuse this man, Jesus Christ, when you see every day in your life what faith in Him can produce? This Christ became a reality to me many years ago; and the freedom from pain, from sickness,

> and from fear, which I have had in these intervening years, is what I am trying to offer you through the medium of these words today. What He has done for me, what He has given me, He is willing to give you, if you will try to practice the magic of faith, the magic of believing.

On the authority of the Bible and of human experience, no matter what your problem may be, or your difficulty, or your defeat, there is enough power in the magic of believing to overcome any or all of it "*if* thou canst believe." And you *can* believe, if you will surrender your life to Him. The magic of believing stimulates a wonderful flow of power. Christianity is a fount of power—of the greatest power in the universe. The Bible is a Book of power that contains techniques of power and formulas of power. Jesus, after His resurrection, said to the disciples, "You shall receive power when the Holy Spirit has come upon you" *(see* Acts 1:8). That was the beginning of the Christian faith: a promise of power.

How much power have you? Are you living on a great flow of power, or are you livng on a miserable little trickle? Do you have a great surging of power, or do you have just a little rivulet that carries you through some things but fails you in others? The law of supply is a great concept, and this law of supply is offered to anyone who will practice the magic of believing.

This doesn't mean you are going to get rich. Christianity isn't designed to make you rich; Christianity isn't interested in whether or not you are rich. The Bible says, "Cast thy bread upon the waters: for thou shalt find it after many days" (Ecclesiastes 11:1). You shall have every one of your needs satisfied, if you practice the magic of believing.

Sometime ago, I heard of a furniture manufacturer in Grand Rapids, Michigan, who learned this lesson.

> *The basic spiritual law of the universe, demonstrated by Jesus Christ, who gave His life, is that blessings come from giving yourself away.*

This man, using the ordinary procedures of business, got into difficulties and almost went broke. He was able to save the factory, but his credit was thin. The bankers wouldn't loan him money. However, he had a few friends who, out of sentiment, loaned him enough to get started again. But he said to himself, "Somehow or other, things elude me. I haven't got what it takes to do a successful job. I'm failing at some point."

Then he began to pray and read the Bible, and he got the idea of tithing—giving ten percent of his income and his time to the Lord. So, when he was ready to start his factory on a thin line of credit, he went to his office and knelt down and said to the Lord, "Lord, this plant, such as it is, is Yours. I accept You now as my partner and I will give the first ten percent, all the rest of my life, to You."

He began to make furniture again, and he kept giving part of his money away. As he gave, more money came back to him. Then his credit got better because his results were better, and the bankers began to loan him money. They were puzzled because part of the money they loaned him he used in his business, but part of it he gave away. They said, "That isn't practical." But his business grew, and he brought blessings to other people.

As you give, you gain—not only monetarily but in all of the more precious blessings of life as well. The basic spiritual law of the universe, demonstrated by Jesus Christ, who gave His life, is that blessings come from giving yourself away. Can you believe this? Have you got what it takes to believe it? If you can believe this, all things are possible.

Try it!

SIX

FILL YOUR HEART WITH HOPE

"Hope springs eternal in the human breast." And it is well that it does, for we cannot live without hope. With it, we can live successfully. It doesn't make any difference how much difficulty people experience; with hope, they can still go forward.

Hope! What a wonderful word it is! Write it indelibly on your mind. H-O-P-E. It is a bright word, shining and scintillating and dynamic, forward-looking, full of courage and optimism. With this word, let us begin tomorrow.

What lies beyond the threshold of today you do not know, nor do I. We can speculate, but we do not know. Inescapably, however, we must cross that threshold and, with the golden gift of hope, we can cross confidently, eagerly, optimistically.

Looking over a list of twenty-five persons who had written to me asking for prayers, I saw requests from Pennsylvania, North Carolina, Michigan, Illinois, Tennessee, Mississippi, California, Maryland, Arkansas, Florida, Indiana, and Ohio.

> *We have . . . three words:* faith, hope, *and* love. *Have that trinity in your mind, live by those shining words, and you have the secret of human life and life eternal.*

Lest you have any doubts about how much people need hope, let me recite at random from that list some of the situations for which people were asking prayers. "Diabetes"... "husband out of a job"... "daughter mentally ill"... "forty thousand dollars in debt"... "bedridden for thirty-eight years." There was a person on the list who had lost the senses of taste and smell; another whose son was in jail; and a woman who asked for prayers to help her overcome hate. There you are—a panorama of human problems!

Now, it is a function of the church of Jesus Christ to have a word for human desperation, human depression, human suffering, and woe. We have the word; or better still, three words: *faith, hope,* and *love.* Have that trinity in your mind, live by those shining words, and you have the secret of human life and life eternal. Faith, hope, and love. "Why art thou cast down, O my soul? and why art thou disquieted within me? hope thou in God: for I shall yet praise him, who is the health of my countenance, and my God" (Psalm 42:11). No matter what difficulties you may face, if you hope in God, the time will come when you will praise Him for your victory and for His goodness.

This life is not easy! It is often fraught with pain and suffering. But hope gives you a lilting upthrust that takes you above the suffering. Storms sweep down upon human beings individually. They sweep down over society. But if you hope in God and do the right thing, storms pass after a while.

No one ought to go through life without developing a philosophy about storms. Storms are to toughen wood; storms are to plow up the earth; storms are to test human beings; storms are hard, but one great thing about storms is that they always pass. And the things that are deeply rooted in the truth of Almighty God endure. So, if you are in harmony with God, you can have hope no matter how furious the storm.

I was once in Columbus, Ohio, to make a speech. I prevailed upon a friend to drive me to Lynchburg, a little town in the southern part of the state, some eighty-five miles from Columbus. I wanted to go to Lynchburg to visit my father's grave. After my father's passing, I ordered a gravestone, and I wanted to see for myself whether it was properly set. So, I found myself in the town where my mother and father grew up, where I had spent many a day as a boy. I went to the cemetery and communed with my father and mother. But it was not because they were there in the cemetery; that is the resting place of their bodies only. They themselves are not there. Neither are any of your loved ones in any grave.

After leaving the cemetery, I went up the street to the house that had been my grandparents' house. It had been sold to a woman named Grace Williams. Each time I visited Lynchburg, I would call and talk with Mrs. Williams. She was always kind to me. I grew fond of her, and I felt sad when she died.

I will never forget my first meeting with her. I went to the house. There was an old-fashioned bell in the door. You twirled it, and it made a musical sound. I twirled the bell, and a sweet-looking woman came to the door. I asked, "Are you Mrs. Williams?"

She replied, "Yes, and you're one of the Peales, aren't you?

I said, "Yes."

"Which one are you, Norman or Robert?"

"I am Norman."

"Aha!" she said. "Do I know you! Your name is written all over my wallpaper. As a youngster, you apparently believed in advertising." From that day, we were wonderful friends.

During that first visit with Mrs. Williams, I told her that I was much attached to the old-fashioned doorbell, which I could remember twirling as a child. "It evokes memories," I said. Well, I had just arrived home a few days later when a package arrived. It was the bell. Mrs. Williams had taken it out of the door and sent it to me. I still have it, and every once in a while I twirl it and go back through the years in memory.

The last time I saw Mrs. Williams, we were standing on the porch, and I said, "I see the old tree is still there. It must be one hundred, maybe one hundred twenty-five years old."

"Yes," she said, "that is a great tree. I love it."

"So do I." And I remembered a night, years ago, when my brother Bob and I were small boys. My grandmother had just put us to bed when a terrible storm came up. We could hear the wind whirling around the house, making a deep, whistling sound as though it came out of the vortex itself. And then the flash of lightning, followed by a clap of thunder. The rain was hurled in great sheets against the windows. The house shook. Bob and I were scared and, from where I lay, I could see, silhouetted against the window, that great tree. Seeing how violently it was being tossed by the storm, I was suddenly filled with terror. I always have loved trees and I loved that one. I turned to Bob and cried, "That tree will never last this out. It will go down." We jumped out of bed and scurried downstairs to where my grandmother was sitting by a kerosene lamp. A dyed-in-the-wool Methodist, she was reading the *Christian Advocate.* We cried, "Grandma! Grandma!"

"What's the matter?" she asked calmly.

"The tree! It's going to go down."

Well, my grandmother was a wise Christian woman. She bundled us up and took us out on the porch in the wind and rain. She said, "Isn't it great to feel the rain on your face? Isn't it great to get out here in the wind? God is in the rain. God is in the wind. Just look at that tree. That tree is having a good time with the storm. It yields to it, bending one way or the other. It doesn't fight it. It cooperates with it. It is playing with the storm. It is laughing with the wind and the rain. I don't think it will go down. It will be there for a long time to come. Now, you go to bed, boys. God is in the storm, and all storms ultimately pass."

So we went back to bed. Storms come and go, but a great tree stands. It stands because it has driven its roots deep down into the earth. That is why it can grow high. That is how it rides out the storms.

When people crash under storms, when they have nervous breakdowns or go to pieces in some other way, they do not have the proper root system. Send down into the soil of your life the three great roots of faith, hope, and love, and nothing in this world can shake you, for you will be living in cooperation with Almighty God.

Shakespeare says, "The miserable have no other medicine, but only hope." He also says of hope, "It is a great and healing potion." Hope is a medicine that gives you power inwardly. When you have hope in your heart, you stand straighter, you throw back your shoulders, you breathe deeply of God's good air, and your mind is filled with healthy thoughts.

The primary function of counseling psychologists is to help people clean their hearts and minds so they may have hope and thereby power.

I once received a letter from my mechanic, telling me my car was in bad shape. It needed to be fixed. On the enclosed card it said, "A clean engine always delivers power." Well, we had to have the valves ground and quite a lot of work done to get that engine clean. That is just as true of a human being as it is of an engine. Get the hate out of your mind, get the fear out of your mind, get the conflicts out of your mind, and hope will flow into it. Then you will have the power to live, for with hope come aliveness, enthusiasm, vibrancy, and vitality.

A friend of mine sent me a quotation from Elbert Hubbard, one of the greatest inspirational writers this country ever produced. He is worth reading. His writings glow with vitality. Here, from Elbert Hubbard, is a priceless piece of writing that is full of the hope and power with which we should live today:

> Whenever you go out of doors, draw the chin in, carry the crown of the head high, and fill the lungs to the utmost; drink in the sunshine; greet your friends with a smile and put soul into every handclasp.
>
> Do not fear being misunderstood and do not waste a minute thinking about your enemies. Try to fix firmly in your mind what you would like to do, and then, without veering of direction, you will move straight to the goal. Keep your mind on the great and splendid things you would like to do, and then, as the days go gliding by, you will find yourself unconsciously

> seizing upon the opportunities that are required for the fulfillment of your desire.
>
> Picture in your mind the able, earnest, useful person you desire to be, and the thought you hold is hourly transforming you into that particular individual.
>
> Thought is supreme. Preserve a right mental attitude—the attitude of courage, frankness, and good cheer. To think rightly is to create. All things come through desire and every sincere prayer is answered. We become like that on which our thoughts are fixed.

These words of Elbert Hubbard are as sound as the good earth on which we stand. How do they apply to you? What do you habitually think about yourself? Do you think of yourself as old and weary, or as sick or discouraged or gloomy? Do you think of yourself as having no ability? Do you think of yourself as defeated? Then, in the name of God, get some hope into your mind and change that thought pattern, for otherwise your living will be as negative as your thoughts.

So pull yourself up—physically, mentally, spiritually. Do it by filling your mind with the Bible and with hope. "Hope thou in God: for I shall yet praise him, who is the health of my countenance" (Psalm 42:11). As you hope in Him, trust in Him, serve Him, you will have health in your countenance because you will have health all through you— body, mind, and spirit.

Pull the fresh air into your lungs and hope into your mind. Remember that you do not go into the world alone but with God, who has walked with you ever since you were a child; and that the Lord Jesus Christ is with you, too. Begin tomorrow with hope. Unlock the mysterious door of the future with the golden key of hope in God.

SEVEN

HEALED—BY THE GREAT PHYSICIAN

At intervals, I feel it is my duty as a Christian minister to deal with the subject of the healing power of faith. This isn't the easiest topic in the world to handle, and it was a long road by which I personally came to a complete belief in the healing power of faith. I was reared in a family of ministers and physicians and always took a rather coldly scientific view of the healing process. I abhorred anything that smacked of quackery. But some years ago, I had a profound experience that changed my attitude.

One night, I was awakened by the insistent ringing of the telephone. I snapped on the light, looked at my clock, and saw that it was 2:00 A.M. Picking up the telephone receiver, I heard the familiar voice of a close friend of mine, a leading physician in Syracuse, New York, where this experience took place. My friend apologized, "Norman, I'm sorry to awaken you, but I have a patient about whom I am greatly concerned. I cannot seem to bring about a crisis. I need help. Will you come and join me here?"

"What in the world could I do to help you, except pray?"

He rebuked me, "What could possibly be more powerful than prayer? Please come."

I went. But I was nervous. Before ringing the doorbell, I stopped and prayed and asked the Lord to guide my faltering efforts. The doctor admitted me. "My patient is very ill. What I want you to do is join me in filling this sickroom to overflowing with the healing power of Jesus Christ." You may think that is a strange way for a physician to talk, but it was not so strange. And this particular physician was a member of many learned societies, one of the most highly respected men of medicine of his time.

I looked at the woman in the bed. Her face was white. She seemed to me to be in a deep coma. I whispered, "What are her chances?"

"I've had consultations," he answered. "I've done all I can. It is now in the hands of the Great Physician. But," he said, "don't minimize Him. He has great power." He motioned me to a seat and took one himself on the other side of the bed. "Let us pray silently and in–depth for her, trying to drive our prayers into her consciousness."

Thus we prayed. I opened my eyes once and looked across at him. I told him later, "If, when I am dying, I can look up and see your face by my bed, I'll have confidence and serenity."

Then the doctor began to quote healing passages of Scripture and nodded to me to do the same. I did. Then he quoted more passages. It seemed as though they just welled up out of him, until we could sense Jesus Christ in that room. I started quoting passages of Scripture that I didn't feel I could remember in their entirety. For some strange reason, I found myself quoting them almost verbatim. They had been buried in my subconscious. My conscious mind didn't know them, but my subconscious mind did, and God gave them back to me.

This went on for some time. Finally, color began to come into the woman's cheeks. Then the most amazing thing happened: She opened her eyes wide, looked at us both, and then started to recite Scripture passages herself.

Later the doctor said to me, "The crisis has passed. She will sleep now. I'm sure she will get well." Which shc did—and lived for many years thereafter.

As I left that house, my friend went to the door with me, commenting, "Jesus isn't dead, is He? He was in this house tonight." Neither of us could speak easily, we were so moved by His presence.

It was by now 5:00 A.M. Sleep was of no concern to me at all; I was so excited. I had never felt more alive, more awake, in my life. I could hardly contain myself. I remember that I walked for a long time, overwhelmed by the wonder and the glory and the majesty of it all, with a whole new consciousness of the power of God dawning in my mind: We heal through God's servants the doctors, and we also heal through our own faith.

I found myself remembering one of the most beautiful scenes described in the New Testament. Jesus was on a plain near the sea. A great multitude had gathered. Great multitudes always gather when He is present, because no one has ever been loved as He is loved. The Bible says,

"And the whole multitude sought to touch him: for there went virtue out of him, and healed them all" (Luke 6:19). In the King James Version of the Bible, from which I have just quoted, the word *virtue* is often used in a larger sense, in which it means the power of goodness or, as one modern dictionary gives it, the "active quality of power." The Revised Standard Version renders this text: "For power came forth from him and healed them all."

The Bible also says that Jesus Christ is "the same yesterday, and to day, and for ever" (Hebrews 13:8). He has not lost His ancient skill. The multitudes still gather today; and I tell you, in His name, that if we really seek to touch Him, power will come out of Him and heal us all!

How does this healing power operate? It heals the body, but that is secondary. The real sickness of man is in his mind and in his soul. And this is the unity that Jesus Christ makes whole. When you are whole in soul, mind, and body, you live with power and joy.

A prominent Japanese physician with whom I am acquainted says he has found that physical disability, or illness, is often traceable to some disorder of mind, heart, or relationship with other people. "The disability," he says, "arises out of this disorder." This physician doesn't happen to be a Christian. He is a Japanese Buddhist. But he makes the statement that if some power could eliminate disorder from people's lives, their health quotient would be high indeed.

There is a physician in the Midwest who said, "If I can get people into the area of pure joy, even for one minute every day, I can keep them well." And what is this area of pure joy? "It is a perfect contact with Jesus Christ, the Great Physician," said the doctor. "There is healing in His touch." So, whatever disorder you have in your life, bring it to the Lord, and ask Him to straighten it out.

I have a book entitled *God Is Able* by a former New York City colleague, Dr. John Ellis Large, who was once rector of the Church of the Heavenly Rest on Fifth Avenue. Dr. Large had much experience in the healing ministry. He told about a man named George. This man's wife, Sarah, was one of Dr. Large' s parishioners, although she never came to church or had anything to do with the religious life of the church, except when she got into trouble. One day she came to see him and said, "Dr. Large, I shouldn't take your time. I've been on your church rolls, but I'm what is commonly known as 'dead wood.' But," she said, "I have a real problem. It is my husband. My husband isn't well. He's irritable; he's irascible; he's full of tension; he's on edge all the time. He's a disappointed, frustrated, unhappy man. And he's developed all sorts of symptoms of poor physical health. He has gone to the doctor, and the doctor says there isn't anything really wrong with him that wouldn't be straightened out if he got his life in order.

"I've tried to talk to him about it," she continued, "but he just swears at me. It's difficult. He misses one promotion after another at the office. All the men he started out with in his company have moved ahead faster than he has. This fills him with indignation and resentment. I talked with his boss. He said, 'George is contentious; he is not cooperative; he doesn't play ball; he has no enthusiasm; and he is full of meanness.'

So Dr. Large suggested to this troubled wife, "Why don't you bring your husband to see me?"

"He would never come," she replied. "He has no use for you, or any minister, or for the church. I can't even get him to pray with me. He says he is fed up with God. He says he doubts there really is a God."

"Well, then," said Dr. Large, "let us give him some treatment at home." And he asked her this peculiar question: "What are your husband's sleeping habits?"

"He tosses most of the night," she said, "wears himself out groaning and moaning, but by five o'clock in the morning he is in a deep sleep. And I have to wake him up to get him to the office."

"All right," the rector said, "at five o'clock every morning, you get up and sit by your husband, and pray for him. Believe that Jesus Christ is there by your husband's side, actually present with you and with him. Imagine your husband as a whole man—happy, controlled, organized, and well. Hold that thought in your mind, for an image will become a fact as you hold it. Think of your prayers as reaching his unconscious. At that time in the morning, his conscious mind is not resisting and you can get an idea into his unconscious.

"Visualize him as kindly, cooperative, happy, creative, and enthusiastic."

"Why," she exclaimed, "I never heard anything like that before!"

"Well, it's time you heard it," he told her. "You go and do it."

She said, afterward, that she soon got so she didn't need an alarm clock. She would wake up promptly at 5:00 A.M. and hover over her husband in the company of Christ, projecting these thoughts and prayers into his unconscious. For many weeks, nothing seemed to happen. Finally, George said to her one day, "You know, it's strange how nice everybody has become—people I used to think were hating me and double-crossing me and everything. What's come over them? They're all so nice. Everything is so different."

Some days later, he came to her when he arrived home from work and said, "What do you know! The boss is making me a division manager. I asked him why in the world he would do that. And he said, 'Because of the great change in you. You're happy; you're cooperative; you play ball; you're enthusiastic—you're becoming one of the best men we have.'

His wife never did tell him how he was reached. But the disorder left his life. The power of Jesus Christ is very skillful. "God moves in a mysterious way, His wonders to perform . . . " said the eighteenth-century poet William Cowper. No wonder the multitudes two thousand years ago sought to touch Him, and power came out of Him and healed them all! And today, twenty centuries later, He is still the greatest healer among all the great healers of the world.

Peret, the great French physician, said, "I treat the patient, but God alone can heal him." And I know a surgeon who, when he has completed an operation and is washing up, says, "Now, it's up to You." So Jesus Christ is still the supreme Master of human illness.

An important factor in the matter is this: Good emotions make us well; bad emotions make us sick. What are bad emotions? Anger, hate, resentment, fear. And what are good emotions? Faith, joy, happiness, love. Dr. John A. Schindler, in his book *How to Live 365 Days a Year,* says, "The Ochsner Clinic in New Orleans published a paper stating that 74 percent of 500 consecutive patients admitted to the department handling gastrointestinal diseases were found to be suffering from emotionally induced illness." Imagine, all those people made ill because of bad emotions. That is not from the pulpit; that is from a clinic.

> *The House of God, ordinarily called a church, is actually a spiritual hospital to which people come with diseases: diseases in their bodies, in their minds, or in their souls. Here, the Great Physician touches them and makes them well.*

Dr. George Crile, who used to run a great clinic in Cleveland, years ago said there are three things that cause more human sickness than anything else: fear, anger, and guilt. They produce weariness and lack of vitality.

The House of God, ordinarily called a church, is actually a spiritual hospital to which people come with diseases: diseases in their bodies, in their minds, or in their souls. Here, the Great Physician touches them and makes them well. I really do believe this. "And the whole multitude sought to touch him: for there went virtue out of him, and healed them all" (Luke 6:19).

From disorder in our lives, and from bad emotions—as contrasted to good emotions—we develop illness. But illness can be cured by the mysterious healing power of faith. I don't pretend to understand this power. I only witness to the fact that it exists and performs wonders.

In some cases, healing doesn't come. That may be because proper conditions are not present in our lives. There comes a time for every man to die, but sometimes we can postpone this through the power of faith.

There is a wonderful book written by Gertrude McKelvey entitled *Finding God's Healing Power.* The author researched every center in this country where spiritual healing is practiced. She talked with men such as the Reverend Dr. Alfred Price, Bishop Austin Pardue, Dr. John Sutherland Bonnell, and other great men in this field.

She tells the story of a man named Wesley Hablett. I want to give it to you in her own words:

> Wesley Hablett opened his eyes to see his surgeon standing quietly by his bed. He realized slowly that the doctor, whom we shall call Dr. Jones, had come to give him the final report on his operation. His thoughts now went back to his conversation with the surgeon just before entering the hospital.
>
> "Dr. Jones, I can take it. I'm a grown man," he had said. "So promise me you will tell me the truth when you know it."
>
> Five full days had passed since he had been wheeled back to his bed from surgery. For other patients about him in the small ward, this period meant healing and recovery. About his own case, he was not so sure, since his operation had been performed to remove a malignant tumor from his spine. Now, he would learn the truth.
>
> Dr. Jones was reviewing the operation. He had found it possible to remove only part of the tumor, since cancer had spread, making it difficult to determine where the diseased cells stopped and the healthy cells began. Fifty-year-old Wesley Hablett, sensing the truth, went right to the point. "How long have I got, Dr. Jones?" he asked.
>
> This outstanding neurological surgeon, a man of great faith, pulled the curtain around his patient's bed to ensure privacy, and sat down. This was not the first time he had been compelled to bring a hopeless report, yet each time it seemed more difficult.

He gave the answer quickly, "If you want to know how long I *think* you will live, then I would say about six months. But we both know that only God knows the answer."

A long silence followed, one of those times when, as so often happens in a doctor-patient relationship, a feeling of trust, compassion and gratitude akin to love possessed each. The surgeon broke the silence by asking: "Would you like me to pray with you?"

Wesley Hablett nodded. The surgeon's hand slipped into his pocket, came up with a small Testament from which he read quietly, then prayed. Another silence followed as these two men thought of their Savior and His redeeming love. They had not asked for healing, but for strength to carry out God's will for their lives.

Two weeks later, Dr. Jones was able to discharge his patient. He has remained in excellent physical condition for the past seven years, and his clinical tests, since the first six months after his operation, have all been negative. Wesley Hablett and his doctor had both felt a wonderful sense of the presence of God as they prayed together.

Do you feel His presence now? I do! In the depth of the stillness, which rests upon us when we truly pray, there is a mystic power by which man, who is both of the earth and of heaven, can be healed. Our lives were given by God. They can be taken by God. They can be healed by God. Let us touch Him.

EIGHT

Anticipate a Good Outcome

All of us want to do the best we can with our lives. Life on earth is short at best, and if there are seventy-five or fifty or even twenty-five years behind you, and you are not satisfied that you have lived a creative life, you'd better get busy. Even though life is uncertain and insecure, it has tremendous possibilities, no matter how old you are or who you are.

Among the great principles that make life worthwhile is the anticipation of a good outcome. This is a subtle principle of creative living. We tend to draw back to ourselves that which we project in thought. If you send out a certain thought pattern continually, you are likely to draw back to yourself that same thought pattern. If you constantly project an image of bad outcomes, this is indeed a dangerous procedure, for it can, in effect, produce the kind of outcomes you project. If, on the contrary, you learn the great, vital, dynamic principle of anticipating good outcomes, then by a subtlety of the mind you set forces in motion that tend to produce good outcomes.

Sometime ago, I was talking with a man who is an industrial psychiatrist. He was telling me about a mutual friend who was having a hard time. Everyone recognized that this fellow had good training, an excellent education, above-average intelligence, and sterling character. The psychiatrist diagnosed his trouble in a picturesque way. He said the man had no knowledge of creative anticipation. I asked him to explain "creative anticipation."

The psychiatrist said that our friend was constantly anticipating bad results, both personally and in connection with his associates, and was thwarting his inherent potential, which was tremendous, by not using creative anticipation. He was, instead, using destructive anticipation, which brought to him destructive results.

Are you thinking in terms of destructive anticipation or creative anticipation? The Bible says much about this in many different ways. In Mark 11:24 it says, "Therefore I tell you, whatever you ask in prayer, believe that you have received it, and it will be yours" (RSV). That is a tremendous offer! And in Mark 11:23 it says, "Whoever … does not doubt in his heart, but believes that what he says will come to pass, it will be done for him" (RSV).

What is meant by "heart"? The heart is the instrument that pumps blood. But here, the Bible means to say that if, in your deep unconscious, you do not doubt what you pray for, you shall receive it. So anticipate good outcomes; do your best; leave it to God and believe it will come right!

I have preached this for years. If I had a tape recording of myself twenty-five years ago, it would say the same thing.

The reason is that it is basic truth, and basic truth never changes. You can think yourself into destructiveness, and many people do. They think themselves into ill health, into weakness, into failure, into old age. They don't really believe enough to think any other way. They anticipate the terrible way it's going to be, and then it actually becomes that way.

But it need not be like that. Remember the words of Jesus: "Whoever ... does not doubt in his heart, but believes that what he says will come to pass, it will be done for him. Therefore I tell you, whatever you ask in prayer, believe that you have received it, and it will be yours."

There are many people who really believe in creative anticipation. They test it out. They put it into effect. A good example is this letter written to me by an advertising man:

> Some weeks ago, my agency was one of several invited to solicit for a substantial international advertising account. It is one of the largest companies in the world, employing over 300,000 people and doing an annual volume in excess of $5 billion.
>
> We were by far the smallest advertising agency invited to solicit for the account and, frankly, I was fearful that we would lose out because the other agencies had much more big-client experience.
>
> This past Tuesday was "Decision Day," and I knew the review meeting would be held in the company's offices at 10:45 A.M. I was haunted by the nagging fear that we were going to wind up as an also-ran, and I had

convinced myself with all of the reasons we wouldn't get this account.

I was awake most of the night before and was in a bad frame of mind on Tuesday morning. I sat in my office and wondered, "What can I do to convince these people that we are the right agency? Should I telephone and put in a final plea? Should I suggest a special fee arrangement that might offer them cash savings?"

Suddenly, I realized I hadn't used the most powerful convincer of all. I closed my office door, opened the Bible, and read and prayed. I also read two of your booklets, *Thought Conditioners* and *Spirit Lifters.* After a few moments, I closed my eyes and concentrated intently on all of the reasons we were ideally suited to handle this business. I saw very clearly that I should not do anything more, that it was in God's hands and He was working with me.

I opened my eyes, and, although the day had started out as a dull, dreary morning, suddenly the sun came out. I felt confident about the decision, which would be forthcoming any minute. An hour went by and I really had to keep a firm thought about the outcome.

Then the telephone rang. The caller said, "It was a tough meeting and a difficult decision. Frankly, we were leaning heavily in another direction, when someone pointed out that a smaller agency could give more personal and dedicated service, which is what our company badly needs. That was the turning point. In a few minutes, we made up our minds to go with your agency. I am happy to tell you that, instead of starting on July 1, you have our account effective today."

> I know this decision was God-directed and God-inspired. It has helped me in my continuing growth to be more loving and understanding, and it has served as an excellent illustration to all of the members of my staff, who also realized that a power far greater than human power helped make this decision. It is the biggest account we have ever secured and has opened up an entirely new field for my firm.

This letter is a perfect illustration that your faith can be involved in everything you do all your life. Of course, good outcomes do not always come suddenly; sometimes a door is shut in your face. And often that is the best thing that can happen to you. For, as my dear mother used to tell me, "Norman, the door will slam in your face sometimes." (And don't think plenty of them haven't.) "This means that God is trying to guide you down the road to the open door that awaits you." So whatever things you ask and pray for, believe that you receive them and, if it is God's will, you will receive them.

To have good outcomes in your life, you also must be a good person. It is true that, sometimes, evil seems to prosper, and some people get away with things. But in the end, God collects His bills. The individual who has been a double-dealer gets it dealt to him. Good outcomes ultimately come to those people who justify good outcomes.

Therefore, we ought to be reminded that what we must develop in our country is a better, cleaner, more decent character in ourselves. A nation, as well as an individual, can go to pieces floundering on the lack of character. This is largely a responsibility of mothers. There is no one closer to a child than a mother. Of course, children also need their fathers—the family structure is important. But a mother is essential. And the kinds of mothers who made this country were gentle, feminine, beautiful, sweet women; but they were awfully tough, too! And they built character into their children. Our country will not continue to be great unless we make children, and all people, for that matter, amenable to the laws of righteousness and honor.

What do I know about children? I've raised three, with the help of my wife. And we're proud of them. Now I'm a grandfather, and this is quite a position.

One day, my daughter Liz deposited her nine-month-old son, Andrew, on my lap and asked, "Daddy, could you baby-sit for two hours with Andy?"

"What about your mother?" I asked.

"She's going shopping with me."

"Isn't there anyone else?" I hinted. "I'm busy; I'm dealing with important things."

She kissed me on the cheek and said, "There isn't anything more important than helping to direct the life of a child."

Well, since I was going to preach this same doctrine on Sunday, I had to get with it. Anyway, my grandson seemed comfortable. He was cooing and gurgling and smiling at me.

"We will be back in two hours," Liz announced. "I'll put him down to sleep now, and if he follows his usual pattern, he won't wake up. In case he does, here's a bottle; all you have to do is give it to him."

"How about diapers?" I wanted to know.

"I think we'll be safe on that," was her reply.

So, they hadn't been gone more than thirty minutes when I heard Andy crying. He screamed to high heaven! I went in and thought, *What's the matter with you? You're supposed to sleep for two hours.*

I picked him up and he stopped crying. I put him down;

> *You don't make great people by spraying them with perfume; you do it by love and discipline.*

he yelled again. So I took him into the kitchen and took out the bottle. I warmed it up and gave it to him. This silenced him, but he gulped down the milk in no time.

I put him down after I'd given him the bottle. I thought that if his stomach was full, he would be satisfied. But he yelled again. I picked him up and he stopped; I put him down and he yelled. So I checked his diaper; he was dry. I sat down with him and said, "Look, Andy, let's have a talk. We must have an understanding. I don't know how your mother raises you, but I can tell you how your grandfather's going to do it. You can yell your head off until you get so tired that you fall down there and go to sleep. I'm not going to pick you up anymore. So get with it."

What do you think happened? The little fellow, not yet a year old, gave me a great big laugh. He didn't cry again. It was as if he understood and said to himself, "I can't fool with this guy, so I'd better obey orders and be good."

Today, I know we have many soft people who don't think that is the way to do things. But you don't make great people by spraying them with perfume; you do it by love and discipline. Now, I wouldn't have strongly disciplined my grandson at that age. He's lovable; he really gets around your heartstrings. But I was firm because I love him.

You know, there is nothing in God's world like this mother-child relationship. Only God could have thought of it. It is so subtle, so profound. A mother who can have rapport with a young child is a genius, and only God can make her so.

I was once driving behind a school bus from Carmel to Pawling, New York, which is an exercise in patience because you have to stop when it does. But I was glad I followed this one. We were stopped beside a lake, and on the other side were some scattered houses. A boy about nine years old got off the bus. He tossed his pile of books to the side as he picked up a flat rock and skipped it across the lake. It was the most beautiful sight, the rock bouncing from wavelet to wavelet. I wanted to grab a rock myself to see if I could go him one better.

Then the boy started walking toward the house, carrying his books. His mother was home waiting for him, which is indeed significant. She waved to him and came bouncing down the walk. She was a beautiful woman and she was smart, too, for she didn't kiss him. There's a time when men like to be kissed, but it isn't at nine years of age. So what did she do? She put up her hands like a prizefighter and she socked him a couple of times in the chest. Then they turned around and went up the walk together. It was the boy who put his arm around his mother's waist. And she, being taller, put her arm around his shoulder. They walked into the house.

Entranced by it all—the bus was almost out of sight—I thought, *What a mother!* And when that boy is an old man, and the years have mounted up, and death is knocking at his door, it wouldn't surprise me if the last name he mentions is the name *Mother.* That kind of a mother builds the anticipation of good outcomes into children. She makes them good so that they're worthy of good outcomes. And people like that make our nation good, and solid, and right. We must keep it that way!

Let us all dedicate ourselves to building good outcomes. Practice the great principle of creative, spiritual anticipation in your life, and it will be full of good outcomes!

NINE

FAITH CAN LIFT YOU UP

Looking over an audience, I often wonder about all the sorrows, the problems, the hopes, the dreams, the frustrations that are represented. How many human heartaches are present?

Once in Japan, I had a nice visit with a Shinto priest who told me he and his coreligionists considered that there are fifteen basic human problems. When I asked him to name them, he replied, "You name them!" Which is to say that my list and his list would be equally valid. Well, whether there are fifteen or fifty, the Gospel of Jesus Christ is the right place to look to for the right answer to any problem.

One of the most remarkable statements ever made, a statement that is almost incredible, and one that offers enormous hope, is found in Matthew 17:20: "If ye have faith as a grain of mustard seed, ye shall say unto this mountain, Remove hence to yonder place; and it shall remove; and nothing shall be impossible unto you." Another version says, "If you have faith as big as a mustard seed, you can say to this hill, 'Go from here to there!' and it will go. You could do anything!" (TEV).

Jesus Christ teaches that many of the greatest things in this world are done not by something big but by something small. But that something small must be packed full of power and reality.

These are words from the most reliable mind that ever appeared on this earth. It is interesting that the great philosophers of the past who are studied today have nothing like the enormous influence on people that Jesus has. All that remains from these scholars is a body of writing; what remains from Him is a Person, a Person with the Truth. Since this passage comes from Jesus, we can believe it. And whatever your difficulty may be, you can gain a victory over it by applying the truth of this passage.

The first thing it tells us is that all it takes is to have faith as a grain of mustard seed. That means not much faith, only a little—yes, just a speck. It isn't necessary to recite all the creeds and doctrines of the church. All you have to have is a little bit of faith, but this must be real. Jesus Christ teaches that many of the greatest things in this world are done not by something big but by something small. But that something small must be packed full of power and reality.

One time, in a newspaper that reported interesting phenomena, I read about a professor who performed a demonstration for some purpose or other. His equipment consisted of a board, a big nail, a bottle, and a small fleck of Carborundum. He took the bottle in his right hand—it was a big, thick, heavy bottle, one of the thickest, heaviest bottles you could get—and he used it as a hammer. With a series of powerful strokes of the bottle, he drove the nail into the board. This didn't fragmentize the bottle. Then the professor took the tiny fleck of Carborundum, which is one of the hardest of the solids, and dropped it into the glass bottle. The bottle was instantly shattered into many pieces. It wasn't size or quantity that did it; it was essence.

So it is with the problems and difficulties of this life. Suppose you bring to bear against your difficulties all the force and power that you can, all the struggling that you can, all the resisting of which you are capable, but it isn't effective. Then take a mustard-seed pinch of faith and drop it with confidence into the problem. The problem shatters, breaks apart; it reveals to you all the elements of the problem, and you put it together for a solution.

No wonder that Jesus Christ, the divine Son of God, the Redeemer, has lived all these years as the *one* great figure who has compelling influence over the human race, because He deals with the essence of things. The essence of the matter, in the beginning of our text, is that the faith referred to isn't genial, Pollyannaish kind of faith; it is faith in-depth. This doesn't come easily. But when you have it, then you have the faith that moves mountains, that can accomplish anything. It is an extraordinary power.

Jesus also tells us, in the same statement, that faith eliminates one of the most overwhelming factors in human experience: the impossible. *It's impossible,* one thinks, *that I could better this situation* or *that I could solve this problem* or *that I could overcome this difficulty* or *that I could conquer this sorrow. It's impossible!* But, when you have this mustard-seed pinch of faith, you no longer see it as impossible.

This doesn't mean that you will get everything you want. That would not be desirable or wise. It does mean that, hereafter, it is no longer impossible that a great life shall be yours. This is what the Bible proclaims.

Let me give you two other quotes. Mark 9:23: "If thou canst believe. ... " The hardest thing in the world, maybe, is to believe. It is a struggle, it doesn't come easily; but when you learn to believe, " ... all things are possible to him that believeth." Now, that is rather difficult. *All* things are possible if you can believe. Again, there is the statement in Luke 18:27: "The things which are impossible with men are possible with God."

Take the social situation in which we live today. Some believe that the only way to correct social injustice is through sociological procedures and legislative action. I personally believe in both sociological and legislative action. But this is not the main thing, or the most important. What would change the social situation in this country and the world today, and change it within a short period of time, would be a great turning of the people to belief in God. For that which is impossible to man is possible with God. That is why we should support every movement, every design, to bring the power not of man but of God into social action.

"Well," you may say, "it sounds good. But you don't know what a tough problem *I* have. You don't know the impossibilities *I* face." Yes, I do! I haven't been a pastor all these years without knowing what people face. I have a deep and profound compassion for human beings. All of us are poor souls struggling in this world of difficulty. I know how hard your problems are, all right. But, however appalling our problems are, we are to have faith in God; for He is equal to them all.

Let me share with you a letter. It is from a nineteen-year-old girl. I will not tell you who she is, for obvious reasons, or even in what part of the country she lives. And I have changed the name of the boy in the letter, since this is highly confidential. Sadly, I receive more and more letters like this all the time. Here is this one:

> Dear Dr. Peale,
>
> If anyone had told me even a week ago that I would be writing this, I would probably have laughed out loud. I'm 19 years old and have for quite some time called myself an atheist. But, last week, I went to a doctor. He told me I am pregnant. I am not married.
>
> This news has, needless to say, changed my life completely. Now I realize how terribly wrong I was in bringing a new life into this world under such wrong circumstances. Also, I'm afraid that Jack's feelings have

changed toward me. I'm sure at one time he loved me, but I am so afraid that he doesn't care anymore. I don't know what I will do if he doesn't care anymore.

But what frightens me even more than all this is that for the past two years I have been taking drugs. I was just after a few kicks, but now I may have ruined another life. God help me. I know I was wrong. I also know I can't retrace my steps and change things. But at least I now realize my mistakes and I'm trying to rectify them.

Night before last, I was sitting in the living room, sulking. I was convinced the whole world was against me, that my life was ruined and that I had no future. My roommate came in with some of your sermon pamphlets. She suggested that I read a couple of them, so, to pacify her, I did. I can't believe how different I am because of those pamphlets. They made me realize how much I need Someone stronger than me. The situation seems so impossible. Is there any hope?

At nineteen one should be happy. For a girl of nineteen, the world should be filled with promise. This terrible thing that we call sin has soured the mixture. We read in certain publications about getting high on drugs and the new morality, how fulfilling it is. The real truth comes out when you come up against a story like this one. And believe me, the woods—or the streets—are full of it.

Is there any hope for this girl? I wrote to her and told her what I now tell you and myself: that if she will commit herself completely, and I do mean completely, to Jesus

Christ and develop in-depth faith, she can reconstruct her life and nothing need be hopeless; that she can eliminate the impossibilities from her life. As a reborn and remade child of God, she can become a beautiful mother and raise a marvelous child. Why? Because God loves her even though she has done a terribly wrong thing.

So you name your impossible problem and take a great big red pencil and write, "I have faith in Christ and I thereby strike a line through that word *impossible*" Jesus deals in the truth about life and people. So, through faith in Him, the impossibility factor can be removed.

The mustard-seed passage is a tremendous text. It is just full of values. First, there is the power of just a little faith—which has to be real. Second, it eliminates impossibility. Third, it eliminates the mountains.

In these passages, the Bible speaks figuratively about mountains. If you walked up a hill and tried to tell it to get out of your way, the hill would say, "The only way you can get me out of the way is to bring a power shovel and bulldozer. That will get me out of the way. " What is meant in the Bible by a mountain is that accumulation of stuff in your life that obstructs you: mistakes, weaknesses, sins, frustrations, mixed-up thinking. All this gets in your way and blocks your path.

And how are you going to get rid of it? Walk up to it with faith! If you have faith even as a grain of mustard seed, you should say to this mountain, "Be thou removed" and believe. There is another passage, in Matthew 21:21, that says if you have faith you can say to the mountain,

The person who has the mustard seed of profound faith never accepts defeat, because he knows he can scatter defeat to the winds.

"Be thou removed, and be thou cast into the sea" and it shall be done. " … cast into the sea. … " That means out of sight, swallowed up, rid of completely.

So what is standing between you and a great life, a beautiful life, a godly life, a life worthwhile? It may be your ability to believe, your acceptance of defeat. Never accept defeat. The person who has the mustard seed of profound faith never accepts defeat, because he knows he can scatter defeat to the winds.

Once, when I was on a speaking trip, I checked in at a certain hotel. It seemed like a nice hotel and, when I went to my room, I was sure it was a nice hotel. Not only was the room attractive but on the dresser was a beautiful arrangement of flowers and on the table an enormous basket of fruit. I thought, *I wonder how much all this is going to cost me?* Then I examined the slip the bellboy had handed me. And what do you know? It said, "Complimentary," which completely changed my attitude toward the whole matter! So, without delay, I went downstairs to call on the manager, who was responsible for all these benefits. "I want to thank you for the fruit and the flowers and the complimentary room," I said. "You didn't need to do all that."

"I wanted to," he replied. "I wanted to do it because of what you have done for me."

"Because of what I have done for you? What in the world did I ever do for you?"

"Oh," he said, "a nurse and you saved my life."

Well, this was interesting and humbling, and I pressed him to tell me the story. He explained: "Some years ago, I had a stroke, which was a great blow to me. It rendered my left side paralyzed, interfered with the left side of my mouth, and disturbed my speech. I lay in bed and thought, *I am just a remnant of a man. I don't amount to anything anymore. I have had it. I am all through.*

"But the doctors took good care of me and I was slowly recovering. One day, our family doctor came to see me and said, 'You are much better. Your reactions are much improved. If you will, you can be a well man.'

He was a wise doctor, for equally as important as medicine is your will to get well. That doctor knew that this man would need a mighty will because he had a great big mountain in front of him. So he told him, "If you make up your mind to do it, you can get out of bed and you can walk."

"But my arm," said the man, "it's limp."

The doctor assured him, "The arm will recover. And your speech is already much improved."

Now the man had a fine nurse. I have great respect for the profession of nursing. Some of the greatest people I have ever met have been nurses—loving, understanding, giving themselves completely to human beings. This nurse brought the man one of my books and he read it and he thought, *This is great, but it doesn't apply to a man in my condition.* He read in that book, he told me, the passage I have quoted. "If ye have faith as a grain of mustard seed … nothing shall be impossible unto you." He thought, *I believe that.* But he didn't really; he only thought he believed; he didn't really believe it would work in his case.

So after a few days, the nurse came and lowered the side of the bed. She pulled back the covers and said, "Get out of bed. Are you a man or are you a worm? Put your hand in mine, think of the Lord Jesus Christ, and get out of bed."

Now, medically, she knew what she was doing, and psychologically and spiritually she also knew. He put his foot down gingerly.

"I followed her," he told me, "in a staggering fashion to the door of my room. There, she let go of my hand, and she said, 'Now go on your own. But remember, Jesus Christ will hold you up.' I looked at her and I knew she believed it, and suddenly I did, too." He then got up from behind his desk and walked around, and all I could see was a slight limp of the left leg. He concluded, "I am manager of this big, fine hotel and have all these opportunities, because I learned to believe." The mountain had melted out of his way.

Faith can indeed lift you up—and hold you up!

TEN

How to Relax

A great many people today are tense and nervous. This is a predominant characteristic of our times. But really, people do not need to be so tense. The tension of modern living has invaded the quiet sanctuary of the soul and of the central nervous system as well. This is an era of crises. When I think back to when I was a boy, it seems a peaceful period compared with this day. No wonder the incidence of nervous diseases has grown so rapidly. It is an age that is afflicted with tension.

This problem is adversely and profoundly affecting the happiness and well-being of people. One cannot believe that the good Lord wants His children to be thus afflicted. Surely He hopes that in our hearts and minds we will find and enjoy the blessings of peace and serenity.

How, then, can we stop being tense? Well, let me tell you about a man who kept calling me long distance about once a week, telling me that he was so tense he could almost "jump out of my skin"—as he put it. He called hoping I might say something peaceful and soothing that would quiet him. Of course I was sympathetic and tried to do my best for him. But he kept calling more and more often. I soon

> *One of the greatest dangers of human nature is to become a leaner, to transfer your own sense of responsibility to someone else.*

realized that he was leaning on me; I had become a kind of father to him, just because I was trying to help him.

One of the greatest dangers of human nature is to become a leaner, to transfer your own sense of responsibility to someone else. It is a human weakness that can get badly out of hand. Anyway, this man did not know what a slender reed he was leaning on.

"Say something to me that will help me stop being tense," he kept repeating with a kind of desperation. "The only way I get any relief is to pick up the telephone and call you," he explained miserably.

One night when he called—and he called at all hours—I said to him, "Instead of dialing me, why don't you dial a Book that you have in your possession? It will save you money and will do you more good." My suggestion mystified him, so I explained that I would give him several passages of Scripture designed to help him escape tension. "Just dial the Book and say those Scripture passages to yourself," I suggested.

I convinced him that this was a good idea, and he agreed to try it. One of the passages I gave him was Psalm 46:10: "Be still, and know that I am God." He told me later that this one verse pulled him out of his difficulty.

"What I discovered," he said, "is that you must have inner stillness to overcome tension. And the way you get inner stillness is to stop your agitation just long enough to realize that God is God, that you are in His hands, that He watches over you and guides you, and that you can depend upon Him. When you are agitated, you forget Him. In fact, you cannot think of anything constructive. But when you become quiet, you begin to understand, you think things out rationally and sensibly, and your tension lessens."

What a tremendous truth! Just be quiet, get calm, and remember, He is God. You will realize that you need not be upset or disturbed; He is with you and can do anything for you. That is the meaning of this Scripture. So get your mind on God: off your troubles, off your hates, off your conflicts. Practice this wonderful tension-reducing technique. "Be still, and know that I am God."

If there is any one quality we must get into our systems, it is stillness. Pascal, seventeenth-century philosopher, said, "One of the ways in which man brings the most trouble upon himself is by his inability to be still." You have to learn to have inner stillness. That does not mean you are not to be active, but you cannot be forever active unless you are also still. Edwin Markham, the poet, said, "At the heart of the cyclone tearing the sky is a place of central calm." That is to say, the cyclone derives its power from a calm center. So does a person. No one can have driving force and energy unless he is also a master of stillness.

A wise bit of advice: "Be still, and know that I am God." Get spiritual stillness in your body, in your mind, and in your soul. This is the trinity that makes up the individual.

The body is the greatest instrument ever made; it is given to you to make your life rich and full; it is given to you to use. As far as we know, you will never have this kind of body again; it is the only one you are ever going to have. The next body you get will be a spiritual one, and the more spiritual you make this body you now occupy, the more natural will be the shift to the spiritual one. Indeed, your body is so sacred that it is often referred to as the temple of the soul.

But it is a complicated instrument. The ability to raise your arm—or to open and shut your eyes, or eat, or speak— is something no earthly inventor knows how to reproduce. In overcoming tension, you can start by practicing quietness and stillness in your physical body.

Note the various nervous movements of the hands—drumming the fingers, stroking the cheek, nail biting—all evidences of muscle tension in the body.

Years ago, I became convinced that muscle tension had so much to do with mental tension that I decided to practice bodily stillness techniques and found them effective. In the course of my study, I went to a Hindu swami's relaxation demonstration. That man sat for one solid hour without twitching a muscle. In trying the same procedure, I could hardly stand it. I could even hear myself swallow.

Later, I developed more ability to reduce muscle tension. The secret is to relax and think of every part of your body as quiet and still—that God is giving His peace to your muscles and nerves. That is a great art to master.

It is even possible to practice stillness of the body in the midst of tumult. One way to do this is to lie down on some fairly flat surface, such as the floor, where you can keep the backbone straight and the organs in proper balance. Start with your feet and say, "The stillness of God is in my toes, my feet … " and come up through every part of your body saying, "The stillness of God is in my heart, my lungs, my stomach, my fingers, my arms; the muscles of my neck, the muscles of my face, the lids of my eyes.… It is as if to say, "Be still, O physical organs, and know that I am God."

A woman told me she practices physical relaxation on the basis of the body being the temple of the soul. As part of this process, she lets her tongue rest for ten minutes on the floor of her mouth. She claims, and I think she is right, that the tongue is related to the muscles of the throat and face and that these, in turn, are related to the general attitude of the body. You may discover some other technique, but however you do it, I strongly recommend that you consciously relax and conceive of the hand of Jesus as touching every part of your body.

How would you feel if you met Jesus when you were tense, and He put His hand on your heart? Wouldn't that be wonderful in its quieting effect? Or if you had pain—to feel His hand where your pain was. Why not? He says He is with us always. He comes to you when you seek Him. He touches your body and gives you stillness.

Then there is the necessity of cultivating stillness in the mind. If you could flush out of your mind all the sins you have ever committed, wouldn't you have stillness? Suppose you could mentally lose any sense of injustice that agitates you—wouldn't you have inner stillness?

The cause of tension is often disturbance due to some sin you have committed that was never forgiven. Or, it may be you are struggling with some temptation or compromise that keeps you tense. If you have a sense of injustice and resentment, or ill will, you can have no stillness. But as the Bible tells us, we can be washed clean and become whiter than snow (Psalm 51:7).

I remember a man who had a virulent hatred for a former employer. Everything the employer had done was wrong. Only vaguely would he admit that anything he himself had done was wrong. That, of course, was inconceivable. This poor fellow was seething. The look on his face, when he talked of the man, made one aware of his intensity of feeling. And he kept telling the bitter story over and over.

Finally, he developed many symptoms of hypertension until a minister took him into a church and made him kneel at the altar. He said to him, "Your trouble is because of the hatred in your system. You are filled with all manner of resentment, and I want you to stay here at the altar until it is all washed out. Unless you do so, your tension will destroy you."

The cleansing took place; the man gained quietness, peace, and composure. His tension was gone.

Developing mental stillness is a great art. The ability to control your mind in the midst of tense circumstances, to send your mind into some area of peace and quietness, is hard to come by. Yet, it is remarkable what you can do with your mind in developing quietness and composure. When you are in a tense situation, by means of your thoughts you can go away from where you are, however hectic, into a place of quietness and peace.

The famous former Brooklyn Dodger pitcher, and my good friend, Carl Erskine, told me how he kept calm and confident in the midst of the confusion and pressure of a ball game.

"I have a little trick," he said. "When I get in a tight spot, I pick up the ball and walk around the pitcher's mound, thinking of a creek in Indiana where I fish. I remember how cool and peaceful it is on a beautiful morning, when I throw a line into the still water. Mentally, I go fishing."

Imagine crowds of fans, sitting wondering what ball Erskine was going to pitch, while he went fishing in Indiana! You can go away in your mind to any place you like—and you can go without buying a plane ticket. You might go up into the North Country, where the aroma of pine and hemlock is in the air. You can go down by the sea, watching the water lap gently on the sand. With your mind, in the turning of a thought, you can be with God, sharing His everlasting peace. Bring this quietness of God into any situation and note the results.

There is a deeper experience of quietness for human nature than even those of the body or mind. It is when, at long last, the soul stands in the presence of God; when the soul yields itself to God; when you take everything in your life and put it into the hands of God, believing that if you do your best, you can safely leave it with Him. Then your tension passes away—like the old Indian's interpretation of the Twenty-third Psalm. He said the phrase "thou anointest my head with oil" (verse 5) means, "He puts His hand on my head and all the tired goes 'way." The oil, symbol of the everlasting peace of God, is given to people who have become still in their bodies, minds, and souls. Then they are no longer in a dither of nervous tension as to what life is going to do for them, or to them. They do the best they can and leave the rest to God. God does the best He can, and that is enough.

Life can be wonderful, victorious, overwhelming, if you will just get this stillness of God into your body, mind, and soul. Do the best you can; do good, be good. Then put it all into His hands and trust Him. Don't be excited; don't be nervous; don't be tense. Just be still. Remember that He is God, and He will give the peace and power of God to you.

Scriptures for Relaxing Tension

Peace, be still. (*Mark 4:39*)

Peace I leave with you, my peace I give unto you. (*John 14:27*)

And the peace of God, which passeth all understanding, shall keep your hearts and minds through Christ Jesus.

(*Philippians 4:7*)

Come unto me, all ye that labour and are heavy laden, and I will give you rest.

(*Matthew 11:28*)

Be still, and know that I am God.

(*Psalm 46:10*)

ELEVEN

DRAW UPON THE HIGHER POWER

Do you ever feel inadequate in the presence of the problems of human existence? Do you ever feel the need for more power within yourself? I am sure it is safe to say that everyone does at one time or another. Well, I want to remind you that God, through faith in Jesus Christ, builds power into people, so that they become equal to whatever life may bring.

I was talking with a man who told me of an experience he had following a game of golf. It was one of the great spiritual incidents of his life. He and two other men were concerned about a friend of theirs who was having a great deal of trouble. "So" he said, "we three fellows ganged up on George and took him out to the golf course with us to get his mind off himself."

They had a pleasant game. Afterward, as they were sitting in the locker room in the clubhouse, George spoke up and said, "I want to thank you fellows. I know what you are up to, getting me out here today to play golf. This was your way of helping me. I want you to know I am touched by it. You certainly are good friends. For the three hours we were on the course, I did sort of forget my troubles for a time. But, whether I can handle the problems I am faced with, I don't know. Life has thrown the whole book at me. I just don't know what to do."

At this point, one of the other men rose, ready to leave. He dropped his hand on George's shoulder and said, "Look, George, I haven't known you too long, but I think I know how you feel. A few years ago, so many things were going wrong for me that I thought no one ever had such troubles. It just seemed that I couldn't handle them at all. I was about to give up. As a matter of fact, I had what you might call the makings of a nervous breakdown. But then I met a man who really had something. This man had had a spiritual experience in-depth, and his whole being was full of power. One day he said to me, 'The only way you will ever solve your problems is to draw upon the higher power.' So look, friend, you do the same. Draw upon the higher power."

The man telling about this said that the phrase struck him, for he, too, had troubles he had not said anything about—and even the good game of golf hadn't dissipated them. He went home thinking about that statement, "Draw upon the higher power." Of course, he knew the reference was to God. *How,* he thought, *can I draw on that power? I know it is of God, but I haven't got it.* Then it occurred to him that God didn't just create us and set us down here by ourselves, isolated: He maintains a contact and He keeps it

> *God didn't just create us and set us down here by ourselves, isolated: He maintains a contact and He keeps it open, always. And through this contact, power—divine power—can flow into us.*

open, always. And through this contact, power—divine power—can flow into us.

"Well," the man continued, "as I was thinking about this one day, I had the most releasing experience. All of a sudden, it seemed I was infused with power from on high. I was able to cast out all my negativisms, all my fears, all my hates, all my weaknesses, all my tension, and my nervousness. I got power over myself right then and there. I tell you, it's a fact: Any human being who really makes the effort, who isn't content just to wallow forever in his weaknesses, but who makes the effort, can draw upon this higher power!"

He then gave me a text. He said it was his personal, private text, but actually it isn't so personal and private, for he shares it with everyone, as he shared it with me. I, too, take it as my text—and I give it to you.

It is Luke 18:27: "The things which are impossible with men are possible with God." It means you do not need to have any impossibles at all. You can draw upon the power from God that moves the impossibles into the area of the possibles. Draw upon that higher power.

Don't take this for granted. Take it as though you had never heard anything like it before. *You do not need to be defeated.* You can draw upon the higher power. *Really* pull it down into yourself, into your life, and spread it out everywhere. This is a tremendous thing! Take it! Listen to it! Grab it!

But you may be wondering how in the world to do it. *How* do you draw on that higher power? Well, you *live* with God. You live with Him every day. You live with Christ. You talk to Him. You walk with Him. You pray to Him. You think about Him. You don't do anything, however seemingly small or insignificant, that you don't bring Him into it. Some people never think of God except in connection with church or some religious exercise. Other people live with Him every minute of the day. The more you do this, the more the power flow increases.

I have a friend in Toronto, for example, a businessman and a good one—top-notch in his line. He prays about everything. He talks with God as he walks down the street. And he prays that every day the Lord will lead him to someone he can help.

He told me he was walking along a Toronto street one day when it occurred to him to go into a certain men's clothing shop. This shop was operated by a young couple, friends of his. He noticed, as he came close to the window, that the place was unpainted, looked drab, and was dimly lighted inside. He knew these young friends carried high quality merchandise, but the place repelled him instead of attracting him. He went in. There were no customers in the store. The wife was attending to something behind the counter toward the back. The husband was upstairs in the office. My friend asked, "Mary, how are things going? I just felt I should come in and see you."

"Oh," she replied, "things are bad. We may have to fold. I don't know if we can hang on to this business."

"What is the trouble?"

"Come upstairs and see John," she said. "He's up there fussing over bills. There are no customers here, so it doesn't make any difference if I go up with you."

She took him up to the office, which was on a balcony. And there was John. He had a great stack of bills he was getting ready to send out. "I don't know what I am going to do," he said. "We can't get anyone to pay us promptly, and our business has fallen off. We put in a big inventory. Our suppliers are pressing us. What are we going to do?"

"Well," my friend said to him, "there's a paint store down the street. One thing you can do is to go down and get a can of paint and a brush and, after you close up at night, just go around and paint all the woodwork an attractive color. It will brighten the place up. And for goodness' sake, get yourself some new light fixtures. Flood the place with light. Anyone who knows how to merchandise anything knows you have to have color; you have to have light; you have to display the goods well. So why don't you get busy doing it?"

"Oh, that wouldn't do any good," the young man answered in a discouraged tone.

"Now, about those bills. Do you know the people you sold these goods to?"

"We know a few of them."

"Can you call them by name?"

"No," said John, "we can call hardly any of them by name."

"Well, this one here: William Smith. How many children has he got?"

"I haven't the slightest idea," replied John.

"Or this Mr. Jones. How's his wife, do you know?"

"Why, I don't even know whether he is married. What's all this got to do with it?"

"What you've got to do," my friend told him, "is to bring God into this business. You've got to get so much God in the heart that you begin to love these people. Don't just be interested in selling them shirts and ties but be interested in them as persons. Maybe they need much more than a shirt or a tie. Maybe they need courage and hope and faith. Why don't you give that to them? What are you going to do right now? Send those bills out?"

"Yes," said the young storekeeper, "we've got to. We've got to get six hundred dollars, and we've got to get it fast. We are that near failing."

"All right," said the older man. "Mary, you come over here. And John, you come over here." He put his hand on the stack of bills and got them to put their hands on top of his. He prayed aloud, "Dear Lord, here are Mary and John. They are running this store, and they really don't know how to do it. They need You as a partner. Help them, won't You?

"Now, they are going to send these bills out to all these people, and we ask You to bless all who receive them. Bless Mr. Jones's wife, if he has one. Bless Mr. Smith's children, if he has any. Be with those among these people who are sick. Send the power of faith down through these bills. And, dear Lord, make us love these people."

Did you ever hear of running a business that way? Well, this was the practical result: One week later, the couple had nine hundred dollars in the till, three hundred dollars more than they desperately needed. And many customers who couldn't pay wrote notes about how kind and patient the owners had been. John and Mary hadn't expressed kindness in any tangible way. They had sent it mentally through the power of God.

Soon, more people began to come to the shop, which, meanwhile, the owners had brightened up. They drew upon the higher power. And, the great thing about it wasn't that their business increased; it was what happened to them personally. They became two of the most vital members of one of the great churches in Toronto.

So make a fresh evaluation of the kind of life you live. How deeply involved is God in your everyday life? Whatever your problem, take God into it. Draw upon the higher power.

There are also the deep, hard experiences in life: great pain, great sorrow, the anguish of bereavement, the tension and anxiety that come when a loved one is seriously ill. Everyone has to face such things at one time or another, in one way or another. There will come a time when you think you just haven't got the strength to meet the situation you face. But you have, really, for Almighty God has put a wonderful power into human beings. He is an astonishing Creator. I am not thinking only of the physical mechanism He has made, the body, but of the resiliency of spirit He put into us.

Greater than anything else, He has given us the capacity to have faith—to let something go and let Him take it over. This is really one of the greatest secrets of human existence: Do all you can about a thing and, having done all, turn it over to God. When there is nothing more you can do about a situation, what more can you do? It is then that you turn it over to God, put it into His hands, leave it with Him; rest it with Him confidently, expectantly, prayerfully, and with faith. He may not give you the answer you want, but He will give you the answer you should have. He will always do right by you. Have the faith to trust Him. Put your problem into His hands and the power will come through.

Years ago, while flying low over Chicago, I looked down and saw the old Edgewater Beach Hotel, where I have made many speeches. In its time, it was a great hotel. Well, I remember speaking in the ballroom of the Edgewater Beach Hotel at a luncheon meeting of a big national convention. The place was packed, and at the end of the room a line of waitresses stood listening. They were all dressed in black, with white collars and cuffs, a very attractive, young group.

When the meeting was over, I had to get away in a hurry because of another commitment. As I was walking across the ballroom entrance, which had a floor of huge squares of marble, I heard someone running behind me, obviously a woman, her heels striking on the stone floor. Turning around, I saw one of the waitresses. She rushed up to me, grabbed my arms, and said, "Oh, Dr. Peale, I really love you!"

I looked at her, and she had such a sweet, happy face that I said, "You know something? I love you, too." Then I said, "But, please enlighten me: Why do we love each other?"

By this time, four or five other waitresses had gathered around. She answered, "Oh, it is because of an idea I got out of one of your printed sermons. I have a little boy. He is a sweetheart, and I love him. His father is gone. I have only the boy left. Well, he became ill. He was so sick that the doctor called me in one day and said, 'Mary, I've got to tell you. I don't think this boy can live. You must strengthen yourself. You may lose your boy. I'll do all I can, but I have to give it to you straight.'

"And I said, 'Oh, doctor, I *can't* lose him! I mustn't lose him! He's all I have! He's all I live for!' " And she told how she went and told her next-door neighbor about it. This neighbor got out one of our sermons. You never know about a piece of printed material, where it may fill a need. The neighbor said, "You read this."

Well, in that sermon was the advice that when a loved one is ill, and you've done all you can, then the thing is to pray, "Lord, You gave me this loved one. I give him back to You. I put him in Your hands. No harm can come to him because Your heart is so loving and Your arms are so strong. So I just put him back in Your hands. I give him to You. I wish You would let me keep him, but if You can't, I'll understand."

The young woman continued, "I had never read anything like that. It astonished me. But somehow it seemed the right thing to do. So I prayed and said, 'Lord, here he is. I give him to You. I put him in Your hands. You take him. If you can just let me have him back, I'll thank You so much. But if You can't, I'll know You will give me the power to take it.'

At this point, I noticed there were tears in the eyes of everyone listening, including myself. I asked, "What happened finally?"

"Thank God," she said, "he did get well! God did give him back to me. But you know, I felt such wonderful power and peace. I've dedicated my boy to being a good Christian. I am going to love him into it."

> *The average individual does not live up to his greatest possibilities more than a few times in his whole life. We are infinitely greater than we ordinarily act.*

I looked at her and said, "You are one of the greatest mothers I've ever met. You have found the answer for you and your child." The other waitresses nodded their heads.

That young woman drew upon the higher power. What is impossible with men becomes possible with God. And this higher power is available to each of us. The average individual does not live up to his greatest possibilities more than a few times in his whole life. We are infinitely greater than we ordinarily act. I wish I could make you see what you really can be through the power of God in Jesus Christ. Put yourself, and everything you love and hope for, in God's hands. Draw upon the higher power.

TWELVE

PRAYER CAN CHANGE YOUR LIFE

There is something that, when you find it, will make your life absolutely wonderful. It is all tied up with Someone you can't see but who is real just the same. And when this Someone gets through to you and me, our lives are changed. I haven't the slightest doubt about this, for many times I have seen people who were defeated, mixed-up, and sinful turn to God, receive Him, and be wonderfully changed. Prayer is fundamental in this life-changing experience, and I strongly recommend that you learn the art of prayer and put it to work in your life.

I once sat in the ballroom of a hotel in Toronto, Ontario, with a gathering of Canadian advertising and sales people. I was the speaker for this occasion, and the audience seemed very sophisticated. I remarked to the man sitting on my right, with whom I had just become acquainted, that I felt power in the room and thought it must be from the quality of these people.

"Oh," he said, "don't be so sure the power is from these people. I've been praying for this meeting."

This was rather startling, because I hadn't expected to encounter such spiritual ardor. I sometimes forget that there is an immense spiritual stirring in people's hearts.

The man then said to me, "I found two things that have made everything in life different for me. The first—and the greatest single experience I have ever had—was finding Jesus Christ and committing my life to Him. The second was that I learned to pray. These two things," he declared, "revolutionized my life." He added, "What a pity so many human beings never find Christ and never learn to pray! They miss the greatest values in this life."

This is what Jesus has been saying to us through the years, and really astute people make this discovery. Prayer can change your life. It has been my privilege to be associated with many people who have had this experience in one way or another.

When I say this of prayer, I do not mean mere mumbling of words. I do not mean formal affirmations, either, although formal prayers sometimes help, and some formal prayers are touched with the glory of God. What I mean is a deep, fundamental, powerful relationship with God, whereby your whole mind and heart become changed and you receive power from the Source. I have seen such prayer change the lives of so many.

Some people think you come to such a change in only one way. Nothing could be more false. Springtime comes in more ways than one. If it were standardized, if you saw the same thing wherever you looked, spring would not have the glory it has.

After the meeting in Toronto, I drove to Buffalo, New York, through the fruit orchards of Ontario. I'd never before been through that region in the springtime. And it was wonderful. The orchards were ablaze with white and pink. The blossoms stretched as far as you could see, from the shores of Lake Erie back inland. The whole atmosphere was full of a subtle fragrance. The air was clear and fresh and cold.

Springtime in some areas is soft and balmy. It is not the same everywhere. And Christ comes like springtime in different ways to different hearts. Sometimes He comes through feelings, sometimes through the mind; sometimes He comes through theology, sometimes through scientific reasoning; sometimes He comes through poetry. Sometimes He comes in simple ways, sometimes in complicated ways. As the human heart and mind are conditioned, so does He come. But however He comes, associated with Him is the life of prayer.

Thinking along these lines, my mind goes back over many experiences. I remember one night when I spoke in a suburban church in a midwestern city. A man came up to me and asked if he could drive me back to my hotel. This man's manner was so appealing that I let my other transportation go and went with him. He was a hail-fellow-well-met kind of person, and I liked him right off. He led me down the street to the most battered automobile I think I've ever seen. "How do you like that for a car?" he asked.

"Oh," I said, "that sure is some car." (It may have been, about twenty years before!)

"Well," he said, "it'll run. Get in." As he opened the door for me, it fell down slightly on one hinge, but he pulled it up, saying, "You have to know how. These are tricky doors." When he got the car in motion, he sat back rather happily. This was long before seat belts, but I sure could have used one! "You know," he said, "some months ago I couldn't have afforded even a car like this. I haven't moved far up the scale, but I'll tell you one thing: this car is paid for."

Then, in a quieter tone, he said, "I want to tell you a story of spiritual victory. I was a failure. I was frustrated. Everything I did ultimately went wrong. I'd start out all right. Then I'd do some stupid thing. I'd get into a wrangle with someone. Or I would say something out of line, or I'd get into some dishonesty. I made a mess of one thing after another. My wife finally got disgusted and left me. Then I took to drink, and what little money I had left disappeared. I was down, completely down.

"At this point, a friend came to me and said, Trank, you don't need to be this way. You have abilities and you can live a successful life, if you'll do one thing.' And he led me to Jesus Christ. I accepted Christ; I took Him into my life; I committed my whole self to Him. My friend said to me, 'Frank, I want you to read the Bible. But I don't want you to read the whole Bible yet, because you'd get mixed up; you'd get lost. I want you to stick to Matthew, Mark, Luke, and John, and read every word of those four books. And when you come to a passage that particularly strikes you, I want you to commit that passage to memory.'

"So I started reading. One day, I came upon a passage where Jesus is saying to Peter, 'I will give unto thee the keys of the kingdom of heaven' [Matthew 16:19]. That fascinated me, because I knew Peter also had messed up his life and even denied the Lord, just as I had. But the Lord said to Peter, 'I will give unto thee the keys of the kingdom of heaven. ' I took it as meaning He would give the keys to me, too, and I began to ask myself what He meant by the kingdom of heaven. I reasoned that the kingdom of heaven must be full of God's love, full of His peace, full of His rightness, full of every good thing. Each day in my prayers, I unlocked the kingdom of heaven, and these marvelous blessings started flowing into my life. This hasn't brought me much money, but it wasn't designed to bring me money."

One way prayer can change your life is by teaching you to think creatively.... Prayer sharpens the mind....

When we rattled up to the door of my hotel and he let me out, he said, "Hang on to those keys." And, when we had said good-night, he slammed the car door (which nearly fell off in the process). I watched him move out into the traffic. In my mind, that battered old car was invested with the splendor of a chariot being driven by a knight in shining armor. That man had had his life changed. He found Jesus Christ and accepted Him as his Savior, and then he learned to pray in such a way that he developed perception and understanding.

One way prayer can change your life is by teaching you to think creatively. The way you think spells the difference between living well and living poorly. Prayer sharpens the mind and thereby brings the believer into harmony with the great Mind.

Prayer is a mental process. If you have the idea that it is merely the mumbling of a few words, I almost think you're better off not to use it at all, for that degrades it. True prayer requires discipline, pain, and agony of thought. But when you do think prayerfully, with Jesus as your guide, you break free from defeats.

I believe any problem, any defeat, and any difficulty can be overcome through prayer. I have a friend who runs a big bakery business that he built from small beginnings. He was the company's first baker. As a matter of fact, he claims he can still make better bread and cakes than most of the present bakers. One day, he described to me a significant experience he had some years ago. He had been faced with an extremely worrisome problem. He would pace the floor trying to figure out a solution. He lay awake nights brooding over it. Then one day, as he sat in his office feeling completely baffled, he chanced to glance at his mother's picture on the wall.

"My mother," he told me, "was a Kansas woman reared on the farm where I was born. She was tall and gaunt. She never was able to beautify herself much. She was just a plain woman all her life. But she was wise. She never had much schooling. But in the hard, good life she and my father lived together, she learned many things in the school of experience. And she used to say to us children, 'When you have a problem, and you've worked as hard as you can at it, given it all you've got, and still you haven't solved it, the thing to do is just walk away from it and think about God. But don't talk to God about the problem. Talk to Him about Himself. Tell Him how much you love Him. Talk to Jesus and thank Him for all He has done for you. Tell Him you want to be His faithful follower. Have fellowship with God and with Jesus.' "

How wise that woman was—maybe wiser than she knew! For when you concentrate on a problem unduly long and do not get the answer, you tense up, your thinking freezes, and neither insights nor ideas come through. You must then let it be for a while, to break the strain. After that, when you talk to Jesus about it, you will find that He lifts you way up so when you go back to the problem, you have grown and the problem shrinks. Then, prayerfully, you can break it open and find the right answer.

So my friend, in his perplexity, looked at the picture of his mother, departed long since but still living and still speaking to him in thought. And he decided to leave the problem for a while. He took out his Bible and read passages his mother had marked in it. He thought about Jesus and he rededicated himself, acknowledging that he felt he had not been growing spiritually as he ought, that he'd been less than himself. After a time, he turned back to the problem. Did he get an answer immediately? No. But now he felt calm about it. He was confident he would somehow be able to handle it. And later he did find a satisfactory solution.

Often a person will complain, "I've prayed and prayed and I didn't get what I wanted." Well, who said you are supposed to get what you want? Prayer isn't a device to get what you want. Prayer is a means of bringing you to the point where you will accept what God wants. If you're using prayer just for getting what you want, you're engaging in an improper use of it. The Lord does want good things for us and, if with all your heart you pray for something that is wholesome and constructive, you are likely to receive it. Sometimes the thing you pray for is something you shouldn't have. We are like children; we want what we want, when we want it. This infantilism is in most of us. To be a Christian means to be a mature person. You learn to say, "This is what I'd like to have, Lord, if You think it's all right for me; but if You don't, then give me what You want me to have, or show me what You want me to do."

I met a lady who said to me, "1 have been to your church twice and heard two of your sermons." She sounded so enthusiastic that I thought she was going to tell me those sermons had done her a lot of good. But she didn't. "I also heard your wife make a speech," she said, "at the church I belong to—and that is what I really remember."

"Well, that is not surprising to me," I said. "I get most of my good ideas from my wife." That's teamwork, you know. If you have a wife you pray with, and work with, and walk the pathway of life with, and she and you try to serve the Lord together, you don't know where one begins and the other leaves off.

At any rate, this woman explained that she had been struggling in prayer for something she wanted, and God wasn't answering her prayers. And Mrs. Peale, in that speech, had remarked that there are three ways God answers prayer: Yes. Wait awhile. No. "And when she said that," the woman told me, "I knew I had my answer. It was no. But I hadn't wanted to take a *no* answer."

"Maybe that *no* answer is going to lead you to some great experience," I said. "And when you love Him enough to trust Him, you humbly say, 'All right, Lord, I accept that, and I look to You for further guidance.' Then some bright day you realize, 'If He had not said no, this wonderful thing I now have would not have come to me.'

The attitude that really leads to life in all its fullness is that of a child walking with Him, loving Him, trusting Him, seeking to serve Him. Prayer, in this attitude, can change your life wonderfully.

THIRTEEN

COME ALIVE!

People have different ideas of the Christian faith. For one thing, it is the way of eternal salvation. I often think of it also as a sort of hospital where any person, wounded in body, mind, or soul, may come for healing and renewal. It is a source of energy, enabling any who are tired, discouraged, or frustrated to receive an injection of power. It is an enthusiasm builder. When you have a down attitude toward yourself or toward life, Christian faith will rejuvenate you.

So many of us suffer from tired, gloomy, desultory thoughts, with the result that our life force is reduced. Of course, we have been infused by the media over a long time with such thoughts. Years ago, there was a popular radio commentator in my neighborhood. He had a great voice. But every time he started a radio program, he would say, "There's bad news tonight, folks." He claimed to be an objective reporter and was merely telling it as it was. It became his trademark: "There's bad news tonight."

His successors have surpassed him. They not only come up with bad news but also are pushing pessimistic and cynical viewpoints. With people telling us "there is bad news" all the time, it is a wonder that the country survives. Here's some bad news I cut from a magazine called *Success:*

> It is a gloomy moment in the history of our country. Not in the lifetime of most men has there been so much grave and deep apprehension; never has the future seemed so incalculable as at this time. The domestic economic situation is in chaos. Our dollar is weak throughout the world. Prices are so high as to be utterly impossible. The political cauldron seethes and bubbles with uncertainty. It is a solemn moment of our troubles. No man can see the end.

I suppose some might agree that this is a fairly accurate picture of today. However, that was first published in *Harper's Weekly* in October 1857. It's a wonder the country has survived all this bad news!

Our ancestors, I believe, were tougher than we are. They had substantial faith and were able to separate the temporary from the eternal. As thinkers, they knew that humanity goes forward by difficulty, pain, and suffering. But they also knew that if you stick it out, if you keep your faith in God, if you do your part as a citizen and as a Christian, no matter how many dark clouds may appear, the sun will shine again. So, let us be rid of those tired and gloomy thoughts and come alive. Get the pollution of negative thinking out of your mind. The world is good. People are good. The future is good. Of course, that is not to say there is no bad news along with it. But humanity has gone forward by overcoming bad news.

Such victories represent much of the history of Christianity. It was born in a bad-news time. Indeed, it has grown great in bad-news eras. It becomes greater whenever it has to deal with bad-news situations. For faith draws upon a power that is of the essence of time. We are in the timeless, not the ephemeral, time equation.

Most of us have been affected by these tired, gloomy thoughts, and all of us would like to be rid of them and come alive. How do you do it? First, an important and effective technique is to constantly practice being *under*-whelmed, not overwhelmed. Everyone, in effect, exclaims, "This overwhelms me. That situation overwhelms me; our country is overwhelmed with problems, taxes, and a huge deficit."

Now, what do you get by being overwhelmed? All you do is create additional tension. The idea is to be underwhelmed. The secret is to *de-emotionalize* yourself. One great trouble with contemporary life is that we have so many superemotionalized people. The antidote to that is to think rather than to be emotional. Any problem can be solved if a person will keep cool and think. That is all you have to do. Just think and pray, for prayer is a form of thought; prayers bring divine intelligence to aid your own intelligence. The human mind will not function effectively when it is superheated by emotion; only when the mind is cool, rational, dispassionate, and underwhelmed will it produce logical concepts. The human mind *can* get answers to difficulties. So don't get into a tizzy. Don't be in a dither. Don't emotionalize. Think!

I was once in a hotel where I was to speak at a luncheon. They told me 910 people were signed up for this luncheon.

I was sitting in the office of the manager, an old friend of mine, when his assistant came rushing in. He was perspiring and red of face. "We are in a bad situation," he said.

The manager calmly said, "Jim, tell me about it."

"We have one thousand twenty people and are prepared for nine hundred ten. What will we do?"

'I'll tell you what to do, Jim," said the manager. "The tables in the ballroom are now too far apart. Put them closer together by six inches and that will give you the space you need. If necessary, put some tables in the foyer outside the dining room."

"Well," the assistant agreed, "maybe we can do that, but what about the food? We don't have enough for a thousand twenty people. We are serving roast beef and it won't go around."

The manager replied, "Set the gauge on the cutting machine and slice the beef a little thinner."

"But we're serving peas."

"Well," the manager asked, "how many peas are you giving a person?"

"We count out one hundred peas to every person." (I thought that was a lot of peas, but that is what he said.)

"Make it ninety," the manager said, "and you're in."

"But," the man still objected, "we don't have enough rolls. We have to put a roll on every plate."

"Oh, no, you don't; pass the rolls. Half the diners won't take a roll."

The assistant manager calmed down, wiped the perspiration from his brow, and went out. The manager sat back, put his feet up on the desk, and said, "You know something? One of the secrets of this hotel business is to know how to be calm in a crisis. Never let anything work you up. There is always an answer to everything if you will just keep calm and think," and then he added, "and pray." Then he said, with a serious look on his face, "I pray about my job every day."

I went into the luncheon and the meat was delicious. (I would have been glad to settle for forty of the peas they had.) Underwhelmed! That's the idea.

Now, the world isn't going to go to pieces; nor is the United States; nor is your business; nor is your life. It never has and it never will—if you get rid of all those old, tired, gloomy thoughts. Isaiah was so right: "In confidence and quietness shall be your strength" (*see* Isaiah 30:15).

In San Francisco, I was a guest on a call-in radio talk show. I don't like talk shows because you never know what kind of question you're going to get and you never know what kind of answer you're going to give. On this show, a man called and asked, "Dr. Peale, is that you?"

"Yes, sir, that's right."

"You're sure it's you?"

"As far as I know it's me."

"You always talk about positive thinking, don't you?"

"Not always. I refer to it occasionally."

"Well," he continued, "I don't buy that positive thinking! I have a problem you can't get around. You might as well fold up on this because you can't handle it."

I replied, "If that is the case, why go further with it?"

"I want to get an answer. Here is the question: Im fifty-two years of age and out of a job. You know yourself that no man fifty-two years old can get a job. Furthermore, I don't have any brains. I haven't had any good experience. I haven't had any education and no one likes me. What are you going to tell me to do about that?"

I asked, "How do you know you haven't any brains?"

"When I was young, I was told I didn't have any brains. The brains in the family all went to my brother."

"Who told you that?"

"My brother."

"But you sound to me as if you have brains."

Then I continued, "Are you telling me that no one fifty-two can get a job? I hired a man just last week who was fifty-nine years old. The trouble is, you're overwhelmed. If you get underwhelmed, I know you can get a job." I took another angle: "Who did you say doesn't like you?"

"No one likes me."

"Do you like yourself?"

"I never thought about that."

"If you will get to like yourself as a child of God, you will realize that you have what it takes to get a job and do a great job." Then I added, "You must love your neighbor as yourself. But you can't love your neighbor until you love yourself."

Finally, he asked, "Will you pray for me?"

"Now you're talking! Of course I'll pray for you, and you pray for yourself."

Then he asked, "Is that positive thinking?"

"No, that's just faith in yourself and faith in a good God, but it certainly isn't *negative* thinking."

About six weeks later, I had a note from this man saying he had a job. He said, "It isn't much of a job, but believe me, by the time I get through with it, I'll make a terrific job out of it!"

That's the way to think and talk! Take what you can get, and do the best you can with it. Work at it until it becomes something great. There are negative-talking, miserable, defeated, unhappy, discouraged people everywhere. It isn't necessary to be that way, either about yourself or about your country or about the time in which you live. So say to yourself and to your husband or wife, "You know something, honey, from now on I am underwhelmed." Of course, you may shake him up for a while, but he'll get used to it. *Underwhelmed* is the word.

Once you become underwhelmed, get excited about life. Are you excited? Could you honestly tell yourself that when you arose on this beautiful morning, you were excited? You weren't? That is indeed a pity! But you may ask, "What do you mean? I can't turn on excitement at will. If you're excited, you're excited. If you're not excited, you're not excited. You can't go to the drugstore and buy a bottle of excitement."

Well, listen. If you are not excited, you can get excited. How? Act as if you are excited. This is one of the greatest psychological principles ever enunciated. It was first mentioned in this country by nineteenth-century philosopher William James, who at one time was a Harvard professor of anatomy, psychology, and philosophy (body, mind, and soul, you might say). He taught the "As If" principle. That is to say, if you're full of fear and you want to be full of courage instead, you must act "as if" you did have courage and, in due course, you will be courageous.

And if you're full of hate and want to change—you want to love people, instead—act "as if" you are loving, and presently, in the very nature of the psychology of the human being, you will begin to take on loving aspects. So if you're not excited, act as if you are excited. Go out and say, "Isn't this a terrific day? Look at that sky! Look at those beautiful clouds! Feel that wonderful rain on my face!" Do this and you will become excited.

This is what our faith is designed to do: lift us up into excitement about life. What is a preacher's job? It is to build people up in faith so they will be excited about God, about Jesus Christ, about themselves, about other people, about their world, about their day and their generation. Get excited! You're never going to live this day again. Never again! So live it to the hilt.

That reminds me of a professor at Syracuse University, Dean Hugh Tilroe of the College of Public Speaking, an outstanding orator in upstate New York. He was one of the men who installed me as pastor of a church in Syracuse. I didn't know who he was, that first Sunday; while sitting with him in the pulpit, I leaned over and asked, "Professor, what do you teach in the university?"

He said, "Public speaking."

"Oh, my," I groaned.

"Don't let me bother you," he said. "I've made speeches for so long I know how nerve-racking it is. I'm not here judging you. I'm your friend. Tell the people out in front what you know about Jesus Christ and tell them to be enthusiastic and excited."

So I tried to do the best I could. And I loved this man from that moment on.

> *The world belongs to the enthusiasts*
> *who can keep cool.*

A few years later, I received a telephone call and was told that he had suffered a stroke. When I visited him, he was lying in bed and not even able to raise his hand. His speech was slurred. He was like a great big oak tree that had fallen.

"I—I can't hunt anymore." (He was a great hunter.) "I can't fish anymore." (He was also a great fisherman.) "I can't teach anymore; can't speak anymore." And he added, "I have a date tomorrow night in Pennsylvania for a commencement. I want you to go and substitute for me."

"What do you want me to tell them, Professor?"

"Tell them to love the Lord and be enthusiastic and excited. Tell them that excitement sweeps every resistance before it. Tell them to love the world, to love people; tell them to be excited."

I could hardly bear seeing him lying there, broken like that. I went out and walked up and down Walnut Avenue, weeping because this great man, my friend, had fallen. And I went to Pennsylvania the next night and talked about excitement and enthusiasm in memory of him.

The two suggestions I have mentioned—underwhelmed and excitement—are important, for the world belongs to the enthusiasts who can keep cool. Never become gloomy; never lose faith. Always believe in the possibilities inherent in human nature. Always believe in the greatness of yourself. Forever believe in the future of mankind. Be a believer, an enthusiast, an excited person who doesn't emotionalize but always keeps cool. Trust the Lord and think!

Whenever I recall my old friend Hugh Tilroe, broken physically but not mentally or spiritually, his advice comes back to me: "In God's name, tell people that they are great souls, that they can be greater people, that life is good, and that it can be greater by overcoming bad news."

Visualize now those tired, gloomy thoughts flowing out of your mind, leaving you underwhelmed by all the bad news. Think objectively and dispassionately. Do not emotionalize but *think.* Be excited and life will be good, very good.

FOURTEEN

"I'll See You in The Morning"

It was a long-distance telephone call, spanning nearly half the continent. The voice at one end was feminine, old, and frail. The voice at the other end was masculine, vital, and crisply strong. It was an aged mother and a beyond-middle-aged son who were speaking.

Strangely and tenderly, sometimes I grant you exasperatingly, men to mothers are always little boys. The conversation, therefore, was pitched on that level, and she talked to him about the simple, humble, endearing things of the family. She was talking from a little midwestern village, from an old-fashioned home on a tree-lined street. He was in a towering office building in throbbing and surging Manhattan. But it was a communication between two people who loved each other more than life itself.

He knew she wasn't well and he said to her, "Mother, I am flying out tonight and we will have a good time together. You just get everything ready and I will be with you tomorrow."

"Ah," she said, "I will have all the things you like to eat. Won't it be nice to have my boy home again?" And then her quavering voice came over the phone, "I'll see you in the morning."

When he arrived the next morning, he was told that, quietly and peacefully during the night, his beloved mother had gone across to the other side. There she lay peacefully. He looked upon her face, upon the lips that would not speak again, and he knew that the last words he had heard her say he would never forget: "I'll see you in the morning."

This man is a longtime friend of mine—modern, businesslike, matter-of-fact; you might even say he is sophisticated. I once asked him what he thought about that phrase, "I'll see you in the morning." He looked at me with a face full of surprise. "Why, of course," he said, "I'll see her in the morning."

"How do you know?" I asked.

"Oh," he replied, "don't you remember how you and I and our other friends used to go to those little country churches long ago?" And I do well remember. I thank the Lord that I had a chance to grow up in little country churches just after the turn of the century. Looking out the windows, you saw no buildings, only fields and hills and woods and the sky.

Those preachers weren't always highly educated men, but they believed everything they said. Furthermore, they had spiritual experience to communicate; they were talking from lives that knew God through Jesus Christ. My friend continued, "Don't you remember the dear old hymn, 'There's a land that is fairer than day, And by faith we can see it afar.' And the refrain: 'In the sweet by and by, We shall meet on that beautiful shore.' Oh, yes," he said, "I haven't the slightest doubt at all that I will see her in the morning. "

When I first began preaching, we had to deal with crass, sophomoric, cocky scientists who had suddenly discovered the amazing things man could do in the universe. They tended to bow God out, or at least reduce Him. They treated the Bible (at least some did) as old wives' tales. People who had a fundamental concept of God were looked upon askance. Thus began a slow but steady abandonment of the precepts of the faith. Science, you see, had to grow up, and it took quite a few years.

I used to think that, in an Easter sermon, I had to spend half my time defending the faith. I got over that a long while ago, and so did science, because science now has reached out in this universe and found that it is a revelation of God rather than a depreciation of Him. It is increasingly apparent that the whole universe is, and can be, characterized by one word, *life,* and not the word *death.* So the

> *No one has to prove the Bible. The Bible has long since proved itself.*

ancient Gospel comes back now with the support of science.

If you are so old-fashioned and outmoded as to want to raise a conflict between science and religion, you ought to go back to school. Science now shows that in this universe is a vast Mind and a great Spirit. The great men have always held this view; it was only the small-fry, scientific infantile who said that science and Christianity were incompatible.

I once went on archeological expeditions in the Holy Land with some of the greatest scholars in this field. I asked one of them, "Are you trying to prove the Bible?"

"We are pure scientists," he replied. "We are working to uncover what is here. We are not digging to prove anything." Then he looked at me and asked, "What is the matter with you? No one has to prove the Bible. The Bible has long since proved itself. But I will tell you one thing for sure: Everything we uncover substantiates what the Bible says about the circumstances of the ancient life with which we are working."

So, if the Bible tells you that there is a land beyond, that there is life after death, that there is immortality, you can be sure it is a fact. And the great minds have always known it. Take John Morely who, at the end of his remarkable book of recollections, writes: "And so to my home and in the gathering twilight." What home? Why, of course, the many mansions beyond this life of mortality.

Years ago, Sir William Osier gave a speech to the students at Yale that has gone down in history as a classic. He has been characterized as the greatest doctor who ever practiced in the United States. Born in Canada, later he taught at Johns Hopkins University and finally in England.

When he decided to leave the United States, the greatest financiers in the country offered large sums to keep him here. He trained the famous Mayo brothers and Harvey Cushing, the great brain surgeon.

Dr. Osier lost a son in World War I. The greatest physicians in the American army tried to save the boy, but his wounds were mortal. Sadly, they had to put in the earth the body of the beloved son of their dear chief. This was the beginning of the end for Osier, for the boy was the apple of his eye, the idol of his life, the center of his dreams. Finally, a few years later, Osier was taken with an illness which he, with his skillful understanding and marvelous diagnostic ability, knew to be a fatal disease. He was observed, in his last hours, writing something on a sheet of paper. When he was dead, they had to take the paper from his cold hands, and this is what it said: "And so the voyage is nearly over and the harbor in view. It has been a glorious journey with such good companions along the way. But, I go gladly, for my boy will be waiting for me over there."

Now, are you willing to presume that a mind like Sir William Osier's was wrong, especially when his faith was

> *There has never been any darkness*
> *that hasn't given way to light.*

built upon the substantiality of the Word of God and the permanency of Jesus of Nazareth, as well as human intellectual and spiritual history? No one anywhere has yet disproved Jesus. He lives, and because He lives, we live also.

So, when you have to come to that sad experience of seeing someone whom you love disappear into the darkness, just listen and you will hear that person say, 'Til see you in the morning." And when the time comes that you, too, shall go into that darkness, realize to your comfort that darkness is only the prelude to light.

Did you ever observe that there has never been any darkness that hasn't given way to light? Light is the ruler of the day, the sun; light is the answer, not darkness. I was at Mount Holyoke College once, visiting my daughter Elizabeth, who was a student there. We were walking around the campus of this lovely New England college and came upon a sundial which had the following inscription: "To larger sight the rim of shadow is the line of light." We meditated on it and discussed it. There was no author's name given and no explanation offered.

With small sight, you see only shadow; to larger sight, the rim of shadow is the line or beginning of light. That is exactly what the Resurrection story teaches.

Let me illustrate this further. I went out to Kennedy Airport one night to take a plane to Paris. We took off quite late due to some mechanical difficulty; in fact, it was one o'clock in the morning. It was a moonless and starless night. There was rain in the air and some mist; it was very black and dark. That is really something, isn't it, to get into a mighty plane and zoom through the dark, heading east over the dark ocean. The attendant came around to pull down the window shades, and I said to her, "Please leave mine up; I to see what I can see."

I sat there looking into the darkness and faintly, far in the distance—you see it was then 6:00 A.M. in Paris—a thin line of golden light appeared. Five hundred miles and one hour later, all of a sudden that line of light burst into the amazing glory of the dawn.

That is the way it is. When the final hour comes, and the deep darkness is there, remember the words on the sundial: "To larger sight the rim of shadow is the line of light."

"I'll see you in the morning."

Many have had mystical experiences along this line. I was preaching in Georgia at a Methodist gathering under the leadership of my good friend Bishop Arthur Moore. He had some Methodist preachers of Georgia there with their church members. It was a real old-time Methodist gathering, and such preaching! Dr. Charles Allen of Houston, Texas, a lanky, dyed-in-the-wool Southerner, was just wonderful, and so was Bishop Moore, one of the truly great preachers of our time. And I came along with my poor little feeble Yankee talk. And there was lots of singing.

At the end of the final meeting, Bishop Moore asked all the preachers in the congregation to come to the platform and form a choir to sing for the folks. As they came, the congregation was singing that old song, "At the cross, at the cross where I first saw the light, And the burden of my heart rolled away." As these preachers walked down from their places, I was sitting on the platform. They all walked down the aisles, singing that old hymn. Then I saw my dear old father.

Before he died, my father had suffered several strokes and could hardly move, and his voice was a whisper. But as I was sitting on that platform, there walked my father down the aisle, singing, with a wonderful light on his face: "At the cross, at the cross where I first saw the light." He seemed about forty; he was trim and vital and healthy and handsome, and he was smiling at me. When he put up his hand in the old familiar gesture, it was so real that I jumped up from my chair. What other people thought, I don't know. But there were only my father and I in that big auditorium. Then I sat down and could see him no more; but the inner feeling of his presence in my heart was indisputable. So I can say to my dear father, "I'll see you in the morning."

There is just one more thing about this great Resurrection truth that I wish to emphasize. Why was Jesus Christ raised from the dead? To prove that nothing can overcome the power of God—nothing—not even death.

What I should like to ask you, and ask myself, is this: Are you, and am I, living in the power of this Resurrection? Or are we defeated? My simple belief about Christianity is that if you really get it in your heart, it gives you an astonishing power. The trouble is that most of us have only a weak version of it. But get the resurrected kind of faith, and you really have something that can defeat anything.

Let me illustrate that possession of power by those who live in the power of the Resurrection. I once sat in my study with a tiny woman. She sat on my couch and her feet didn't even touch the floor. She was dressed in a Chinese costume, but she was British. She had that wonderful cockney speech that I always liked. One day, in London, she went to a Salvation Army street meeting and was converted; and when I say converted, I mean converted. She became a resurrected person. Then she developed an avid interest. The gentleman for whom she worked had a wonderful library on China and she began reading.

One day, her employer came in and found her reading and reproached her. He said, "I hired you to dust and clean, not to read my books. Besides, you didn't ask if you might read my books."

"Ah, sir," she said, "I am so fascinated with China."

"Read the books, but not until after you get the housework done," he replied.

Then she received the call. She believed that God wanted her to go as a missionary to China. She went to the Mission Board and, of course, they were all highly intellectual, highly educated ecclesiastics, and they gave her an intellectual test that she couldn't pass. They said no, you do not measure up to our intellectual standards; you can't go. But did that faze her? Not at all. She had received her commission from a higher Source than a Mission Board.

So remarkable was the career of the missionary Gladys Aylward that, years later, a motion picture was made of it called *Inn of the Sixth Happiness.* And it was a fascinating movie. This Gladys Aylward, sitting in my study, told me about the times she used to preach on the streets in Yencheng and other Chinese cities. The little British cockney woman told the people that no power on earth could overcome the Christian, that God was with him and Jesus Christ was with him and that, if he would become a resurrected soul, he could triumph over the world. This went on, week after week.

One day, the governor summoned her and said, "We have a terrible situation. There is a riot in the prison, where murderers and vicious men are guarded by only twelve soldiers. We can't go in; they will kill us. And one of the worst men in the prison is berserk. He has a huge meat cleaver in his hand and has already killed two men and terrified the others. We want you to go in and take the meat cleaver out of his hands."

"You must be out of your mind, sir," she said.

"I have listened to you in the street telling that your God is always with you, about Daniel in the lion's den, and how Jesus Christ, in your heart, will protect you."

"Ah, but you misunderstand, sir."

"Oh, you haven't been telling the truth," he replied. "I only know what I heard you say and I believed you."

She knew then that, if she ever wanted to preach again, she would have to go into that prison. She asked the Lord to go with her and she felt strangely peaceful. She stood at the prison door; they unlocked it, quickly shut it, so fearful were they. She found herself in a long, narrow tunnel. At the end, she could see men wildly running about, shouting and cursing. She prayed, "Be within me, Jesus."

She walked to the end of the tunnel and saw the madman, the meat cleaver dripping with blood, chasing a man. Suddenly he was in front of her. They stood facing each other, the little woman and the giant. She looked into his wild and feverish eyes and calmly said, "Give me that weapon. " There was a moment of hesitation; then, with utter docility, he handed it to her. "Now," she said, "get in line, all of you men—get back in line." Quietly, they lined up.

Addressing them, she asked, "What are your complaints? I will tell them to the governor and I assure you in his name that, where possible, they will be corrected."

The resurrected life, the Resurrection of Jesus Christ, is to give us spiritual power for ourselves and all the world, and the power to make a better world in His name. All who live with Him can be sure of meeting again those you love and have lost awhile. You may confidently say to them, "I'll see you in the morning."

FIFTEEN

MIRACULOUS LOVE

A group of us stood on a hillside overlooking some fields where occurred one of the greatest events in the history of mankind. In those fields, on a mystic and starlit night long ago, some simple shepherds saw the heavens filled with a chorus of angels proclaiming peace on earth, goodwill to men.

I contemplated those fields, remembering that the shepherds, after viewing that angelic sight, said, "Let us now go even unto Bethlehem, and see this thing which is come to pass" (Luke 2:15). And then our group, too, went to Bethlehem, a short distance away.

In that land, changes take place slowly. Camel trains are still silhouetted against the sky; people still ride little donkeys; shepherds still watch over their flocks by day and night, on rocky hillsides and in stony pastures.

There is, in the Holy Land, a strange blending of the old with the new. I saw a train of fifty camels, laden with merchandise and led by an Arab in flowing white garments with a voluminous headdress shielding his face from the sun. The camel train pulled up and stopped for a red light at the Jerusalem airport to let an airplane taxi in from a faraway place. The Arab was unmoved by the airplane.

> *The miracle is not only His birth*
>
> *but also what He does.*

When the light changed to green, the camels moved on.

At another place, I saw a sweet-faced young mother riding a donkey and holding a baby in her arms. The donkey was led by a sturdy young man clad in traditional costume. The couple seemed to me for all the world like Mary and Joseph coming into that ancient walled town.

At Bethlehem, our group lingered silently and thoughtfully at the place where Jesus was born. The land is honeycombed with the caves in which people then lived. Jesus probably wasn't born in a wooden stable as we know stables here but in a cave where the animals were sheltered.

It is the same little town of Bethlehem over which the star stood, where the everlasting light proclaimed that here had taken place the greatest miracle of all. And the miracle is not only His birth but also what He does. From time to time, people tell me that miracles never happen. I used to agree with them because I wanted to be scientific. But I finally decided that the highest form of science is spiritual science, for it follows laws the same as physical science does; and Jesus Christ releases powers in history greater than any that physical science has ever released.

A miracle is a wonder that we find difficult to explain. After we have learned to explain it, we no longer regard it as a miracle. One of these miracles is the miracle of love.

Haven't you ever noticed the strange things that seem to happen to people at Christmastime? On Christmas Eve, for example, amid the throngs on the city streets, irritation is softened and stridencies become less. There is a flow of love, a community of understanding. Prejudice weakens and, for twenty-four hours, cities, towns, and villages everywhere are different because people's hearts are different. I have never known this to fail. In all my years, I have often wondered why all of us could not be this way throughout the year. It is the miracle of love working magical transformations.

When I began preaching, businesspeople and scientists —indeed almost everyone—thought of love as something theoretical. Now, however, scientists and the so-called realistic thinkers tell us that the only practical way to live is by practicing love and goodwill.

Yet I have always known that love really works. On one of our early trips to Jerusalem, the Holy City, we saw people fighting one another. In the center of the city there was an eight-hundred-foot stretch of desolation called No Man's Land. On one side were warring Arabs, on the other, warring Jews.

I was waiting at this No Man's Land checkpoint to meet Father Patrick, a famous Franciscan priest. Finally, an old car chugging along was stopped by the sentry. Out of the car stepped a priest with a face that made you love him at once. Father Patrick was one of the best-known Christians in the Middle East. He could even cross the border unchallenged. At this meeting, the sentries gathered around him and he put his arm around them, saying, "Hi, boys! How are you all?"

I said to one of the sentries, "You fellows seem to love Father Patrick."

"Oh, yes, we all love him," he replied.

One of them waved an arm toward the other side. "They love him over there," he said, "just as we do here."

This Franciscan was going back and forth, weaving strands of love that no politician could weave, that no United Nations commissioners could bring about! It was a living demonstration that on those very roadways where Jesus walked, there was occurring a miracle of love. A modern disciple, Father Patrick demonstrated that people can learn to live together in goodwill.

Perhaps the idea of love working internationally in the relationships between peoples may surprise you. It should not. Have you ever actually, wholeheartedly, tried love instead of hate? When someone has done something that has annoyed or offended you, have you ever tried loving him into a good relationship instead of fighting him back? Did you ever bless people for the mean things they have done to you? Have you ever overcome your prejudices and preconceived notions about people by learning to know and love them?

A man spoke to me once in a city where I was scheduled to speak. I recognized him as the assistant to a seemingly very difficult executive in a midwestern business. This assistant, Bill, I will call him, had to report to his boss every day. "I would actually stand outside his door feeling cold all over," Bill told me. "My hands were clammy. I could feel chills going up and down my spine. And I knew he would either bark at me or receive me in stony silence.

"'There, sir, there it is,' I would say, placing my report before him.

"He would look at it, then at me, and never say a word. Sometimes he would grumble, 'All right. Get going. I have it.'"

Of course this attitude stimulated a feeling of hatred within the assistant. He asked me what he ought to do. "Perhaps, if we were of the same faith, we might get together," he said.

"Well," I replied, "you are of the same faith in God. That makes you his brother. Have you brought the Bible to bear on the situation? I suggest that you try loving that man into a pleasant relationship."

"No one can love him," he protested. "There isn't a soul in the world who loves him."

"Then perhaps he is suffering from an inferiority complex," I suggested. "Maybe he is lonely and shy, and his spirit has retreated behind this domineering personality. Why don't you try an experiment? Pray for him, asking that you may understand him and be able to help him. Put tomorrow's meeting with him in God's hands. Think of this unhappy man and forget yourself, and when you stand outside his door in the morning, project thoughts of love toward him. Ask the Lord how you can help him."

Bill tried the experiment for a long time without results. Then, while they were discussing a problem in cost accounting, a subject in which Bill was an expert, they were bending over the desks, their heads close together. "Suddenly I felt a surge of love like a wave of compassion sweeping over me," Bill told me later. "And when we had finished our discussion, the boss put his hand on my shoulder and said, 'Bill, I've come to depend upon you more and more. You mean a lot to me.' In that moment I saw, behind the stern exterior, the unhappy, lonely man you had suggested he might be."

Bill is no longer shrinking and inarticulate. "I want to tell you," he declared, "this power of love works. People I once disliked or looked down upon, I now appreciate and get along with."

That is what the Baby, born in a manger long ago, came to tell us. I have often wondered about the wondrous power given Him at birth, which He exercised over human beings. Some mysterious quality was put into Jesus—into His smile, into His voice—so that people, when they came close to Him, were changed completely. As they yielded themselves to Jesus, no matter what their weaknesses and failures had been, they were taken away. This is the greatest miracle of all—this new birth that takes place within human beings.

I don't know what your life struggle may have been, what weakness, what sense of defeat, or what prejudice has plagued you. You know what they are. You may have struggled with them all your life and been defeated by them. But the minute you yield yourself to the Spirit of Him who first came as a Baby in a manger, you can be changed.

Most unhappy people simply need the love and understanding of others who have the spiritual answer.

A wonderful story showing the application of brotherhood and love is revealed by an incident that occurred in a hospital when a hopeless, battered, would-be suicide was brought in. A nurse, in talking to him, discovered that he knew a great deal about medicine. She spoke to the attending physician. "I think this poor fellow is a doctor," she said.

"Where did you get your medical information?" the doctor asked the patient.

"Never mind," was the answer. But the doctor pursued the subject. "You interest me. You have learned a lot somewhere." Eventually, the man opened up and told his story.

"I was a lieutenant colonel in the medical department of the army," the man admitted. "I practiced medicine in a large city before the war."

"What happened to you?" the physician asked.

"My wife was unfaithful to me, and it knocked the props out from under me. From then on, I didn't care and I just let myself go. I became an alcoholic. Now I'm licked, hopeless. I wish you would let me die."

The physician remembered that Freddie, an orderly, had been brought into the hospital in the same hopeless condition. But Freddie had found Christ. So the doctor sent for Freddie to talk to the man.

Freddie told the patient, "You can never do anything for yourself. But if you will just let Jesus heal you, He can put you right back where you were; maybe He'll do even better by you."

The patient stared intently at Freddie's face. "I heard that as a boy," he said, "but I never gave myself to Jesus."

"You will never know peace until you do," the orderly insisted.

"How do you do it?" asked the man.

Freddie told him. "All you need to say is, 'Dear Jesus, I am weak and can't handle my life. I give myself to You.' "

Sometime later, that patient was successfully practicing his profession again. That is why, all over the world, people are singing about Jesus. That is the reason we love Him so. What is His power? It is the power of God, who created us and is always re-creating us. Most unhappy people simply need the love and understanding of others who have the spiritual answer.

If you are doing what you know is wrong or mean or unkind, if you feel weakness or inability within yourself, just give yourself to Him. These things will fall away and you will be made new in Christ. That is why the shepherds said, "Let us now go even unto Bethlehem, and see this thing which is come to pass."

Miracles do happen, even today.

महीप सिंह
की
लोकप्रिय कहानियाँ

महीप सिंह

प्रभात प्रकाशन, दिल्ली
ISO 9001:2008 प्रकाशक

प्रकाशक • **प्रभात प्रकाशन**
4/19 आसफ अली रोड,
नई दिल्ली–110002

संस्करण • प्रथम, 2016
मूल्य • दो सौ पचास रुपए
मुद्रक • आर–टेक ऑफसेट प्रिंटर्स, दिल्ली

MAHEEP SINGH KI LOKPRIYA KAHANIYAN
Published by Prabhat Prakashan, 4/19 Asaf Ali Road, New Delhi-2
e-mail: prabhatbooks@gmail.com ISBN 978-93-5186-901-6
₹ 250.00

अनुक्रम

उलझन

कॉलेज से आते ही प्रोफेसर महेंद्रसिंह ने अपना कोट और टाई उतारकर पलंग पर फेंक दिए। पप्पी पलंग पर सोई हुई थी और सुरजीत कौर पास ही बैठी खाना गरम कर रही थी। 'आँ–हाँ! अभी पगड़ी न उतारिएगा।'' वह वहीं बैठी–बैठी चिल्लाई, ''दो मिनट बैठकर साँस ले लीजिए। बाहर से गरम–गरम आते हैं और आते ही पगड़ी उतार देते हैं, सिर में सीधी हवा लगती है और फिर जुकाम हो जाता है।···कितनी बार कहा। मेरी तो कोई सुनता ही नहीं।''

महेंद्रसिंह अब तक पगड़ी उतारकर मेज पर रख चुके थे और शीशे के सामने खड़े अपने केशों पर कंघा फेर रहे थे। सुरजीत कौर ने खाना मेज पर लगा दिया और कोट व टाई को हैंगर पर टाँगते हुए झुँझलाए स्वर में कहा, ''इतना भी नहीं होता कि आकर अपने कपड़े तो हैंगर पर टाँग दें। बस पलंग पर फेंक दिए। क्रीज खराब हो जाती तो कल कॉलेज क्या पहनकर जाते?''

महेंद्रसिंह कुछ बोले नहीं, थोड़ा मुसकरा भर दिए और तौलिए से अपने हाथ पोंछते हुए खाने की मेज पर बैठ गए। पानी के गिलास भरकर सुरजीत भी बैठने को ही थी कि पलंग पर पतले दुपट्टे के अंदर लेटी हुई पप्पी थोड़ी सी कसमसाई।

''और गुरीबत!'' कहती हुई सुरजीत झट से पलंग की ओर बढ़ी और उसे सुलाने के लिए थपकियाँ देने लगी।

''अब आओ भी।'' महेंद्रसिंह चम्मच से सब्जी का रसा पीते हुए बोले, ''दो बज रहे हैं और मुझे बड़े जोर से भूख लग रही है। तुम यह क्या ले बैठीं?''

''भूख क्या मुझे नहीं लगी है?'' सुरजीत जरा झुँझलाकर बोली, ''पप्पी जाग जाएगी तो दोनों का खाना हराम हो जाएगा, आप शुरू कीजिए।''

किंतु पप्पी को सुलाने के सभी प्रयत्न विफल रहे और आखिर उसे साथ लेकर बैठना पड़ा। उसने प्लेट से रोटियाँ निकालकर नीचे फेंक दीं, सब्जी की कटोरी को मेज

पर उलट दिया। महेंद्रसिंह अरे-अरे! करते रहे, सुरजीत खीझती-झुँझलाती रही और दोनों किसी प्रकार खाते रहे।

महेंद्रसिंह को कॉलेज में प्राध्यापक हुए दो वर्ष ही हुए थे। अपने घर से काफी दूर बंबई जैसे नगर में उन्हें नौकरी मिली। पहले वर्ष तो वह अकेले एक होटल में रहते रहे, क्योंकि लगातार प्रयत्न करते रहने पर भी उन्हें रहने योग्य कोई उचित स्थान नहीं मिल सका। दूसरे वर्ष बड़ी चेष्टा करने पर उन्हें अपने कॉलेज से लगभग दस मील दूर एक खोली मिली, अर्थात् एक कमरा, जिसमें लकड़ी का परदा लगाकर एक रसोई बनाई गई थी। किराया छह मास का पेशगी देना पड़ा था। कुशल इतनी ही थी कि कुछ पगड़ी नहीं देनी पड़ी। महेंद्रसिह का बस चलता तो ऐसे मकान की ओर आँख उठाकर भी नहीं देखते, किंतु वह अनुभव कर चुके थे कि उनके जैसे वेतन पानेवाले व्यक्ति को बंबई जैसे नगर में इससे अच्छे स्थान की आशा नहीं करनी चाहिए।

खाना खाकर महेंद्रसिंह पलंग पर लेट गए और एक पत्रिका के पन्ने उलटने लगे। सुरजीत ने पप्पी को उनके पास बैठा दिया और स्वयं जूठे बरतनों को समेटने में लग गई। महेंद्रसिंह कई बार कह चुके थे कि क्यों न एक नौकर रख लिया जाए, जो बरतन माँजने, कपड़े धोने और पप्पी को खिलाने में मदद कर दिया करे, किंतु सुरजीत सदा यही कहकर टालती रही कि इतने वेतन में बंबई जैसे नगर में नौकर रखने की गुंजाइश कैसे हो सकती है। आखिर दस-बीस पीछे भी तो डालने चाहिए। समय-कुसमय में कुछ पास न होगा, तब किसके सामने हाथ फैलाएँगे? महेंद्रसिंह इस तर्क पर चुप हो जाते? फिलहाल एक बाई काम करती थी, जो दोनों समय बरतन माँज जाती और कमरे में झाड़ू-कटका कर जाती। बंबई में कटका का अर्थ होता है—गीले कपड़े से कमरे के फर्श को साफ कर देना।

सुबह महेंद्रसिंह की नींद खुली तो उन्होंने देखा कि सुरजीत नहाई-धोई रसोई में बैठी स्टोव जला रही है। वह पलंग से उठकर कुरसी पर बैठ गए और बोले, "एक गिलास पानी देना।" सुरजीत ने चाय का पानी स्टोव पर चढ़ा दिया था। उसने उठकर एक गिलास बासी पानी, जो उनको नित्य प्रात: पीने की आदत थी, उनके सामने रख दिया और कहा, "जल्दी नहा-धो आइए काफी देर हो गई है?" महेंद्रसिंह ने पानी पीकर मेज पर रखी टाइमपीस की ओर देखा। साढ़े छह बजनेवाले थे। उन्होंने दैनिक पत्र उठाया और उसकी मोटी-मोटी सुर्खियाँ देखने लगे। सुरजीत ने रसोई में से ही कहा, "चाय तैयार है। फिर कॉलेज को देर हो जाए तो मुझे न कहिएगा?"

महेंद्रसिंह जमुहाई लेते हुए उठे और इधर-उधर देखते हुए बोले, "तौलिया कहाँ है?"

"तार पर नहीं टँगा है क्या?"

उन्होंने कमरे में आर-पार बँधे हुए तार पर दृष्टि डाली और उस पर से तौलिया उतार लिया। फिर उन्होंने कमरे के एक कोने के आले से साबुनदानी और पेस्ट उठाया, पर देखा कि वहाँ ब्रुश नहीं है। ''मेरा ब्रुश कहाँ है?'' वह जोर से चिल्लाए।

''वहाँ आले में नहीं है?'' सुरजीत ने रसोई में ही बैठे-बैठे उत्तर दिया।

''यहाँ तो कहीं नहीं है।''

''वहीं कहीं इधर-उधर होगा। देखिए न?''

महेंद्रसिंह ने इधर-उधर देखा, किंतु उन्हें कहीं दिखाई न दिया। बोले, ''आओ जरा ढूँढ़ दो, मुझे तो नहीं मिलता।''

इधर पप्पी भी जाग गई। सुरजीत ने उसे पलंग से उठाया और उनकी गोद में देते हुए कहा, ''पकड़िए, मैं देखूँ।'' महेंद्रसिंह ने पप्पी को ले लिया। वह अपने छोटे से हाथ से उनके मुँह की ओर ताकती हुई उनकी लंबी नाक को पकड़ने की कोशिश कर रही थी और महेंद्रसिंह बुत बने खड़े थे।

''यह लीजिए।'' सुरजीत ने ब्रुश अपने हाथ में लेते हुए कहा, ''उस कोने में पड़ा था, मगर यह नहीं हुआ कि जरा कमर झुकाकर ढूँढ़ लें। एक आदमी तो खाली आपके कामों के लिए होना चाहिए।''

महेंद्रसिंह हँस दिए, बोले, ''तुम्हारे सामने तो सचमुच मेरी सारी चलत-फिरत मारी जाती है। पता नहीं, पिछला साल कैसे कट गया। अब तो तुम्हारे बिना मुझसे तिल भर भी करते-धरते नहीं बनता। देखो न, जरा-जरा सी बात के लिए तुम्हारे सहारे पड़ा रहता हूँ।''

सुरजीत जब कभी महेंद्रसिंह के मुख से इस प्रकार के शब्द सुनती, उसे एक प्रकार का आत्मिक आनंद मिलता। यह अनुभूति उसे एक अजीब सा सुख देती कि कोई उस पर इतना आश्रित है कि अपनी छोटी-से-छोटी बात के लिए उस पर निर्भर रहता है। फिर भी वह नाराजगी भरे स्वर में बोली, ''अच्छा, जाइए और जल्दी निपटिए। ऐसा भी क्या आलस?''

□

महेंद्रसिंह सचमुच बड़े आलसी थे या यों कहिए कि अब हो गए थे। सुबह उठते ही चिल्लाना शुरू कर देते थे—पानी, तौलिया, ब्रुश, पेस्ट। नहाने जाते समय जब कच्छा भूल जाते, तब या तो सुरजीत स्मरण कराती या फिर गुसलखाने से कच्छे के लिए पुकार आती और सुरजीत को रसोईघर में जलते हुए स्टोव और उबलते हुए दूध को वैसे ही छोड़कर भागना पड़ता। आगे बढ़ते हुए प्रत्येक कदम पर वह पीछे घूमकर देखती जाती कि इस बीच कहीं पप्पी रसोईघर में घुसकर सब उलट-पुलट न कर दे। महेंद्रसिंह जब नहाकर आते तब उन्हें दाढ़ी फिक्स करने के लिए एक कटोरी पानी, धुला हुआ ठाठा

(दाढ़ी पर बाँधनेवाला कपड़ा) और काला धागा तैयार मिलता। ऐसे समय जब कभी पप्पी आकर उनसे उलझने लगती, तब वह चिल्ला उठते, "अरे, इसे पकड़ो, नहीं तो फिक्सो की शीशी उलट डालेगी?"

और तब सुरजीत रसोई से ही उसे आवाजें देना शुरू करती या फिर पकड़ने के लिए स्वयं आती।

एक दिन महेंद्रसिंह कॉलेज जाने के लिए तैयार हो रहे थे। पगड़ी बाँध चुके थे, कपड़े पहन चुके थे। बूट पहनने लगे तो देखा कि उसमें पड़े हुए मोजे कुछ गंदे हैं। उन्होंने इधर-उधर देखा, सुरजीत कहीं पास दिखाई नहीं दी। दूसरे मोजे ढूँढ़ने के लिए उन्होंने दो-तीन संदूकों के कपड़े इधर-उधर पलट डाले, किंतु सब बेकार। वह खड़े-खड़े झुँझला ही रहे थे कि सुरजीत हाथ में धुले हुए कुछ गीले कपड़े लिये वहाँ आ गई।

"अरे क्या खोज रहे हैं?" संदूकों के उलटे-पुलटे कपड़ों को देखकर उसने पूछा।

"तुम कहीं गई थीं? मुझे मोजे चाहिए। सब देख डाला, पर कहीं नहीं मिले।"

"गुसलखाने में पप्पी के दो फ्रॉक ही तो धोने गई थी। इतनी देर में मानो प्रलय आ गई।" कहते हुए उसने उघड़े हुए एक संदूक के कोने से मोजे निकालकर उनके हाथ में दे दिए। फिर कहा, "जरा ध्यान से देखते तो वहीं मिल जाते, मगर आपको तो खाली उलट-पलट करना आता है। सारे कपड़ों की तह खराब करके रख दी।"

देर हो जाने की आशंका से महेंद्रसिंह वैसे ही खीझे हुए थे, सुरजीत की इस बात से उनका पारा और चढ़ गया। बड़े गंभीर स्वर में बोले, "देखो, जब तक मैं कॉलेज चला न जाया करूँ, तब तक तुम एक क्षण के लिए भी मेरे सामने से न हटा करो। तुम्हें मालूम तो है कि तुम्हारे बिना जरा सी देर के लिए भी, एक क्षण के लिए भी मेरा काम नहीं चलता।"

महेंद्रसिंह के इस क्रोध में भी सुरजीत को हँसी आ गई, बोली, "जब मैं नहीं आई थी, तब आपका काम कैसे चलता था?"

"तब मैं अपना सब काम स्वयं कर लेता था। तुम्हीं ने तो मेरी आदतें बिगाड़ दी हैं।"

कभी-कभी सुरजीत घर के काम से बहुत खीझ जाती थी। महेंद्रसिंह का आलस और पप्पी उसके मुख्य कारण होते। पप्पी जब से बंबई आई थी, पहले दिन से ही उसे यहाँ के दूध से ऐसी अरुचि हो गई थी कि एक बार में पाँच औंस पी जानेवाली वह लड़की अब दूध की बोतल को मुँह नहीं लगाती थी। महेंद्रसिंह ने डिब्बे का दूध लाकर दिया, किंतु उसे वह भी नहीं भाया। इसलिए अब वह अधिकतर माँ के दूध पर रहने लगी थी और दिन में एक क्षण के लिए भी सुरजीत का पिंड नहीं छोड़ती थी। महेंद्रसिंह

जितनी देर भी घर पर रहते, या तो कुछ पढ़ते रहते या लिखते रहते। जब कभी सुरजीत तंग आकर पप्पी को उनके हाथ में पकड़ा जाती, वह उसे पाँच मिनट से अधिक नहीं टिका पाते। या तो वह उनकी पुस्तकों के पन्ने नोचने शुरू कर देती या फिर रोने लगती और महेंद्रसिंह झुँझलाकर किसी काम में लगी सुरजीत के पास उसे बैठा आते। वह झट माँ का कंधा पकड़कर खड़ी हो जाती और उसकी गोद में पहुँचने का प्रयत्न करने लगती।

उस दिन महेंद्रसिंह जब कॉलेज से लौटे, तब सुरजीत बहुत झुँझलाई और परेशान बैठी थी। पप्पी उसकी गोद में पड़ी दूध पी रही थी। आज उसने उसे बहुत परेशान किया था। खाना बनाते समय वह बार-बार रसोईघर में घुस आती और सुरजीत की पीठ का सहारा लेकर ऊधम मचाने लगती। एक बार वह बगल से होकर जलते हुए स्टोव के पास पहुँच गई। सुरजीत चमचे से सब्जी हिला रही थी। पप्पी का हाथ जलते हुए स्टोव पर पड़ने ही वाला था कि उसने देख लिया और वह हड़बड़ाकर उसे पकड़ने के लिए लपकी। पप्पी का हाथ जलने से तो बच गया, किंतु हड़बड़ाहट में सुरजीत की कोहनी स्टोव पर रखे बरतन से लगी और वह उलटकर नीचे आ गिरा। सारी सब्जी फर्श पर बिखर गई। सुरजीत के कपड़े पीले हो गए। दो-चार छींटे पप्पी पर आ पड़े और वह जोर-जोर से रोने लगी। फर्श पर पड़ी हुई सब्जी के रसे में सने हुए कपड़ों और पप्पी की चीखों ने उसे एक साथ पागल सा बना दिया। किसी प्रकार उसने अपने कपड़े बदले, पप्पी के बदन पर जहाँ छींटे पड़े थे, वहाँ नीली रोशनाई लगाई और फिर उसे चुप कराने के लिए वह दूध पिलाने लगी। इस घटना ने उसे इतना भ्रमित कर दिया कि उसे इस बात का ध्यान ही नहीं रहा कि महेंद्रसिंह के आने का समय हो गया है और उसे उनके लिए अब तक कुछ खाना बना लेना चाहिए था।

महेंद्रसिंह ने आते ही अपनी आदत के अनुसार कोट और टाई उतारकर पलंग पर डाल दिए और कमीज उतारते हुए बोले, ''जल्दी खाना लगाओ, भूख अपना पूरा जोर दिखा रही है।''

सुरजीत जैसे नींद से जागी। उसने पप्पी की ओर देखा। वह दूध पीते-पीते गोद में ही सो गई थी। उसे पलंग पर लिटाते हुए सुरजीत ने कहा, ''आज खाने में कुछ देर है। अभी बन नहीं पाया है।''

''अभी बन नहीं पाया है, क्यों?'' महेंद्रसिंह ने जरा तीखे स्वर में पूछा, ''मुझे तो भूख बड़े जोर से लग रही है।''

''अभी बन जाता है'' के अतिरिक्त सुरजीत ने और कुछ नहीं कहा। एक गुबार सा उसके हृदय में भरा हुआ था, जिस पर उसके मौन ने आवरण डाल रखा था। वह जैसे ही रसोईघर में जाने को हुई पप्पी जागकर रोने लगी। शायद उसकी जलन की पीड़ा

उसे सोने नहीं दे रही थी। सुरजीत ने पप्पी की ओर देखा और फिर महेंद्रसिंह की ओर कुछ तीखी दृष्टि से देखते हुए कहा, ''आप जरा इसे उठा लीजिए?''

एक तो महेंद्रसिंह वैसे ही पप्पी को बहुत कम लेते थे और अकसर सुरजीत को उसे गोद में लिये ही खाना बनाना पड़ता था, पर आज तो महेंद्रसिंह की मन:स्थिति भी ठीक नहीं थी। कुरसी पर बैठे और एक पत्रिका के पन्ने उलटते हुए वह बिगड़कर बोले, ''ना बाबा, यह काम मुझसे नहीं होगा।''

पप्पी तथा घरेलू कार्यों के प्रति महेंद्रसिंह के ये उद्‌गार सुरजीत के लिए नए नहीं थे। किंतु आज के उनके इन शब्दों ने उसे वह ठेस पहुँचाई कि उसका अंतरतम तिलमिला उठा। हृदयागार में चिरसंचित कुछ मानो अब फटकर बाहर निकल आना चाहता था। उसके नेत्र डबडबा आए और उसके मुख से कुछ अस्फुट शब्दों के निकलते-न-निकलते आँसुओं की धारा वेगवती होकर बह चली। पप्पी को पलंग से उठाते हुए उसने कहा, ''आप इसे नहीं लेंगे तो आज मुझसे खाना नहीं बन सकेगा?''

महेंद्रसिंह ने मूक दृष्टि से सुरजीत की ओर देखा। वह अपनी आँखें पोंछती हुई कह रही थी, ''आप पुरुष लोग यह समझते हैं कि जीविका कमाने के लिए आप तो मेहनत करते हैं और ये स्त्रियाँ घर में बेकार बैठी रोटियाँ तोड़ती हैं। इसलिए घर-गिरहस्ती का और अपना जितना भी बोझ इन पर डाला जाए, उतना ही ठीक, किंतु हम औरतें घर में अपना दिन किस तरह गुजारती हैं, यह हमें ही पता है। आपकी नौकरी तो कुछ घंटों की होती है, किंतु हम चौबीस घंटे के नौकर हैं और ऐसे नौकर कि जिनके काम को काम नहीं समझा जाता। आप अपने मालिकों से दया और सहानुभूति की आशा रखते हैं, किंतु हम पर आप शायद भूलकर भी दया दिखाना नहीं चाहते। आज मेरा जरा सा ध्यान चूक जाता तो पप्पी स्टोव से जल जाती और पता नहीं कितनी मुसीबतें उठानी पड़तीं। इसको बचाने में सारी सब्जी जमीन पर गिर गई। मेरे कपड़े खराब हो गए और इस पर भी कई जगह गरम छींटे पड़ गए। तब से यह लगातार रो रही है।''

महेंद्रसिंह ने खेद और उत्सुकता मिली दृष्टि से पप्पी की ओर देखा। उसकी बाँहों पर दो-तीन जगह नीली दवा लगी हुई थी। महेंद्रसिंह क्रोध से उबल पड़े और बोले, ''मैंने तुमसे कई बार कहा कि एक नौकर रख लो, लेकिन तुम हो कि मेरी बात सुनती ही नहीं।''

सुरजीत बोली, ''मुझे क्या नौकर से कोई चिढ़ है? अगर मैं यह खर्च बचाना चाहती हूँ तो क्या अपने लिए? कल अगर हमारे पास दो-चार पैसे न हुए तो आपके माता-पिता आपको नहीं, मुझे दोष देंगे कि इसने समय-कुसमय के लिए चार पैसे भी बचाकर नहीं रखे।''

सुरजीत ने देखा, पप्पी उसके कंधे पर सिर रखे सो गई है। उसने उसे धीरे से पलंग

पर लिटा दिया और अपना मुँह पोंछती हुई रसोईघर में चली गई।

महेंद्रसिंह की दृष्टि तो पत्रिका के पृष्ठों पर लगी थी, किंतु विचारों का झंझा कहीं और चल रहा था। अपने तीन-चार वर्ष के विवाहित जीवन में उन्होंने सुरजीत के नेत्रों में इस प्रकार के आँसू कभी नहीं देखे थे। आज की उसकी बातों ने उन्हें झकझोर दिया था और वह सोच रहे थे—क्या कॉलेज के अलावा घर के लिए मेरी कोई जिम्मेदारी नहीं है? क्या सुरजीत ने ठीक नहीं कहा कि हम पुरुषों के काम के घंटे तो सीमित होते हैं, पर स्त्रियाँ चौबीस घंटे की गुलाम होती हैं? हमें सप्ताह में एक दिन छुट्टी मिलती है, लेकिन उस दिन इन्हें और दिनों से ज्यादा काम होता है।

पता नहीं, कितनी देर वह इसी प्रकार सोचते रहे। उनकी विचार-शृंखला तब टूटी, जब सुरजीत ने उन्हें खाने के लिए बुलाया।

□

उस दिन के बाद से महेंद्रसिंह के व्यवहार में एक विचित्र सा परिवर्तन दिखाई देने लगा। उन्होंने मन-ही-मन निश्चय कर लिया था कि अब वे अपने छोटे-मोटे व्यक्तिगत कार्य स्वयं कर लिया करेंगे और जितना हो सकेगा, घर के काम में सुरजीत का हाथ बँटाएँगे। सुबह उठते ही उन्होंने स्वयं घड़े से एक गिलास पानी लेकर पिया। स्नान करने गए तो वहीं से अपना बनियान और कच्छा धोते लाए। कॉलेज जाने से पहले जूतों पर उन्होंने स्वयं ही पॉलिश कर ली। सुरजीत उनके इस व्यवहार पर चकित अवश्य हुई, किंतु बोली कुछ नहीं।

दो-चार दिन ऐसे ही बीत गए। अब महेंद्रसिंह कॉलेज से आकर अपने कपड़े पलंग पर फेंकते नहीं, बल्कि व्यवस्थित रूप से हैंगर पर टाँग देते। शाम को सुरजीत जब खाना बनाने लगती, तब वह पप्पी को लेकर छज्जे पर निकल जाते। एक दिन जब सुरजीत ने पूछा, तब उन्होंने कहा, ''मैंने सोच लिया है कि अब मैं अपने छोटे-मोटे काम स्वयं करूँगा और घर के काम में भी तुम्हारी मदद करूँगा।''

सुरजीत ने हँसते हुए कहा, ''हो चुका आपसे।''

''देख लेना।''

''तब तो बड़ी अच्छी बात है।''

उस दिन इतवार था, छुट्टी का दिन था। इतवार को केश धोना महेंद्रसिंह का नियम था। साधारणतः सुरजीत प्रातः उठते ही उनसे केश धोने के लिए कहना शुरू कर देती थी, पर वह छुट्टी के मूड में अपने सभी काम खूब बेफिक्री के साथ करते रहते थे। शौचादि से निवृत्त होकर वह चाय पी लेते, अखबार पढ़ते रहते और पड़ोसियों से गप्पें लगाया करते। जब सुरजीत कहते-कहते परेशान हो जाती और बिगड़ने लगती, तब वह तौलिया, साबुन और दही आदि लेकर गुसलखाने में जाते। आज भी उस क्रम में कुछ

विशेष अंतर नहीं पड़ा, किंतु जब वह केश धोकर बाहर आए और उन्हें सुखा चुके, तब स्वयं ही तेल लगाने लगे। सुरजीत पप्पी को गुसलखाने में नहला रही थी। लौटकर आई तो उसने देखा कि वह केशों में तेल लगा, कंघा कर जूड़ा बाँध रहे थे।

सुरजीत के हृदय को गहरी चोट लगी। जब से उसका महेंद्रसिंह से विवाह हुआ था और जब भी वह उनके निकट रही थी, रविवार को केश धोने के बाद उन पर तेल लगाने का कार्य वह स्वयं ही करती थी। महेंद्रसिंह के अन्य व्यक्तिगत कार्यों की अपेक्षा इस कार्य में शायद वह अधिक सजग रहती थी। आज उन्होंने स्वयं तेल लगा लिया है, यह देखकर उसे बड़ी ठेस लगी। किंतु वह बोली कुछ नहीं।

दूसरे दिन महेंद्रसिंह स्नान करने जाने लगे, तब वह बोली, ''कच्छा-बनियान धोने की जरूरत नहीं है, वहीं छोड़ दीजिएगा, मैं बाद में धो दूँगी।''

''क्या फर्क पड़ता है?'' कहते हुए महेंद्रसिंह गुसलखाने की ओर चले गए और जब वह लौटकर आए, तब उनके हाथ में धुले हुए कच्छे-बनियान के अतिरिक्त दो ठाठे भी थे।

□

जब से महेंद्रसिंह अपने व्यक्तिगत कार्यों को स्वयं करने में रुचि दिखाने लगे थे, सुरजीत को एक विचित्र प्रकार का असंतोष सा रहने लगा था। वह स्वयं नहीं समझती थी कि यह कैसी उलझन है, किंतु उसे लगता था, जैसे उसकी कोई मूल्यवान निधि प्रतिदिन लुटती जा रही है। जब महेंद्रसिंह अपने सारे काम उसी पर डाले रहते थे, तब कई बार वह खीझ उठती थी, किंतु उसकी उस खीझ में भी उसे एक सुख की अनुभूति होती थी। अब भी उसके कान इसी प्रतीक्षा में रहते कि महेंद्रसिंह कब उसे किसी चीज के लिए पुकारेंगे, किंतु अब वह उससे कुछ नहीं कहते थे। ठाठा, बनियान, कच्छा, टाई और रूमाल आप ही ढूँढ़ लेते थे। पप्पी को स्वयं ही लेकर छज्जे पर घूमने लगते थे। घर के वातावरण में एक विचित्र सी मूकता आने लगी थी। अब न महेंद्रसिंह की चिल्लाहट ही सुनाई देती थी, न सुरजीत की खिझलाहट ही।

अगले इतवार को महेंद्रसिंह केश धोकर छज्जे पर सुखाने लगे। थोड़ी देर में उन्हें पप्पी के रोने का स्वर सुनाई दिया और वह उसे घुमाने ले जाने के लिए अंदर गए।

''रहने दीजिए, अभी इसे दूध पिलाना है।'' सुरजीत ने कहा और महेंद्रसिंह चुपचाप बाहर आकर फिर बाल सुखाने लगे। थोड़ी देर में उन्होंने हाथ लगाकर देखा। केश सूख गए थे। वह कमरे में आए और अलमारी में से तेल की शीशी निकालकर कुरसी पर बैठकर उसका ढक्कन खोलने लगे।

सुरजीत बैठी यह सब देख रही थी। वह धीरे से उठी और पास आकर तेल की शीशी पकड़ते हुए बोली, ''लाइए, मैं लगा दूँ।''

''मैं लगा लूँगा।''

''लाइए न, लगाऊँ।'' सुरजीत ने जरा आग्रह से कहा।

''नहीं, मैं स्वयं लगाऊँगा।''

कहकर महेंद्रसिंह उसके हाथ से तेल की शीशी खींचने लगे, किंतु उन्होंने अनुभव किया कि सुरजीत की पकड़ कुछ कड़ी हो गई है। उन्होंने उसकी ओर देखा। सुरजीत की स्थिर दृष्टि उन पर गड़ी हुई थी। उनकी दृष्टि भी स्थिर हो गई। देखते-ही-देखते सुरजीत के नेत्र डबडबा आए और आँसुओं की एक अविरल धार बह निकली।

''अरे क्या हुआ?'' महेंद्रसिंह ने अचंभे में पूछा।

''कुछ नहीं।'' सुरजीत ने आँखें पोंछते हुए कहा, ''तेल मैं लगाऊँगी।''

महेंदसिंह हँस पड़े और बोले, ''तुम स्त्रियों को समझना तो शायद भगवान् के भी बस में नहीं।''

और यह कहते हुए उन्होंने तेल की शीशी सुरजीत के हाथ में देकर सिर आगे बढ़ा दिया।

□

पानी और पुल

गाड़ी ने लाहौर का स्टेशन छोड़ा तो एकबारगी मेरा मन काँप उठा। अब हम लोग उस ओर जा रहे थे, जहाँ चौदह साल पहले ऐसी आग लगी थी, जिसमें लाखों जल गए थे और लाखों पर जलने के निशान आज तक बने हुए थे। मुझे लगा, हमारी गाड़ी किसी गहरी, लंबी अंधकारमय गुफा में घुस रही है और हम अपना सबकुछ इस अंधकार को सौंपे दे रहे हैं।

हम सब लगभग तीन सौ यात्री थे। स्त्रियों और बच्चों की भी संख्या हममें काफी थी। लाहौर में हमने सभी गुरुद्वारों के दर्शन किए। वहाँ हमें जैसा स्वागत मिला, उससे आगे अब पंजासाहब की यात्रा में किसी प्रकार का अनिष्ट घट सकता है, ऐसी संभावना तो नहीं थी, परंतु मनुष्य के अंदर का पशु कब जागकर सभी संभावनाओं को डकार जाएगा, कौन जानता है?

यही सब सोचते-सोचते मैंने माँ की ओर देखा। देखा, हथेली में मुँह टिकाए कोहनी को खिड़की का सहारा दिए वे निरंतर बाहर की ओर देख रही थीं। खेत कट चुके थे। दूर-दूर तक सपाट धरती दिखाई दे रही थी। मुझे लगा, माँ की आँखों में से उतरकर यह सपाट़ता मन में पूरी तरह छा गई है। फिर मैंने अपने डिब्बे के दूसरे यात्रियों की तरफ देखा। उन पर गहरी उदासी छाई हुई थी। समझ में नहीं आ रहा था कि एकाएक ऐसी उदासी सब पर क्यों छा गई है?

''तुम्हें तो यह रास्ता अच्छी तरह याद होगा?'' मैंने माँ का ध्यान तोड़ते हुए पूछा, ''सैकड़ों बार आना-जाना हुआ होगा तुम्हारा?''

माँ मेरी ओर देखकर मुसकराई। वह मुसकराहट सब कुछ खोकर पाई हुई मुसकराहट थी। बोलीं, ''मुझे तो इस रास्ते का एक-एक स्टेशन तक याद है, पर आज यह इलाका कितना बेगाना-बेगाना सा लग रहा है। आज चौदह साल बाद इधर से जा रही हूँ। पहले भी ऐसे ही जाती थी। लाहौर पार करते ही अजीब सी उमंग नस-नस में दौड़ जाती थी।

सराई हमारा गाँव, जैसे-जैसे निकट आता जाता, वहीं की एक-एक शक्ल मेरे सामने दौड़ जाती, स्टेशन पर कितने लोग आए होते···

माँ की आँखों में चौदह साल पहले की याद तरल हो आई थी। पिताजी ने अपना रोजगार उत्तर प्रदेश में ही जमा लिया था। हम सब भाई-बहनों का जन्म पंजाब के बाहर ही हुआ था। मुझे याद है, पिताजी तो शायद साल में एकाध बार ही पंजाब जाते हों, पर माँ के दो-तीन चक्कर जरूर लग जाते थे। हममें जो छोटा होता, वह माँ के साथ जाता और जब से मुझे याद है—मेरी छोटी बहन ही उनके साथ जाया करती थी।

उन दिनों, जब पंजाब का विभाजन घोषित हो चुका था, पंजाब की पाँचों नदियों का जल उन्माद की तीखी शराब बन चुका था, माँ ने फिर पंजाब जाने का फैसला किया था। सभी ने ऐसे विरोध किया, जैसे वे जलती आग में कूदने जा रही हों और वह सचमुच आग में कूदने जैसा ही तो था, परंतु पिताजी सहित हम सब जानते थे कि माँ को अपने निश्चय से डिगाना कोई आसान काम नहीं। उन्होंने सबकी बातों को हँसकर टाल दिया। बीस-बाईस दिनों में वह वापस आ गईं, गाँव के घर का बहुत सा सामान वे बुक करा आई थीं। अपने साथ वे अपना पुराना चरखा और दही मथने की बड़ी मथानी ले आई थीं।

फिर सारे पंजाब में आग लग गई। घर-के-घर, गाँव-के-गाँव और शहर-के-शहर उस आग में जलने लगे। आग रुकी तो लगा, इधर तक सपाट फैली हुई जमीन अमृतसर और लाहौर के बीच से फट गई है और उस पार का फटा हुआ हिस्सा बीच में गहरी खाई छोड़कर न जाने कितना उधर खिसक गया है। हम सब भूल से गए कि उस गहरी खाई के उस पार हमारा अपना गाँव था, पक्की सड़क के किनारे, पीछे की ओर एक नहर थी, और पास ही जेहलम नदी अल्हड़ लड़की की तरह उछलती-कूदती बहती थी।

आज मैं माँ के साथ उस खाई पर राजकीय औपचारिकता के बाँधे हुए पुल से गुजरकर उसी ओर जा रहा था, जो कल कितना अपना था, आज कितना पराया है।

मैं एक पुस्तक के पन्ने उलट रहा था। माँ ने पूछा, "यह गाड़ी सराई स्टेशन पर रुकेगी?"

मैंने कुछ सोचा, फिर कहा, "हाँ, शायद रुके, पर पहुँचेगी रात के एक-दो बजे। हम लोग गहरी नींद में सो रहे होंगे। स्टेशन कब आकर निकल जाएगा, पता भी नहीं लगेगा। और अब अपना रखा ही क्या है वहाँ?"

माँ के चेहरे पर खिसियाहट सी फैल गई। बोलीं, "तुम्हारे लिए पहले भी वहाँ क्या रखा था?"

मेरी बात से माँ को चोट पहुँची थी। बिना और कुछ बोले मैं सिर झुकाकर अपनी पुस्तक के पन्नों में उलझ गया।

धीरे-धीरे अँधेरा छाने लगा। माँ ने पोटली खोलकर खाने के लिए कुछ निकाला।

मेरे एक दूर के मामाजी हमारे साथ थे। तीनों ने मिलकर कुछ खाया और सोने की तैयारी करने लगे। मामाजी तो दस मिनट में ही खर्राटे भरने लगे। मैं भी एक ओर लुढ़क गया। माँ वैसी ही बैठी रहीं।

कुछ देर बाद एकाएक मेरी आँख खुली तो देखा, माँ वैसे ही बाहर फैले हुए अँधेरे की ओर अपलक देखती हुई बैठी हैं। घड़ी देखी, साढ़े दस बज गए थे। मैंने कहा, "माँ, तुम लेट जाओ न!"

"अच्छा।" उनके मुँह से निकला और वे अधलेटी सी हो गईं।

उस अधनींदी अवस्था में मैंने कोई स्वप्न देखा, ऐसा तो मुझे याद नहीं आता, पर उस नींद में भी कुछ घबराहट अवश्य होती रही थी। शायद किसी अस्पष्ट स्वप्न की ही घबराहट हो। कोई लाल सी तरल चीज मुझे अपने चारों ओर फिरती अनुभव होती थी। और मुझे लग रहा था, उस लाल-लाल गाढ़ी सी चीज पर मेरे पैर फच-फच पड़ रहे हैं। फिर एकाएक मैं हड़बड़ाकर उठा। माँ मुझे झकझोर रही थीं। अजीब सी घबराहट और उत्तेजना से उनके हाथ काँप रहे थे।

"क्या है?"

"देखो, यह बाहर शोर कैसा है?"

मैंने बाहर झाँककर देखा। हमारी गाड़ी छोटे से स्टेशन पर खड़ी थी। प्लेटफॉर्म पर लैंप-पोस्टों की हल्की-हल्की रोशनी थी और अजीब सा कोलाहल छाया हुआ था। एकबारगी मेरा रोयाँ-रोयाँ काँप उठा था। चौदह साल पहले की अनेक सुनी-सुनाई घटनाएँ बिजली बनकर कौंध गईं, जब दंगाइयों ने कितनी गाड़ियों को जहाँ-तहाँ रोककर लोगों को गाजर-मूली की तरह काट डाला था। मामाजी भी जागकर मेरा कंधा हिला रहे थे।

"अरे क्या बात है?"

तभी मेरे कानों में आवाज पड़ी। उस भीड़ में से कोई चिल्ला रहा था, "अरे, इस गाड़ी में कोई सराई का है?"

"यह कौन सा स्टेशन है?" मैंने माँ से पूछा।

माँ ने कहा, "सराई···अपने गाँव का स्टेशन।"

बाहर से फिर आवाज आई, "अरे, इस गाड़ी में कोई सराई का है?"

मैंने माँ की ओर देखा। उनका चेहरा पूरी तरह आश्वस्त था।

"पूछो इनसे, क्या बात है?"

मैंने खिड़की से गरदन निकाली। बहुत से लोग घूमते हुए पुकार रहे थे, "अरे, कोई सराई का है?"

पास से जाते हुए एक आदमी को बुलाकर मैंने पूछा, "क्या बात है जी? आप में कोई इस गाँव का है?"

"हाँ, हम हैं इस गाँव के···" माँ आगे आकर बोलीं।

"तुम सराई की हो?" उस आदमी ने जोर देकर पूछा।

"हाँ जी?"

माँ के इतना कहते ही स्टेशन पर चारों ओर शोर मच गया। इधर-उधर घूमते हुए बहुत से आदमी हमारे डिब्बे के सामने जमा हो गए। फिर कई आवाजें एक साथ आईं।

"तुम सराई की हो?"

"हाँ जी, हम सराई के ही हैं···" माँ ने जोर देकर कहा, "इसी गाँव के।"

उपस्थित जनसमुदाय में एक कोलाहल सा हुआ। किसी की आवाज आई, "तुम किसके घर से हो?"

माँ ने मेरी ओर देखा। मैंने कहा, "मेरे पिताजी का नाम सरदार मूलासिंह है। ये मेरी माँ हैं?"

"तुम मूलासिंह के बेटे हो," कई लोग एक साथ चिल्लाए, "तुम मूलासिंह की बीवी हो···रवेलसिंह की भाभी? कैसे हैं सब लोग···?" कहते-कहते कितने ही हाथ हमारी ओर बढ़ने लगे। लोग हमारे संबंधियों में सबकी कुशल-क्षेम पूछते हुए अपने हाथ की पोटलियाँ मुझे और माँ को थमाते जा रहे थे। उनमें बादाम, अखरोट, किशमिश आदि सूखे मेवे बँधे हुए लग रहे थे। मैं और माँ गुमसुम से उन्हें ले-लेकर अपनी सीट पर रखते जा रहे थे। देखते-देखते हमारी बर्थ छोटी-छोटी कपड़ों की पोटलियों से भर गई।

मैं हक्का-बक्का सा यह सब देख रहा था। माँ अपने सिर का कपड़ा बार-बार सँभालती हुई हाथ जोड़ रही थीं। खुशी से उनके होंठ फड़फड़ा रहे थे। मुँह से कुछ भी निकल नहीं रहा था और लगता था, आँखें अभी चू पड़ेंगी।

वहीं खड़े गार्ड ने हरी लालटेन ऊपर उठाई और कोट की जेब से सीटी निकाली। मैंने देखा, तीन-चार आदमियों ने उसे पकड़ सा लिया।

"अरे बाबू! दो-चार मिनट और खड़ी रहने दे न गाड़ी को। देखता नहीं, यह बीबी इसी गाँव की है।" और एक ने उसका लालटेनवाला हाथ पकड़कर नीचे कर दिया।

"भरजाई, सरदारजी कैसे हैं? उन्हें क्यों नहीं लाईं पंजेसाहब दर्शन कराने?" एक बूढ़ा सा मुसलमान पूछ रहा था।

माँ ने दोनों हाथों से सिर का कपड़ा और आगे कर लिया। उनके मुँह से धीरे से निकला, "सरदारजी नहीं रहे···"

"क्या···? मूलासिंह गुजर गए? क्या हुआ था उन्हें?"

माँ चुप रहीं, मैंने जवाब दिया, "उनके पेट में रसौली हो गई थी। एक दिन अचानक फूट गई और दूसरे दिन पूरे हो गए।"

"ओह! बड़े ही नेक बंदे थे! खुदा उन्हें अपनी दरगाह में जगह दे!" उनमें से एक ने अफसोस प्रकट करते हुए कहा। कुछ क्षणों के लिए सब में खामोशी छा गई।

"भरजाई, तेरे बच्चे कैसे हैं?"

"वाहेगुरु की किरपा है, सब अच्छे हैं?" माँ ने धीरे से कहा।

"अल्लाह उनकी उम्र दराज करे।" कई आवाजें एक साथ आईं।

"भरजाई, तुम अपने बच्चों को लेकर यहाँ आ जाओ।" किसी एक ने कहा और कितनों ने दुहराया, "भरजाई, तुम लोग वापस आ जाओ...वापस आ जाओ।" प्लेटफॉर्म पर खड़ी कितनी आवाजें कह रही थीं—

"वापस आ जाओ।"

"वापस आ जाओ।"

मैंने सुना, मेरे पीछे खड़े मामाजी कुढ़ते हुए कह रहे थे, "हूँ...बदमाश कहीं के! पहले तो हमें मार-मारकर यहाँ से निकाल दिया, अब कहते हैं, वापस आ जाओ...लुच्चे!"

प्लेटफॉर्म पर खड़े लोगों ने उनकी बात नहीं सुनी थी। वे कहे जा रहे थे—

"भरजाई, तुम अपने बच्चों को लेकर वापस आ जाओ। बोलो भरजाई, कब आओगी? अपना गाँव तो तुम्हें याद आता है? भरजाई, वापस आ जाओ... ।"

माँ के मुँह से कुछ नहीं निकल रहा था। वे सिर का कपड़ा सँभालते हुए हाथ जोड़े जा रही थीं।

दूर खड़ा गार्ड हरी लालटेन दिखाता हुआ सीटी बजा रहा था।

इंजन ने सीटी दी। गाड़ी फक-फक करती हुई चल दी। भीड़-की-भीड़ हमारे डिब्बे के साथ चल दी।

"अच्छा भरजाई, सलाम...अच्छा बेटे, सलाम...रवेलसिंह को हमारा सलाम देना...सबको हमारा सलाम देना।"

माँ के हाथ जुड़े हुए थे और मुँह से गद्‌गद स्वर में धीरे-धीरे कुछ निकल रहा था। धीरे-धीरे गाड़ी कुछ तेज हो गई। हम दोनों खिड़की से सिर निकाले हाथ जोड़े रहे। भीड़ के लोग वहीं खड़े हाथ ऊपर उठाए चिल्लाते रहे।

गाड़ी स्टेशन के बाहर निकल आई तो मैंने बर्थ से पोटलियाँ हटाकर एक ओर कीं और माँ से कुछ कहने के लिए उनकी ओर देखा।

माँ की आँखों से आँसुओं की अविरल धारा बह रही थी, बहे जा रही थी। वे बार-बार दुपट्टे से आँखें पोंछे जा रही थीं, पर टूटे हुए बाँध का पानी बहता ही जा रहा था।

हमारी गाड़ी जेहलम के पुल पर आ गई थी। रात्रि की उस नीरवता में खडर...खडर की तेज आवाज आ रही थी। मैं खिड़की से झाँककर जेहलम का पुल देखने

लगा। मैंने सुना था, जेहलम का पुल बहुत मजबूत है। पत्थर और लोहे के बने उस मजबूत पुल को अँधेरे में मैं देख रहा था। मेरी दृष्टि और नीचे की ओर भी जा रही थी। वहाँ घुप अँधेरा था, पर मैं जानता था—वहाँ पानी है, जेहलम नदी का कल-कल करता हुआ स्वच्छ और निर्मल पानी, जो उस पत्थर और लोहे के बने हुए पुल के नीचे से बह रहा था।

□

कील

इकतीस दिसंबर है और फिर वही अजीब सी परेशानी। जब यह दिन आता है तो मोना को लगता है कि उसके हाथ से कुछ फिसलकर नीचे गिर जाता है और देखते-देखते पारे की तरह बिखर जाता है। उस रात को बारह बजने की प्रतीक्षा में लोग लहरों की तरह सड़कों पर भागते-फिरते हैं। सब 'कल' का स्वागत करने की ओर दौड़ रहे होते हैं, पर इस 'कल' का अहसास मोना को दिन भर बेचैन किए रहता है और बार-बार उसके अंदर ध्वनित होता रहता है, वह एक साल और बड़ी हो गई है।

इस बार पहली जनवरी को डैडी ने सुबह-सुबह 'हैपी बर्थ-डे' कहा तो छब्बीस की संख्या, जो कल से घंटियों की हल्की-हल्की आवाज की तरह उसके चारों ओर खनक रही थी, धमककर उसके अंदर उतर गई।

मम्मी का पत्र भी सुबह की डाक में मिला। उन्होंने भी उसके बर्थ-डे का जिक्र किया है, पर ऐसे जैसे वह उसे बस कनखियों से देखकर निकल जाना चाहती हो। पत्र के शेष भाग में उन्होंने वही सब कुछ लिखा है, जो वह चाहती है कि मम्मी लिखें, अधिक विस्तार से लिखें, पर विस्तार से लिखी हुई इस बात को पढ़कर मोना खीझ उठती है। एक कड़वाहट उसकी रग-रग में करंट की तरह गुजरने लगती है। मम्मी लिखती हैं—''मोना, अब और ज्यादा रुकना ठीक नहीं। हर काम की एक उम्र होती है। फिर लड़की तो एक ऐसा फूल है कि अपनी डाल पर लगे-लगे मुरझा जाता है और अगर उसे तोड़कर किसी के कोट पर लगा दिया जाए तो उसकी ताजगी खत्म होने में ही नहीं आती। अब तुम्हें फैसला कर ही लेना चाहिए। अब तो मुझे तुम्हारे डैडी की बात बिल्कुल समझ में नहीं आती। यह ठीक है कि तुम लाखों में एक हो। वैसे मोना, हर माँ-बाप की बेटी लाखों में एक होती है, परंतु अब ऐसा लड़का, जो तुम्हारे डैडी को भी पसंद हो और तुम्हें भी पसंद हो, कहीं से ढूँढ़ा जाएगा और यह ढुँढ़ाई कब तक चलती रहेगी? मेरे खयाल से सुरेश सब तरह से तुम्हारे काबिल है। वह तुम्हें चाहता भी बहुत

है और तुम्हारी कितनी इज्जत करता है।''

सुरेश उसकी बहुत इज्जत करता है। डैडी भी कहते हैं, वैसे सुरेश ठीक है। धीरे-धीरे उसका वकालत का धंधा भी जम जाएगा, पर वह थोड़ा दब्बू स्वभाव का आदमी लगता है। मोना कोई मामूली लड़की तो है नहीं कि शादी की, घर बसा लिया और पति पर रोब गाँठ-गूँठकर हँसते-खेलते जिंदगी गुजार दी। मोना को तो ऐसा लड़का चाहिए, जो उसके अंदर छिपी उन अनंत शक्तियों को पहचान सके और उनके फलने-फूलने के सभी साधन जुटा सके। दब्बू स्वभाव का लड़का यह काम नहीं कर सकता।

डैडी से वह लगातार सुनती आ रही है कि वह कोई मामूली लड़की नहीं है। यह बात उसके अंदर इतनी गहराई तक बैठ गई है कि उसे हर लड़की बहुत मामूली नजर आती है और कोई लड़का अपने काबिल नजर नहीं आता।

जब कभी किसी लड़के के बारे में बात चलती है, सबकुछ विचार करने, देखने-सुनने के बाद जब मम्मी की आँखें मोना और उसके डैडी पर उठती हैं, तब डैडी के मुख पर एक बहुत परिचित मुद्रा उभर आती है। वह लंबी कुरसी पर थोड़ा अधलेटे हो जाते हैं। उनकी आँखें सुबह के पढ़े हुए अखबार में से कुछ अनपढ़ी खबरें ढूँढ़ने लगती हैं और वह बहुत रुक-रुककर कहते हैं, ''मोना से पूछ लो। अगर यह लड़का उसे अपने काबिल लगे तो मुझे कोई एतराज नहीं है।''

और मोना जान जाती है कि डैडी की मरजी क्या है। उसे लगता है, वह लड़का जो अभी उसे देखकर गया है, जरूर उसके काबिल नहीं है। वह मना कर देती है। मम्मी खोई-खोई सी उन्हें देखती रहती हैं।

डैडी की सेहत ऐसी है कि न ज्यादा गरमी बरदाश्त होती है, न सर्दी। इसीलिए सर्दियों में वह बंबई चले जाते हैं और गरमियों में किसी पहाड़ पर। दिल्ली में बड़ी मुश्किल से उनके तीन-चार महीने ही गुजरते हैं। पिछले कितने सालों से लगातार मोना उनके साथ जा रही है। मोना की तीमारदारी से डैडी बहुत खुश रहते हैं। वह सुबह उन्हें चाय पिलाकर अखबार पढ़कर सुनाती है। जब उनकी कोई और कंपनी न हो तो वह उनके साथ बैठकर शतरंज या रमी खेलती है। डैडी अनेक पत्र-पत्रिकाओं के पन्ने उलटते हैं। उनमें छपी हुई कहानी की दो-चार पंक्तियाँ पढ़ते हैं और यदि वह अच्छी लगे तो मोना से पूरी पढ़वाकर सुनते हैं। मोना उन्हें दिन में तीन-चार बार कप में रगड़कर बनाई हुई ऐस्प्रेसो कॉफी पिलाती है। उनका विश्वास है कि ऐसी कॉफी मोना के अलावा और कोई नहीं बना सकता। मोना जानती है, मम्मी के साथ उनकी पटरी नहीं बैठती। रीता को अपने घर और दो बच्चों से बिल्कुल फुरसत नहीं मिलती और चंदर अकेला ही इतना बड़ा मेडिकल स्टोर सँभालता है। इस स्थिति में डैडी की देखभाल के लिए रह जाती है सिर्फ मोना।

डैडी घूमने के लिए बाहर गए हैं और वह मम्मी के पत्र को मरोड़ती हुई गुमसुम सी बैठी है। पता नहीं उसे क्या चाहिए? पता नहीं वह पुरुष कैसा है? पता नहीं वह किसकी तलाश कर रही है? और वह उठकर वार्डरोब में लगे आदमकद शीशे के सामने आ खड़ी होती है। वह अपने आपको देखती है, अपना व्यक्तित्व। फिर उनकी कल्पना करती है…सुरेश की…उसकी…उसकी…उसकी। उसे लगता है—सभी उसकी साड़ी का पल्लू पकड़े बड़ी श्रद्धा से उसके मुख की ओर ताक रहे हैं, बिल्कुल बौने आदमियों की तरह।

नैनीताल में डैडी के परिचितों की संख्या बढ़ती जा रही है। उनमें एक कर्नल साहब हैं, एक बैरिस्टर साहब, दो-तीन अवकाश-प्राप्त सरकारी अफसर हैं। सबकी उम्र एक जैसी है। सबकी आदतें एक जैसी हैं। सबके पास अपनी गुजरी हुई जिंदगी में से दूसरों को सुनाने के लिए बहुत कुछ है। सबको अपने लड़के-लड़कियों से कुछ खास शिकायतें हैं। इसलिए डैडी की सुबहें और शामें यहाँ बहुत भरी-भरी गुजर रही हैं, पर मोना तो और अकेली होती जा रही है, और उस अकेलेपन में वह अपने में ही कहाँ-कहाँ भटकती रहती है। भटकते-भटकते थक जाती है। तीखी अकुलाहट उसकी रग-रग से फूटने लगती है और वह शीशे के सामने आकर खड़ी हो जाती है। अपने आपको देखती रहती है, अपना पाँच फीट छह इंच का कद अपनी बड़ी-बड़ी आँखें, अपनी सुडौल बाँहें अपना भरा हुआ शरीर और…बहुत अंदर तक बैठी हुई एक मोना…एक बहुत जाग्रत् मोना।

□

वह पलंग पर लेटी हुई कोई किताब पढ़ने का उपक्रम कर रही है। उसने अपने आपको बिल्कुल ढीला छोड़ दिया है। उसकी साड़ी से उसकी पिंडलियाँ बाहर निकल गई हैं। उसकी अलकें इधर-उधर बिखरी हुई हैं। डैडी बाहर के कमरे में अपने दोस्तों के साथ शतरंज में डूबे हुए हैं और ऐसी अस्त-व्यस्त पड़ी हुई मोना आज अपने को बड़ा हल्का-हल्का महसूस कर रही है। इतना अस्त-व्यस्त हो जाना कितना अच्छा है? उसका मन कर रहा है—वह कुछ और शिथिल हो जाए, कुछ और अस्त-व्यस्त हो जाए। बस पलंग पर लेटे-लेटे कसकर अँगड़ाई ले। अपना अंग-अंग मरोड़कर रख दे, परंतु बाहर डैडी हैं। वह जानती है, डैडी एकाएक अंदर नहीं आएँगे। फिर भी वह बाहर ही तो बैठे हैं। डैडी के साथ वह अस्त-व्यस्त नहीं हो सकती और उसके साथ रहते कितने वर्ष बीत चुके हैं। डैडी के साथ रहना उसकी आदत बन चुकी है। उस आदत में एक संकोच, एक मर्यादा भी इस तरह घुल-मिल गई है कि अस्त-व्यस्त होना उसे भूल सा गया है।

उसने लेटे ही लेटे अपनी साड़ी को ठीक कर लिया है। उसने डैडी की आवाज सुनी है। वह कह रहे हैं, "कर्नल साहब, मोना मेरी लड़की नहीं, लड़का है। मेरा

कितना खयाल रखती है। इसकी शादी हो जाएगी तो मैं अकेला रह जाऊँगा··· मैं कहता हूँ, मेरे घर में मोना के रूप में किसी देवी ने जन्म लिया है···शी इज ए गॉडेस।''

कर्नल साहब पूछ रहे हैं, ''पर चोपड़ा साहब, अभी तक आपने उसकी शादी क्यों नहीं की? अब तो वह काफी सयानी हो गई है।''

''आप ठीक कहते हैं, कर्नल साहब!'' डैडी कह रहे हैं, ''इस उम्र तक अकसर लड़कियों की शादी हो जाती है, पर मोना कोई मामूली लड़की नहीं है। आपने उसकी पर्सनैलिटी तो देखी ही है। उसे म्यूजिक का बेहद शौक है। लिटरेचर में उसकी गहरी दिलचस्पी है। उसके लिए कोई मामूली लड़का नहीं चाहिए। सच कहूँ, कर्नल साहब, मुझे उसकी शादी की कोई जल्दी नहीं। पर यह जरूर चाहता हूँ कि लड़का ऐसा हो, जो उसका मैच हो।''

मोना डैडी के मुख से ऐसी बातें बहुत बार सुन चुकी है। पिछले कितने वर्षों से लगातार सुनती चली आ रही है···यह देवी है गॉडेस डैडी सभी से कहते रहते हैं— मोना मामूली लड़की नहीं···उसके लिए मामूली लड़का नहीं चाहिए··· ।

आज वह कर्नल साहब से कह रहे थे—मुझे मोना की शादी की कोई जल्दी नहीं है···क्यों जल्दी नहीं है? मोना के मन में बार-बार उठ रहा है। आखिर वह गैर-मामूली लड़का मिलेगा कहाँ···कब? उसे कौन ढूँढ़कर लाएगा? या एकाएक वह किसी अवतार की तरह प्रकट हो जाएगा? मम्मी लिखती हैं—लड़की वह फूल है, जो ज्यादा देर डाल पर रहने से मुरझा जाता है। क्या वह भी मुरझा जाएगी? छह महीने की दूरी पर सत्ताईसवाँ साल मुसकराते हुए संकेत कर रहा है···और उसके पीछे दूर खड़ा अट्ठाईसवाँ साल भी उसे मद्धिम-मद्धिम सा नजर आ रहा है···और उसके पीछे गहरा अँधेरा है, जहाँ कुछ भी नजर नहीं आता।

वह फिर शीशे के सामने आ खड़ी हुई। उसे लगता है, वह बहुत सुंदर है···वह अभी भी बहुत सुंदर। थोड़ा इससे कम भी सुंदर होती तो कोई अंतर न पड़ता। उसे लगता है, वह बहुत स्वस्थ है। कभी बीमार ही नहीं पड़ती। ऐसी भी क्या तंदुरुस्ती कि आदमी कभी बीमार ही न पड़े। डैडी बीमार रहते हैं, वह उनकी तीमारदारी करती है। पिछले सात-आठ साल से वह लगातार डैडी के साथ जुड़ी हुई है। बी.ए. के बाद उसका कितना मन था कि वह म्यूजिक में एम.ए. करे। उसने एम.ए. जॉइन कर लिया था, पर बीच में ही छोड़ना पड़ा। तब से उसे बस एक ही काम है, डैडी के साथ रहना। उनके साथ बंबई, दिल्ली और नैनीताल के बीच झूलते रहना।

और डैडी लगातार उसकी कितनी प्रशंसा करते चले आ रहे हैं···मोना मेरी लड़की नहीं, लड़का है···मोना के रूप में मेरे घर किसी देवी ने जन्म लिया है···मोना कोई मामूली लड़की नहीं है··· ।

मम्मी ने अपने पत्र में फिर वही बात लिखी है···कुछ फैसला करो···सुरेश अभी भी तुम्हारी प्रतीक्षा कर रहा है।

फैसला···? किसे करना है फैसला···? उसे? क्या उसे फैसला करना है? कौन करता है फैसला?

बाहर डैडी की हँसी गूँज रही है। उन्होंने कर्नल साहब के बादशाह पर शह लगा दी है।

□

"मोना···?" डैडी की आवाज है। वह उसे साथ की कुरसी पर बैठने का इशारा करते हैं, "मोना, क्या तुम सुरेश से शादी करने को तैयार हो?"

वह उनकी ओर देखती है। सामने की छोटी मेज पर गिलास के नीचे एक पत्र दबा हुआ है। डैडी की नजरें सुबह के पढ़े हुए अखबार पर दौड़ रही हैं। पता नहीं क्यों दौड़ रही हैं? क्या कोई ऐसी खबर है, जो सुबह के दो-तीन घंटों के पारायण के बाद भी बच गई है? या उन्हें अखबार पर दौड़ने की सिर्फ आदत पड़ गई है?

"तुम्हारी मम्मी का पत्र आया है," डैडी बोल रहे हैं, पर उनकी नजरें अभी भी अखबारी कागज पर सरपट दौड़ रही हैं, "उसने लिखा है कि तुम सुरेश से शादी करने को तैयार हो। तुमने उन्हें लिखा था···?"

"जी···।"

"बड़ी अजीब बात है।" उनकी सरपट दौड़ती नजरें अखबार से उठकर मोना के चेहरे पर दौड़ने लगी हैं, "तुमने तो खुद एक दिन कहा था कि उसमें कोई खास बात नहीं है।"

"पर मुझमें ही क्या खास बात है, डैडी?"

"तुममें···?" डैडी गंभीर हो जाते हैं, "तुममें तो वह बात है, जो लाखों में नहीं होती। हाँ, यह बात जरूर है कि आदमी को खुद मालूम नहीं होता कि वह क्या है? खैर···मैं चाहता हूँ कि तुम खूब सोच-समझकर फैसला करो। मैं नहीं चाहता कि किसी दबाव में आकर तुम अपनी मरजी के खिलाफ कोई फैसला कर लो। कहीं तुम अपनी माँ की इच्छा तो पूरी नहीं कर रही हो, मोना?"

"नहीं डैडी, यह फैसला मैंने खुद किया है।"

"तब तो बड़ी खुशी की बात है," डैडी बहुत सँभल-सँभलकर बोल रहे हैं, "मैं तो बस इतना ही चाहता हूँ कि मेरी हीरे जैसी बेटी किसी ऐसी जगह जड़ी जाए, उसकी पूरी कद्र हो। तुम इस रिश्ते से खुश हो तो मैं भी खुश हूँ···बहुत खुश हूँ।"

□

मोना शीशे के सामने खड़ी है। अकसर वह शीशे के सामने अपने आपको बहुत

चुप-चुप देखती रही है···बहुत गंभीर होकर। आज उसे लग रहा है, वह मुँह चला-चलाकर, आँखें घुमा-घुमाकर, गरदन को थोड़ा टेढ़ा करके देखे। अपनी ऐसी बहुत सी बातें देखें जो उसने पहले नहीं देखी थीं।

एकाएक उसे अपने दाहिने गाल के ऊपर एक कील सा दिखाई देता है। वह नजदीक होकर उस कील पर उँगली रगड़-रगड़कर देखती है। उसे आश्चर्य होता है। उसके मुँह पर यह कील कब निकल आया? वह उसे खुरचने लगती है।

बाहर से कर्नल साहब की तेज हँसी सुनाई दे रही है, ''चोपड़ा साहब, आखिर आज मात दे ही दी। अगले साल जब फिर आएँगे तो शतरंज के और ताजे जौहर दिखाऊँगा आपको···हा···हा···हा···!''

डैडी बहुत धीरे-धीरे बोल रहे हैं, ''कर्नल साहब अगले साल यहाँ आना नसीब होगा या नहीं, कौन जाने? मोना बहुत सयानी हो गई है। उसकी शादी अब जल्दी ही करनी है। फिर यह अपने घर चली जाएगी, मेरे साथ कौन आएगा?''

मोना ने कील खुरचकर फेंक दिया है और उस स्थान को मुँह बिचकाकर, गरदन टेढ़ी करके देख रही है।

वहाँ खून छलछला आया है।

□

सीधी रेखाओं का वृत्त

इसी तरह एक बार वह पाँच-एक साल पहले भी अचकचाया था, पर उस समय वह इतना भौंचक्का नहीं हुआ था। सवी की बात सुनकर वह सिर्फ चुप भर रह गया था और काफी देर तक कुछ भी नहीं बोल सका था। सवी सामने बैठी उसे देख रही थी। वह उसकी उन आँखों से अपने को लगातार चुरा रहा था। सवी ने अपनी आँखें कहीं और गड़ा रखी थीं, फिर भी उसे सवी की आँखें दिखाई दे रही थीं। उन आँखों में कैसी तरलता झाँक रही थी, लगता था सवी की आँखें अभी पिघलकर इधर-उधर फैल जाएँगी। और आज···आज भी वह सवी से आँखें चुरा रहा है। आज भी वह सवी की तरफ नहीं देखना चाहता है। आज सवी की आँखों से हल्की-हल्की चिनगारी फूट रही हैं। उस दिन सवी के होंठ बहुत धीरे-धीरे हिल रहे थे, पर आज उसके होंठ उत्तेजना से फड़फड़ा रहे हैं और सारा चेहरा जैसे पाँच साल पहले के मासूम, पूरी तरह से समर्पित हो जाने को व्याकुल चेहरे का मजाक बन उठा है।

आज वह चुपचाप बैठा है। पाँच साल पहले के दिन की तरह उसके बोलने की किसी को प्रतीक्षा नहीं है। आज वह कुछ बोलकर कुछ सुनने के लिए कतई उत्सुक नहीं है। आज तो सवी सुनाना चाहती है कि बस वह भी याद रखे। वे दिन गए, जब सवी उसके सामने गिड़गिड़ाई थी। अब क्यों गिड़गिड़ाए? होंगे आप लाट साहब, तो अपने घर के होंगे।

सारी बात कुल पाँच साल की परिधि में घिरी हुई है। उसने देखा, सामने जो औरत बैठी हुई है, तमतमाई हुई, अपने दो साल के लड़के को गोद में डाले हुए, वह वह नहीं है, जो तीन-एक साल पहले थी। पास में पैडस्टल लैंप रखा है, उस पर फ्रेम में मढ़ी हुई एक फोटो रखी है। उस फोटो में सवी अपने पति के साथ खड़ी है। तीन साल पहले जब उसने इस तसवीर को देखा था तो हँसते हुए कहा था, 'इसमें तुम्हारा व्यक्तित्व बड़ा निखरा सा लग रहा है।'

'यह और भी निखरा हुआ लगता, यदि बिंद्रा की जगह पर तुम होते?' सवी ने बड़ी बेबाकी से कहा था और फिर उसे बहुत सी बातें एक-दूसरे से उलझी हुई, एक-दूसरे में मिली-जुली याद आने लगीं। शायद सवी ने उस समय यह भी कहा था—'मिनी, तुम मुझे अपना नहीं बना सके, तुमने मुझे इस लायक नहीं समझा, पर तुम्हारी दोस्ती, तुम्हारा सहारा मुझे इस नए जीवन में भी चाहिए, नहीं तो मैं घबड़ा जाऊँगी।'

फिर शादी के बाद भी साल-दो साल तक सवी उसे बराबर पत्र लिखती रही थी—वैसे ही बेबसी, बेताबी, बेचैनी भरे पत्र।

आज वह उसके घर से निकल आया है तो जैसे कुछ उसे बड़ी तेजी से कचोट रहा है। उसे लग रहा है—वह बुरी तरह से अपमानित हुआ है। और अपमानित भी किसके हाथों हुआ? उसके हाथों, जो उसके द्वारा सैकड़ों बार अपमानित होने पर भी बुरी तरह उसके पीछे पड़ी रही थी। उसे बार-बार सवी की मुद्रा याद आ रही है, उसके शब्द याद आ रहे हैं और सबकुछ इतनी तेजी से चुभ रहा है कि उसे महसूस हो रहा है कि उसका अपना हर एक रोआँ खड़ा होकर काँटा बन गया है।

घर आकर भी उसे महसूस हो रहा है, उसके रोएँ उसी तरह खड़े हैं। पत्नी से बात कर चुका, अलमारी से निकालकर डबल पैग रम पी चुका, खाना खा चुका, पर रोएँ हैं कि जैसे के तैसे खड़े हैं। बार-बार खयाल आता है—सवी की बच्ची। अब मेरा इस तरह अपमान कर सकती है?

वह अपनी मेज के सामने बैठा है। सब लोग सो चुके हैं, पर रम का डबल पैग भी आज उसे सुला नहीं पा रहा है। सवी···सवी की बच्ची···शादी हो गई, पति मिल गया, बच्चा मिल गया···अब घरवाली बन गई है···घरवाली।

और उसे लग रहा है, उसकी साँस बड़ी तेज-तेज चल रही है, इतनी तेज कि साँस का स्वर उसके कानों में हथौड़े की तरह बजता हुआ महसूस हो रहा है। वह सोच रहा है, आज नींद नहीं आएगी, और वह सोचे जा रहा है, उस सबके बारे में, जो पिछले कुछ दिनों में हुआ था। फिर वह सोचने लगा, यदि वह यह सब कुछ सोचेगा तो बेचैनी और बढ़ेगी। जो रोएँ अभी काँटों की तरह चुभ रहे हैं, वे छुरियों की तरह काटने लगेंगे। फिर वह सोचने लगा, पाँच साल पहले की बात, जिस दिन वह बुरी तरह अचकचा गया था।

वह कॉलेज पहुँचा ही था कि स्टाफ रूम के चपरासी ने उसे एक बंद लिफाफा दिया था। लिफाफे के ऊपर लिखी राइटिंग देखकर ही वह जान गया था कि पत्र किसका है और उसमें क्या लिखा होगा। उसने लिफाफा जेब में डाल लिया था और हाजिरी-रजिस्टर सँभालता हुआ अपनी क्लास की ओर चल दिया था। क्लास खत्म करके उसने बड़े अनमने ढंग से लिफाफा खोला था, इस उम्मीद से कि सवी ने फिर वही सबकुछ लिखा होगा—'मैं तुम्हारे बगैर जी नहीं सकती···तुम मेरी बिल्कुल परवाह नहीं करते···'

परंतु आज का पत्र बहुत छोटा था—''मिनी, तुमसे कुछ बहुत जरूरी बात करनी है। आज तुम्हारा सिर्फ एक पीरियड है। इसे खत्म करके 'हिमालय' में आ जाना। मैं वहाँ हूँ। बैरा बता देगा कि किस कैबिन में हूँ। बात बहुत जरूरी है, इसलिए टालना मत।''

क्या जरूरी बात हो सकती है, वह सोचने लगा था। आज सवी से मिलने का उसका बिल्कुल मन नहीं था। कल ही वह उसके साथ था। एक दिन में ही ऐसी क्या खास बात हो गई? बस में धक्के खाते हुए चार मील दूर के 'हिमालय' रेस्त्राँ में जाना आज उसे बहुत खल रहा था।

वह रास्ते भर सोचता रहा, ऐसी क्या बात हो सकती है। क्या सवी की शादी का कहीं से प्रस्ताव आया है? ऐसा हो तो बहुत अच्छा है। अब उसकी शादी हो ही जानी चाहिए, पर सवी भी तो बहुत बेवकूफ है। कोई लड़का इसकी नाक से उतरता ही नहीं। किसी की पर्सनैलिटी नहीं जँचती, कोई इंटेलैक्चुअल नहीं लगता, कोई ऐसे धंधे में है, जिसका कोई भविष्य नहीं···और बस की रॉड पकड़े खड़े-खड़े उसे यह सब सोचकर झुँझलाहट होने लगी थी। फिर उसे लगा था कि कुछ और बात तो नहीं है। उसे कँपकँपी सी महसूस हुई। कॉलेज में स्टाफ के लोगों को तो कुछ-कुछ शक होने लगा था। कहीं बात और दूर तक न चली गई हो। यह सोचकर उसे फिर झुँझलाहट हुई थी।

बैरे ने इशारा किया था कि वह एक नंबर कैबिन में है। वह जानता था कि वह उसी कैबिन में होगी। एक नंबर की कैबिन खाली हो तो वह और किसी में नहीं बैठती। कैबिन की ओर जाती सीढ़ियाँ चढ़ते हुए उस झुँझलाहट में भी वह मुसकरा रहा था।

उसने कुरसी पर बैठते हुए पूछा था, 'कितनी देर से बैठी हो?'

'आधा घंटा हो गया?'

उसने महसूस किया था—सवी का चेहरा आज कुछ पुख्ता सा है। जैसे वह कुछ निर्णय करके आई है।

बैरा चाय का सेट रख गया था। वह प्याले में डालते हुए बोला, 'कहो, क्या बात है?'

'कोई खास नहीं।' वह प्यालों में चीनी डालने लगी थी। उसने उसका चेहरा देखा तो लगा था कि कुछ क्षण पहले उसे गलतफहमी हुई थी। सवी के चेहरे पर कोई पुख्तापन नहीं है। उसके पास कोई निर्णय नहीं है। वह बिल्कुल हर रोज की तरह है। वही शिकायत भरी अतृप्त आँखें, वही उदास मुद्रा, वही तेज चलती हुई ठंडी साँसें, वही सूनापन, वही बुझापन, जिसे वह पिछले एक-डेढ़ साल से लगातार देखता आ रहा था।

'फिर भी, कुछ बात तो होगी ही।'

'मुझसे मिलना ही बहुत जरूरी बात नहीं है?' सवी की आवाज में उसे बड़ा दर्द महसूस हुआ था। सवी की आँखें भरी हुई थीं। उसकी खीझ और झुँझलाहट एकदम

नीचे बैठ गई थी। वह सवी के प्रति एकदम करुण हो उठा था। वह कुछ बोला नहीं था। उसने सिर्फ उसके दोनों हाथ थाम लिये थे। सवी ने अपना सिर उसकी गोद में रख दिया था और सुबकने लगी थी।

उसने बहुत धीरे से उसे उठाया था, उसकी आँखें पोंछी थीं, उसे प्यार किया था और कहा था, 'पगली कहीं की! अभी कल ही तो हम लोग मिले थे।'

'तुम्हारे बिना···।' सवी की आँखों में फिर आँसू उमड़ आए थे।

'लगी न फिर से रीतिकालीन नायिकाओं की भाषा बोलने?' वह हँसते हुए बोला था, 'वैसे कहती हो कि मुझे इंटेलैक्चुअल आदमी पसंद हैं, क्योंकि मैं एम.ए. हूँ, इकोनॉमिक्स की लेक्चरर हूँ, पेंटिंग का शौक रखती हूँ। मार्क्स और फ्रायड से लेकर रसल और सार्त्र तक सभी का सिर चाट सकती हूँ, और आँसू इस तरह बहा रही हो कि···जैसे अभी कैबिन में सैलाब उमड़ आएगा।'

सवी का चेहरा उसी तरह उदास था, 'तुम इस बात को नहीं समझ सकते। मैं तुम्हें कितना चाहती हूँ, इसका तुम शायद अंदाजा भी नहीं लगा सकते। मेरा पीरियड एक बजे शुरू होता है, पर मैं रोज सुबह दस बजे कॉलेज आ जाती हूँ। सिर्फ इसलिए कि तुम्हारी आवाज सुन सकूँ। तुम्हारी क्लास के सामने चक्कर काटती हूँ, सिर्फ इसलिए कि तुम्हारी आवाज सुन सकूँ। स्टाफ-रूम की जिस कुरसी पर तुम बैठते हो, मैं रास्ता देखती हूँ कि तुम कब उठो और मैं उस पर बैठकर तुम्हारी गरमाहट को महसूस कर सकूँ। पर तुम···! एक-एक बार मिलने के लिए तुम्हें दस-दस बार कहना पड़ता है।'

उसे लगा था, सवी ने उसे अपराधी के कठघरे में खड़ा कर दिया है। शायद उसने सवी को कुछ समझाने की कोशिश की थी—'हम लोग कितनी कठिन परिस्थितियों में रहते हैं। स्टाफ की दो सौ और विद्यार्थियों की चार हजार आँखें सदा हमें घेरे रहती हैं। बात का बतंगड़ बनते देर नहीं लगती। और फिर तुम तो अभी प्रोबेशन पर हो, तुम्हारी नौकरी खतरे में पड़ सकती है।'

'मैं अपनी नौकरी की परवाह नहीं करती।' वह काफी तुनककर बोली थी।

'बस तुम्हारा यही पागलपन तो मुझे अच्छा नहीं लगता, जब तुम्हें इसका दौरा पड़ता है, तुम अच्छे-बुरे का विचार छोड़ देती हो।'

वह और तुनक उठी थी, 'मैंने क्या पागलपन दिखाया है? कब तुम्हें या और किसी को राह चलते पकड़ लिया है?'

'अब तुम्हीं बताओ। क्या यह पागलपन नहीं है कि तुम दिन में दस-दस बार चपरासी के जरिए मुझे पत्र भिजवाती रहती हो? वह बूढ़ा क्या सोचता होगा? फिर कभी-कभी तुम छात्र-छात्राओं का भी इस काम में इस्तेमाल कर लेती हो। और उस दिन तो तुमने हद ही कर दी। जब स्टाफ-रूम में तुमने बड़ी मेज की उस तरफ से

फेंककर अपना पत्र दिया था। खैरियत यह थी कि उस समय वहाँ कोई था नहीं।'

सवी चुप बैठी सुन रही थी। उसके हाथ का चम्मच चीनीदानी में बराबर चल रहा थां।

उसने पूछा, 'और चाय पीयोगी?'

सवी ने गरदन हिला दी थी, 'नहीं।'

मगर उसने घंटी बजाकर बैरे को बुलाया था और चाय मँगवाई थी।

तब सवी ने कहा था, 'मैं बड़ी गंभीरता से तुमसे एक बात कहना चाहती हूँ।'

'कहो।' पर पता नहीं क्यों उसे डर सा लगने लगा था।

सवी चुपचाप बैठी रही थी। बैरा चाय रख गया था। वह चाय बनाने लगी थी। उसने पूछा था, 'बोलो न क्या बात है?'

सवी ने चाय का प्याला उसकी ओर सरका दिया था। वह प्याले में चम्मच हिलाता हुआ बोला था, 'कहो न, क्या बात है?' और फिर एकाएक अनजानी बेचैनी सी महसूस करने लगा था।

'मिनी, तुम मुझसे शादी कर लो।'

'क्या''?' उसके मुँह से बहुत धीरे से निकला था। चम्मचवाला हाथ वहीं रुक गया था। वह एकटक सवी को देख रहा था। वह प्याले को ताक रही थी, ताके जा रही थी।

'पर सवी, सोचो, यह कैसे हो सकता है? मैं विवाहित हूँ और एक पत्नी के रहते दूसरी शादी गैर-कानूनी है।'

'कानून सिर्फ उस हालत में दखल देता है, जब पहली पत्नी आपत्ति करे। और मैं जानती हूँ कि तुम चाहोगे तो कमल आपत्ति नहीं करेगी।' सवी ने बहुत तौल-तौलकर अपनी बात कही थी।

उसे लगा था—वह निरुत्तर हो गया है। वह भाग उठना चाहता था। बस किसी तरफ भी दौड़ पड़ना चाहता था। 'अच्छा, मैं किसी वकील से पूछूँगा।' जैसे यह भाग उठने की भूमिका थी।

'मैं पूछ चुकी हूँ।' और सामने ऊँची दीवार की तरह थी सवी।

'क्या पूछ चुकी हो?' वह उस ऊँची दीवार को इधर-उधर सरकाने की कोशिश कर रहा था।

'यही, जो तुम पूछना चाहते हो।'

वह चुप हो गया था।

वह भी चुप थी।

एकाएक उसकी नजर सवी की ओर उठी तो जैसे वह जड़ हो गया था। सवी की

आँखें बेहिसाब करुण हो आई थीं। वह कह रही थी, 'एम आई नॉट फिट टू बी योर वाइफ?' और उसके होंठ इस तरह फड़फड़ा रहे थे, जैसे किसी चिड़िया के नवजात बच्चे के पंख हों।

'नहीं, ऐसी तो कोई बात नहीं?' वह बहुत सँभलकर बोला था, 'इस बारे में मेरे मन में कोई शक नहीं है, परंतु यह बहुत मश्किल है। कमल पर क्या गुजरेगी? उसे एक ऐसे अपराध की सजा मिलेगी, जो उसने किया ही नहीं है।'

और वह कह रही थी, 'कमल तुम्हारी पत्नी है। इसलिए उसका इतना ध्यान है। मैं तो तुम्हारी कुछ भी नहीं हूँ। मुझ पर क्या गुजर रही है, इससे तुम्हें क्या गरज है?'

'सवी···प्लीज···मुझे समझने की कोशिश करो।' मुझे माफ करो वाले स्वर में वह बोला था।

सवी का करुण चेहरा विकृत होने लगा था। उस पर वही सबकुछ फिर से उभर आया था, जो रोज उभरा रहता था। वह बिफर उठी थी, 'साफ कहो कि तुम शादी करना नहीं चाहते। तुममें गट्स नहीं हैं। तुम दुनिया को फेस नहीं कर सकते।'

'हार मानता हूँ' की मुद्रा में वह बोला था, 'शायद यही बात हो।'

बैरा कैबिन के बाहर से कई बार गुजर चुका था। आज उन्हें अंदर बैठे बहुत देर हो चुकी थी। वह उठना चाहता था, पर सवी वहाँ जड़ बनी बैठी थी—न बोल रही थी, न हिल-डुल रही थी। उसकी आँखें भी बहुत देर-देर से झपक रही थीं।

वह उस दिन सवी को वहीं कैबिन में बैठा छोड़ आया था। उसे लगा था, उसने सवी का अपमान किया है। सवी के साथ ही जैसे उसने जाने कितनी औरतों को अपमानित कर दिया है। फिर उसे लगा था, वह बुरी तरह से झकझोर दिया गया है। बार-बार सवी की शक्ल उसकी आँखों में घूमने लगती थी, बार-बार सवी के शब्द उसे बींधने से लगते थे—

एम आई नॉट फिट टू बी योर वाइफ···

एम आई नॉट फिट···

एम आई नॉट··· योर वाइफ···वाइफ···वाइफ···कमल···वाइफ···सवी···एम···आई नॉट फिट···

वह बेहद परेशान हो उठा था। फिर उसे याद आया था कि वह सवी को वहाँ कैबिन में छोड़ आया है। उदास, बुझी हुई, टूटी हुई सवी वहीं कैबिन में बैठी होगी। कैबिन में बैठी सवी की जैसे-जैसे वह कल्पना करता, एक बड़ी करुण शक्ल, इतनी करुण कि वह डरावनी सी लग रही हो, उसके अंदर उभर आती थी।

फिर कुछ महीने बाद सवी की शादी हे गई थी—मिनी, तुम मेरे दोस्त बने रहना, मेरे नहीं, 'हमारे' दोस्त रहना। और इसी तरह बीच में दो-तीन साल जाने कैसे हर

किसी की आँख बचाकर निकल गए थे। और गेहुँए रंग की दीखने वाली सवी एकदम गोरी-चिट्टी हो गई और स्टाफ-रूम में उसकी खिलखिलाहट का स्वर बहुत तेज सुनाई देने लगा था।

एक दिन फिर उसे एकाएक महसूस हुआ था, जब वह उसे 'सवी' कहकर बुलाता है तो सवी को शायद अच्छा नहीं लगता। वह कुछ कुनमुनाने सी लगती है, उसके चेहरे पर अजीब सी उलझन, अजीब सी अस्वीकृति उभर आती है। उसने कोशिश की कि वह उसे मिसेज बिंद्रा कहे, पर हर कोशिश के बावजूद उसके मुँह से मिसेज बिंद्रा नहीं निकलता था।

फिर एकाएक उसे यह भी लगा था कि सवी ने भी उसे जाने कब से मिनी नहीं कहा है, और एक तरह से वह भूल ही चुका था कि सवी ने उसे मिनी नाम दिया था। उसने यह भी महसूस किया था कि सवी उसे किसी नाम से नहीं पुकारती, जब भी कहती है सिर्फ 'आप' कहती है—और जब उसने भी सवी को 'आप' कहना शुरू कर दिया तो उसे आश्चर्य हुआ था, और कुछ कचोट भी गया था कि सवी ने इस बात पर बिल्कुल आपत्ति नहीं की थी।

फिर एक दिन बड़ी छोटी सी बात हुई और सवी जैसे आग-बबूला हो गई। बात इतनी छोटी थी कि वह सवी की ऐसी प्रतिक्रिया सोच भी नहीं सकता था।

सवी अपना रजिस्टर लेकर स्टाफ-रूम से निकल रही थी कि उसने उसे रोककर कहा था—'सवी··· !' और तभी महसूस हुआ था कि उसके चेहरे पर कुछ रेखाएँ बल खा गई हैं। वह सँभल गया था, 'सुनो, तुम्हारी थर्ड ईयर की क्लास में एक लड़की है—सुनीता···शायद सुनीता लांबा। उसकी कुछ अटेंडेंस शॉर्ट हैं, जरा देख लेना।'

उसने कुछ मुँह बिचकाकर कहा था, 'देखूँगी।' और वह एकदम मुड़कर स्टाफ रूम से बाहर चली गई थी।

दूसरे हफ्ते कॉलेज के नोटिस बोर्ड पर 'अटेंडेंस शॉर्ट स्टूडेंट्स' की लिस्ट में सुनीता लांबा का नाम देखकर उसे धक्का सा लगा था। फिर उसे पता लगा था कि सुनीता की अटेंडेंस इकोनॉमिक्स में शॉर्ट हुई हैं। आँखों में आँसू भरे हुए सुनीता उससे कह रही थी, 'मिसेज बिंद्रा ने मेरा एक साल बरबाद कर दिया।'

वह तड़प उठा था। सवी ने मेरी इतनी सी बात नहीं मानी! उसने उसे कॉलेज में ढूँढ़ा था, फिर उसके घर जा पहुँचा था। सवी अपने मुन्ने को एबीसी लिखना सिखा रही थी।

उसे देखकर सवी कुछ अचकचा सी गई थी। पिछले कई महीनों से वह उसके घर नहीं आया था।

'आइए?' फीकी सी मुसकराहट में उसने अपना पल्ला सँभालते हुए कहा था

और उसके मन में उठा था—सवी कितनी गदरा गई है, कितनी मांसल हो गई है।

उसने कुरसी पर बैठते हुए कहा था, 'सवी, बड़े अफसोस की बात है। तुमने मेरी एक छोटी सी बात नहीं मानी।'

'क्या बात?' उसने आश्चर्य झलकाते हुए पूछा था।

'आखिर तुमने उस लड़की की अटेंडेंस शॉर्ट कर ही दीं।'

'कौन सी लड़की…?' उसने इस तरह कहा जैसे बड़ी मामूली बात हो। 'वो लांबा? बड़ी गैर-जिम्मेदार लड़की है। कैंटीन में बैठी लड़कों से गप्प लगाती रहती है और क्लास में आती नहीं। ऐसी लड़कियों को सबक मिलना चाहिए।'

उसे लगा था, वह जिस कुरसी पर बैठा है, किसी ने उस पर पेट्रोल छिड़ककर आग लगा दी है।

'पर उसके बारे में मैंने तुम्हें कहा था?' 'मैंने' शब्द पर उसने बहुत जोर दिया था।

'हाँ…तुमने कहा तो था।' सवी ने नौकर को आवाज दी थी, 'मदन, जरा गैस जलाकर चाय का पानी तो रख दे।'

'मेरा कहना तुम्हारे लिए अब कोई अर्थ नहीं रखता…क्या?'

वह कुछ नहीं बोली थी। मुन्ने की स्लेट पर एक्स वाई जेड लिखने लगी थी। फिर बोली थी, 'उस लड़की में तुम्हारी कोई खास दिलचस्पी है?'

और उसे लगा था, सवी के सारे अंगों से एक काट देनेवाली मुसकराहट झर रही है और उसने महसूस किया था, जैसे तेज जहर सा उसके सारे शरीर में दौड़ गया है।

'लड़कियों में मेरी खास दिलचस्पी हो भी तो क्या होता है? तुममें भी तो मेरी दिलचस्पी थी।'

इससे पहले कि वह अपनी कड़वी बात की ठंडक खुद महसूस कर सकता, सवी की आँखें उसकी ओर उठ गई थीं और सारा चेहरा एकदम खिंच सा गया था… 'मुझमें तुम्हारी कब दिलचस्पी थी?'

'मेरी तुममें कोई दिलचस्पी नहीं थी…?'

'कैसी दिलचस्पी…?' और उसे लगा था, आसपास कोई बम फूट गया है या भूचाल आ गया है या कोई नदी सारे कगार तोड़कर उमड़ पड़ी है। सवी के नथुने फड़क रहे थे। उसके होंठ फड़फड़ा रहे थे, उसकी आँखों से लाली जैसे बाहर फूट पड़ना चाहती थी, 'तुम समझते हो, तुमने मुझमें दिलचस्पी दिखाकर कोई बहुत बड़ा उपकार किया था मुझ पर। पर यह तो मैं ही जानती हूँ कि तुम्हारी कितनी दिलचस्पी थी मुझमें। तुमने मुझे कुचला था, दुत्कारा था, अपमानित किया था। तुम समझते हो, तुम बड़े महान् हो। तुम किसी के साथ कैसा भी व्यवहार कर सकते हो। सब लोग तुम्हारे जरखरीद गुलाम हैं।

तुम समझते हो, मैं अभी भी तुम्हारे पीछे उसी तरह दुम हिलाती हुई घूम रही हूँ। तुम्हारी कही हर एक बात को भगवान् का वचन मानकर सिर-माथे चढ़ाए फिर रही हूँ…'

और पता नहीं वह क्या-क्या बोलती चली जा रही थी। और उसे लग रहा था कि उसे किसी ने उठाकर पानी से भरे तालाब में फेंक दिया है, जहाँ उसकी सारी गुरुता नष्ट हो गई है, वह सिर्फ काठ के एक टुकड़े की तरह ऊपर-ऊपर उतरा रहा है।

फिर उसे सुनाई दिया था। सवी कह रही थी, 'अच्छा है, तुम मुझे उन दिनों की याद न कराओ। मैं उन दिनों को, उन कड़वी यादों को बहुत नीचे दफना चुकी हूँ।'

उसे लगता है, सवी उसके सामने खड़ी है—गुस्से से बल खाती हुई सवी एकदम सीधी खड़ी है। पहले जब वह खड़ी होती थी तो उसकी पीठ दोनों कंधों से आगे की तरफ कुछ सिकुड़ जाती थी। आज वह बिल्कुल तनी खड़ी है… स्साली… उसके अंदर गालियाँ घुमड़ती हैं, घुमड़ती रहती हैं और उसे लगता है—सवी कितनी मादक हो उठी है, कितनी निखर आई है। उसके भरे-पूरे अंग उसकी आँखों में तिरने लगते हैं। सालों पहले 'हिमालय' में मिलनेवाली सवी की आकृति पर यह सवी पूरी तरह फैलती जा रही है। वह बैठा-बैठा कसमसाने लगता है और इस सवी को एक बार पा लेने की ललक बड़ी शिद्दत से उसके अंदर जाग उठती है।

□

शोर

जब वे अंदर आए तो उन्हें महसूस हुआ कि वहाँ उतना अँधेरा नहीं है, जितना हमेशा हुआ करता था और खास बात यह थी कि सामनेवाली वह जगह, जो गाँव के कुएँ के आकार की बनी थी और जिसके अंदर बैठकर कभी कोई ग्रामोफोन पर अंग्रेजी धुनें बजाया करता था, आज ज्यादा आबाद थी। वहाँ चार-पाँच हिप्पी खड़े थे। उनके हाथों में वाद्य यंत्र थे। ऐसा लग रहा था कि ऑर्केस्ट्रा कुछ देर पहले ही पूरे यौवन पर था और अब किसी नई धुन की तैयारी हो रही थी। उस जगह ज्यादा रोशनी का होना जहाँ उन्हें खला था, वहीं वह रौनक उन्हें अच्छी लगी थी।

वे पहले बाईं तरफ की मेज की ओर बढ़े। पर उन्हें लगा कि इस तरह वे ऑर्केस्ट्रा के बिल्कुल सामने होंगे और आने-जानेवाले सभी उन्हें देखेंगे। वे दाहिनी ओर मुड़ गए और सामने की कैबिननुमा जगह की तरफ बढ़ गए, जिन्हें टाट के पार्टीशनों द्वारा अलग-अलग विभाजित किया गया था।

उस तरफ बढ़ते हुए मर्द की नजर उसके साथवाली कैबिन की तरफ चली गई। वहाँ उसे एक परिचित आकार का आभास हुआ। अरे, वह तो नरूला था। उसके सामने बैठी लड़की उसे नजर नहीं आई। पर क्षण भर में ही उसने अंदाजा लगा लिया—वह शमा होगी।

मर्द जरा दाहिने दब गया। उसे लगा, नरूला ने उसे देखा नहीं है। वह नरूला की तरफ पीठ करके बैठ गया। औरत उसके सामने बैठ गई। मर्द को उस हॉल की ज्यादा रोशनी का अहसास हुआ—नहीं तो वह औरत को अपनी बगल में बैठा लेता।

ऑर्केस्ट्रा पर तेज धुन बजने लगी थी।

मर्द ने देखा—औरत उसे एकटक देख रही थी।

वह मुसकराया।

फिर उसने अपनी गरदन आगे बढ़ाकर औरत से कहा, ''जानती हो, मेरे पीछे की तरफ कौन बैठा है?''

औरत ने आँखें चौड़ी करके टाट के परदे के उस ओर झाँकना चाहा। उस तरफ आकृति होने का आभास तो उसे लगा होगा।

नरूला की आवाज बहुत साफ सुनाई दे रही थो। वह किसी मजाहिया ड्रामे का एक हिस्सा सुना रहा था और लड़की (शायद शमा) बार-बार हँस रही थी।

मर्द ने धीरे से कहा, ''यह नरूला है—थियेटर यूनिटवाला।''

औरत एकाएक घबरा उठी, ''चलो, यहाँ से चलें। यह आदमी मुझे जरा भी अच्छा नहीं लगता।''

ऑर्केस्ट्रा के ड्रम पर तेज थाप पड़ने लगी। दूसरे यंत्र भी झनझना उठे। सब कुछ शोर में डूब गया।

मर्द ने शब्दों से कम और मुद्रा से अधिक बोलकर कहा, ''परवाह न करो। उसने हमें देखा नहीं है।'' पर उसे लगा, औरत बहुत घबरा रही है। वेटर को उसने चीज-सैंडविच और कॉफी लाने को कहा।

वह बोली, ''आओ कहीं और चलें।''

''अब कहाँ जाएँगे?'' आदमी बोला, ''दफ्तर छूट चुके हैं। बाहर बहुत भीड़ होगी।''

उसे फिर लगा, औरत घबरा रही है।

''तुम तो किसी से डरती नहीं। आज तुम्हें इतना डर क्यों लग रहा है?''

उसने देखा, औरत के चेहरे पर कुछ पुख्तापन आ गया है। वह बोली, ''मुझे यह जगह ही अच्छी नहीं लगती। रेस्त्राँ है या अँधेरी गुफा? जबरदस्ती का गाँव बना रखा है। क्या गाँव ऐसा ही होता है? मुझे यहाँ की हर चीज डरावनी लगती है।···और यहाँ आज शोर कितना है?''

ऑर्केस्ट्रा के यंत्रों के साथ शायद हिप्पियों के गाने की आवाज भी आने लगी थी।

वह सैंडविच खाने लगा। उसे लगा, औरत कुछ खा नहीं रही है और उसे एकटक देख रही है।

''खाओ न!''

औरत ने मुसकराने की कोशिश की और छुरी से सैंडविच काटने लगी।

'गाँव' में आने से पहले मर्द ने महसूस किया था कि उसे भूख लगी है। बाहर सड़क पर औरत का इंतजार करते हुए उसने दस पैसे के भुने चने लेकर खाए थे।

औरत को कुछ न खाते देखकर उसे कोफ्त हुई। उसकी प्लेट में सैंडविच और कटा टुकड़ा उसी तरह पड़ा था और उसे टुकुर-टुकुर ताक रही थी।

''तुम कुछ खाती क्यों नहीं?''

''तुम खाओ न···।''

"मैं तो खा रहा हूँ। तुम क्यों नहीं खातीं?"

"मुझे भूख नहीं है।"

"नहीं खातीं तो मत खाओ।" मर्द झुँझलाया और उसने औरत की प्लेट में पड़ी सैंडविच को अपनी प्लेट में सरका लिया।

"तुम जब भी मेरे साथ आती हो, कुछ भी नहीं खातीं। देखो, तुम्हारा कॉफी का प्याला भी पूरा भरा हुआ है।"

औरत ने प्याले की तरफ देखा। एस्प्रेसो कॉफी की झाग नीचे बैठ चुकी थी। उसने प्याला उठाकर एक सिप लिया।

"क्या यह जिंदगी ऐसे ही गुजरेगी?" औरत बोली।

कॉफी पीते हुए मर्द ने प्याला रखकर औरत की तरफ देखा।

ऑर्केस्ट्रा का शोर एकदम तेज हो उठा।

दोनों एक-दूसरे की तरफ देख रहे थे। दोनों कुछ बोले नहीं। शोर इतना था कि कुछ बोला ही नहीं जा रहा था।

"यह जिंदगी और किस तरह गुजर सकती है?" मर्द बोला।

पता नहीं औरत ने मर्द की बात सुनी या नहीं, बस वह उसे देखती रही। मर्द को भी पता नहीं था कि औरत ने उसकी बात सुनी है या नहीं, पर वह महसूस कर रहा था कि उसने औरत की बात का उत्तर दे दिया है।

कुछ देर तक कोई कुछ नहीं बोला।

"क्या ऐसा नहीं हो सकता···?"

"कैसा?"

औरत अपनी अधूरी बात पूरी नहीं कर रही थी।

"बोलो न···क्या नहीं हो सकता?"

वह कुछ बोल नहीं रही थी, बस उसे देखे जा रही थी।

मर्द कॉफी पीने लगा।

पीछे से नरूला और लड़की की आवाज आ रही थी—बहुत धीमी-धीमी।

और ऑर्केस्ट्रा भी धीरे-धीरे बज रहा था।

"क्या मैं तुम्हें पा नहीं सकती?"

मर्द उसे एकटक देखने लगा।

"जितना पा चुकी हो, क्या उससे ज्यादा पाना चाहती हो?"

"क्या इतना पाना काफी है? प्यास से तड़पते हुए के लिए आधा घूँट पानी।"

"इससे ज्यादा और क्या हो सकता है?"

मर्द के यह कहते-कहते ऑर्केस्ट्रा की आवाज तेज हो चुकी थी।

"क्या यह नहीं हो सकता कि···?" औरत ने फिर बात अधूरी छोड़ दी। उसके होंठ बार-बार इस तरह हरकत करने लगे, जैसे वह कुछ निगल रही थी। वह बार-बार आँखें मिचका रही थी।

ऑर्केस्ट्रा के यंत्र दनदनाकर बज रहे थे। सारा वातावरण शोर से झनझना उठा था।

"आगे क्यों नहीं बोलतीं? क्या नहीं हो सकता···?"

औरत कुछ बोल नहीं रही थी। बस कुछ निगल रही थी और आँखें मिचमिचा रही थी।

"अच्छा, मैं बताता हूँ?" मर्द बोला, "तुम शायद यह कहना चाहती हो कि क्या हम शादी नहीं कर सकते?"

औरत बिना किसी प्रतिक्रिया के उसे देखती रही।

"यह नहीं···? अच्छा तो तुम शायद यह कहना चाहती हो कि क्या मैं तुम्हें किसी दूसरे देश में भगाकर नहीं ले जा सकता, जहाँ तुम्हारा पति हमारा पीछा न कर सके।"

औरत कुछ बोली नहीं। उसी तरह कुछ निगलती रही और आँखें झपकाती रही।

"यह भी नहीं···? अच्छा यह भी नहीं तो तुम शायद यह कहना चाहती हो कि क्या हम दोनों जहर नहीं खा सकते?"

औरत थोड़ा सा कसमसाई।

"मैं मरना चाहती हूँ, पर एकदम नहीं। क्या कोई ऐसा जहर नहीं, जिसे खाकर मैं धीरे-धीरे मरूँ। किसी को पता भी न लगे कि मैं जहर खाकर मरी हूँ।"

"हैं," मर्द मुसकराया, "दाल-रोटी खाती रहो। इसी को खाते-खाते एक दिन मर जाओगी?"

"तुम मुझे बुजदिल समझते हो?"

"नहीं, अपने आपको तुमसे ज्यादा बुजदिल समझता हूँ।"

मर्द ने देखा, औरत के प्याले में तीन-चौथाई से ज्यादा कॉफी भरी है।

"इसे तो पियो। पैसे बरबाद करने से क्या फायदा?"

औरत ने प्याला उठाकर मुँह से लगा लिया।

मर्द ने अपने प्याले का आखिरी घूँट भरा।

ऑर्केस्ट्रा जोर-जोर से दनदनाने लगा।

औरत के अंदर फ्लैश की तरह गुजरा, उसकी बिटिया ने कहा था—मम्मी, दफ्तर से लौटते समय ऊन जरूर लेती आना। सुपर बाजार और जनपथ की ऊन से भरी दुकानें उसके इर्द-गिर्द हो आईं और यह तिलमिलाने लगी।

"कुछ समझ में नहीं आता कि क्या हो सकता है।" औरत बोली, "पर मुझसे इस तरह जिया नहीं जाता।"

हिप्पी जोर-जोर से गा रहे थे। मर्द उधर देखने लगा। वाद्य-यंत्र बजाते हुए वे नाच रहे थे। बढ़ी हुई दाढ़ियाँ, मटमैले उलझे बाल, गंदे कपड़े—तीन लड़के दो लड़कियाँ।

बीच-बीच में उनकी किलकारी गूँज रही थी।

''सुनो!'' मर्द बोला, ''उस दिन तुम टेलीफोन पर कह रही थीं—बिटिया को तुम अपनी माँ के पास छोड़ दोगी...फिर...?''

''फिर...फिर क्या...? आगे तुम सोचो?''

''मैं सोचूँ...?'' मर्द ने सोचा, वह सोचने की कोशिश कर रहा है, पर वह कुछ सोच नहीं पा रहा है। उसकी सोच में बार-बार जो बात आ रही है, वह उसकी हिप पॉकेट में पड़ा हुआ पर्स है और उस पर्स में दस का इकलौता नोट है और वह सोचता है कि यहाँ का बिल चुकाने के बाद उसकी जेब में बस दो-तीन रुपए ही रह जाएँगे। और वह सोचता है, कल से उधार माँगने का चक्कर शुरू हो जाएगा।

औरत ने दूसरी ओर मुँह घुमा लिया।

ऑर्केस्ट्रा चुप था।

दो जोड़े हिप्पी कमर में हाथ डाले नाच रहे थे। एक हिप्पी दोनों हाथ ऊपर उठाकर झूम रहा था।

पीछे की कैबिन में नरूला और शमा भी चुपचाप बैठे थे।

औरत मर्द की ओर देखने लगी। वह देखती जा रही थी। जैसे देखती-देखती बोल रही थी। बार-बार एक ही बात बोले जा रही थी।

हिप्पियों ने अपने यंत्र फिर सँभाल लिये और ऑर्केस्ट्रा कानों को फाड़ देनेवाली आवाज में बजने लगा।

मर्द बोल रहा था, ''सुनो...कुछ भी नहीं हो सकता। हम जैसे जी रहे हैं, वैसे ही जिएँगे। इसमें हम कोई फर्क नहीं ला सकते।''

ड्रम पर थाप इतनी तेज पड़ रही थी कि मर्द की समझ में नहीं आया कि औरत ने उसकी बात सुनी है या नहीं। उसे लगा, उसने अपनी बात कह दी है। औरत के सुनने या न सुनने से उसका कोई सरोकार नहीं है। औरत उसे उसी तरह देखे जा रही थी। देखते हुए कुछ सुन रही थी—कुछ निगल रही थी।

मर्द ने देखा, औरत की कॉफी का प्याला अभी भी आधा भरा है।

औरत भी प्याले की तरफ देखने लगी। फिर उसने प्याला उठाया और सारी कॉफी एक ही घूँट में पी गई।

तेज-तेज बजता ऑर्केस्ट्रा धीरे-धीरे मद्धिम पड़ने लगा।

दोनों चुप बैठे थे। दोनों को लग रहा था, कोई चीज बड़ी तेजी से इधर-से-उधर दौड़ रही है। दौड़ती हुई चीज न पकड़ी जा पा रही थी, न पहचानी जा पा रही थी।

ऑर्केस्ट्रा रुक गया था। हिप्पी वहीं जमीन पर टाँगें फैलाकर बैठ गए थे। पिछली कैबिन से नरूला और शमा की कोई आवाज नहीं आ रही थी।
'गाँव' पूस की रात की तरह एकदम चुप था।
दोनों एक-दूसरे की तरफ देख रहे थे।
उन्हें लग रहा था—चारों तरफ बेहिसाब शोर फैला हुआ है।

□

सन्नाटा

सब मिलाकर शायद छत्तीस बिल्डिंगें थीं और जिस बिल्डिंग में उसे जाना था—उसका नंबर था उनतीस। उनतीस बटा चौबीस का मतलब है—उनतीस नंबर बिल्डिंग में चौबीस नंबर फ्लैट। चूँकि हर फ्लोर पर चार फ्लैट बने हुए हैं, इस हिसाब से चौबीस नंबर फ्लैट को छठे फ्लोर पर होना चाहिए।

इतना हिसाब तो सीधा-सादा था और किसी के भी समझाने से समझ में आ सकता था, पर उसकी मुश्किल कुछ और थी। बॉम्बे सेंट्रल पर गाड़ी आ गई थी पाँच बजे। वह कॉलोनी स्टेशन के बिल्कुल पास है, इसलिए जब उसने टैक्सी से सामान उतारकर पैसे दिए तो अभी साढ़े पाँच बजने में तीन-चार मिनट बाकी थे···बावजूद इसके कि टैक्सीवाला इस बिल्डिंग को ढूँढ़ने के लिए कॉलोनी के दो-तीन चक्कर लगा चुका था। अटैची को लिफ्ट पर रखकर छठे माले पर ले जाने में ज्यादा-से-ज्यादा पाँच मिनट लगेंगे, पर क्या पाँच-पैंतीस पर किसी के फ्लैट की बेल बजाना ठीक रहेगा? इस समय तो वह गहरी नींद में सो रही होगी।

फिर?

छह बजे से पहले उसे फ्लैट की कॉलबेल नहीं बजानी चाहिए, पर आधा घंटा इस तरह खड़ा भी तो नहीं रहा जा सकता। लोगों का आना-जाना जारी था। सैर के लिए जाते हुए, दूध की बोतलें लेकर आते हुए लोग उसे देख रहे थे और आँखों-ही-आँखों में पूछ रहे थे—किसके पास जाना है?

उसे मिसेज वर्मा के पास जाना है। मिसेज वर्मा···कैसा लगता है! पर उसे वह क्या कहकर सोचे? उसका ध्यान आते ही उसके सामने एक व्यक्तित्व उभरता है···एक औरत उभरती है, जिसे आज तक वह कितने नाम दे चुका है, पर सचमुच वह कोई नाम नहीं दे सका है। उसने उसके साथ कभी 'भाभी' जैसा संबंधसूचक नाम भी बनाया था, पर यह कुछ ज्यादा देर नहीं चला। वह उसे इस संबंधसूचक नाम से नहीं याद कर पाता।

उसका अपना घरेलू नाम कुछ फूलमती, चमेली या गुलाबो तर्ज का है, जिसे वह कभी स्वीकार नहीं कर सका। उसका पति उसे राधा कहता था, पर यह नाम भी उसे उसके लिए बहुत नाकाफी लगा था। तब एक बार उसने उसे बिना बताए एक नाम दे दिया था—दिवा। और फिर वह जब भी उसके बारे में सोचता, वह दिवा के बारे में सोचता।

पर दिवा को यह कहाँ मालूम था कि वह दिवा है। यह तो किसी को भी नहीं मालूम। लोग जानते हैं कि वह मिसेज वर्मा है। वह भी जानती है कि वह मिसेज वर्मा है। साल-छमाही शायद ही कहीं कोई व्यक्ति, कोई स्मृति कोई संबंध उससे टकराता हो, जो उसे उसके असली नाम से बुलाता हो।

अब वह उसके फ्लैट के सामने खड़ा था। बाहर नेम-प्लेट लगी थी···मिसेज सी. वर्मा···चमेली वर्मा, चंचल वर्मा, चाँदनी वर्मा। उसने घड़ी देखी। छह बजने में अभी कुछ मिनट बाकी थे। वह कुछ समय और काटने के लिए छठी मंजिल से नीचे सीढ़ियों पर झाँकने लगा। घुमावदार सीढ़ियाँ एक गहरे कुएँ की तरह नीचे तक चली गई थीं। साथ की लिफ्ट बार-बार ऊपर-नीचे आ-जा रही थी और उसमें से निकलनेवाले उसे घूर-घूरकर देख रहे थे।

अब छह बज चुके थे। एक-एक पल उसे भारी लग रहा था। उसने कॉलबेल पर अपनी उँगली रख दी···डिंग···डिंग···डिंग।

घंटी बड़ी मधुर आवाज में बज उठी थी। वह कुछ क्षण प्रतीक्षा करता रहा। उधर से कोई हलचल सुनाई नहीं दी। उसने सोचा, वह सो रही होगी। वह कुछ देर वैसे ही खड़ा रहा। फिर···डिंग···डिंग···डिंग।

दरवाजे पर हैंडल की कुछ खटपट हुई। वह सामने खड़ी थी···हाउसकोट पहने, बिखरे बाल, अलसाया चेहरा, बोझिल पलकें और सूखे होंठ।

''ओह!···येलकम···जेलकम···आज यह सूरज किधर से निकला···श्यामा भी साथ में है न?''

''नहीं···अकेला आया हूँ।''

''उसे क्यों नहीं लाए···? मैंने तुम्हें लिखा था, श्यामा को भी साथ लेकर आना···यू स्काउंड्रल···बीवी को साथ लेकर निकलने में शर्म लगती है?''

''अंदर आने दोगी?''

वह वहीं खिलखिलाकर हँस पड़ी, ''कम इन···कम इन।''

वह दाएँ मुड़कर उसे ड्राइंगरूम में ले गई। ड्राइंगरूम बहुत बढ़िया सजा हुआ था। कमरे में गलीचा बिछा हुआ था, डाइनिंग टेबल, मोटे शीशेवाली सेंटर टेबल, बाईं तरफ रखा हुआ रेडियोग्राम, सामने रखा हुआ टेलीविजन तथा डनलप पिलोवाला चमचमाता नया सोफासेट। वह आतंकित और डरा हुआ सा महसूस करने लगा।

वह सोफे पर बैठता बोला, "बहुत अच्छा फ्लैट है तुम्हारा और तुमने इसे सजाया भी खूब है।"

वह मुसकराई—एक परितुष्ट सी मुसकराहट। झटका देकर उसने आगे आई लट को पीछे कर लिया।

"चाय लाऊँ?"

"किटी कहाँ है?"

"अपने कमरे में सो रही होगी।"

वह उठकर किचन की ओर चली गई। वह सुबह स्टेशन पर खरीदे गए अखबार को हाथ में लेकर देखने लगा। अखबार देखते-देखते उसकी नजर बार-बार ड्राइंगरूम की चीजों पर फिसल जाती थी और वह सोचने लगा था…दिवा, अब बहुत आराम की जिंदगी जी रही है…दिवा अपने पूर्व-जीवन की सारी कड़वाहटें, सारे कष्ट, सारे लांछन समेट चुकी है और अब वह बहुत थमा-थमा सा बहुत संतुष्ट सा, बहुत शांत सा जीवन बिता रही है।

"तुमने श्यामा का हाल-चाल तो बताया ही नहीं?" वह कप में चाय डालती हुई बोली।

"तुम जानती ही हो कि उसकी जिंदगी में हाल-चाल नहीं, सिर्फ हल्की सी चाल भर है, जिसे वह सधे कदमों से लगातार चलती चली जा रही है।"

वह बड़ी फीकी सी मुसकान मुसकराने लगी।

"तो तुम अपने ही हाल-चाल बताओ।"

"तुम यह भी जानती हो कि मेरी जिंदगी हाल-चाल की नहीं, भाग-दौड़ की जिंदगी है," वह बोला, "और भागते हुए आदमी को कदम गिनने की फुरसत नहीं होती।" दोनों कुछ देर तक चुप बैठे रहे।

"तुम्हारा क्या हाल-चाल है?" उसने पूछा।

"बस…जी रहे हैं।" वह बड़ी थकी हुई मुसकराहट मुसकराई और फिर आँखें बंद करके होंठ कुछ इस तरह सिकोड़ लिये जैसे कोई लंबी यात्रा पूरी करने के बाद अपने घर की छत के नीचे सुस्ता रही हो।

"किटी कहाँ है?" उसे याद नहीं रहा कि वह यह बात पहले भी पूछ चुका है। फिर खुद ही बोला, "शायद अभी सो रही है।"

इतने में उसने देखा, मैक्सी पहने एक लंबी सी लड़की उसके सामने खड़ी है। वह बिस्तर से उठकर आई लगती थी और उसे देखकर थोड़ा अचकचा गई थी। वह किटी थी। उसे वह कई साल बाद देख रहा था। वह बहुत लंबी हो गई थी।

"हलो किटी…मुझे पहचाना?"

तब दिवा भी मुड़कर उसकी तरफ देखने लगी, "अरे, अपने जॉली अंकल को भूल गई क्या?"

वह मुसकराई, "हलो अंकल! आप कब आए?"

"अभी।"

"आंटी कैसी हैं?"

"ठीक हैं...पर तुमने दिल्ली न आने की कसम खा रखी है क्या?"

"मामा मुझे ले ही नहीं जातीं। बस खुद ही चली जाती हैं।"

"मैं तुझे नहीं ले जाती?" दिवा बोली, "तेरा खुद ही कहीं जाने का मन नहीं करता है?"

"क्या कर रही हो आजकल?" वह बीच में ही बोल पड़ा।

"गेवेज ट्रेवल्ज में काम कर रही हूँ।"

"पढ़ाई पूरी कर ली?"

उसे लगा यह बात कहीं बीच में ही अटक गई है। किटी एकाएक अखबार पलटने लगी और दिवा उठती हुई बोली, "अच्छा, नहा-धो लो। मैं नाश्ता बनाती हूँ।"

नौ बजनेवाले हुए तो उसने देखा, दिवा भी तैयार है, किटी भी तैयार है। दोनों के हाथों में पर्स है, दोनों के हाथों में चाबियों के गुच्छे झूल रहे हैं, दोनों ही बार-बार अपनी साड़ी की सलवटों या चुन्नटों पर हाथ फेर रही हैं, दोनों अपने होंठों की लिपस्टिक को एक सुर कर रही हैं।

"हमारे पास अपनी-अपनी चाबी है।" दिवा बोली, "यह तीसरी चाबी तुम सँभालो। ठीक से बंद करके जाना।"

□

रात को जब वह वापस आया तो दिवा घर आ चुकी थी। दरवाजा खोलकर वह पीछे हटी तो उसे एक भभका सा पीछे हटता महसूस हुआ। फ्लैट के अंदर आने पर लगा, सिगरेट का धुआँ इधर-उधर तिर रहा है और सारे फ्लैट में एकदम खामोशी छाई है।

"कहाँ घूमते रहे सारा दिन?"

"आज का सारा दिन तो चंदर को ढूँढ़ने में ही निकल गया।" वह बोला, "वह कल्याण कैंप में रहता है। तेज और चिलचिलाती धूप में ऊबड़-खाबड़ छितरे-बिखरे कल्याण कैंप में—जो मीलों में फैला हुआ है—उसका घर ढूँढ़ने के बाद लगा जैसे कोलंबस की तरह मैंने किसी नई दुनिया का पता लगाया है?"

"खाना?"

"खा आया हूँ। चंदर की बीवी पराँठे बहुत अच्छे बनाती है।"

ऊपर की ओर उठी हुई खामोशी फिर धीरे-धीरे नीचे सरकने लगी।

वह उठकर अपने बेडरूम की ओर गई और वापस आई तो उसके हाथ में सिगरेट की डिब्बी और दियासलाई थी। पास के सोफे पर बैठकर उसने सिगरेट जलाई और पीने लगी।

तभी एकाएक उसे लगा, उसे किटी के बारे में पूछना चाहिए।

''किटी भी अभी तक नहीं आई। शायद अपनी सहेलियों के साथ मूवी देखने चली गई हो।'' वह उबासी लेते हुए बोली।

वह उसे एकटक देखने लगा। उसे लगा, दिवा किटी के बारे में बहुत उदासीन है या बहुत निरपेक्ष है।

''किटी अब काफी सयानी हो गई है।'' वह बोला।

''हाँ...।'' वह बोली, जैसे यह तो होना ही था।

''उसकी शादी-वादी के बारे में तुमने क्या सोचा है?''

''अपनी शादी के बारे में वह खुद सोचेगी।'' दिवा ने बची हुई सिगरेट को राखदानी में दबाते हुए कहा, ''जब, जहाँ, जिससे चाहेगी, शादी कर लेगी।''

वह सोचने लगा। उसे लगा, किटी अपने किसी बॉय फ्रेंड के साथ मूवी देखने गई होगी। फिर उसे लगा, किटी बहुत सीधी है, बहुत मासूम। क्या वह 'जब, जहाँ, जिससे' की स्थिति का सामना कर सकेगी?

इतने में बेल हुई। दिवा बड़ी अलसाई सी उठी। दरवाजा खुलने, किसी के अंदर आने और फिर दरवाजा बंद होने की आवाज आई।

दिवा आकर फिर अपनी जगह बैठ गई।

''किटी आ गई?'' उसने पूछा।

''हाँ...।''

उसने सोचा, किटी सीधी अपने कमरे में चली गई होगी। फिर उसने सोचा, किटी कपड़े बदलकर इस कमरे में आएगी और कुछ देर बैठकर बातें करेगी।

दिवा दो-तीन सिगरेट और फूँक चुकी थी। उसे लगा, इस बीच काफी समय गुजर गया है। वह उठा। उसने अटैची से कुरता-पाजामा निकाला और बाथरूम की ओर कपड़े बदलने चल दिया। बाथरूम को जाते हुए वह किटी के कमरे के सामने से गुजरा। दरवाजे पर परदा था, पर उसे उसकी झलक दिखाई दी। वह अपने बेड पर लेटी कुछ पढ़ रही थी।

कपड़े बदलकर वह आया तो उसने देखा—दिवा ने ड्राइंगरूम का दीवान उसके सोने के लिए ठीक कर दिया है।

''पीने के लिए पानी रख देती हूँ।'' कहती हुई दिवा पानी लेने चली गई।

वह बेड पर बैठकर कमरे की एक-एक चीज को घूरने लगा। टेलीविजन, रेडियोग्राम, डाइनिंग टेबल, सोफासेट—सब निर्जीव चीजें अपनी-अपनी जगह पर रखी हुई थीं। किसी को एक-दूसरे से कोई मतलब नहीं था। वह सोचने लगा, 'क्या इस कमरे में इन चीजों की पोजीशन को बदला जा सकता है? डाइनिंग टेबल वहाँ न रखकर उस दीवार के साथ रख दिया जाए तो कैसा रहे? सोफासेट उधर रखा जा सकता है। दीवान उधर खिसकाया जा सकता है।' टेलीविजन···? वह कमरे में इधर-उधर देखने लगा। फिर उसे लगा—वह जहाँ रखा है वहीं ठीक है। फिर उसे लगा, जो चीज जहाँ रखी है, वहीं ठीक है।

□

दिवा की लरजती हुई आवाज सुनाई दी, "गुड मॉर्निंग! नींद आई?"

"नींद मुझे हर जगह आ जाती है। शी इज वेरी काइंड टू मी।"

वह खिलखिलाकर हँस पड़ी।

नाश्ते की टेबल पर उसने कहा, "आज नाइट-शो के तीन टिकट मैं ले आऊँगा।" वह किटी की तरफ मुड़ा, "तुम्हें ऑफिस के बाद कहीं जाना तो नहीं?"

किटी अपने टोस्ट पर बटर लगा रही थी।

"कहीं खास नहीं, अंकल?"

उसने दिवा की ओर देखा, "घर से जरा जल्दी निकल चलेंगे। कुछ देर चौपाटी की सैर करेंगे।"

फिर वे बातचीत करने लगे···कहाँ कौन सी फिल्म लगी हुई है। अधिकतर फिल्में देखी हुई थीं—कुछ दिवा की···कुछ किटी की।

"तुम लोगों ने साथ-साथ कौन सी फिल्म देखी है?"

एकाएक उसे लगा, उसने बड़ी गलत बात पूछ ली है। दिवा के चेहरे पर एक बड़ी रूखी सी मुसकराहट फैल गई, जो कुछ भयावह सी नजर आ रही थी। किटी का चेहरा भी हल्की सी उलझन से भर गया लगता था

"तुम्हारे हाथ के आलू के पराँठे मुझे नहीं भूलते। इतने स्वादिष्ट पराँठे मैंने और कहीं नहीं खाए। सच कहता हूँ कि कुकिंग का कोई 'नोबेल प्राइज' हो तो वह तुम्हें सिर्फ तुम्हारे आलू के पराँठे के लिए मिल सकता है।" वह बोला।

दिवा और किटी दोनों हँसने लगीं।

"अंकल, आप बड़े चालाक हैं।" किटी बोली, "मामा को मक्खन लगा रहे हैं न···। पर मामा, कितना अरसा हो गया, तुमने आलू के पराँठे नहीं बनाए। रोज सुबह वही ब्रेड, बटर, अंडे खा-खाकर मैं तो बोर हो गई हूँ।"

"कल नाश्ते में आलू के पराँठे बनाऊँगी।" दिवा का चेहरा खिल उठा था। किसी

कोने में छिपा हुआ मातृत्व उसके चेहरे पर इधर-उधर से ताक-झाँक करने लगा था। उसने एक स्लाइस पर मक्खन की खासी मोटी परत लगाकर किटी की प्लेट में रख दी।

''ओ···नो मामा···मैं नहीं खाऊँगी?''

''डोंट बी सिली···। कहकर वह दूसरे स्लाइस पर मक्खन लगाने लगी।

वह फिर अखबार पलटने लगा और फिल्मों की बातें करने लगा। दो-तीन फिल्में अभी अनदेखी थीं, पर उन्हें रिलीज हुए दो-एक दिन ही हुए थे। इसलिए उनके टिकट मिलने की उम्मीद कम थी।

उसने कहा, ''इनमें जिसके भी टिकट मिलेंगे, मैं लेता आऊँगा।''

□

शाम को वे चौपाटी की रेत पर बैठे हुए थे।

एकाएक दिवा बोली, ''साल-छमाही कहीं एक ऐसा दिन आता है।''

उसने दिवा की ओर देखा। वह सामने समुद्र में खड़ी एक किश्ती की ओर देख रही थी। फिर वह उसकी तरफ देखने लगी, ''तब कहीं हल्का सा महसूस होता है, मेरा भी कोई परिवार है···मैं और किटी माँ-बेटी हैं।''

वह हँसी और किटी की ओर देखने लगी। किटी मुट्ठी में रेत भर रही थी और उसे अपनी उँगलियों के बीच से निकाल रही थी।

''कैसी अजीब बात है। हमारे बीच जब तक कोई तीसरा व्यक्ति न आए, हमें यह अहसास ही नहीं होता कि हम माँ-बेटी हैं। हमें आपस में कोई बात किए हफ्तों गुजर जाते हैं। फ्लैट में एक-दूसरे की छाया देखकर हमें बस एक-दूसरे के होने का अहसास होता है। अलग-अलग कमरे, अलग-अलग बाथरूम, यहाँ तक कि टूथपेस्ट भी अलग-अलग।''

किटी बड़े सूने-सूने, बड़े गुमसुम ढंग से उसकी बात सुन रही थी।

''आओ भेल-पूड़ी खाएँ।'' उसने कहा। सब उठकर भेल-पूड़ीवाले की तरफ बढ़ लिये।

फिर सब धीरे-धीरे चलकर लेमिंगटन रोड पर आकर फिल्म देखने लगे। वह किनारे बैठना चाहता था, पर दिवा और किटी ने ऐसी स्थिति बना दी कि वह उनके बीच में बैठा।

फिल्म देखकर निकले तो किटी बोली, ''अंकल, आइए थोड़ी देर के लिए फिर चौपाटी पर चलें। रात को वहाँ बैठने में बड़ा मजा आता है।''

उसने दिवा की ओर देखा।

''चलो न मामा···!'' किटी दिवा से लिपट सी गई।

वह हँसी, ''कल दफ्तर नहीं जाना है?''

"कल की कैजुअल ले लेंगे···।" वह बहुत उमंग से बोली, "और कल सारा दिन अंकल के साथ पिकनिक मनाएँगे। और अंकल, कल के आपके सारे प्रोग्राम कैंसल।"

दिवा ने उसकी ओर देखा—बड़ी गहरी, बड़ी डूबी, बड़ी मोहक नजर से। जैसे वह 'वह' नहीं है। वह 'वह' है···यह···यह···किटी का अंकल···किटी का पिता···।

□

गाड़ी सुबह सात-पैंतीस पर छूटती थी, वी.टी. से। दिवा ने दिन के लिए आलू के पराँठे बना दिए थे। साथ में कई किस्म का अचार और सलाद काट दिया था। सुबह का नाश्ता भी जल्दी-जल्दी बन गया था। किटी को भी वह इधर-उधर डोलते देख रहा था। किटी बीच-बीच में उसे याद कराती थी और कहती थी—"मद्रास से आप मेरे लिए कुछ शंख खरीद लीजिएगा। एक तो चौड़े पंजेवाला, पर खयाल रखिएगा, कोई कहीं से जरा सा भी टूटा हुआ न हो। और दूसरे बड़ेवाले शंख जो मंदिरों में बजाए जाते हैं। और आप तो मद्रास से सीधे दिल्ली चले जाएँगे। वहाँ मेरी चीजें सँभालकर रखिएगा। मामा जब अगली बार दिल्ली जाएँगी तो उन्हें दे दीजिएगा।"

"तुम दिल्ली नहीं आओगी···?" उसने दाँतों से टोस्ट काटते हुए पूछा।

"इस बार मैं भी मामा के साथ आऊँगी···नहीं मामा के साथ नहीं, अकेली आऊँगी। आप मुझे दिल्ली की खूब सैर कराएँगे न? सब जगह घुमानी पड़ेंगी।"

दिवा ने चाय की केतली टेबल पर रखते हुए कहा, "किटी बेटा, अंकल की गाड़ी का वक्त हो रहा है। तुम जरा सड़क से टैक्सी तो बुला लाओ।"

किटी टैक्सी लेने चली गई।

दिवा उसी के साथ कुरसी पर बैठ गई।

सामान बँध चुका था।

वह कपड़े पहनकर तैयार था।

उसने चाय का आखिरी घूँट पिया और दिवा की ओर देखने लगा। वह सूनी आँखों से मुसकराने की कोशिश कर रही थी।

उसने उसके दोनों हाथ अपने हाथों में ले लिये।

दिवा की आँखें और सूनी हो गईं।

टैक्सी चली तो दोनों ने हाथ हिलाए और उसने देखा दोनों लिफ्ट की तरफ मुड़ गई हैं।

दो-एक मोड़ लेकर टैक्सी सड़क पर आ गई। सड़कें अभी सूनी थीं। सन्नाटा अभी पूरी तरह टूटा नहीं था। बड़ी मस्त हवा चल रही थी। पीछे छोड़े हुए फ्लैट के कुछ बिंब उसके सामने उभरने लगे।

लिफ्ट में दिवा और किटी खामोश हैं···लिफ्ट से निकलकर दिवा फ्लैट का दरवाजा खोलती है···किटी सीधे अपने कमरे में चली जाती है···दिवा बरतन साफ करनेवाली बाई को डाइनिंग टेबल साफ करने के लिए कहती है। किटी अपने बिस्तरे पर लेटकर किसी पत्रिका के पन्ने पलटने लगती है···फिर उठकर नहाने चली जाती है···दिवा अपने कमरे में आकर सिगरेट सुलगाती है और अखबार की सुर्खियाँ देखने लगती है···फिर वह भी नहाने चली जाती है···बाई टेबल पर नाश्ता लगा देती है···ब्रेड, बटर, उबले अंडे, दूध···

फिर नौ बजते हैं। दोनों अपने-अपने पर्स सँभालती हैं···अपने चाबियों के गुच्छे सँभालती हैं···अपनी साड़ियों की चुन्नटों पर हाथ फेरती हैं···लिपस्टिक लगे होंठों को शीशे में देखती हैं और फ्लैट से निकल पड़ती हैं।

उसे सामने वी.टी. स्टेशन का भव्य भवन दिखाई देने लगा था।

□

सहमे हुए

हाशमी के ठीक सामने हरजीत बैठता है। हरजीत के दाईं ओर लोबो और बाईं ओर शर्मा। वर्मा की जगह निश्चित नहीं है। कभी वह शर्मा के बाईं ओर बैठता है, कभी लोबो के दाईं ओर।

दफ्तर की यह चौकड़ी नहीं, पंचकड़ी है—जनाब इकबाल हाशमी, सरदार हरजीत सिंह मिस्टर जॉन लोबो, पंडित रघुनाथ शर्मा और श्री बी.आर. वर्मा, पर यह बी.आर. क्या हुआ? जब सभी के नाम पूरे-पूरे हैं तो वर्मा के ही 'इनीशल' क्यों? यह भी सही है कि इसमें कोई कुछ नहीं कर सकता, वर्मा अपने आपको बी.आर. वर्मा ही कहलाना पसंद करता है।

जब पाँचों व्यक्ति अपना-अपना लंच बॉक्स खोल लेते हैं तो किसी-न-किसी बात को लेकर बहस शुरू हो जाती है। जॉन लोबो यह कहकर भी अपनी बात शुरू कर सकता है, ''यार वर्मा, तुम न बी.आर. हो, न वर्मा। तुम हो बुधराम कोरी। कोरी होने से तुम शेड्यूल्ड कास्ट में आ गए और आजकल शेड्यूल्ड कास्ट की तो चाँदी-ही-चाँदी है। पर यार, तुम बी.आर. वर्मा की नकाब के पीछे अपनी असलियत कितने दिन छिपाते रहोगे? मेरी समझ में यह नहीं आता कि तुम खुलकर कहते क्यों नहीं कि मैं कोरी हूँ...एंड आइ एम प्राउड ऑफ इट...!''

बस यों समझिए कि लंच का पूरा वक्त इसी चर्चा में निकल जाता है। वर्मा आर्यों और अनार्यों के संपूर्ण इतिहास को उन्हीं मिनटों में अपनी सब्जी की कटोरी में समेट लेता है। वर्ण-व्यवस्था के नाम पर कुछ लोगों को 'अछूत' बना दिए जाने की साजिश पर पूरा भाषण दे डालता है और कहता है, ''मैं तो बी.आर. वर्मा ही लिखता हूँ। मेरा बेटा सीधे-सीधे अपने आपको ब्रह्मकुमार शर्मा लिखेगा।'' यह कहकर वह रघुनाथ शर्मा की ओर मुड़ता है और मुसकराता है।

महफिल बरखास्त होती है। हाशमी अपनी मेज की दराज से सुपारी-इलायची

निकालकर सबको देता है और सब लोग अपनी-अपनी मेजों पर चले जाते हैं।

इस पंचकड़ी में एक हिंदू, एक मुसलमान, एक ईसाई, एक सिख और एक हरिजन होने का यह अर्थ नहीं है कि यह कोई देश की भावात्मक एकता बढ़ानेवाला दफ्तर है। इसको बस एक संयोग ही मानना चाहिए। संयोग से एक और बात याद आती है। आपको नई दिल्ली की बैंक वैन डकैतीवाली बात भूली नहीं होगी। चार युवकों ने मिलकर दिन-दहाड़े एक बैंक की मोटरगाड़ी को लूट लिया था, खजांची और ड्राइवर युवकों की गोली के शिकार हो गए थे। लंबे समय तक इस डकैती का सुराग नहीं मिला था। और जब सुराग मिला, चारों युवक पकड़े गए तो पता लगा कि वे भावात्मक एकता का खासा प्रतिनिधित्व करते थे। उनमें दो हिंदू थे, एक मुसलमान और एक सिख।

यह दफ्तर किताबें प्रकाशित करने का एक बड़ा व्यावसायिक संस्थान है। इसका मुख्य कार्यालय बंबई में है। उत्तर-पश्चिमी भाग का कार्यालय दिल्ली में है। यह संस्थान अनेक भाषाओं में पुस्तकें प्रकाशित करता है। हर भाषा के अपने-अपने संपादक हैं। पं. रघुनाथ शर्मा हिंदी के, जनाब इकबाल हाशमी उर्दू के, सरदार हरजीत सिंह पंजाबी के और मिस्टर जॉन लोबो अंग्रेजी के संपादक हैं। पहले यह संस्था एक ब्रिटिश फर्म का अंग थी। अब इस पर पूरी तरह भारतीयों का अधिकार है, परंतु ब्रिटिश लोगों ने इस संस्थान में जो परंपराएँ डाली थीं, आज के मालिक भी उन्हें पूरी तरह निभाए जा रहे हैं। यह भी शायद इसी परंपरा का एक अंग है कि मालिक लोग समझते हैं कि संस्कृत-हिंदी का काम कोई ब्राह्मण ही ठीक ढंग से कर सकता है, उर्दू का काम कोई मुसलमान ही कर सकता है, पंजाबी के लिए एक सिख होना चाहिए और अंग्रेजी किसी शुद्ध हिंदुस्तानी के बस का रोग नहीं। उसके लिए ब्रिटिश व्यक्ति ही होना चाहिए। वह न हो तो एंग्लो-इंडियन हो। और वह भी न हो तो कम-से-कम क्रिश्चियन तो होना ही चाहिए।

एक परिवर्तन जरूर आया है। पहले हिंदी का संपादक गाँठ लगी चोटीवाला, धोती-कुरताधारी, त्रिपुंडधारी पंडित होता था। इसी तरह उर्दू का संपादक 'मौलवीनुमा' और पंजाबीवाला 'ज्ञानीनुमा' होता था। अब यह बात नहीं रही है। अब लोग काफी 'उदार' हो गए हैं। यह बात अलग है कि शर्मा, हाशमी और लोबो की शक्ल देखकर उन्हें हिंदू, मुसलमान और ईसाई बताया जा सकता है। हरजीत की तो बात ही अलग है। उसकी मैरून रंग की पगड़ी उसके 'खालसा' होने की घोषणा करती रहती है, परंतु इसमें संदेह नहीं कि ये पाँचों लोग उदार हैं। इनकी उदारता का इससे बड़ा प्रमाण क्या होगा कि ये पाँचों मित्र हैं, एक-दूसरे के घर आते-जाते हैं, वहाँ चाय-वाय पीते हैं। ये लोग नियमित रूप से हाशमी की मेज पर अपने लंच-बॉक्स खोलते हैं। यहाँ भी इनकी 'उदारता' कभी सँकरी गलियों और कभी चौड़े पाट से होकर बहती है।

यह स्थिति भी कुछ कम मजेदार नहीं। शर्मा दूसरों के लंच-बॉक्स में से अचार

और सलाद-खीरा, गाजर, मूली, प्याज आदि ले लेता है। हाशमी के लंच-बॉक्स में अकसर कबाब होते हैं और हरजीत के लंच-बॉक्स में तली हुई कलेजियाँ। हाशमी हरजीत की कलेजियाँ खा लेता है और हरजीत हाशमी के कबाब खा जाता है। यहाँ दोनों अपने-अपने धार्मिक आदेशों की कुछ अवहेलना कर जाते हैं, क्योंकि हाशमी के कबाब हलाल किए हुए बकरे के मांस के बने होते हैं और सिखों में हलाल खाना वर्जित है। इसी तरह हरजीत की कलेजियाँ 'झटका' किए हुए बकरे की होती हैं, जिसे एक मुसलमान नहीं खा सकता। खान-पान की इस 'उदारता' के बावजूद हाशमी और हरजीत के मन को एक शंका अंदर-ही-अंदर घेरे रहती है। हरजीत हलाल बकरे के कबाब खाने जितना उदार तो हो गया है, पर 'बीफ' नहीं खा सकता। इसलिए वह कभी-कभी हाशमी से कह देता है, ''यार हाशमी, तेरे कबाब इतने लजीज होते हैं कि मैं उन्हें छोड़ नहीं सकता, पर कभी मुझे 'बीफ' खिलाकर मेरा धरम भ्रष्ट न कर देना।''

इसी तरह हाशमी भी एक बात की ओर से पूरी तरह सतर्क है। वह हरजीत के लंच-बॉक्स की कलेजी खा लेता है, क्योंकि बकरे का कलेजी की स्वाद उसे हलाल या झटका किए जाने से नहीं बदलता, पर वह 'पोर्क' नहीं खा सकता। वह अकसर कह देता है, ''सूअर का मांस कोई इनसानों के खाने की चीज है...लाहौल विला कूवत... !''

लोबो और वर्मा ने खाने-पीने के मामले में कभी हुज्जत नहीं की। लोबो सबकुछ खा लेता है। वैसे उसका लंच-बॉक्स सिर्फ उसी का रहता है, क्योंकि उसमें कभी टमाटर वाली, कभी 'चीज' वाली और कभी-कभी हैमवाली सैंडविच होती हैं। वर्मा को दूसरों के लंच-बॉक्स से कुछ भी लेते संकोच होता है। वह अपने साथ सलाद खूब लाता है और एक अखबारी कागज पर डालकर मेज के बीचोबीच रख देता है। सब वहीं से लेकर खाते रहते हैं।

हाशमी और हरजीत कभी-कभी अपने लंच-बॉक्स से कबाब या कलेजी निकालकर उसके लंच-बॉक्स में डाल देते हैं।

एक दिन हरजीत बोला, ''यार हाशमी, आज फिर अखबार में खबर आई है कि लखनऊ में शिया-सुन्नियों में झगड़ा हो गया है। मेरी समझ में यह नहीं आता कि शिया-सुन्नियों में आखिर झगड़ा किस बात का है?''

खबर सुबह के ही अखबार में थी और सभी ने पढ़ी थी। इससे पहले भी इस पंचकड़ी में इस विषय पर कितनी ही बार चर्चा हो चुकी थी, क्योंकि साल में एक-दो बार तो ऐसी खबर अखबारों में आती ही है। हाशमी ने कई बार इसकी पृष्ठभूमि भी बताई है, पर वह किसी को याद नहीं रहती। जब भी अखबार में यह खबर छपती है, यह बात नए सिरे से शुरू होती है।

आज हाशमी ने जवाब नहीं दिया, बल्कि सवाल किया, ''तुम यह बताओ कि यह

अकालियों और निरंकारियों का झगड़ा क्या है? इस झगड़े में कुछ ही अरसे में कितने लोग हलाक हो चुके हैं।''

शर्मा, वर्मा लोबो सभी हरजीत की ओर देखने लगे। इन दिनों अकाली-निरंकारी संघर्ष की खबरें अखबारों को घेरे हुए थीं। हरजीत ने कुछ बताना चाहा, पर उसकी समझ में नहीं आया कि इतनी देर में वह क्या बता दे। वह इतना ही बोला, ''इस झगड़े की पृष्ठभूमि जरा लंबी है। मैं किसी दिन विस्तार से बताऊँगा।''

शर्मा ऐसे विवादों में बहुत उत्साह से भाग नहीं लेता। वह लोगों की बातें सुनता है और अपनी सारी प्रतिक्रिया आँखों से, भौंहों से, चेहरे की रेखाओं से और गरदन को आगे-पीछे या इधर-उधर हिलाने से ही व्यक्त करता है।

वह बोला, ''हरजीत ठीक कहता है। झगड़ों के बीज हमारी पृष्ठभूमि में पता नहीं कब, किसने और क्यों बो दिए थे? उस बोई हुई फसल को हम कब से काट रहे हैं, काटते चले जाएँगे। मनुष्य अवश्य लड़ेगा। वह अकेले-अकेले लड़ता है तो लोग उसे झगड़ालू, गुंडा और बदमाश कहते हैं। वह झुंड बनाकर लड़ता है तो देशभक्त, धर्मवीर और गाजी कहलाता है, उसे सम्मानित किया जाता है। आखिर मनुष्य यह सम्मान क्यों न ले?''

''जी, हाँ...इसी सम्मान के लिए वह सामूहिक रूप से घृणा करता है...व्यक्ति से नहीं, बल्कि एक पूरे समूह से...उसे गाँव में बसने नहीं देता, कुएँ से पानी नहीं भरने देता, मंदिर में नहीं जाने देता, उसकी छायामात्र पड़ जाने से वह अशुद्ध हो जाता है।'' वर्मा प्रायः बात करते-करते उत्तेजित हो जाता है।

□

इन दिनों के अखबार सांप्रदायिक दंगों की खबरों से भरे पड़े हैं। मुरादाबाद की ईदगाह में सूअर घुस गया था। वाराणसी के किसी मंदिर में गोमांस मिला था। इलाहाबाद की एक मसजिद में सूअर का गोश्त पाया गया था।

दिल्ली में भी छिटपुट वारदातें हो गई हैं। हाशमी बल्लीमारान में रहता है। वहाँ कर्फ्यू लगा हुआ है। हरजीत तुर्कमान गेट में रहता है। वहाँ भी कर्फ्यू लगा हुआ है। लोबो और वर्मा ही दफ्तर आ रहे हैं। शर्मा कुछ दिन के लिए अपने भाई से मिलने चंदौसी गया था। उस क्षेत्र में दंगा कुछ इस तरह भड़का हुआ है कि वहाँ से उसकी कोई खबर नहीं आ रही है।

हरजीत कितने ही वर्षों से रोज शाम को किसी भी समय शीशगंज गुरुद्वारे में मत्था टेकने जाता है। सन् सैंतालीस में जब उसके माँ-बाप, बड़े भाई-बहन गुजराँवाला से उजड़कर दिल्ली आए थे तो वह गर्भ में था। उसकी माँ कितने ही दहशत भरे दिन और कितनी डरावनी रातों को अपनी कोख में समेटे हुए दिल्ली पहुँची थी। उसके परिवार ने

कितने ही दिन इधर-उधर भटकते हुए और शीशगंज गुरुद्वारे में 'लंगर' खाते हुए गुजारे थे। बाद में उसके पिता ने तुर्कमान गेट में एक मकान खरीद लिया था, जिसका मुसलमान मालिक पाकिस्तान जाने की उतावली में उसे कौड़ियों के मोल बेच रहा था। तब से उसका परिवार इसी मकान में है। उस मकान का पूरा हुलिया ही बदल गया है। उसके पिता और भाइयों ने मिलकर धीरे-धीरे उसे एक अच्छी-खासी कोठी में बदल दिया है। पर उस क्षेत्र में आज भी मुसलमानों की बहुतायत है। 'सरदारों' के परिवार की गली-मुहल्ले में बड़ी इज्जत है, पर जब भी देश के किसी हिस्से से दंगे-फसाद की खबरें आती हैं, मन की किन्हीं तहों में बैठा हुआ सहम उनके चारों ओर फैलने लगता है।

हरजीत को आजकल कितना घूमकर गुरुद्वारे जाना पड़ता है। जब भी दंगों की खबर जोर पकड़ती है, हरजीत अपनी बुश्शर्ट के नीचे छोटी कृपाण पहनना शुरू कर देता है।

हाशमी इलाहाबाद का रहनेवाला है। देश के विभाजन के समय उसकी उम्र तीन-चार वर्ष की थी। उसके कई नजदीकी रिश्तेदार पाकिस्तान में रहते हैं, जो विभाजन के समय उधर चले गए थे। इलाहाबाद विश्वविद्यालय से उर्दू में एम.ए. करने के बाद वह नौकरी की तलाश में दिल्ली आया। वर्षों तक छोटे-मोटे उर्दू अखबारों में नौकरी करने के बाद उसे इस प्रकाशन संस्थान में अच्छी नौकरी मिली। वर्षों से बल्लीमारान की बदबूदार गलियों के गवाह बने दो कमरों के सीलनदार मकान में रहता है। कितनी ही बार उसका मन हुआ है कि वह भी दिल्ली की किसी आधुनिक कॉलोनी में एक फ्लैट लेकर रहे, उसके बच्चे किसी अच्छे पब्लिक स्कूल में पढ़ें, उसकी बीवी इन गलियों का खाना खाती, फूहड़ बातें करती और टाट के परदों के पीछे जिंदगी जीती औरतों से कुछ अलग होकर जीवन जिए, परंतु वह इसी गली में जीवन जिए जा रहा है। यहाँ वह एक अजीब किस्म की सुरक्षा अनुभव करता है। उसे बार-बार लगता है—यदि वह ग्रीन पार्क, हौजखास, साउथ एक्सटेंशन या लाजपत नगर जैसी कॉलोनी में, जहाँ से उसका दफ्तर बहुत नजदीक है, मकान लेकर रहेगा तो उसके हिंदू-सिख पड़ोसी कभी उससे खुलकर व्यवहार नहीं करेंगे। उनकी औरतें उसकी बीवी नसरीन से वैसा बहनापा नहीं बनाएँगी, जैसा वे आपस में बना लेती हैं, और उसके बच्चे दूसरे बच्चों से हमेशा दूर-दूर रहेंगे। इन गलियों में बदबू तो है, पर उन कॉलोनियों में एक घुटन होगी, जो उसे और उसके परिवार को लगातार महसूस होती रहेगी।

□

आज कई दिन बाद यह पंचकड़ी फिर जमी है। शर्मा चंदौसी से वापस आ गया है। उसके चेहरे पर गहरा खिंचाव है। लोबो पूछता है, "क्या हाल है उस तरफ?"

"हाल क्या होना है," शर्मा भर्राई आवाज में कहता है, "पाकिस्तान बन गया, पर पाकिस्तान जिंदाबाद के नारे अब भी उसी तरह लग रहे हैं, जैसे अभी एक और

पाकिस्तान बनना है। मसजिदें गोला-बारूद और चाकू-छुरों की भंडार बनी हुई हैं। पाकिस्तानी एजेंट सरेआम दंगे करवा रहे हैं। दुःख की बात तो यह है कि पनाह उन्हें यहाँ के मुसलमानों से मिल रही है। दंगाई खुलकर पुलिस और फौज पर हमले कर रहे हैं और इसमें मशीनगनों और ऑटोमैटिक राइफलों का प्रयोग हो रहा है…ये हथियार इन्हें कहाँ से मिल रहे हैं?''

शर्मा की बात से एक अजीब सन्नाटा सा छा जाता है। शर्मा, हरजीत, लोबो सभी कनखियों से हाशमी की ओर देखते हैं, जैसे जो कुछ शर्मा ने कहा है, उसकी कुछ-न-कुछ जिम्मेदारी हाशमी के सिर पर भी है।

हाशमी कुछ नहीं बोलता। चुपचाप खाना खाता रहता है।

वर्मा कहता है, ''यह भी कैसी अजीब बात है कि हरिजन सभी तरफ से पिटते हैं। मराठवाड़ा में सवर्ण हिंदुओं के हाथों पिट रहे हैं, क्योंकि अछूत हैं। मुरादाबाद इलाके में मुसलमानों ने हरिजन बस्तियाँ जला दी हैं, क्योंकि उनकी नजर में हम हिंदू हैं।''

लोबो कहता है, ''तुम सब लोगों ने यह खबर तो पढ़ी ही होगी…असम में कुछ ईश्वर-भक्तों ने एक पुलिस सब-इंस्पेक्टर को पकड़कर इतना पीटा कि वह वहीं मर गया।''

सभी लोबो की ओर देखने लगते हैं।

''कैसी जहालत है?'' लोबो जैसे अपने आप से कहता है, ''एक मुसलमान पुलिस सब-इंस्पेक्टर अपने एक हिंदू साथी को ढूँढ़ता हुआ मंदिर के अहाते में चला गया। वहाँ कुछ लोगों ने उसे पहचान लिया…अरे, यह तो मुसलमान है, और फिर इतना पीटा…इतना पीटा कि वह वहीं ढेर हो गया।''

सभी शर्मा की ओर देखते हैं। जैसे वह मुसलमान सब-इंस्पेक्टर क्यों मारा गया, इसका पूरा स्पष्टीकरण शर्मा के पास है।

सभी खाना खत्म कर लेते हैं। आज वर्मा का लाया हुआ सलाद बच जाता है, क्योंकि शायद सभी ने उसमें से मूली या प्याज के टुकड़े नहीं उठाए थे। आज यह भी हुआ कि हाशमी ने अपने कबाब और हरजीत ने अपनी कलेजियाँ खुद ही खाईं।

आजकल हाशमी और हरजीत कुछ ज्यादा ही नजदीक दिखाई देते हैं। तुर्कमान गेट और बल्लीमारान के इलाके भी पास-पास हैं। प्रायः शाम को दोनों साथ-साथ लौटते हैं। लाल किले पर बस से उतरकर दोनों चाँदनी चौक की तरफ चल देते हैं। हरजीत शीशगंज गुरुद्वारे में मत्था टेकने के लिए रुक जाता है। हाशमी आगे चला जाता है। दोनों साथ-साथ रहते हैं तो एक-दूसरे का सहारा अनुभव करते हैं।

हाशमी कहता है, ''किसी भी मुल्क में माइनॉरटीज की जिंदगी महफूज नहीं होती। पता नहीं कब मैजॉरिटी कम्युनिटी में किसी भी सबब से पागलपन सवार हो जाए

और वह माइनॉरटीज के पीछे हाथ धोकर पड़ जाए।''

हरजीत उसकी बात का समर्थन करता है, ''कम गिनतीवाली कम्युनिटी के आदमी को तो एक अच्छी नौकरी भी नहीं मिलती। मुझे पता है, इस नौकरी को पाने के लिए मुझे कितने धक्के खाने पड़े।''

उस दिन लंच के बाद हाशमी ने हरजीत को अपने कमरे में बुलाया।

''बोलो।'' हरजीत ने देखा, हाशमी कुछ घबराया हुआ है।

''गाँव से वालिद साहब का खत आया है। अम्माँ बहुत बीमार हैं···बस आखिरी वक्त समझो। मरने से पहले वे मुझे एक नजर देखना चाहती हैं। सोचता हूँ, दो-चार दिन के लिए चला जाऊँ।''

''हाँ···हाँ···हो आओ, इसमें इतना सोचने की क्या बात है? तुम्हारी छुट्टी तो बाकी होंगी?''

''छुट्टी की तो कोई बात नहीं है, पर यार, चारों तरफ फसाद फैले हुए हैं।'' हाशमी कुछ सकुचाते हुए बोला।

''हाँ, फसाद तो हैं। पर ऐसी चिंता की कोई बात नहीं है। आजकल हालात बेहतर हैं और अब तो दंगाग्रस्त इलाकों में फौज तैनात है।'' हरजीत बोला।

''हाँ, यह ठीक है।'' हाशमी कुछ रुक-रुककर बोला, ''पर यह भी तो होता कि लोग रास्ते में ट्रेन रोक लेते हैं और बस फिर काट-पीट शुरू कर देते हैं।''

हरजीत ने देखा, हाशमी के चेहरे पर पसीने की बूँदें झलक आई हैं।

''नहीं, ऐसी कोई बात नहीं। इस बीच दंगाइयों ने कहीं ट्रेन रोककर काट-पीट की हो, ऐसी कोई खबर नहीं है। तुम ऐसा करो, रात की गाड़ी से सफर करो। तुम्हें इलाहाबाद जाना है न, कालका मेल से चले जाओ। गाड़ी सुबह चलती है। तुम दिन-दिन में ही इलाहाबाद पहुँच जाओगे।''

हरजीत की बात सुनकर हाशमी कुछ सोचने लगा। फिर बोला, ''इसमें एक और उलझन है। हमारा गाँव इलाहाबाद से तकरीबन बीस मील दूर है। वहाँ बस से जाना पड़ता है। इलाहाबाद की हालत तो तुम जानते ही हो। बस-अड्डे तक पहुँचते-पहुँचते किसी ने छुरा भोंक दिया तो अपन गए काम से।''

दोनों सोच में पड़ गए और कितनी ही देर सोचते रहे। हाशमी गाँव नहीं गया। पंचकड़ी में उससे किसी ने नहीं पूछा कि उसकी माँ की हालत कैसी है। उसकी माँ सख्त बीमार है, यह बात सभी को पता थी, पर अब उसकी हालत कैसी है, यह पूछते जैसे सभी को अंदर-ही-अंदर डर लग रहा था।

लंच टाइम में खाना तो सबका साथ-साथ चल रहा है, जगह भी वही है, खाना भी पहले जैसा ही है, पर पता नहीं क्यों, एक-दूसरे के लंच-बॉक्स से चीजें लेना लगभग

बंद सा हो गया है। वर्मा अपना सलाद जरूर उसी तरह लाता है और कागज पर फैलाकर मेज के बीचोबीच रख देता है। लोग बड़े अनमने ढंग से उसमें से एक-आध टुकड़ा उठा लेते हैं, पर खाना सभी लोग अपने-अपने लंच-बॉक्स से ही खाते रहते हैं, जैसे दूसरे के खाने में जहर मिला हुआ हो।

अब पहले जितनी बातचीत भी नहीं होती। एक चुप्पी सी छाई रहती है। इस चुप्पी को प्राय: लोबो ही तोड़ता है—"यार, हिंदू-मुसलमानों के दंगों में हम ईसाइयों की बड़ी मुसीबत होती है। मुसलमान हमें हिंदू समझकर छुरा भोंक देता है और हिंदू हमें मुसलमान समझकर हमारी गरदन काट देता है। जब तक हम बताएँ-बताएँ कि हम क्या हैं—पेट चाक हो चुका होता है। हमें तो साला कुछ दिखाने का मौका ही नहीं मिलता।"

उसकी इस बात पर ऐसा ठहाका लगता है कि पूरा कमरा गूँजने लगता है।

पटना में होनेवाले 'बुक फेयर' की तारीख नजदीक आ गई है। इस प्रकाशन संस्थान ने उसमें अपने लिए काफी बड़ी जगह ली है। वर्मा चूँकि बिक्री विभाग में है, इसलिए वह एक सप्ताह पहले ही वहाँ चला गया था। शर्मा, हाशमी, हरजीत, लोबो को भी वहाँ जाने का आदेश मिला है। 'अपर इंडिया एक्सप्रेस' में फर्स्ट क्लास के डिब्बे में सभी का रिजर्वेशन हो चुका है। चारों की बर्थ एक ही कैबिन में है, इसलिए सभी संतुष्ट हैं—रात को खूब मौज रहेगी। हरजीत ने सबसे कह दिया है, "दोस्तो, घर से खाना खाकर मत आना। अपना-अपना खाना साथ लाना। आठ बजकर दस मिनट पर गाड़ी छूटती है। गाजियाबाद निकल जाने के बाद 'जश्ने-जमहूरियत' शुरू करेंगे। बोतल लोबो लाएगा, सलाद मास्टर वर्मा साथ नहीं है, कोई बात नहीं, शर्माजी, सलाद आप लाएँगे। हाशमी, देख यार, कबाब काफी होना चाहिए...और हरजीत सिंह लाएगा कम-से-कम आधा किलो तली हुई कलेजी।"

□

आज का अखबार दंगे-फसाद की खबरों से फिर भर गया है। अलीगढ़ में चौबीस घंटे का कर्फ्यू लग गया है। सारे शहर में सेना गश्त कर रही है। दंगाइयों ने कितने ही दुकान-मकान जलाकर खाक कर दिए हैं। कितनी ही लाशें जले हुए मकानों के मलबों के नीचे से निकाली गई हैं। सारा शहर आतंक में डूबा हुआ है।

स्टेशन पर सबसे पहले शर्मा पहुँच जाता है। कुछ देर में हाशमी पहुँचता है। दोनों अपनी कैबिन में आमने-सामने बैठे हैं। शर्मा कहता है, "यह बुक फेयर सफल नहीं होगा। वैसे भी कौन पुस्तकें खरीदता है? फिर आजकल तो आम आदमी ऐसे ही घर से निकलने से डरता है।"

हाशमी सिगरेट सुलगाकर पीने लगता है। बैठे-बैठे बार-बार उसकी नजर प्लेटफॉर्म पर जाती है। आज ज्यादा भीड़ नहीं है। वह आते-जाते लोगों को देखता है और

अनायास ही उनमें हिंदू और मुसलमान चेहरे ढूँढ़ने लगता है।

लोबो और हरजीत एक साथ आते हैं। चारों लोग आ गए हैं, इस बात पर सभी खुशी प्रकट करते हैं। लोबो कहता है, "घर से स्टेशन तक आते-आते लगा, जैसे मुझे सैल्यूट मारने के लिए जगह-जगह पर सिपाही तैनात हैं। लाजपत नगर से कोई स्कूटरवाला इधर आने को तैयार ही नहीं होता था। सब कहते थे—उधर कर्फ्यू लगा हुआ है।"

गाड़ी चलने में अभी दस-पंद्रह मिनट बाकी हैं। हरजीत प्लेटफॉर्म पर खड़ा है। प्लेटफॉर्म पर रोशनी बहुत मद्धिम है और उमस बहुत ज्यादा।

गार्ड की सीटी सुनाई देती है तो वह अपनी कैबिन में आकर हाशमी की बगल में बैठ जाता है। चारों चुप-चुप बैठे हैं। अलीगढ़ के दंगे की खबर आज की सबसे ताजा खबर है। शाम के अखबार में खबर है कि आसपास के जिलों में भी तनाव बढ़ गया है। शाम का अखबार दोनों खिड़कियों के बीच की टेबिल पर रखा हुआ है।

हरजीत बोलता है, "कल अलीगढ़ में दंगाई एक मकान में घुस गए। घर में उस समय एक बूढ़ा था—सत्तर साल का और एक लड़की थी—आठ साल की। दंगाइयों ने दोनों को छुरों से गोद-गोदकर मार डाला। पिताजी बताते हैं कि सन् सैंतालीस के दंगों में दंगाई छोटे-छोटे बच्चों को नेजों की नोक पर उछाल देते थे⋯क्या वही दिन वापस आ रहे हैं?"

ऐसा लगा, जैसे सभी के चेहरों पर पसीने की बूँदें झलक आई हैं।

गाड़ी चल देती है। धीरे-धीरे वह प्लेटफॉर्म से बाहर निकल आती है। यमुना पुल पर गाड़ी आती है तो हाशमी उठकर कैबिन का दरवाजा बंद करके चिटकनी लगा देता है। फिर सभी लोग कुछ-न-कुछ पढ़ने में तल्लीन हो जाते हैं।

किसी ने कैबिन का दरवाजा खटखटाया है। लोबो दरवाजा खोलता है। कंडक्टर आकर टिकट चेक करता है और पूछता है, "आप लोग बेड-टी कहाँ लेंगे?"

"कानपुर में।" लोबो कहता है।

"नहीं," हरजीत कहता है, "यह गाड़ी कानपुर तो सुबह चार बजे ही पहुँच जाती है⋯चाय फतेहपुर में भिजवाइएगा।"

"ठीक है साब।" कहकर कंडक्टर कैबिन से बाहर निकल जाता है और दरवाजा बंद करता जाता है।

हाशमी उठता है और दरवाजे की चिटकनी लगा देता है।

गाजियाबाद के प्लेटफॉर्म को छोड़कर गाड़ी आगे बढ़ती है तो लोबो अपने बैग से बोतल निकालकर मेज पर रख देता है। कहता है, "बड़ी मुश्किल से आज इसका इंतजाम हुआ। मुझे ध्यान नहीं था कि आज 'ड्राइ डे' है।"

शर्मा अपना टिफिन कॅरियर खोलता है, जिसके ऊपरी डिब्बे में कटा हुआ सलाद

रखा है। हाशमी और हरजीत भी अपने-अपने डिब्बे खोलते हैं। लोबो बोतल रखकर थोड़ी व्हिस्की सबके गिलासों में डाल देता है। हरजीत वाटर बॉटल से गिलासों में पानी डालता है।

सब गिलासों को टकराते हैं और पीने लगते हैं। दो-तीन घूँट पीने के बाद शर्मा बोलता है—"यार हाशमी, बुरा मत मानना। मुसलमान इस देश के प्रति वफादार नहीं हो सकता।"

हरजीत और लोबो को इस समय यह चर्चा अच्छी नहीं लगती। हाशमी शर्मा की बात सुनता है और चुप रहता है। फिर वह बची हुई शराब को गले में उतार देता है और गिलास को मेज पर रख देता है, "शर्मा, एक बात मैं भी कहूँ। यह देश क्या है? नदियाँ! पहाड़! जमीन! नहीं, यह देश नहीं है। देश है...यहाँ के बसनेवाले लोग...तुम...तुम जो अपने आपको हिंदू कहते हो। हिंदू के मन में हमारे लिए नफ़रत है और उसके दिल से यह नफरत नहीं जा सकती।"

लोबो गिलास फिर भर लेता है।

"देखो," वह कहता है, "शर्मा हाशमी से नफरत नहीं करता और न ही हाशमी कभी शर्मा के प्रति बेवफाई करेगा। पर जब हम अपने-अपने मजहबी माहौल में पहुँचते हैं तो हम बदलने लगते हैं। तब हरजीत पक्का अकाली बन जाता है और मुझे अपना कैथोलिक होना याद आने लगता है।"

हरजीत एक घूँट में गिलास खत्म कर देता है, "दोस्तो, मुझे लगता है, सारी लड़ाई ताकत और दौलत की लड़ाई है। आदमी सत्ता के लिए लड़ता है और सत्ता के पीछे-पीछे दौलत आती है। अब इस लड़ाई को चाहे धर्म के नाम पर लड़ो, चाहे देश के नाम पर लड़ो, चाहे किसी चमकदार वाद के नाम पर लड़ो...बस लड़ो...लड़ो और लड़ते चले जाओ।"

बोतल आधी से ज्यादा खत्म हो चुकी है। गाड़ी अपनी पूरी रफ्तार से भागती चली जा रही है। लोबो ने बातचीत का रुख दूसरी तरफ मोड़ दिया है। अब बातचीत के केंद्र में प्रकाशन संस्थान के मैनेजिंग डायरेक्टर मिस्टर रामानी आ गए हैं। लोबो ने अपनी अनेक स्रोतों से प्राप्त उस जानकारी को फिर दुहरा दिया है कि मिस्टर रामानी पहले इस फर्म में प्रूफ रीडर के तौर पर भरती हुए थे। धीरे-धीरे वे अंग्रेज मालिकों के चहेते बनते चले गए। उसी जमाने में वे कंपनी के एक डायरेक्टर बन गए। जब अंग्रेजों ने इसे छोड़ने का फैसला किया तो सब कुछ मिस्टर रामानी के पास आ गया।

आज मिस्टर रामानी लाखों में खेल रहे हैं।

अलीगढ़ से पहले सभी ने खाना खा लिया है। यहाँ तक किसी ने सोने की बात नहीं कही है। सभी के मन में था—पहले अलीगढ़ निकल जाए।

अलीगढ़ स्टेशन पर लगभग सन्नाटा सा छाया हुआ है। शर्मा ने खिड़कियों के शीशे नीचे कर दिए हैं। चारों लोग शीशे से ही बाहर झाँकने की कोशिश कर रहे हैं, इक्का-दुक्का चायवाला आवाज लगाता हुआ घूम रहा है। पुलिस के दो-चार सिपाहियों के बूटों की आवाज उस सन्नाटे में बज सी रही है।

गाड़ी अलीगढ़ स्टेशन छोड़ती है तो सभी राहत की साँस लेते हैं। सभी अपने-अपने बिस्तर बिछाने लगते हैं। शर्मा और हाशमी नीचे की बर्थों पर हैं। सोने से पहले शर्मा उठकर हल्की नीली रोशनी छोड़कर बाकी बत्तियाँ बुझा देता है।

लोबो के खर्राटों की आवाज सबसे पहले आती है। फिर हरजीत की नाक भी हल्की-हल्की बजने लगती है। शर्मा और हाशमी एक-दूसरे की ओर पीठ किए सोने की कोशिश करने लगते हैं। उन्हें भी नींद का पहला झोंका आ गया है।

तभी शर्मा की आवाज सुनाई देती है, ''हाशमी···हाशमी!''

हाशमी एकदम चौंककर उठता है, ''क्या है···?''

गाड़ी रुकी हुई है। शर्मा खिड़की से कुछ देखने की कोशिश करता है।

हाशमी झटपट उठकर बत्ती जलाने के लिए स्विच ऑन करता है, पर बत्ती नहीं जलती। तभी वह अनुभव करता है कि कैबिन के पंखे भी बंद हैं और उमस बढ़ गई है। लोबो और हरजीत की नींद भी गरमी के कारण टूट जाती है।

लोबो लेटे-लेटे ही कहता है, ''शर्मा, गाड़ी रुकी हुई है क्या? और इतनी गरमी क्यों हो रही है?''

हरजीत कहता है, ''अरे हाशमी, लाइट तो ऑन कर दो।''

''लाइट गायब है?'' हाशमी और शर्मा के मुँह से एक साथ निकलता है।

लोबो और हाशमी नीचे उतर आते हैं।

गाड़ी खड़ी है। चारों ओर घुप अँधेरा है। आकाश में एक भी तारा टिमटिमाता नजर नहीं आ रहा है।

हाशमी अपने पास बैठे हरजीत को कंधे से हिलाते हुए कहता है, ''तुम्हें कुछ शोर नहीं सुनाई दे रहा है?''

सभी कान लगाकर सुनने लगते हैं। आँखें फाड़-फाड़कर दूर अँधेरे में कुछ देखने की कोशिश करते हैं। दूर से साँय-साँय की आवाज आ रही है, जैसे कहीं शोर हो रहा हो।

लोबो उठकर दरवाजा खोलने लगता है।

''दरवाजा मत खोलो···'' हाशमी चीख उठता है।

कैबिन में इतना अँधेरा है कि किसी को किसी की शक्ल साफ दिखाई नहीं दे रही है। शर्मा लोहे के सरियों की खिड़की से इंजिन की ओर देखने की कोशिश कर रहा है,

पर अँधेरे में आगे के डिब्बों की खामोश कतार के अलावा और कुछ दिखाई नहीं देता।

"यार, बाहर निकलकर पता तो लगाएँ कि आखिर बात क्या है?" हरजीत कहता है।

"जरा कंडक्टर से ही पूछ देखें।" लोबो कहता है।

"चुपचाप बैठे रहो।" शर्मा कड़ककर कहता है।

सभी को लगता है, शोर बढ़ता जा रहा है और पास-पास आता जा रहा है।

तभी एक बहुत जोर का धमाका होता है। कोई भारी और सख्त चीज शर्मा की खिड़की से लगे सरियों से टकराती है और नीचे गिर जाती है। एक चीख और दहशत कैबिन में भर जाती है। शर्मा और हाशमी जल्दी-जल्दी अपनी खिड़कियों के शटर और शीशे नीचे गिरा देते हैं।

कैबिन में घुप अँधेरा छा जाता है।

सभी को एक-दूसरे की साँसों की आवाज साफ सुनाई दे रही है।

कैबिन चारों ओर से बंद है। फिर भी ऐसा लग रहा है, जैसे बाहर बेहिसाब शोर फैला हुआ है।

पसीने से तरबतर और सहमे हुए आठ हाथ आपस में एक-दूसरे को पलोसते चले जा रहे हैं।

□

धूप की उँगलियों के निशान

वह स्टेशन से बाहर निकल आया। धूप बहुत तेज थी। उसने पास के पीपल की ओर देखा। हर पत्ता चुपचाप मुँह लटकाए हुए था। हिल-डुल बिल्कुल नहीं रहा था। गरमी में जब तीखी उमस का उसे अहसास करना होता है तो वह किसी वृक्ष की ओर देखता है। उसने अपनी बुशर्ट की कॉलर को गरदन से पीछे करके सिर दाएँ-बाएँ घुमाया—उफ''। पसीने की लकीरें उसके चेहरे पर बराबर चल रही थीं और वह अपने गुड़ी-मुड़ी रूमाल से उन्हें पोंछता जा रहा था।

इस क्षेत्र का भूगोल उसे अच्छी तरह याद है। सड़क पार सामने दिल्ली पब्लिक लाइब्रेरी है। उसके साथ ही सड़क पर एक-दूसरे में गुँथी मिनी बसें दूर तक खड़ी दिखती हैं, परंतु बसों का यह जमघट सुबह-शाम ही ज्यादा नजर आता है। उसने देखा, इस समय तो वहाँ बस दो-तीन ही बसें खड़ी थीं।

वह अपनी अटैची उठाकर सड़क पार कर गया। सड़क पार कहीं रत्तीभर भी छाँह नहीं थी। दिल्ली पब्लिक लाइब्रेरी के दरवाजे पर थोड़ी सी छाँह थी। वह लाइब्रेरी के चबूतरे पर चढ़ गया और वहीं से दूर खड़ी बसों में से अशोक विहार जानेवाली बस को पहचानने की कोशिश करने लगा। उसे कुछ दिखाई नहीं दिया। वह जानता था कि अशोक विहार जानेवाली मिनी बस का रंग हरा होता है और पंजाबी बाग जानेवाली बस नीले रंग की होती है; परंतु इतनी कड़ी धूप में उसे रंग की पहचान नहीं हो पार रही थी।

वह सड़क पर उतर आया। उसे लगा जैसे किसी ने सिर पर आग जला दी हो। वह धीरे-धीरे बसों की ओर बढ़ा।

पहली बस हरे रंग की थी। उस पर जनकपुरी लिखा हुआ था। अंदर पाँच-छह सवारियाँ बैठी हुई थीं। कुछ दूरी पर दूसरी बस खड़ी थी। उस पर विनय नगर लिखा था। उसमें कोई भी सवारी नहीं थी। दो-एक लोग बस के आसपास मँडरा रहे थे। पीछे ठंडे पानी की रेहड़ी लिये लड़का खड़ा था। एक औरत छतरी लगाए वहाँ पानी पी रही थी।

वह भी रेहड़ी के पास जा खड़ा हुआ।

पानीवाला लड़का उसे देखकर गिलास भरने लगा तो वह बोला, ''गिलास जरा अच्छी तरह साफ कर लो।''

उसे लगा, उसकी बात सुनकर छतरीवाली औरत कुछ कसमसाई है। उसने उसे कनखियों से देखा, फिर पूरी तरह देखा, वह वही थी।

औरत ने भी उसे देखा। उसकी आँखों पर धूप का काला चश्मा चढ़ा हुआ था, फिर भी उसे लगा, जैसे औरत की आँखें एकाएक टिमटिमाने लगी हैं और चेहरे पर ऐसी लकीरें उभर आई हैं, जो एक साथ कुछ बोलना चाहती हैं और चुप भी रहना चाहती हैं, जो पहचानना भी चाहती हैं और अनपहचाना भी रहने देना चाहती हैं।

वह बोला, ''नीता, कैसी हो?''

''तुम...आप...।'' वह कुछ हकलाती सी बोली, ''यहाँ कहाँ...इस समय?''

''मैं अभी गाड़ी से उतरा हूँ, सोच रहा था, शायद अशोक विहार जानेवाली मिनी बस मिल जाए।'' वह बोला, ''पर...तुम...आप...इस समय...इस धूप में कहाँ से?''

''स्कूल से...।'' उसने काला चश्मा उतारकर साड़ी के पल्लू से अपना मुँह पोंछा, ''यह समय और यह धूप मेरे लिए नई नहीं है...इतना तो आपको याद ही होगा।''

''हाँ...हाँ...पर...।'' उसकी समझ में नहीं आ रहा था कि वह उसे 'तुम' कहे या 'आप' कहे, ''स्कूल इधर कहाँ...?''

वह मुसकराई—''डेढ़-दो साल से इधर ही हूँ। कोशिश कर रही हूँ कि कहीं उधर ही ट्रांसफर हो जाए।''

''काफी परेशानी होती होगी...।'' उसने ध्यान से औरत को देखा। धूप में गोरा रंग लाल-काला मिश्रित जैसा लग रहा था—बाँहें, ब्लाउज के ऊपर और नीचे से झाँकता हुआ शरीर, वह शरीर जिसकी हर नीली नस को वह अपनी हथेलियों पर आज भी महसूस कर सकता है।

''आप अशोक विहार किसके पास जाएँगे?'' उसने चश्मा लगा लिया और पल्लू माथे तक ले आई।

उसने सड़क की ओर देखा। जनकपुरी की बस जा चुकी थी। विनय नगर वाली बस में दस-बारह सवारियाँ आकर बैठ गई थीं। उसके पीछे पंजाबी बाग जानेवाली बस आ खड़ी हुई थी।

''सुदेश है वहाँ...तुम उसे जानती हो। वहाँ उसे फ्लैट मिल गया है। सोचा, आज रात उसके पास बिताऊँ...कल शाम की गाड़ी से वापस चला जाऊँगा।''

''सुदेश की शादी हो गई।''

''हुई थी...पर वह भी उसी हादसे का शिकार हुआ, जिसका कि मैं। आजकल

अकेला ही रहता है?'' वह बहुत फीके ढंग से मुसकराया।

''हादसा,'' वह बहुत मद्धिम स्वर में फुसफुसाई, ''क्या वह इस समय घर में होगा? वह तो किसी दफ्तर में काम करता है न?''

''हाँ···वहीं कहीं रेस्तराँ में बैठकर उसका इंतजार करूँगा।''

दोनों के चेहरों पर एक छाया उभर आई। कुछ क्षण के लिए एक सन्नाटा दोनों के मध्य व्याप गया।

''आप चाहें तो मेरे पास भी ठहर सकते हैं।'' नीता फुटपाथ से नीचे उतर आई।

''तुम्हारे साथ···मेरा मतलब आपके साथ?''

''हाँ···!'' वह बोली, ''हम पति-पत्नी नहीं हैं, पुराने रिश्ते टूट चुके हैं···पर हम एक-दूसरे के दुश्मन भी नहीं हैं···नहीं हैं न?''

''नहीं···नहीं।'' वह जल्दी-जल्दी बोला, ''दुश्मनी तो उस समय भी नहीं हुई, जब हम लोग टूट रहे थे। अजीत कैसा है?''

''अच्छा है।'' नीता बस की ओर बढ़ने लगी, फिर वहीं ठिठक गई। वह वहीं खड़ा था—अनिश्चय-ऊहापोह-अनिर्णय-असमंजस में घिरा सा।

''क्या सोच रहे हैं?'' वह बोली, ''कोई आपत्ति है? मैं पिछली कोई बात नहीं कुरेदूँगी।''

वह अटैची उठाकर उसके पीछे-पीछे बस में चढ़ गया। तीन व्यक्तियोंवाली सीट पर वे बैठ गए, खुले-खुले, फिर भी एक भूली-बिसरी, परंतु बहुत परिचित गंध दोनों के बीच तिर आई। उसने फिर अजीत की बात छेड़ी, ''अजीत तो मसूरी में ही होगा?''

''हाँ···इस बार उसने नौवीं की परीक्षा दी है। स्कूल बंद होते ही मैं भी मसूरी चली जाऊँगी?''

''वह छुट्टियों में यहाँ नहीं आता?''

''इतनी गरमी में उसे यहाँ बुलाकर क्या करूँ और फिर इस बहाने मैं भी वहाँ घूम आती हूँ···कभी हम शिमला चले जाते हैं···पिछले साल हम दोनों कश्मीर चले गए थे?''

दोनों को कुछ याद आया। पीछे छूटे हुए लंबे रेगिस्तान में कहीं कुछ चमचमाती सी चीज दिखाई दी—बिल्कुल दूधिया रोशनी की तरह कुछ चीज झिलमिला रही थी।

वह बोला, ''जब हम पहली बार कश्मीर गए थे, अजीत बस साल भर का था।

वह खिड़की से बाहर झाँकने लगी। गरमी से सड़क का तारकोल कहीं-कही पिघला दिखाई दे रहा था।

बस चल दी।

दोनों चुप थे। कभी बेमतलब खिड़की से बाहर देखने लगते या हर स्टॉप से

चढ़नेवाली सवारियों के चेहरे मापने लगते।

''संतोष कैसी हैं—तुम्हारी पत्नी?''

''अच्छी है।''

''दो बच्चे हैं न?''

''हाँ, दोनों लड़कियाँ हैं?''

नीता ने ऐसे सिर हिलाया जैसे वह सब कुछ जानती है।

''अजीत को देखे मुझे तीन-चार साल हो गए हैं।'' वह बोला।

''इसी तरह और भी कितने साल निकल जाएँगे।'' वह बहुत गुमसुम सी बोली। बस में सवारियाँ भरती चली जा रही थीं। उनके कंधे जुड़ से गए थे और बीच-बीच में दोनों की कोहनियाँ कमर पर चढ़ी हुई मांसलता का जायजा लेने लग जाती थीं। ऐसा लग रहा था, बहुत दूर, एकदम सुनसान में, बंद दरवाजों पर हल्की-हल्की दस्तक पड़ रही हो।

बस स्टॉप से उतरकर वे पैदल चल दिए।

''कितनी दूर है तुम्हारा फ्लैट?'' उसने पूछा।

''ज्यादा नहीं···बस पाँच-सात मिनट पैदल चलना पड़ता है।'' नीता का ध्यान उसकी अटैची की ओर गया—''अटैची भारी हो तो साइकिल रिक्शा कर लेते हैं।''

''नहीं···ऐसी भारी नहीं है।''

सामने बिल्डिंग नजर आने लगी। नीता ने अपनी छतरी बंद कर ली और बाईं ओर मुड़कर कुछ आगे जाकर दाईं ओर मुड़ी। वह उसके पीछे-पीछे चल रहा था। सामने ऊपर जाने की सीढ़ियाँ दिखाई देने लगीं।

''मेरा फ्लैट तीसरी मंजिल पर है।'' वह कुछ संकोच करती हुई बोली, ''आपको परेशानी तो होगी।''

उसने मुसकराने की भरपूर कोशिश की, परंतु उसे महसूस हुआ कि अंदर काफी टूट-फूट हो गई है, वह एकदम उखड़ गया है। उसके मन में आ रहा था, उसे नीता के साथ नहीं आना चाहिए था। सात-आठ वर्ष के टूटे संबंधों के बाद इस अचानक भेंट को सहेज पाना वैसे भी आसान नहीं था, परंतु वह तो उसका मेहमान बनकर उसके साथ आया है—यहाँ रात गुजारने—ऐसे फ्लैट में जहाँ नीता अकेली रहती है।

तीसरी मंजिल तक आते-आते वह सचमुच हाँफने लगा। नीता की साँस भी तेज हो गई थी।

आगे बढ़कर वह अपने फ्लैट का दरवाजा खोलने लगी। दरवाजे से बाहर कई गमले रखे हुए थे। सभी में अलग-अलग किस्म के खूबसूरत कैक्टस लगे थे। अंदर आते ही एक बड़े कमरे में दाईं ओर सोफासेट, टेलीविजन और किताबों की एक अलमारी रखी थी। बाईं ओर डाइनिंग टेबल रखा था।

''बैठिए, मैं कुछ ठंडा लाती हूँ।''

वह सोफे पर बैठ गया। नीता ने पंखा चला दिया। गरमी, उमस और तपिश में ठंडी हवा के झोंके आने लगे।

नीता शर्बत का जग और दो खाली गिलास लेकर आई तो उसने देखा, वह हाउस कोट पहने है। उसने अपने बाल खुले छोड़ दिए हैं, मुँह पर ताजे पानी की नमी फैली हुई है।

''पानी पी लो, फिर कुछ देर आराम कर लो…शाम को कहीं जाना तो नहीं?''

''सोचता हूँ, सुदेश से मिल लूँ।''

''ठीक है, पर धूप ढल जाने के बाद जाना।''

दोनों शर्बत पीने लगे।

वह उठी। एक सफेद चादर लाकर उसने दीवान पर बिछे मखमली कवर के ऊपर बिछा दी, सिरहाने एक तकिया रख दिया, जिस पर दूध की तरह लकलकाता लिहाफ चढ़ा था।

''लो, थोड़ी देर लेट जाओ।'' कहकर वह सेंटर टेबल पर रखा जग और गिलास उठाने लगी।

''बाथरूम किधर है?'' उसे लगा, वह एक निरीह व्यक्ति है। सामने खड़ी औरत बहुत बड़े व्यक्तित्व की स्वामिनी है—ऊँची, रोबदार, शक्तिसंपन्न।

''आओ… ।''

वह उसके पीछे-पीछे चल दिया। छोटे से गलियारे में दाईं ओर रसोईघर, बाईं ओर एक बेडरूम, दाईं ओर वाश बेसिन, बाईं ओर एक और बेडरूम और उसके सामने बाथरूम।

वह बाथरूम से निकलकर वाश बेसिन पर हाथ धोने लगा। फिर जब वह बड़े कमरे की ओर आ रहा था, उसने कनखियों से देखा, नीता पलंग पर लेटी कुछ पढ़ रही थी।

वह लेट गया। पता नहीं कितनी गड्डमड्ड स्मृतियाँ उसे मथ रही थीं। इस औरत के साथ उसने सात वर्ष से अधिक का समय पति के रूप में गुजारा था। शादी के पहले दिन से ही उसे लगा था, सब कुछ वैसा नहीं था जैसा उसने सोचा था। उसे लगा था, नीता में कुछ अजीब तरह का दर्प है। जब वह 'नहीं' कहती है तो उसका अर्थ 'नहीं' होता है। और वह 'नहीं' कभी नहीं कहती। उसका 'नहीं' न कहना ही 'हाँ' होता है। 'हाँ' के क्षणों में भी वह उन्मुक्त नहीं होती। पता नहीं, कौन सी छाया उसे घेरे रहती है, ढके रहती है, जिससे वह बाहर नहीं निकलती। उसे लगा था, नीता बहुत कम हँसती है। वह बस मुसकराती है। उसकी मुसकराहट में भी गर्व-गुमान सा झरता है।

उसके पुरुष को गहरी चोट लगी थी। वह अंदर-ही-अंदर चीख सा उठा था— इतना ही मिजाज है तो मुझसे शादी करने की क्या जरूरत थी? उसे लगा था, नीता ने उससे बड़ी अनिच्छा से शादी की है।

फिर यह कशमकश सात वर्ष तक लगातार चलती रही। वह कहता—तुमने किसी मजबूरी से, अपनी इच्छा के विरुद्ध, किसी दबाव में मुझसे शादी की है। नीता का एक ही उत्तर होता, 'मैंने किसी मजबूरी में तुमसे शादी नहीं की। मेरे और तुम्हारे माता-पिता में बातचीत हुई थी। उन्होंने मुझसे भी पूछा था। मुझे इनकार करना होता तो मैं इनकार कर देती। मुझ पर कोई दबाव नहीं था।'

'क्या तुमने अपनी इच्छा से मुझसे शादी की है?' वह पूछता था।

'इस शादी के लिए मैंने कभी अपनी अनिच्छा नहीं जताई।' वह कहती।

'अनिच्छा न जताना एक बात है और इच्छा से कोई काम एकदम करना दूसरी बात है।' वह बहुत जोर देकर कहता।

'देखो...शादी से पहले तो हम एक-दूसरे को जानते भी नहीं थे, इसलिए तुम्हारे साथ शादी करने की इच्छा मुझमें कहाँ से हो जाती?' वह कहती, 'उस हालत में अनिच्छा का न होना ही काफी था। किसी भी चीज में इच्छा उसे जानने, उसके संपर्क में आने के बाद पैदा होती है।'

'पर अब तो तुम मुझे जानती हो...मेरे संपर्क में हो। फिर भी मुझे नहीं लगता कि तुम कभी मेरी इच्छा करती हो?'

इस बात पर नीता चुप हो जाती। वह कुछ भी उत्तर नहीं देती। उठकर घर के कामकाज में लग जाती या नन्हे अजीत को खिलाने लगती।

उसे लगता, बड़ी दिमागदार औरत है। पता नहीं, अपने आपको क्या समझती है।

उन सात वर्षों के दौरान नीता पहले से ज्यादा अपने घेरों में घिरती चली गई और वह लगातार छोटा होता जा रहा है ऐसा महसूस करता रहा। अजीत के जन्म के बाद तो वह नीता के 'नहीं' न कहने के एक-एक दिन को तरसने लगा। घर के बाहर वह बेचैन सा रहता। घर आता तो उसकी नसें चटखने सी लगतीं। कभी उससे शीशे का गिलास टूट जाता, कभी चाय का प्याला हाथ से गिर जाता। पर नीता कुछ न कहती। वह चुपचाप टूटे हुए टुकड़े कूड़ेदान में डाल देती और पोचा उठाकर फर्श साफ कर देती।

फिर पता नहीं क्या हुआ, वह अजीत के प्रति हिंसक हो उठा। वह उसे बात-बात पर डाँटता या थप्पड़ जड़ देता। अजीत भी उससे सहमने लगा। जब कभी वह उसे प्यार से गोद में बैठाने की कोशिश करता तो वह छिटककर दूर निकल जाता।

उसे याद आया, एक दिन उसने अजीत को थप्पड़ मारा था। उसकी पाँचों उँगलियाँ अजीत के कोमल गाल पर पूरा नक्शा बना गई थीं। नीता ने दौड़कर उसे अपने वक्ष में सहेज

लिया था और बड़े गुस्से से उसकी ओर देखकर पूछा था, "किससे बदला ले रहे हो?"

वह भी गुमसुम सा हो गया था। फिर धीरे से बोला था, 'अपने आपसे।'

'उसका माध्यम इस मासूम को न बनाओ।'

वह उसे लेकर दूसरे कमरे में चली गई थी।

फिर सब कुछ बड़ी तेजी से टूटने लगा था। जब बिल्कुल टूटने की नौबत आई तो नीता ने इतना ही कहा था, 'कोर्ट-कचहरी के चक्कर काटने में मेरी रुचि नहीं है। मुझे तुमसे कुछ नहीं चाहिए। अपनी नौकरी में अपना और अजीत का गुजारा अच्छी तरह चला लूँगी, मेरी तरफ से तुम आजाद हो।'

उस समय वे रमेश नगर के डबल स्टोरी मकान में रहते थे। वह अपना थोड़ा सा सामान लेकर सुदेश के घर चला गया था।

सुदेश ने बिगड़ी बात बनाने की काफी कोशिश की। दोनों परिवारों के लोगों ने भी कुछ करने का यत्न किया था, परंतु बात नहीं बनी। नीता पहले से ज्यादा गंभीर हो गई थी। उसकी यह गंभीरता उसके पुरुष अहं को गहरी चोट पहुँचाती थी। वह तिलमिला उठता था।

उसका तबादला सहारनपुर के जोनल ऑफिस में हो गया और समय उमस भरी रातों की तरह सताता और गलाता हुआ गुजरने लगा। तीन साल बाद उसने संतोष से शादी कर ली। दफ्तर के बड़े बाबू की छह लड़कियों में से एक, एकदम सीधी-सादी मामूली लड़की, जो क्षण भर में हँस देती और दूसरे क्षण मुँह फुलाकर पलंग पर औंधी जा पड़ती।

एकाएक वह चौंककर उठ बैठा, "अरे, लगता है, मैं काफी देर तक सोता रहा।"

नीता उसके सामने सोफे पर बैठी करेले छील रही थी। वह मुसकराई, वही मुसकराहट, जिसमें सदा उसे उसका दर्प झरता हुआ दिखाई दिया था।

"आप सुबह बहुत जल्दी निकले होंगे।"

"हाँ···!" वह उठा और बाथरूम की ओर चला गया। लौटकर आया तो नीता चाय, पकौड़े और ब्रेड स्लाइस ले आई।

"आपको भूख लगी होगी।" वह बोली।

"नहीं, कुछ खास नहीं।" वह दो स्लाइसों के बीच पकौड़े दबाता हुआ बोला, "संतोष ने दोपहर के लिए पराँठे बना दिए थे।"

नीता ने भी एक पकौड़ा उठा लिया—"मुझे यह देखकर अच्छा लगा कि आपका स्वास्थ्य ठीक है। संतोष आपका काफी खयाल रखती है।"

उसने नीता के चेहरे को पढ़ना चाहा। वहाँ क्या था? व्यंग्य, उपहार, कटाक्ष या बस सामान्य कथन, उसी पुराने दर्प के धागे में पिरोया हुआ, जैसे कोई अफसर किसी

दूसरे दफ्तर में काम करनेवाले पुराने मातहत से कहे, शाबाश, मुझे पता लगा है कि तुम उस दफ्तर में अच्छी तरह से काम कर रहे हो।

वह संतोष के बारे में सोचने लगा—वह सचमुच बड़ा खयाल रखती है···पराँठे बनाती है···पूड़ियाँ बनाती है···कपड़े धोती है··· घर की सफाई करती है···उसके जूते भी पॉलिश कर देती है, लेकिन···! हाँ, यह लेकिन क्या है? क्या है यह लेकिन···? संतोष किसी बात के लिए 'न' नहीं करती। यह सब कुछ करने को तुरंत मान जाती है। यही नहीं पता लगता कि उसकी अपनी इच्छा कहीं है, अनिच्छा कहाँ है। जैसे वह बस रबड़ की एक लुगदी है—जब चाहो, जैसी चाहो, शक्ल दे लो।

एकाएक उसे महसूस हुआ, नीता इस फ्लैट में अकेली रहती है।

वह बोला, "सुदेश घर आ गया होगा। मैं अपनी अटैची भी ले जाता हूँ···रात वहीं गुजार लूँगा।"

"क्यों···?" उसने ऐसे पूछा जैसे वह कोई बड़ी अनहोनी बात कर रहा हो।

"मैं सोचता हूँ, तुम्हें असुविधा होगी?"

"आप सुदेश से मिलना चाहते हैं तो मिल आइए, मैं खाना बना रही हूँ। उससे मिलना जरूरी न हो तो मत जाइए। टी.वी. लगा देती हूँ, बैठकर देखिए।" कहकर वह वहाँ से उठ गई, जैसे और कुछ कहने-सुनने की जरूरत नहीं है।

वह वहीं बैठा कुछ सोचता रहा। फिर उसने फैसला किया, वह सुदेश के यहाँ नहीं जाएगा···यहीं बैठेगा···टी.वी. देखेगा।

उसने महसूस किया, कितने वर्षों बाद वह घर में किसी स्त्री का होना महसूस कर रहा है। जैसे सिर्फ एक नीता से ही यह सारा घर भरा हुआ है। घर के हर कोने में उसके होने का गहरा अहसास भरा हुआ है। एक ही समय उसे ड्राइंगरूम में, बेडरूम में, रसोईघर में अनुभव किया जा सकता है।

तब भी उसे ऐसा ही महसूस होता था। नीता उसे सारे घर में भरी हुई दिखाई देती थी, जैसे वह कोई पीपल का वृक्ष हो, जिसकी डालियाँ घर के हर कोने से झाँक रही हों, और वह मात्र एक पीला पत्ता हो, जो हवा के झोंके के साथ कभी यहाँ गिर पड़ता है कभी वहाँ।

उसने अटैची से कुरता-पाजामा निकाला और बदलने बाथरूम में चला गया। लौटकर आया तो दिन की पहनी पैंट-बुश्शर्ट तहाकर अटैची में रख दी। फिर उसने स्वयं ही टेलीविजन का बटन 'ऑन' कर दिया। बच्चों की कोई फिल्म दिखाई जा रही थी। उसने सामने के टेबल पर पैर फैला लिये, अपना सिर सोफे पर टिका लिया और देखने लगा।

सिर के ऊपर पंखा चल रहा था। रसोई से बरतनों की आवाज आ रही थी।

टेलीविजन से बच्चों का शोर उभर रहा था। उसने देखा, आसपास कोई नहीं है। इस घर में सिर्फ नीता है और वह है। फिर भी पता नहीं, कैसा शोर था, जो वह लगातार महसूस कर रहा था।

नीता ने उसके सामने चाय का गिलास रख दिया। तब भी वह टेलीविजन देखते समय चाय जरूर पीता था।

कुछ देर में नीता भी वहाँ आकर बैठ गई।

उसे लगा, शोर कुछ और बढ़ गया है।

दोनों टेलीविजन देखते रहे। कोई नाटक आ रहा था—महाभारत की पृष्ठभूमि पर धृतराष्ट्र और गांधारी की कहानी थी। वह गांधारी···जो अपने पति के अंधे होने के कारण अपनी आँखों पर पट्टी बाँध लेती है। बाहर का कुछ भी नहीं देखती और अंदर पूरा एक लहराता हुआ समुद्र समेट लेती है और फिर एक-दो नहीं, पूरे सौ बच्चों को जन्म देती है।

"खाना तो समाचारों के बाद खाओगे न?"

उसने नीता की ओर देखा। नीता को सब कुछ याद है। जैसे बीच के इतने बरस बिना किसी खरोंच के, बिना किसी दाग के सिर्फ हवा के एक गरम झोंके का स्पर्श देते हुए निकल गए हों।

खाना खाते समय उसे लगा, समय एकदम सिमट आया है। वही भरे हुए करेलों की सब्जी, कच्चे आम की खटाईवाली अरहर की दाल, खीरे वाला रायता, धनिये-पुदीने की चटनी और इन सबके अंदर एक अछूती गंध, एक बिल्कुल अलग ढंग का स्वाद।

नीता ने उसके विषय में कुछ ज्यादा न पूछा—बस यही कि लड़कियाँ कितनी बड़ी हो गई हैं, सहारनपुर में अच्छे स्कूलों का क्या हाल है, दफ्तर में उसकी अगली तरक्की कब होगी। जो कुछ उसने पूछा, उसका जवाब भी बहुत थोड़ा था—नीता को पी.जी.टी. ग्रेड मिल चुका है। तीन-चार साल तक प्रिंसिपल बन जाने की उम्मीद है, अजीत को वह आई.ए.एस. के कंपीटीशन में बैठाएगी।

"तुमने दूसरी शादी क्यों नहीं की?"

"बस ऐसे ही···।" वह बोली थी, "आपके लिए दूसरी शादी करना आसान था—आपको सिर्फ एक औरत चाहिए थी, परंतु मुझे सिर्फ एक मर्द नहीं चाहिए···और संसार में ज्यादातर पुरुष सिर्फ मर्द दिखाई देते हैं। फिर भी···कभी कुछ ठीक-ठाक लगा तो शायद शादी कर लूँ।"

ड्राइंगरूम के दीवान पर ही नीता ने उसका बिस्तर लगा दिया। बीच की मेज पर पानी का जग और गिलास रख दिया था। जब तक टेलीविजन चलता रहा, दोनों देखते रहे और बिना बोले बातचीत करते रहे। फिर टेलीविजन की उद्घोषिका ने कहा—हमें

कल शाम छह बजे तक के लिए इजाजत दीजिए।

''अच्छा, अब आप आराम कीजिए।'' कहकर नीता अपने कमरे की ओर जाते हुए बोली, ''मैं सुबह सात बजे निकल जाती हूँ। आप बाद में निकलना चाहें तो ताला बंद करके चाबी पड़ोस में दे दीजिएगा?''

''नहीं-नहीं...।'' वह बोला, ''मैं तुम्हारे साथ ही निकल चलूँगा। पहले सुदेश के पास जाऊँगा, फिर दफ्तर का काम निपटाकर सहारनपुर वापस चला जाऊँगा।''

सारे फ्लैट की बत्तियाँ बुझ गई थीं। वह सोने की कोशिश कर रहा था, परंतु नींद कहीं दूर-बहुत दूर वीरानों में भटक रही थी। उसे लगा, नीता भी अपने पलंग पर लेटी हुई जाग रही है, शायद वह भी किन्हीं वीरानों में भटक रही हो...पता नहीं, शायद सो गई हो। तब भी वह सो जाया करती थी और वह खंदकों-खाइयों में भटकता रहता था।

सुबह उसकी नींद खुली तो फ्लैट की खिड़की से सूरज की किरणें झाँकने लगी थीं।

नीता उसके सामने चाय का गिलास रखते हुए बोली, ''यदि साथ ही निकलना है तो जल्दी नहा-धो लीजिए।''

उसने सब कुछ ऐसे किया, जैसे पहले किया करता था या जैसे आजकल किया करता है—चाय का प्याला, टॉयलेट, शेव, बाथरूम थोड़ा-सा टेल्कम पाउडर, बालों में कंघी, कपड़े और फिर नाश्ता।

दोनों बस स्टॉप पर आ गए तो नीता बोली, ''मेरी बस आती होगी, लेकिन आपको रिंग रोड से मिलेगी। थोड़ा सा पैदल चलना पड़ेगा।''

''अच्छा!'' वह चलने के लिए हुआ तो ठिठक गया। नीता ने आँखों पर चश्मा चढ़ा लिया था। उसने 'धन्यवाद' कहना चाहा, परंतु उसे यह पता नहीं लग पा रहा था कि नीता की आँखों का रंग कैसा है। उसे सिर्फ उसके होंठ दिखाई दे रहे थे, जो जुड़े हुए थे, जिनमें कोई हरकत नहीं थी, जिनसे कुछ भी फूटता नहीं दिखाई दे रहा था।

□

दिल्ली कहाँ है

लाहौर की सड़कों पर घूमना भी एक अजीब अनुभव है। व्यक्ति अकेला हो तो यह अनुभव और भी मजेदार हो जाता है। अपने होटल से निकलकर मैं माल रोड के फुटपाथ पर पैदल ही चल पड़ा था। दिल्ली वापस आने की फ्लाइट शाम को पाँच बजे की थी। बीच में तीन-चार घंटे का समय गुजारना था। पीछे से आवाज आई, ''सरदारजी, सस्त्रीकाल!''

मैंने देखा, दो साइकिलों पर चार लड़के मेरे पास से गुजर रहे थे और हाथ मिलाते हुए बड़े खुश दिखाई दे रहे थे। मैंने मुसकराकर जवाब में अपना हाथ हिलाया। उन्होंने साइकिलों की गति धीमी कर दी। उनमें से एक बोला, ''पाकिस्तान केहो जेहा लग्गा?'' (पाकिस्तान कैसा लगा।)

मैंने कहा, ''बड़ा चंगा, बड़ा सोहणा ते निग्घा।'' (बहुत अच्छा, बहुत सुंदर और बहुत स्नेहपूर्ण!)

मेरी बात सुनकर उनके चेहरे खिल गए। यह पाकिस्तान की वह पीढ़ी थी, जिसने भारत के नाम पर जंग, नफरत और खिंचाव ही सुना था, जिसने हिंदी फिल्मों और उनमें काम करने वाले कलाकारों के नाम सुने थे।

मैं चलते-चलते असेंबली के भवन तक पहुँच गया। इस बीच रास्ते में मुझे बहुत लोग मिल चुके थे। प्रौढ़ आयु के मरदों ने मुझे बहुत संकोच से देखा था। औरतों ने अपने दुपट्टों की कनखियों से झाँका था, मुसकराई थीं और फिर आपस में बातें करने लगी थीं। किशोर-जवान लड़कों ने मुझे घेर लिया था और बारी-बारी से मुझसे हाथ मिलाया था। पाकिस्तान की अपनी यात्रा में मुझे लगा था, वहाँ का हर नौजवान लड़के और लड़की के दिल में दिल्ली और बंबई देखने की बड़ी लालसा है, वैसे ही जैसे हमारे नौजवानों में लंदन, पेरिस या न्यूयॉर्क देखने की है। कल जब मैं अनारकली से अपने होटल वापस आया था तो स्कूटरवाला मुझसे भाड़ा नहीं ले रहा था और मैं भाड़ा

देने की लगातार जिद कर रहा था।

वह बोला, "देखिए साहब, मैं आपसे पैसे तो नहीं लूँगा, पर इसके बदले में आप मेरा एक काम कर दीजिए।"

मैंने कहा, "बोलिए, मैं आपका क्या काम कर सकता हूँ?"

उसकी आँखों में बेहिसाब अनुनय भर आया था, "देखिए साहब, आपके घर में किसी बच्चे की शादी हो तो दावतनामे का एक कार्ड मुझे भी भेज दीजिएगा।"

मैं उसका मनोरथ नहीं समझ सका था।

वह बोला, "हुजूर, मैं जबरदस्ती आपका मेहमान नहीं बनूँगा। मैं आपके दावतनामे की बिना पर इंडियन हाई कमीशन से वीजा ले लूँगा। दिल्ली, बंबई देखने की मेरी बड़ी तमन्ना है। यकीन कीजिए, मैं आपको किसी तरह की तकलीफ नहीं दूँगा।"

मैंने उसका हाथ दबाया था। अपना पता उसे दिया था और उसका पता ले लिया था। उसे यह भरोसा भी दिलाया था कि मेरे घर में जब भी कोई शादी होगी, मैं उसे जरूर दावतनामा भेजूँगा।

असेंबली भवन के पास पहुँचकर मैंने सोचा, अब क्या करूँ? दोपहर का एक बजा था। होटल मुझे चार बजे तक लौटना था। मैं दुकानों में घुसकर चीजें देखने लगा। खरीदारी मुझे करनी नहीं थी, क्योंकि पिछली रात अनारकली बाजार से मैं बहुत कुछ खरीद चुका था। दुकानदार बड़ी रुचि से मुझे चीजें दिखा रहे थे, पर अनारकली से यहाँ का बाजार काफी महँगा दिख रहा था, वैसे ही जैसे दिल्ली में करोल बाग और कनाट प्लेस के भावों में अंतर साफ दिखाई देता है।

फुटपाथ पर ही 'कोल्ड ड्रिंक' बेचनेवालों की अनेक रेहड़ियाँ लगी हुई थीं। उनके पास से निकला तो लगभग सभी ने आवाज दी, "भ्राजी आओ, कुछ ठंडा-शंडा पी लवो।"

जब से लाहौर आया था, मैं लगातार पेप्सी कोला पी रहा था।

मैं सोच रहा था कि उनका शुक्रिया अदा करते हुए उनके पास से निकल जाऊँगा। तभी एक अधेड़ से व्यक्ति ने मेरा रास्ता रोक लिया, "भ्राजी, हमारे पास से कुछ पी लो और हमारा दिल ठंडा कर दो।"

उसने अपने दोनों हाथों से मेरा दाहिना हाथ थाम लिया। उसके हाथों में कुछ ऐसी जकड़ थी कि मुझे लगा कि मुझ पर वशीकरण हो गया है। मुझे लगा कि जैसे गहरे पानी के बीच उसने मुझे अपने बलिष्ठ हाथों में उठा लिया है। मैं अपना सारा भार खो बैठा हूँ।

उसने कोला की दो बोतलें खोलकर एक जग में उड़ेल दीं। फिर उसने सोडे की दो बोतलें खोलकर उसमें डाल दीं। फिर उसने एक बड़ा सा नीबू काटकर उसमें

निचोड़ा और नमक मिलाया। मैंने कहा, ''इतना कौन पिएगा?''

उसने मुझे इस तरह देखा, जैसे सारे आकाश को उसने अपनी आँखों में समेट लिया हो, ''मैं भी तो पिऊँगा, बिछुड़े हुए भाई के साथ दो घूँट ठंडा पानी पीने का सुख अल्लाह पता नहीं फिर कब देगा!''

कितने ही लोग हमारे आसपास जमा हो गए थे। बड़े गिलासों में हम दो लोग ठंडा पी रहे थे और बाकी लोग हमें देख रहे थे।

दो बजने वाले थे। मैंने सबका शुक्रिया अदा किया और वापस मुड़ गया। सबकुछ बहुत अजीब सा लग रहा था। एक ओर खून में डूबी हुई जंग और नफरत से सराबोर कुछ वर्ष पहले की यादें, दूसरी ओर कोला, सोडा और नीबू के ठंडे पेय में तैरता हुआ वर्तमान। दोनों सच्चाइयों को अपने कंधों पर लादे हुए लोग कैसी अजीब लड़खड़ाती चाल चलते जा रहे हैं।

चौराहा पार करने के लिए मैं हरी बत्ती की राह देख रहा था। एक व्यक्ति मेरे पास से निकला और ठिठककर खड़ा हो गया। लाहौर में ऐसे बहुत से लोगों से मिलने और उनकी जिज्ञासाओं को शांत करने का मुझे पिछले तीन-चार दिनों में खासा अनुभव हो चुका था, इसलिए मैंने उसकी तरफ विशेष ध्यान नहीं दिया, पर वह एकदम मेरे सामने आ गया, ''मैं आपके दो-चार मिनट ले सकता हूँ?''

मैंने कहा, ''बड़ी खुशी से।''

''आप हिंदुस्तान में कहाँ रहते हैं?''

''दिल्ली में।'' मैं बोला, पर उसी के साथ मैंने महसूस किया, उसकी आँखें एकदम तरल हो आई हैं।

''करोल बाग में।'' मैं बोला।

''मैं फैज रोड पर रहता था।''

''आप यहाँ कब आए?'' मैंने पूछा।

''मुल्क के बँटवारे के वक्त। बँटवारा क्या हुआ, हमारा तो खानदान ही बँट गया। आधे रिश्तेदार यहाँ, आधे वहाँ। हम एक-दूसरे के लिए परदेसी बन गए हैं।''

उसका गला काफी भर्राया हुआ था।

''आपके पास थोड़ा वक्त हो तो आप दिल्ली के बारे में मुझे कुछ बताइए।''

मैंने उसकी आँखों में झाँका, ''क्या आप उसके बाद एक बार भी दिल्ली नहीं गए?''

उसने अपनी गरदन हिला दी।

''लेकिन इतने साल बाद भी दिल्ली मेरे दिल में धड़कती है।'' उसने मेरा हाथ उठाकर अपनी छाती पर रख दिया, ''आप मेरे दिल की धड़कन महसूस कर रहे हैं?''

कौन किसके दिल की धड़कनों को महसूस करे? कौन किसकी आँखों का रंग देखे? दिल्ली में मैंने कितने ही लोगों को लाहौर के लिए मरते देखा है। लाहौर का नाम सुनते ही कितनों की बाँछें खिलती हैं और आँखों का रंग एकदम लाल हो जाता है। कल ही मुझे मेरे लाहौरी दोस्त मुहम्मद शाहीन ने पाकिस्तान के मशहूर पंजाबी कवि उस्ताद दामन की एक कविता की दो पंक्तियाँ सुनाई थीं—

''लाली अँखिया दी पई दसदी ए,
रोए तुसीं वी हो रोए असीं वी हाँ।''

(आँखों की लाली बता रही है कि तुम भी रोए हो, हम भी रोए हैं।)

मैंने कहा, ''पिछले साठ सालों में दिल्ली बहुत बदल गई है; बहुत दूर-दूर तक फैल गई है।''

''अच्छा, जामा मसजिद ठीक है न? हम उसकी सीढ़ियों पर बैठकर कबाब खाते थे।'' उसने बड़ी उत्सुकता से पूछा।

मैंने कहा, ''जामा मसजिद अब पहले से ज्यादा खूबसूरत लगती है। उसके चारों ओर का बाजार—ढाबे, कबाब की दुकानें—सब वहाँ से हटा दिए गए हैं। वहाँ बहुत खूबसूरत बगीचे लगा दिए गए हैं।''

''अच्छा!'' उसकी आवाज कुछ मद्धिम सी पड़ गई। ''फूलवालों की सैर का मेला तो अब नहीं लगता होगा?''

मैंने कहा, ''नहीं, फूलवालों की सैर को अब भी धूमधाम से मनाया जाता है। अब महरौली जाने के लिए वीराने से होकर नहीं गुजरना पड़ता। अब तो वहाँ तक शहर आबाद हो गया है—खूबसूरत कॉलोनियाँ, सड़कें, मकान, और बड़े-बड़े बाजार।''

वह बड़े उत्साह से बोला, ''छुटपन में हम लोग रामलीला देखने जाया करते थे। रामलीला की सवारी निकलती थी तो हम उसके साथ-साथ चलते थे। बड़ा मजा आता था। एक बार की बात बताऊँ—मुझे अच्छी तरह याद है, जैसे बस कल की बात हो।'' प्रौढ़ चेहरे की कितनी ही लकीरें एक जगह सिमट आईं। ''मेरा एक दोस्त था परसू, वैसे उसका नाम परसराम था, पर सब लोग उसे परसू कहते थे। राम और सीता की सवारी निकल रही थी—परसू उनकी बगल में नकली मूँछें लगाए हाथ में एक जड़ाऊ डंडा लिये खड़ा था। मैंने उसे पहचान लिया और सड़क से चीखा—'परसू, ओए परसू!' परसू ने कनखियों से इधर-उधर देखा। भीड़ में वह मुझे नहीं देख पाया। मैंने फिर बुलाया, 'अबे परसू, साले इतनी बड़ी मूँछें कहाँ से लाया?' अब उसकी नजर मुझ पर पड़ गई। मैंने नीचे से ही हाथ हिलाया। उसने वहाँ से हाथ हिला दिया। इतने में पीछे से किसी ने उसे एक घूँसा मारा और परसू की मूँछें नीचे गिर गईं। हम लोग हँसते-हँसते सड़क पर ही लोटपोट हो गए।''

वह जोर-जोर से हँसने लगा। आसपास आते-जाते लोग हमारे पास ठिठक गए।

"सुना है, दिल्ली की आबादी बहुत बढ़ गई है?" उसने पूछा।

"हाँ!" मैं बोला, "आबादी बढ़ती जा रही है और शहर भी बढ़ता चला जा रहा है।"

"अब अगर मैं दिल्ली आऊँ तो उसे पहचान भी नहीं सकूँगा, लेकिन मरने से पहले मैं एक बार दिल्ली जरूर देखना चाहता हूँ। पता नहीं, अल्लाह मेरी यह तमन्ना पूरी करेगा भी या नहीं?" उसकी आवाज एकदम उदास हो गई थी।

मैंने कहा, "आपकी मुराद जरूर पूरी होगी। जब भी दिल्ली आने का प्रोग्राम बन जाए, मुझे जरूर खबर कीजिएगा।" मैंने जेब से अपना कार्ड निकाला और घड़ी देखी। कार्ड उसके हाथ में थमाकर मैं चलने को हुआ तो उसने मुझे फिर रोक लिया, "आपका बेशकीमती वक्त ले रहा हूँ," कहते-कहते उसकी आँखें डबडबा गईं, "क्या करूँ, उस हरामजादी धरती की याद नहीं भूलती, जहाँ मैंने जन्म लिया था, जहाँ मेरा बचपन गुजरा था, जहाँ मेरी जवानी परवान चढ़ी थी।"

उसने दोनों हाथों से मेरा हाथ पूरी ताकत से दबाया, फिर एकदम झटके के साथ छोड़कर आगे बढ़ गया।

मैं एकटक उसे जाता देखता रहा।

मैं सड़क पार करके होटल की ओर चल दिया। एकाएक मुझे अपने चाचा नारायण दास की याद आ गई। उन्नीस सौ इकहत्तर की भारत-पाकिस्तान लड़ाई में ढाका में हजारों पाकिस्तानी सिपाहियों ने आत्मसमर्पण कर दिया था। ये पाकिस्तानी सिपाही भारत के किसी रेडियो स्टेशन से सुबह-शाम बोलकर पाकिस्तान में अपने परिवारवालों को अपना संदेश भेजते थे—"मेरा नाम—मैं पाकिस्तान के जिला-तहसील-गाँव का रहने वाला हूँ—मेरे वालिद का नाम—है, अगर कोई पाकिस्तानी भाई मेरी बात सुन रहा हो तो उनसे गुजारिश है कि मेरी खैर-खैरियत की खबर मेरे घरवालों को पहुँचा दे।"

चाचा नारायणदास को पता नहीं क्या खब्त थी कि सुबह-शाम यह प्रोग्राम जरूर सुनते थे। एक दिन कोई गुलाम रसूल बोल रहा था—"मैं सूबेदार गुलाम रसूल वल्द अल्लारक्खा, गाँव कुंजाह, तहसील फालिया, जिला गुजरात का रहने वाला हूँ, मैं खैर-खैरियत से हूँ, अगर कोई पाकिस्तानी भाई मेरी आवाज सुन रहा हो तो मेरे वाल्दैन को इसकी इत्तला दे दे।"

यह नाम सुनते ही चाचा नारायणदास एकदम चीख उठे थे। मेरे पिताजी को आवाज देते हुए बोले थे, "सुना तुमने, कुंजाह के अल्लारक्खा का पुत्तर गुलाम रसूल बोल रहा था, वह भी पाकिस्तानी फौज का कैदी है।"

मेरे पिताजी के मुँह से तुरंत कुछ निकला नहीं था, पर चाचा नारायणदास की उत्तेजना सभी हदें तोड़ रही थीं—"अपने गाँव कुंजाह का लड़का गुलाम रसूल। मेरे यार अल्लारक्खा का लड़का है—सूबेदार रसूल!"

घर में हम सब लोगों को लग रहा था कि कुंजाह की रट लगाए बूढ़े चाचा नारायणदास सचमुच पागल हो गए हैं।

□

शोक

टेलीफोन के सामने बैठकर सागरजी कुछ देर सोचते रहे। फिर टेलीफोन की डायरी उठाकर उसके पन्ने पलटने लगे। उनके मन में बार-बार उठने लगा—कहाँ से शुरू करूँ। तभी उनके मन में आया कि इधर-उधर से शुरू करने से हो सकता है, कुछ लोग रह जाएँ, इसलिए एल्फाबेटिकली शुरू करना ही अच्छा रहेगा। उन्होंने डायरी का एकदम शुरू का पन्ना निकाला। 'ए' में पहला नाम अमरनाथजी का था। उन्हें लगा—यह महत्त्वपूर्ण नाम है। चाहे यह नाम राजनीति का नहीं है, फिर भी इस व्यक्ति की अपने समाज में बड़ी इज्जत है। पैसेवाला होने के कारण कितने स्कूलों, सभा-सोसाइटियों के साथ जुड़ा हुआ है।

सागरजी ने अमरनाथ का नंबर मिलाया, "अमरनाथजी...?"

उधर से आवाज आई, "जी बोल रहा हूँ।"

"मैं सागर बोल रहा हूँ...जी सुबह-सुबह आपको परेशान कर रहा हूँ...मेरे पिताजी गुजर गए...बस कुछ घंटे पहले...उन्हें दिल का दौरा पड़ा...नहीं पहले तो ऐसी कोई शिकायत नहीं थी...उमर...? बस यही बहत्तर-तिहत्तर थी, लेकिन उनकी सेहत बहुत अच्छी थी...रोज सुबह चार बजे सैर करने निकल जाते थे, आज सैर करके आए तो कुछ घबराहट महसूस हुई...मैं तो अपने कमरे में सो रहा था...रात को ऑल पार्टी मीटिंग बड़ी देर तक चलती रही...होम मिनिस्टर ने बुलाई थी...देश की जैसी हालत है, सो तो आप जानते ही हैं...माँ ने मुझे जगाया...इससे पहले कि मैं डॉक्टर बुला सकूँ... उनके प्राण-पखेरू उड़ गए...(गला भर्रा जाता है), उनका मुझे बड़ा सहारा था...मेरे सार्वजनिक जीवन की जो भी उपलब्धियाँ हैं, सब उन्हीं की बख्शिश से थी...मैं तो एकदम बेसहारा महसूस कर रहा हूँ...जी निगम बोध घाट पर...दोपहर बाद पाँच बजे तक वहाँ पहुँच जाएँगे...बड़ी कृपा होगी...मुझे हमेशा ही आपसे बल मिलता रहा है...जी...जी..." सागरजी ने घड़ी देखी। एक व्यक्ति को इस बात की खबर देने में ही

पाँच-सात मिनट लग गए थे। कुछ इधर-उधर की बातें भी तो करनी ही पड़ती हैं। उन्होंने झटपट दूसरा नाम देखा—अमरजीत सिंह। इसे भी खबर करनी चाहिए। इतना बड़ा ट्रांसपोर्टर है।

चुनाव के मौके पर बड़े काम का आदमी है। उन्होंने नंबर मिलाया। संयोग से अमरजीत सिंह भी फोन पर मिल गए। उनसे भी लगभग उसी तरह की बात हुई। हाँ, एक खास बात यह हुई कि अमरजीत सिंह ने गहरी हमदर्दी दिखाते हुए अपनी ओर से एक पेशकश की—"सागरजी, निगम बोध घाट तक अरथी ले जाने का क्या इंतजाम है?"

"एक बड़ी वैन का प्रबंध मैंने कर लिया है!"

"परिवार के लोग श्मशान घाट तक कैसे पहुँचेंगे?" अमरजीत सिंह ने बड़ा सरोकार दिखाते हुए पूछा।

"दो-तीन गाड़ियों की व्यवस्था तो है, लेकिन...?"

"आप चिंता न कीजिए। मैं एक मिनी बस भेज देता हूँ। पच्चीस-तीस लोग उसमें आसानी से बैठ जाएँगे।"

सागरजी एकदम प्रफुल्ल हो उठे, "यह तो बड़ी अच्छी बात है, अमरजीत सिंह जी...मैं सोच रहा था कि इतने लोगों को इस गरमी में श्मशान तक कैसे ले जाऊँ? घर मेहमानों से भरा पड़ा है...शवयात्रा तक और लोग भी पहुँच जाएँगे। आप मिनी बस भेज देंगे तो बड़ी सुविधा हो जाएगी...बहुत-बहुत धन्यवाद।"

फोन रखकर सागरजी सोचने लगे—'अमरजीत सिंह मौके पर काम आनेवाला आदमी है। लेकिन मैंने भी तो उसके कितने काम किए हैं।' उन्हें याद आने लगा—अमरजीत सिंह की टूरिस्ट बसों को ऑल इंडिया परमिट दिलवाने में कितनी भाग-दौड़ करनी पड़ी थी, ट्रांसपोर्ट मिनिस्टर तक गोट न बैठाई गई होती तो काम नहीं बन सकता था। तभी उनका ध्यान अगले नाम पर गया। अनीस अहमद, अनिल अरोड़ा, अनूपसिंह...फिर उन्हें खयाल आया कि इस तरह चलने से तो बहुत देर हो जाएगी, बहुत से महत्त्वपूर्ण लोग, जिनका नाम म, र, स, व आदि में आता है, वे अपने-अपने घरों से चले जाएँगे...तब उन्हें ढूँढ़ना बहुत मुश्किल होगा। इसलिए बेहतर यही होगा कि पहले महत्त्वपूर्ण लोगों...विशिष्ट लोगों को फोन कर लिये जाएँ...राह-संस्कार के समय कुछ जानी-मानी हस्तियाँ निगम-बोध घाट पर दिखाई नहीं दीं तो लोग क्या सोचेंगे।

सागरजी को विशिष्ट लोगों के नाम याद करते हुए डायरी के पन्ने पलटने पड़े। सबसे पहले उन्हें परिवहन मंत्री का ही नाम याद आया। उन्होंने उनका नंबर घुमाया तो बड़ी अपरिचित सी आवाज सुनाई दी—"जी...ई...ई...ई।"

"आप परिवहन मंत्रीजी के यहाँ से बोल रहे हैं?"

फिर वही, "जी···ई···ई···ई···"

"मैं एस.पी. सागर बोल रहा हूँ···आप कौन बोल रहे हैं?"

"मैं मंत्रीजी का पी.ए. बोल रहा हूँ···शर्मा।"

सागरजी ने आवाज में एकदम मिठास भर ली, "शर्माजी, शायद आपने मुझे पहचाना नहीं···मैं एस.पी. सागर हूँ···मंत्रीजी के साथ आपने मुझे अकसर देखा होगा···मैं अपनी पार्टी के उद्यमी और व्यवसायी सेल का संयोजक हूँ···आपको याद होगा···पिछले ही महीने अमरजीत सिंह ऐंड कंपनी के नए शोरूम का उद्‌घाटन हुआ था···मंत्रीजी उसमें आए थे···शायद आप भी उनके साथ थे···अच्छा, उनके साथ नहीं थे? उस दिन कोई और पी.ए. उनके साथ था? खैर, लेकिन आपने मुझे मंत्रीजी के साथ देखा कई बार होगा···जरा उनसे मेरी बात करा दीजिए···कुछ बड़ी जरूरी बात करनी है।"

चोंगा हाथ में थामे हुए सागरजी प्रतीक्षा करने लगे। दूसरी ओर से कोई आवाज नहीं आ रही है, यह सोच-सोचकर उनके मन में खीझ पैदा होने लगी। वे सोचने लगे, दो-चार मंत्रियों का दाह-संस्कार के समय निगम बोध घाट पर होना बड़ा जरूरी है···नहीं तो बड़ी भद हो जाएगी। तभी अपने घोर प्रतिद्वंद्वी सरूपचंद का चेहरा उनके सामने घूम गया। कुछ महीने पहले ही उसकी माँ की मृत्यु हुई थी। तब निगम बोध घाट पर कितनी भीड़ थी। अपनी पार्टी के कितने ही बड़े नेता वहाँ उपस्थित थे। यहाँ तक कि विपक्षी दलों के कितने जाने-माने चेहरे वहाँ दिखाई दे रहे थे। लेखकों-पत्रकारों का भी वहाँ पर अच्छा-खासा जमावड़ा था···और सबसे बड़ी बात···उस समय सरूपचंद के चेहरे पर कैसा गर्व झलक आया था, जब सफेद ऐंबेसडर कार अंदर तक चली आई थी और उसमें से दो लोग फूलों का कितना बड़ा चक्कर लेकर उतरे थे। लोगों की आँखों में उस समय कैसा भाव झलक आया था, जब उन्हें यह पता लगा था कि प्रधानमंत्री ने सरूपचंद की माँ के लिए ये श्रद्धा-सुमन भेजे हैं।

तभी सागरजी एकाएक चौंक उठे। टेलीफोन पर दूसरी तरफ मंत्रीजी बोल रहे थे, उनकी तो जैसे घिग्घी बँध गई, "जी, मंत्रीजी अच्छा···? आप नाश्ता कर रहे थे···आय एम सो सॉरी···इस वक्त आपको तकलीफ दी···।" फिर उनका गला भर्रा आया। उन्होंने बड़ी करुणा भरी आवाज में पिता की मृत्यु के कारण उन पर हुए वज्रपात की बात मंत्रीजी को सुनाई। उनके चेहरे से लग रहा था कि मंत्रीजी को इस दुःखद समाचार से बहुत कष्ट पहुँचा है और वे सागरजी गहरी संवेदना व्यक्त कर रहे हैं।

सागरजी की आँखें सचमुच भर आई थीं। एक हाथ से चोंगा पकड़े हुए, उन्होंने दूसरे हाथ से कुरते की जेब से रूमाल निकाल लिया था। वे मंत्रीजी से बातें भी कर रहे थे और अपनी आँखें भी पोंछते जा रहे थे, "आप यदि दो मिनट के लिए वहीं दर्शन देंगे तो मुझे बड़ा ढाढ़स मिलेगा···बहुत बल मिलेगा···आपकी सदा ही मुझ पर बड़ी कृपा

रही है···यह दृष्टि हमेशा बनाए रखिएगा।"

चोंगा रखकर उन्होंने ठंडी साँस ली, "लो, एक मंत्री का आना तो पक्का हुआ।"

फिर टेलीफोन डायरी के पन्ने पलटने और डायल पर उँगलियाँ घुमाने की गति एकाएक तेज हो गई। उनकी नजर बार-बार दीवार पर लगी घड़ी की ओर उठती थी और बार-बार उन्हें अपने अंदर एक बड़ी हड़बड़ी अनुभव होती थी।

"अब बंद भी करिए ये टेलीफोन करना।" सागरजी की पत्नी झुँझलाई हुई उनके पास खड़ी थीं, "पिताजी के अंतिम संस्कार के लिए कितने सारे इंतजाम करने हैं···आप हैं कि सुबह से टेलीफोन लिये बैठे हैं?"

सागरजी ने बहुत घूरकर पत्नी की ओर देखा। उनके मन में उभरा—यह तो बिल्कुल मूर्ख है···इसे पता नहीं···मैं कितना जरूरी काम कर रहा हूँ। यही तो दो-चार मौके होते हैं, जब आपका जन-संपर्क बनता है और दिखता है। उन्होंने उसका एक हाथ पकड़कर अपने दोनों हाथों से दबाया। उन्हें लगा, घर में पत्नी के साथ साधा गया संपर्क बड़े-बड़े नेताओं या हजारों लोगों से किए गए जनसंपर्क से कुछ कम मुश्किल काम नहीं है।

"शीलजी!" अपनी आवाज में बिल्कुल आजमाई मिठास भरकर बोले, "आप चिंता न कीजिए···सारा प्रबंध हो जाएगा, जो काम मैं कर रहा हूँ, वह बड़ा जरूरी है। आप सरूपचंद की माँ के दाह-संस्कार में गई थीं न? कितने लोग···कितने स्टेट्सवाले···श्मशान भूमि में आए थे···हमें भी तो समाज में अपनी इज्जत देखनी है कि नहीं?"

"यह सब तो ठीक है।" शीलजी पूरी तरह द्रवित हो गई थीं, "लेकिन अगर दोपहर से पहले अरथी को घर से बाहर निकालना है तो सारा इंतजाम तुरंत करना पड़ेगा···समय ही कहाँ है?"

"देखो···।" सागरजी ने सोचते हुए कहा, "अरथी तो दोपहर बाद ही यहाँ से निकलेगी। इससे पहले तो लोगों को खबर ही नहीं मिल पाएगी। अगर पिताजी की मृत्यु शाम को हुई तो मैं अखबारों में दे देता, जो दूसरे दिन सभी जगह छप जाती। उसी के साथ दाह-संस्कार का कार्यक्रम भी छप जाता। लेकिन···पिताजी तो सुबह-सुबह ही गुजर गए···शाम के अखबारों में तो मैंने खबर भिजवा दी है···पर जो बात सुबह के अखबारों से बनती है, वह भला शाम के अखबारों से कैसे बन सकती है। मुश्किल यह है कि शाम के अखबारों को लोग सीरियसली लेते ही नहीं।"

अरथी के लिए आवश्यक सामग्री का प्रबंध सागरजी के साले साहब कर रहे थे। तीनों बच्चे अभी बहुत छोटे हैं। सबसे बड़ा लड़का कँवल अभी दस साल का भी पूरा नहीं हुआ। तीनों बच्चे अपने मामा से इतना हिले हुए हैं कि हमेशा मामा-मामा कहते

हुए उसके पीछे लगे रहते हैं।

"किरपाल…!" सागरजी ने उसे पास से गुजरते हुए देखा तो आवाज दे दी।

"जी…जीजाजी।" उसकी आवाज में बेहिसाब हड़बड़ाहट थी।

"देखो भाई, यह सारा इंतजाम तुम्हारे कंधों पर है। मुझे तो यह भी पता नहीं कि ऐसे मौकों पर किन-किन चीजों की जरूरत पड़ती है…देखना किसी बात की कमी न रह जाए, नहीं तो ऐन मौके पर खिल्ली उड़ जाएगी।"

"आप बिल्कुल फिकर न करिए, जीजाजी, कोई कमी नहीं रहने पाएगी।" कहकर उसने शील की तरफ देखा, "दीदी, जरा एक बात सुनना।"

डायल घुमाते-घुमाते सागरजी ने देखा, किरपाल और शील एक कोने में कुछ गुपचुप बात कर रहे हैं और शील अपने ब्लाउज में से पर्स निकाल रही है।

सागरजी ने जो नंबर मिलाया था, वह बार-बार ऐंगेज आ रहा था। वे दूसरा नंबर मिलाने लगे। उन्होंने देखा, शील पर्स में से सौ-सौ के कुछ नोट निकालकर किरपाल को दे रही हैं।

डायल घुमाते-घुमाते सागरजी को बड़ी उलझन होने लगी। उन्हें लगा इस सारे प्रबंध में किरपाल दो-चार सौ रुपए जरूर मार लेगा।

दो-चार लोगों को और फोन करने के बाद सागरजी उठ खड़े हुए। कुछ सोचते हुए धीरे-धीरे वे अंदरवाले कमरे में गए। पिताजी की देह जमीन पर सफेद चादर से लिपटी हुई रखी थी। उनकी माँ और कुछ रिश्तेदार बड़े उदास भाव से बैठे हुए थे। मृत देह के सिरहाने एक पुजारी धीरे-धीरे किसी धर्मग्रंथ का पाठ कर रहा था।

सागरजी मृत देह के पैरों के पास बैठ गए। उन्होंने अपने दोनों हाथ पिता के पैरों पर रखे और सिर झुकाकर फफक-फफककर रोने लगे। आसपास बैठे कुछ लोग उनके पास खिसक आए। उन्हें अपने कंधों और पीठ पर अनेक स्त्री-पुरुष हाथों का स्पर्श अनुभव हुआ।

शाम को निगम बोध घाट पर काफी भीड़ थी। सागरजी अपनी सूजी हुई आँखों से सबके संवेदना भरे स्वर सुन रहे थे और हाथ जोड़कर सबके सामने सिर झुका रहे थे। उनकी नजरें बार-बार सामने से आनेवाले लोगों की तरफ उठ जाती थीं।

सागरजी ने मन-ही-मन में पूरा हिसाब लगा लिया था। पार्टी के स्थानीय नेताओं में से कुछ लोग आ गए थे, किंतु प्रदेश के अध्यक्ष, उपाध्यक्ष या महासचिव के चेहरे अभी तक नहीं दिखे थे। नगर निगम के दो-तीन भूतपूर्व सदस्य तो आ गए थे, लेकिन केंद्रीय नेतृत्व में से किसी के दर्शन नहीं हुए थे…न पार्टी में से, न सरकार में से।

लोग सागरजी के पास आकर अपनी संवेदना व्यक्त कर रहे थे। वे उन्हें बड़े विनम्र भाव से अपना धन्यवाद भी दे रहे थे, पर उनका मन बहुत उदास हो गया था।

नजदीकी रिश्तेदार चिता के लिए लकड़ियाँ उठा-उठाकर ला रहे थे। संस्कार करवाने वाला पुरोहित चिता की लकड़ियाँ ठीक ढंग से लगवा रहा था। सागरजी के बड़े भाई दोपहर को ही दिल्ली पहुँच गए थे, इसलिए पिता के मुखाग्नि देने का दायित्व उनके कंधों पर चला गया था। किरपाल दौड़-दौड़कर सारी सामग्री इकट्ठी कर रहा था।

तभी भीड़ में से एक चेहरा उभरा। सागरजी ने देखा, उपमंत्री आनंदजी हाथ में गुलाब की माला लिये कुछ लोगों से घिरे हुए चले आ रहे हैं। सागरजी के बुझे चेहरे पर हल्की सी चमक दौड़ गई। वे बड़ी फुरती से आगे बढ़े। उन्हें अपनी ओर बढ़ता देखकर आनंदजी रुक गए। उन्होंने मुँह में भरा हुआ पान-मसाला एक ओर थूक दिया और दोनों हाथ बढ़ाकर सागरजी को अपने कलावे में ले लिया।

''पिताजी के स्वर्गवास से बहुत आघात लगा···सागरजी··· ।''

''जैसी भगवान् की मरजी।'' सागरजी ने बड़े शोक भरे शब्दों में कहा। फिर वे उपमंत्रीजी को बड़े आदर से अरथी के पास ले गए। मंत्रीजी ने अरथी पर माला डाली और बड़ी श्रद्धा से दोनों हाथ जोड़कर प्रणाम किया।

□

आज चौथा दिन था। घर के प्रमुख लोगों को अस्थियाँ चुनने के लिए श्मशान भूमि पर जाना था। यह निश्चित हुआ था कि वहीं से एक वैन अस्थियाँ लेकर गंगा में प्रवाहित करने के लिए हरिद्वार चली जाएगी। लेकिन सागरजी अस्थियों के साथ हरिद्वार नहीं जा रहे थे। पिछले दो दिन से वे बहुत उदास थे। किसी काम में उनका मन नहीं लग रहा था। उन्होंने ठीक से कुछ खाया-पीया भी नहीं था। शील ने बार-बार उन्हें समझाने की कोशिश की, ''किसी के माता-पिता हमेशा तो साथ नहीं रहते···इस तरह हिम्मत हारने से कैसे चलेगा···पिताजी अपनी सभी जिम्मेदारियाँ पूरी कर गए। पीछे भरा-पूरा परिवार छोड़कर गए हैं···आपको हौसला रखना चाहिए···इसी से उनकी आत्मा को शांति मिलेगी।''

लेकिन सागरजी की उदासी दूर नहीं हो रही थी। उनकी आँखों के सामने श्मशान भूमि का दृश्य बार-बार घूम रहा था···बस केंद्र का एक उपमंत्री आया···उस कैबिनेट मिनिस्टर को क्या हो गया था···? उसने वहाँ आने का पूरा वादा किया था···पर इनके वादे का क्या है···नहीं आना था तो कम-से-कम अपने पी.ए. के जरिए फूल माला ही भिजवा देते···श्मशान भूमि के लोग भी उम्मीद से बहुत कम थे···कम-से-कम हजार-डेढ़ हजार की भीड़ तो होनी ही चाहिए थी···बड़ी मुश्किल से चार-पाँच सौ लोग होंगे···उनमें ज्यादातर तो गली-मोहल्लेवाले ही थे—वी.आई.पी. कितने थे? मुश्किल से एक-दो होंगे···अगर आनंदजी भी न आते···जो बस सब बंटाढार हो जाता··· ।

अस्थियाँ लेकर एक गाड़ी हरिद्वार चली गई थी। सुबह अफसोस करने आए लोग

भी चले गए थे। घर में सन्नाटा छाया हुआ था। माँ एक कोने में उदास बैठी हुई थी। शील रसोईघर में उलझी हुई थी। बच्चे खा-पीकर सो गए थे।

दूर कुरसी पर बैठे सागरजी माँ की ओर टकटकी लगाए देख रहे थे। एकाएक उन्हें लगा—अब माँ भी ज्यादा दिन जिंदा नहीं रहेंगी। फिर उनके अंदर भविष्य की कितनी ही कल्पनाओं का जैसे ज्वार सा उमड़ पड़ा। उन्हें लगा—माँ की अरथी श्मशान भूमि पहुँच गई है। प्रधानमंत्री सहित मंत्रिमंडल के सभी सदस्य वहाँ आए हुए हैं···सारे निगम बोध घाट पर बस सिर-ही-सिर दिखाई दे रहे हैं··इतने में एक बड़ी लंबी गाड़ी वहाँ आकर रुकती है···उसमें से राष्ट्रपति का ए.डी.सी. फूलों का बड़ा गुलदस्ता लेकर उतरता है और अपनी फौजी वरदी में खट-खट चलता हुआ अरथी के पास पहुँचकर सैल्यूट करता है। फिर उसे अरथी पर रख देता है।

सागरजी माँ को एकटक देखने लगे। फिर धीरे से उठकर उसके पास जाकर बैठ गए। माँ के पास बैठे-बैठे उनकी आँखों में आँसू छलक आए।

□

कौन तार ते बीनी चदरिया

उसके सामने पति का शव पड़ा हुआ था। शाम को जब वह घर लौटा था, उसने बहुत पी रखी थी। वह लड़खड़ाता हुआ चारपाई पर लेट गया था। फिर वह एकाएक उठा और उल्टियाँ करने लगा। सारा फर्श गंदा हो गया। वह झटपट रसोई से एक बाल्टी ले आई। वह बाल्टी में उल्टी करने लगा। कमरे में बहुत बदबू फैल गई। शराब की गंध के साथ कितने ही पचे-अनपचे टुकड़े बाहर निकल गए।

जब उसकी उल्टियाँ कुछ रुकीं तो उसने गिलास में उसे पानी दिया, फिर एक पुराने तौलिए से उसका मुँह पोंछने लगी। उसके मुँह और कपड़ों से बहुत बदबू आ रही थी। उसे उसने चारपाई पर लिटा दिया और फर्श साफ करने लगी।

एकाएक वह फिर उठा। ऐसे लगा जैसे वह फिर उल्टी करेगा। उसने वही बाल्टी उसके आगे कर दी। बदबू का एक भभका उठा और उसने फिर उल्टी कर दी। उसने पानी दिया, मुँह पोंछा और धीरे से उसे लिटा दिया।

पर वह बहुत छटपटा रहा था। दोनों हाथों से बार-बार अपना सिर पकड़ता था और हाय···हाय कर रहा था। बार-बार उसे उबकाई आ रही थी। उसे लगता कि फिर उल्टी होगी। वह उसके पास ही चारपाई पर बैठी कभी उसकी पीठ पर हाथ फेरने लगती, कभी उसका सिर दबाने लगती।

उसके मुँह से निकला—''सिर फटा जा रहा है··· ।''

वह उसका सिर दबाने लगी।

उसकी बेचैनी और छटपटाहट वैसी ही थी।

दोनों बच्चे बाहर खेलकर अंदर आ गए थे और चुपचाप खड़े देख रहे थे। वह आँखें बंद किए लेटा था और तेज-तेज साँस ले रहा था। बीच-बीच में वह आँखें खोलकर बच्चों की ओर देखता था, फिर आँखें बंद कर लेता था।

पत्नी ने पूछा, ''चाय पियोगे?''

उसने हलके से सिर हिलाया—"बस थोड़ी सी।"

वह चाय बनाने चली गई।

उसने बच्चों को इशारे से बुलाकर अपने पास बैठा लिया। लड़की का हाथ पकड़कर बोला, "मुन्नी, स्कूल गई थी?"

"जी पापा···।"

वह कुछ सोचने लगा—"मुन्नी, तू किस क्लास में है?"

मुन्नी हँस दी—"पापा, आपको यह भी नहीं मालूम···मैं चौथी में हूँ।"

उसने अपना सिर झटका। झटककर जैसे वह नशा उतार रहा था।

वह हलके से मुसकराया—"मुन्ना···तू पाँचवीं में है?"

वह भी हँस दिया—"नहीं पापा, मैं छठी में हूँ···मुन्नी से दो साल बड़ा हूँ ना।"

उसने आँखें बंद कर लीं। उसे उखड़ी-उखड़ी, धुँधली-धुँधली याद थी—कल शाम उसे रणधीर अपने घर ले गया था। वह छड़ा-छाँट है। न कोई आगे, न पीछे। दोनों ने जमकर पी थी। रणधीर संतरा ब्रांड ठर्रे की दो बोतलें ले आया था। साथ में ढेर सारी भुनी हुई कलेजियाँ थीं। दोनों ने खूब गंदे-गंदे मजाक किए थे और खूब हँसे थे। जब दूसरी बोतल खत्म हो गई तो रणधीर ने अपने गिलास पर निचोड़ने की क्रिया करते हुए कहा था—'देख संजय, इसमें से आखिरी बूँद तक निचोड़ दूँगा।'

वह भी अधमुँदी आँखों से देखता हुआ बोला था—'स्साला! बोतल को निचोड़ रहा है।'

उसे याद है···अपने ऑटो को किसी तरह स्टार्ट करके वह घर पहुँच गया था।

वह नींद में डूब रहा था। उसे लग रहा था, वह सचमुच डूब रहा है। उसके चारों ओर पानी-ही-पानी है। वह बड़े हाथ-पैर मार रहा है, उसे थाह नहीं मिल रही है, वह बहता चला जा रहा है। बार-बार उसे लगता, बच्चे पापा-पापा चिल्ला रहे हैं। अधनींद में ही वह सोचता है—सुजाता कहाँ है? वह बच्चों के साथ क्यों नहीं है? पर उसे वह कहीं दिखाई नहीं देती···उसकी घबराहट बहुत बढ़ गई है, साँस तेज चल रही है। उसकी नींद खुल जाती है। वह महसूस करता है, वह पसीने से तर-बतर हो गया है। सारा शरीर बहुत दर्द कर रहा है।

सुजाता को इस बात का अहसास नहीं था कि उसका पति इस तरह उसे छोड़कर चला जाएगा। वह रोज पीता था, मिल जाए तो अंधाधुंध पीता था। उसका अपना ऑटो रिक्शा था। सारा खर्च निकालकर वह दो-तीन सौ रुपए बचा लेता था। शाम होते ही उसका सिर भन्नाने लगता था। शराब की हुड़क उसकी नस-नस से बाहर निकलने लगती थी और आँखें देसी शराब की दुकान तलाशने लगती थीं।

एक शाम वह एक सवारी को लेकर लाजपत नगर जा रहा था। रास्ते में उसे एक

दुकान दिख गई। बाहर मोटे-मोटे अक्षरों में लिखा था—देसी शराब का ठेका। उसने अपना ऑटो दुकान की ओर मोड़ दिया और बड़ी मिन्नत भरे स्वर में सवारी से बोला, 'साब, मैं अपना राशन-पानी ले लूँ···बाद को दुकान बंद हो गई तो मैं मर जाऊँगा।'

सवारी ने हँसकर कहा, 'जाओ, ले आओ।'

वह दौड़कर गया और एक बोतल ले आया। बोतल उसने अपने औजारों की डिग्गी में कपड़े में लपेटकर रख दी और ऑटो स्टार्ट करके सड़क पर ले आया।

सवारी ने पूछा, 'रोज पीते हो?'

'रोज···कम-से-कम एक अधिया।'

'क्यों पीते हो?'

'इसका क्या जवाब दूँ, बस इसकी लत पड़ गई है।'

'परिवार में कौन है?'

'बीवी है, दो बच्चे हैं।'

सवारी ने आगे कुछ नहीं पूछा।

□

संजय का अंतिम संस्कार हो गया। उसका भाई पास के ही दूसरे शहर में था। उसने आकर सारी व्यवस्था की। दूर-पास के पाँच-दस रिश्तेदार भी आ गए थे। सुजाता ने संजय के सारे कपड़े टटोले। अपने पास भी देखा। कुल साढ़े तीन सौ रुपए थे।

उस दिन बहुत गरमी थी। बच्चे कुछ खा-पीकर सो गए थे। घर्र-घर्र करता हुआ पुराना पंखा उसे बोलता सा लगा—आगे क्या···आगे क्या···आगे क्या? सचमुच आगे क्या? सभी रिश्तेदार वापस चले गए थे। जैसे-तैसे तेरहवीं भी हो गई थी। सुजाता ने कमरे की सभी खिड़कियाँ खोल रखी थीं। उसे लग रहा था, सारा शरीर भीगा हुआ है। लेकिन उसे लग रहा था, कमरे में वैसी गंध नहीं है जैसी हुआ करती है। संजय का शराब पीना, फिर कच्चे प्याज के साथ तीन-चार रोटियों को दाल में डुबो-डुबोकर निगलना उसने बरसों तक देखा था। सारा दिन ऑटो चलाकर वह भी चूर हो जाता था। पसीने से उसके कपड़े भी गँधाने लगते थे। खाना खाने के बाद वह चारपाई पर औंधे मुँह गिरकर खर्राटे भरने लगता था।

गंध उसकी साँसों में घुल-मिल गई थी। इसी गंध से गुजरते हुए उसने दो बच्चों को जन्म दिया था। यह गंध उसके जीवन के सुख-दुःख के क्षणों की साक्षी बन गई थी।

आज गरमी थी, उमस थी, पर वह गंध नहीं थी। उसे बहुत अजीब लग रहा था। आगे की उम्र का रास्ता बहुत लंबा था। उसने जीवन के पैंतीस वसंत देखे थे। पर सभी तो वसंत नहीं थे। पिछले पंद्रह बरसों में वसंत की महकती बहार शायद ही कभी उसे छूकर निकली हो।

उसे लगा, पंखा घर्र-घर्र करता हुआ वही बात बोल रहा है—आगे क्या…?

उसके माँ-बाप हैं, भाई भी है, दो छोटी बहनें भी हैं। दोनों ब्याही हुई हैं, अपने-अपने घरों में हैं। एक का पति सुबह-सुबह साइकिल से निकलता है आवाज लगाता हुआ—कबाड़ी…कबाड़ी…रद्दी-लोहा-पीतल-बोतल…की गुहार लगाता हुआ कितनी गलियों से गुजरता है। शाम तक दो-तीन सौ रुपए कमा लाता है। कभी कोई अच्छी चीज हाथ लग जाए तो पाँच-सात सौ रुपए भी बन जाते हैं।

दूसरी का पति फलों की रेहड़ी लगाता है। वह भी दो-तीन सौ रुपए कमा लेता है।

दोनों ही कभी-कभी पी लेते हैं…जब कभी मौका मिल जाए या मुफ्त की मिल जाए। पर संजय की तरह गँधाते नहीं हैं। उनकी पत्नियों ने ऐसी शिकायत कभी नहीं की। दोनों यह जरूर कहती हैं कि उनके आदमी मर्द हैं। दूसरे-चौथे दिन वे उन्हें दो-चार थप्पड़ लगा देते हैं। यह मानते हैं कि वह मर्द ही क्या जो कभी-कभी अपनी औरत पर हाथ न उठाए। औरत को उसकी औकात में रखने के लिए यह जरूरी है।

भाई एक प्राइवेट कंपनी में ड्राइवरी करता है। उसका अभी विवाह नहीं हुआ है। किसी तरह बूढ़े माँ-बाप का पालन करता है।

इनमें ऐसा कौन है जो सुजाता के लिए कुछ कर सके।

सुजाता को लगता है, एक बड़े वृक्ष की खोह में उसका घोंसला बना हुआ था। उसका चिड़ा भी था और दो नन्हे-नन्हे चूजे भी। लेकिन उस वृक्ष पर साँप बहुत लिपटे हुए थे। उसके घोंसले पर एक दिन एक साँप ने फुफकार मार दी। घोंसला टूटकर धरती पर गिर गया। चिड़ा मर गया। चिड़िया और बच्चे बच गए। वृक्ष के तने में एक खोह थी! चिड़िया और बच्चे उस खोह में घुस गए। वृक्ष पर घोंसला तो था, पर साँपों का डर हमेशा बना रहता था।

खोह में घुसी चिड़िया को अब डर नहीं लगता।

सुजाता ने दो घरों में काम पकड़ लिया। सुबह बच्चों को स्कूल भेजकर वह धवन बीबीजी के घर में सफाई-पोंचे का काम करने लगी। बीबीजी कॉलेज में पढ़ाती हैं। धवन साहब दो बरस पहले गुजर गए थे। दोनों बेटे कॉलेज में पढ़ते हैं। बीबीजी करीब ग्यारह बजे कॉलेज जाती हैं। सुजाता उससे पहले इस घर का काम निपटा देती है। यहाँ से उसे एक हजार रुपए महीना मिलते हैं।

इसके बाद वह कोहली साहब के घर जाती है। कोहली साहब और उनका लड़का सुबह दस बजे तक अपने-अपने धंधों पर चले जाते हैं। कोहली बीबीजी कई बरस से बीमार चल रही हैं। उनके सारे शरीर में हमेशा दर्द होता रहता है। बहुत इलाज करा चुकी हैं, पर खास फायदा नहीं हुआ।

अपनी देखभाल के लिए हमेशा उन्हें एक मेड की जरूरत रहती है। पुरानी मेड

किसी कारण चली गई तो यह काम सुजाता को मिल गया। वह सारा दिन कोहली बीबीजी की सेवा करती, उनका बदन दबाती, मालिश करती, खाना बनाती और उन्हें चाय-कॉफी बनाकर देती। धवन बीबीजी के घर वह नाश्ता करती थी। इस घर में अपने लिए खाना बना लेती थी। बच्चे दोपहर को स्कूल से आ जाते थे। उनके लिए वह सुबह कुछ बनाकर रख आती थी।

कोहली परिवार से उसे दो हजार रुपए प्रति माह मिलने की बात हो गई थी।

धूप कितनी तीखी होती है। तन-बदन को झुलसा देती है। उससे बचने के लिए आदमी छाँव की तरफ भागता है। सुजाता का जीवन धूप में तपते हुए गुजरा था। विवाह के बाद जिस छाया तले वह आई थी वहाँ वह तपी थी। जब तपी नहीं थी, वह हुमस में बहुत गली थी।

सुजाता को पता लगा—धूप गुनगुनी भी होती है···सुख का अहसास भी देती है।

वह शाम को घर लौटती थी। बार-बार उसे यह लगता था—संजय शीशे के गिलास में देसी शराब ढालकर पी रहा होगा। उसके सामने कच्चे प्याज और मूली के कटे हुए टुकड़े किसी प्लेट में पड़े होंगे। उसे याद आया वह दिन, जब उसने बहुत ज्यादा पी ली थी। उसने उल्टियाँ की थीं। सारा कमरा शराब और उल्टी की सड़ाँध से भर गया था। फर्श पर गिरी उल्टी साफ करते हुए उसे कितनी उबकाई आई थी। उसे लगा था, वह भी उल्टी कर देगी। उसने सभी खिड़कियाँ खोल दी थीं। उस सड़ाँध में उसने किस तरह रात काटी थी। चारपाई पर औंधा लेटा संजय लगातार कराह रहा था। उसे वह किसी मरियल कुत्ते जैसा लग रहा था। फिर बुरे-बुरे सपने देखते हुए उसकी आँख लग गई थी। रात में संजय के प्राण कब निकल गए थे, उसे पता भी नहीं लगा था।

घर आई तो दोनों बच्चे स्कूल का होमवर्क करते हुए दिखे। मुन्ना बहुत खुश होकर बोला, "मम्मी, मैंने गैस जलाकर चाय बनाई, मैंने भी पी, मुन्नी ने भी।"

मुन्नी बहुत चहकती हुई बोली, "हाँ मम्मी, भैया ने बड़ी अच्छी चाय बनाई, बड़ा मजा आया।"

सुजाता उनके पास बैठ गई। वह उनके सिर पर हाथ फेरने लगी। उसे बहुत अच्छा-अच्छा लग रहा था। कोहली बीबीजी ने आज पकौड़े खाने की इच्छा जाहिर की थी। उसने गोभी, बैंगन, आलू, प्याज के पकौड़े तले थे। शाम को चलने लगी तो बीबीजी ने कहा, "कुछ पकौड़े बच्चों के लिए भी ले जा।"

बच्चे पकौड़े खा रहे थे। वह उन्हें एक टक देखती जा रही थी। बहुत अच्छा लग रहा था। बिलकुल शरद की गुनगुनी धूप की भाँति। उसने महसूस किया, बच्चों के शरीर से कितनी अच्छी गंध आती है। उसे सारा कमरा महकता हुआ लगा।

□

पटकथा

वह अस्पताल पहुँचा। रजनी अपने नवजात शिशु के साथ पलंग पर लेटी हुई थी। उसे देखकर उसने नजरें झुका लीं और बच्चे पर चादर ओढ़ाने लगी। उसने पास आकर बच्चे को देखा। अंदर तक एक टीस विष के घूँट सी उतरती चली गई। बच्चे का रंग, नैन-नक्श बिलकुल अलग थे, उसके पहले दो बच्चों की तरह नहीं। उसे लगा, बच्चे के नैन-नक्श अलग तो हैं, पर अनपहचाने नहीं हैं। इतने में बलबीर आ गया। उसने उसे बेटे के जन्म की बधाई दी और अपने दोनों हाथों से उसका दायाँ हाथ दबाने लगा।

हरचरण ने उसे कनखियों से देखा। फिर वह बच्चे की ओर देखने लगा। बलबीर रजनी की ओर बढ़ा तो उसने मुसकराते हुए बच्चे के मुँह से चादर हटा ली। उसने बड़ी कोमलता से बच्चे के एक गाल पर उँगली छुआई और रजनी से बोला, ''बेटा मुबारक!''

रजनी ने मुसकराती आँखों से बलबीर को देखा और नजरें झुकाकर बच्चे को देखने लगी।

बलबीर हरचरण से बातें करने लगा—''रजनी भाभी तो अब कुछ दिन दफ्तर आ नहीं सकेंगी। तुम जरा ज्यादा ध्यान दो तो अच्छा है।''

हरचरण हँसा। उसकी हँसी बड़ी फीकी और खिसियाई हुई थी। उसे लगा, पिछले कई सालों से वह उस तरह खुलकर नहीं हँसा है, जैसे पहले हँसता था।

बलबीर चला गया। हरचरण पास रखी कुरसी पर बैठ गया। उसने अपना चश्मा उतारा, जेब से एक मुड़ा-तुड़ा गंदा रूमाल निकालकर उसे साफ करने लगा। रजनी उसे देख रही थी। उसने अपना दुपट्टा उसकी तरफ बढ़ा दिया। वह फिर उसी ढंग से मुसकराया फीका...खिसियाहट भरा। उसने दुपट्टे के एक छोर से चश्मा साफ किया और लगा लिया।

''शाम को आओगे?''

''तुम्हारे लिए कुछ खाना लेकर आऊँगा न।''

''थोड़ी सी खिचड़ी ले आना। विन्नी बना देगी।''

''खिचड़ी तो मैं भी बना सकता हूँ।'' वह फिर उसी तरह मुसकराया।

''मैं जानती हूँ, तुम क्या-क्या कर सकते हो···मैं जानती हूँ।''

रजनी के व्यंग्य ने उसे झनझना दिया। लंबे समय से वह उसकी हिकारत भरी नजरों की आरी से कट रहा था। कोई पल, कोई पहर ऐसा नहीं था जब आरी के तेज दाँतों की चुभन उसे महसूस न हुई हो। ऐसे में उसे कुछ नहीं सूझता, सिवा इसके कि वह इस चुभन से भी ज्यादा तेज कोई चीज अपने अंदर उतार ले और उस समय तक उतारता रहे जब तक होश की मद्धिम किरण भी उसके सामने से ओझल न हो जाए। फिर जो कुछ भी हो, वह हो···दुनिया भाड़ में जाए।

वह बहुत तिलमिलाता सा चुपचाप बैठा रहा

''शाम को बच्चों को साथ ले आना।''

बच्चों की बात सुनते ही उसे लगा, वह कुछ क्षण पहले ही तपती हुई रेत पर खड़ा था। एकाएक उसके सामने कोई घना पेड़ आ गया हो।

वह सोचने लगा—विन्नी दस साल की हो गई है। अपनी उम्र से ज्यादा बड़ों जैसी बातें करती है। घर पहुँचूँगा तो वह स्कूल से आ चुकी होगी। फिर एकदम उसका मुँह कसैला हो गया। उसका पहला सवाल होगा—'पापा, मुन्ना किस पर गया है?'

शाम को विन्नी और पाँच साल का बीनू बड़े चाव से उछलते-कूदते अस्पताल पहुँचे। खिचड़ी का डिब्बा मेज पर रखते हुए उसने देखा, दोनों मुन्ना के पास खड़े उसे एकटक देख रहे हैं। बीनू के सिर पर हाथ फेरते हुए रजनी बोली, ''बीनू, देख तेरा भैया आया है?''

बीनू बोला कुछ नहीं। वह बड़े ध्यान से बच्चे को देखने लगा। फिर वह विन्नी को देखने लगा, जैसे उससे कुछ पूछना चाहता हो। विन्नी आगे बढ़कर बच्चे को प्यार करने लगी। उसका चेहरा अजीब सी उलझन से भरा हुआ था। वह बड़ी भोली नजरों से माँ को देखने लगी।

''मम्मी, भैया कितना प्यारा है!''

''बिलकुल तेरे पर गया है।'' रजनी को लगा, विन्नी की आँखों में कुछ सवाल चक्कर काट रहे हैं।

''बिलकुल तेरे जैसा है।''

''पर दीदी तो कितनी गोरी है।'' बीनू सहज नहीं हो पाया था—''मुन्ना का रंग कैसा है?''

रजनी जानती थी, अस्पताल से बाहर निकलते ही कितनी आँखों में उभरा यह सवाल उसे बींधने लगेगा।

"भगवान् का खेल है।" रजनी ने बड़ी तेजी से अपनी ओर बढ़ते सैलाब से बचने के लिए एक सहारा ढूँढ़ा—"वह किसी को गोरा बना देता है, किसी को काला।"

उसने इधर-उधर नजर दौड़ाई। हरचरण नहीं दिख रहा था।

"तुम्हारे पापा कहाँ गए?"

दोनों बच्चों ने इधर-उधर देखा—"अभी तो यहीं बैठे थे।"

विन्नी ने देखा। वह वार्ड में बिछी चारपाइयों में से झूमता हुआ आ रहा था। पास आया तो सभी ने देखा, उसकी आँखें लाल हैं और पैर लड़खड़ा रहे हैं। रजनी के चेहरे पर हिकारत उभर आई। उसने अपना मुँह दूसरी ओर फेर लिया।

हरचरण, बलबीर, रजनी···इस पटकथा का यह त्रिकोण कैसे बना? कोई नहीं कह सकता कि त्रिकोण कैसे बन जाते हैं। बड़ी धूमधाम से हरचरण और रजनी की शादी हुई थी। वह जब ससुराल आई तो सभी चकाचौंध हो गए थे। गोरा रंग इतना भी गोरा हो सकता है! वह ठंडी धूप का उमगता हुआ झरना लगती थी। बरसों तक अड़ोस-पड़ोस में उसके गोरेपन को लेकर चर्चा होती रही।

हरचरण में भी कमी नहीं थी। तीखे नैन-नक्श, खुलता गेहुँआ रंग और कद-काठी में वह बड़ा भरा-पूरा लगता था। अपने शहर में उसके पिता ने जब महाराजा रेस्तराँ की शुरुआत की थी तो उस जोड़ का वहाँ दूसरा रेस्तराँ नहीं था। देखते-देखते रेस्तराँ नगर के अमीरों, रसिकों, पीनेवालों का अड्डा बन गया। पिता भी पीने के शौकीन थे, उनके दोनों बेटे गुरुचरण और हरचरण उनसे दो कदम आगे थे। बाप-बेटे साथ-साथ पीते थे और अलग-अलग भी। अलग पीते-पीते हरचण बहुत अलग हो गया। पिता और बड़े भाई के लिए पीना-पिलाना अपने दोस्तों, ग्राहकों, नगर के नेताओं, अधिकारियों के लिए शाम के ढलने का एक शौक था। हरचरण के लिए वह सूरज के निकलने का ऐलान बन गया।

पक्के काले रंगवाला बलबीर इसी दौर में उसका मित्र बना था। शाम को दोनों एक साथ पीते थे, रेस्तराँ में नहीं, घर में। रजनी उनके लिए सलाद काटती, अंडे की भुजिया बनाती और साथ बैठकर कोई सॉफ्ट ड्रिंक पीती। बलबीर जब बहुत जोर देता तो ड्राईजिन ले लेती।

यहाँ आकर पटकथा ने एक बड़ा मोड़ काटा। हर अच्छी पटकथा उन बिंदुओं की राह देखती है, जहाँ से कहानी कुछ गति पकड़ती है। पिता हृदयगति रुक जाने से एक दिन अचानक चल बसे। फिर दोनों भाइयों में बँटवारा हो गया। रेस्तराँ बड़े भाई ने ले लिया। हरचरण अपने हिस्से की रकम और एक मकान लेकर अलग हो गया।

बलबीर ने प्रस्ताव रखा—"तुम मेरी फैक्टरी में मेरे पार्टनर बन जाओ।"

मोटरगाड़ियों में लगने वाले रबड़ पार्ट्स बनाने की फैक्टरी में साझीदार बनने की

बात रजनी को भी अच्छी लगी।

इस बिंदु से त्रिकोण बनना शुरू हुआ।

पिता और भाई का अंकुश पहले ही हरचरण पर नहीं था। पर बाप के सामने वह आँख का कुछ लिहाज रखता था। वे अकसर कहते थे—"देख चन्नी, शाम को थोड़ी सी पी लेने में कोई हर्ज नहीं है। पर तू तो सुबह होते ही पीने लग जाता है। यह बुरी बात है।"

उसे भी मालूम था कि यह बुरी बात है। लेकिन उसके लिए सबसे बुरी बात तब होती जब यह बुरी बात उससे कभी कुछ दूर हो जाती। वह बुरी तरह तड़पता, उसके अंग-अंग बुरी तरह दुखने लगते और जब उसकी हालत बहुत बुरी हो जाती तो यही बुरी चीज उसे राहत देती। उसे अपने चारों ओर सबकुछ अच्छा लगने लगता।

फिर उसे लगने लगता, यह अच्छा लगना उसे बहुत भारी पड़ रहा है। वह फैक्टरी में बैठा होता। बलबीर माल बेचने, उधारी वसूल करने, कभी कच्चा माल खरीदने के लिए बाजार चला जाता। कभी-कभी विन्नी उसे बताती—"आज जब मैं स्कूल से आई तो बलबीर अंकल घर आए हुए थे। मम्मी के साथ बैठे खाना खा रहे थे।"

बलबीर का खाना दोपहर को उसका नौकर फैक्टरी ले आता था। हरचरण का डिब्बा सुबह रजनी तैयार करके साथ ही दे देती थी। अकसर दोनों साथ-साथ ही लंच करते थे। किंतु अब बलबीर को बाजार के कुछ ज्यादा ही काम याद आने लगे थे। उसका लंचबॉक्स शाम तक उसी तरह पड़ा रहता था। हरचरण उससे पूछता, "आज भी तुम्हारा लंचबॉक्स उसी तरह बंद पड़ा रहा। खाना कहाँ खाया?"

वह किसी डीलर का नाम बता देता, उसके साथ लंच कर लिया था। कभी कच्चे माल के किसी होलसेलर का नाम बता देता। कभी-कभी वह यह भी कहता—"उधर से निकला तो सोचा, रजनी भाभी को मिलता चलूँ। लंच का समय हो तो मुझसे रहा नहीं जाता। उनके बनाए खाने का कोई जवाब नहीं है। चन्नी, तुम बड़े खुशनसीब हो।"

इस 'खुशनसीब' शब्द को बहुत दिन उसने अपनी मुट्ठी में बंद करके रखा था। शादी के बाद कितनी बौराई, ललचाई और गरमाई आँखों ने यह शब्द उगला था। तब वह मुसकरा दिया करता था। ईर्ष्या भरी ऐसी आँखें उसे अच्छी लगती थीं। फिर यह शब्द उसे चुभने लगा। यह चुभन कितनी तीखी हो सकती है, उसका गहरा अहसास उसे तब हुआ, जब बलबीर के मुँह से उसने सुना।

दोपहर को वह अकेला लंच करने लगता तो हर निवाले के साथ उसे अपना घर याद आ जाता। उसे लगता, बलबीर और रजनी साथ-साथ खाना खा रहे होंगे। बच्चे अभी स्कूल से नहीं आए होंगे। तभी उसकी सोच अनगिनत संभावनाओं के बिंब बनाने शुरू कर देती। उसी बेचैनी में वह अपने मेज की दराज से बोतल निकालता और खाना

खाते तीन-चार पेग गले में उड़ेल लेता।

एक दिन बलबीर ने उससे कहा, ''देखो चन्नी, रेस्तराँ चलाना एक बात है, फैक्टरी चलाना एकदम दूसरी बात। वहाँ लोग चलकर तुम्हारे पास आते हैं। यहाँ हमें खुद चलकर उन दुकानदारों के पास जाना पड़ता है, जो हमारा माल बेचते हैं। तुम जानते ही हो कि इसके लिए मुझे दूर-दूर के शहरों के टूर भी करने पड़ते हैं। मैं समझता था, मेरे पार्टनर बन जाओगे तो तुम फैक्टरी में पूरा ध्यान देकर प्रोडक्शन सँभालोगे और मैं उसकी मार्केटिंग देखूँगा। पर देखता हूँ कि तुम यहाँ पीकर आने लगे हो, सारा दिन पीते रहते हो। न किसी से ठीक से बात कर पाते हो, न वर्करों से पूरा काम ले पाते हो। ऐसे कैसे चलेगा?''

उसकी समझ में नहीं आता कि वह क्या कहे। वह शर्मिंदा होता। दिन में न पीने का वायदा करता। लेकिन एक तीखी चुभन उसका साथ नहीं छोड़ती। दूसरे ही दिन अपने वायदे को गिलास में ढालकर पी जाता।

बलबीर इसकी शिकायत रजनी से करता—''देखिए भाभी, चन्नी फैक्टरी के दफ्तर में ही बैठकर पिए यह ठीक नहीं है। वहाँ कितने ही लोग आते हैं, कितने मजदूर वहाँ काम करते हैं। उनके सामने आँखें सुर्ख करके बैठना और ऊलजलूल बोलना कितना खराब लगता है।''

रजनी के सम्मुख जैसे किसी फिल्म की पटकथा लिखी जा रही थी। वह समझ रही थी कि यह पटकथा कितनी लिखी जा चुकी है, कहानी में कितने मोड़ आ चुके हैं। आगे कैसे मोड़ आने वाले हैं, इससे भी वह अनजान नहीं थी।

वह हरचरण के लिए बहुत बुरा-भला कहती, अपना गुस्सा भी जताती, लेकिन यह भी समझती थी कि सब बात उसी दिशा में आगे बढ़ रही है, जिस तरह उसे आगे बढ़ना था। वह जानती थी कि बलबीर क्या चाहता है। वह यह भी समझती थी कि बलबीर का रोज शाम उसके घर आना, पीना-पिलाना, हरचरण से दोस्ती की पीगें बढ़ाना, उसे अपना पार्टनर बनाना किस लक्ष्य को पाना था। बलबीर की नजर पेड़ पर बैठी चिड़िया की एक आँख पर थी, जिस पर उसका निशाना सधा हुआ था।

उसे यह भी पता था कि वह चिड़िया कौन है।

एक दिन बलबीर ने कहा, ''फैक्टरी सँभालना चन्नी के बस की बात नहीं है। मुझे इसकी कोई उम्मीद नहीं कि वह अपनी आदत सुधार लेगा।''

रजनी उसके मुँह से अगली बात सुनने के लिए एकटक उसे देखने लगी।

''एक बात कहूँ—मैं चाहता हूँ कि आप मेरी पार्टनर बन जाइए।''

'पार्टनर' शब्द की गूँज बहुत दूर तक सुनाई देने लगी। दोनों एक-दूसरे को देखते हुए इस शब्द के अर्थ-विस्तार को पकड़ने की कोशिश कर रहे थे।

फिर वह अपने कहे की व्याख्या करने लगा—"मेरा मतलब है कि आप फैक्टरी में रुचि लेना शुरू कर दीजिए। आपकी योग्यता में मुझे कोई संदेह नहीं है। आप चीजों को बहुत अच्छी तरह सँभाल सकती हैं।"

आगे की पटकथा में न कुछ अनहोना है, न नया है।

दूसरे दिन से रजनी फैक्टरी जाने लगी। उसके लिए एक अलग कैबिन बनवाई गई। धीरे-धीरे उसने वह सारा काम समझ लिया जो हरचरण के हिस्से का था। शुरू में हरचरण कुछ भौंचक्का हुआ—यह सब क्या हो रहा है। फिर वह निर्लिप्त हो गया। बिलकुल संतों जैसी निर्लिप्तता उसने ग्रहण कर ली। कहीं से बरसों पहले सुनी एक पंक्ति उसकी सोच में चक्कर काटने लगी—'जैसे जल में कमल निरालम।'

एक ही छत के नीचे रजनी के तीनों बच्चे बड़े हो रहे थे।

यमुना जब प्रयाग में गंगा से मिलती है तो दो धाराओं के रंग अलग-अलग दिखते हैं। किंतु जब वह काशी और पटना पहुँचती है तो एक जैसी हो जाती है। किंतु रजनी के बच्चों के साथ ऐसा नहीं था। वहाँ दो बच्चों वाली गंगा और एक बच्चे वाली यमुना का रंग अलग-अलग दिखता था।

बलबीर की फैक्टरी अच्छी चल रही थी। सभी कहते थे—बलबीर और रजनी की पार्टनरशिप खूब फल-फूल रही है।

हरचरण सुर्ख आँखों के साथ सबकुछ देखता था। कभी-कभी उसकी आँखें ज्यादा सुर्ख हो जाती थीं। सब समझते थे कि हरचरण ने आज ज्यादा ही चढ़ा ली होगी। लेकिन रजनी और बलबीर सुर्खी के इस अंतर को समझते थे।

□

सफाई

इस कहानी के पात्रों के नामों के बारे में मैं कई दिन तक सोचता रहा। नाम कुछ भी हो सकते थे—राम, श्याम, मोहन, अहमद, राबिन। महिलाओं के नाम भी वैसे ही हो सकते थे—कमला, विमला, नसरीन, डॉली।

लेकिन मैंने नाम रख लिये हैं—इक्का, दुक्का, तिक्का, चौका। जरूरत पड़ने पर इसे आगे भी बढ़ाया जा सकता है। महिलाओं को इक्की, दुक्की, तिक्की, चौकी कहा जा सकता है। खन्नी, चोपड़ी, पंडितानी, सरदारनी करने की आदत हम सबको है ही।

ये सभी लोग एक मल्टी-स्टोरी बिल्डिंग में रहते हैं। इनमें सरकारी अफसर हैं, अध्यापक हैं, पत्रकार हैं, निजी कंपनियों में काम करनेवाले हैं। बिल्डिंग में परिवार तो और भी हैं, पर इन चार परिवारों की आपस में खूब पटती है। इन्हें जोड़ने में खास भूमिका पंजी की है। चार तो सही-सही जोड़े हैं—इक्का-इक्की, दुक्का-दुक्की, तिक्का-तिक्की और चौका-चौकी। लेकिन पंजी अकेली है। वह कहती है—"अभी तक ऐसा कोई मजबूत पंजा नहीं मिला, जो मेरी बंद मुट्ठी को खोल दे।" आयु चालीस को पार कर गई है। खूब गोरी, लंबी और स्वस्थ। सहशिक्षा वाले कॉलेज में पढ़ाती है। रिकॉर्ड यह है कि किसी उद्दंड लड़के की बदतमीजी की शिकायत लेकर वह कभी प्रिंसिपल के पास नहीं गई। उसका दावा है—"ऐसे मुरगों की गरदन तो मैं खुद ही मरोड़ सकती हूँ। किसमें इतनी जुर्रत है कि मेरे सामने कुसक भी जाए।"

ये सभी लोग हर शनिवार को किसी एक के फ्लैट में मिलते हैं। ये लोग वहाँ ताश नहीं खेलते, कैरम भी नहीं खेलते, किसी पार्टी जैसे कोई चीज भी नहीं करते। चाय के साथ गरम पकौड़े या समोसे इनके लिए काफी होते हैं।

सवाल है—ये लोग करते क्या हैं?

जवाब है—ये लोग बातें करते हैं। यह भी कहा जा सकता है कि इन्हें बातें करने की, बहस करने की 'झस' है। 'झस' शब्द पंजाबी का है। मुझे इसका हिंदी समानार्थी

शब्द याद नहीं आ रहा है। मोटे तौर पर इसे दीवानगी भरी आदत या व्यसन कहा जा सकता है। ऐसी बहस में पंजी को छोड़ अन्य महिलाएँ बहुत सक्रिय भूमिका नहीं निभातीं। इन्हें शुद्ध गृहिणियाँ कहा जा सकता है। शनिवार को जिस घर की बारी होती है, उसकी गृहिणी अपने आपको सबकी आवभगत में लगाए रखती है। पंजी औरत जरूर है, लेकिन पूरी बिल्डिंग की औरतें उसे मर्दों का भी मर्द मानती हैं। शुरू-शुरू में मर्दों के बीच इस तरह उन्मुक्त भाव से उठने-बैठने वाली औरत से उन्हें खतरा भी महसूस हुआ था। किंतु पंजी ने बहुत जल्दी सारी बिल्डिंग की औरतों को मौसी और भाभी बना लिया और खुद सभी की दीदी बन गई कि अब उससे किसी को डर नहीं लगता।

यह बहस अपनी बिल्डिंग की सीवर-प्रॉब्लम से लेकर अंतरिक्ष-युद्ध की संभावनाओं तक फैली हुई है। इक्काजी बहुत सोच-सोचकर बोलते हैं, जैसे हर समस्या पर चाहे जितना बहसा जाए, आखिर ताले की चाबी तो उन्हीं के पास है। दुक्काजी हर समस्या पर अपनी बात इस तरह शुरू करते हैं—"देखिए, इस समस्या के दो पहलू हैं—एक, यह बात इस तरह हुई, दो—अगर यह बात इस तरह न होकर उस तरह हुई होती तो उसका नतीजा इस तरह न निकलता जैसे निकला।"

तिक्काजी दो बात की एक बात जानते हैं—हर समस्या का समाधान डंडा है— "जरा इन ब्लैकिए व्यापारियों को सड़क के बीचोबीच खड़ा करके सरकार इनके…" फिर पंजी का खयाल करके वे अपने वाक्य की बनावट में कुछ संशोधन कर देते हैं— "इनकी पीठ पर चार डंडे मारो। देखिए भाव नीचे आते हैं कि नहीं। आखिर बड़ी बिगड़ी हुई पंजाब समस्या कैसे दुरुस्त हुई? असम में सेना गई और उसने उल्फावालों का कुल्फा बना दिया।" उनका तर्क पंजाबी की इस उक्ति पर आकर रुकता है— "डंडा पीर है बिगड़िआं-तिगड़िआं दा।"

उनके इस तर्क पर कभी-कभी पंजी खीझ उठती है—"कश्मीर-समस्या ऐसे ही हल होगी, तिक्काजी?"

"जी, बिलकुल इसी तरह। कुछ दिन के लिए मुझे कश्मीर का गवर्नर बनाकर भेज दीजिए। देखिए, मैं किस तरह उनकी…" फिर वे अपने वाक्य के दौड़ते हुए घोड़े की लगाम दूसरी तरफ मोड़ देते है—"मैं उनके नथुनों में लाल मिर्च भर देता हूँ।"

चौकाजी बहुत कम बोलते हैं। वे लोगों की बातें सुनते हैं। फिर कंधे से ऊपर के सारे सिर को इस तरह बाएँ-दाएँ हिलाते हैं कि यह पता नहीं लगता कि वे बात का समर्थन कर रहे हैं कि विरोध। ज्यादातर उनकी मुसकराहट से उनकी मंशा जाहिर हो जाती है। कभी-कभी वे चुभती-सी कोई बात बोल देते हैं, जैसे तिक्काजी की डंडे वाली बात पर वे बोले, "तिक्काजी, लगता है, जलियाँवाला बाग वाले जनरल डायर से दूर-पास की आपकी कोई रिश्तेदारी जरूर होगी।"

उनकी इस बात पर बड़े जोर का ठहका लगा था, जिसमें पंजी की आवाज सबसे तेज सुनाई दी थी।

वाद-विवाद की इनकी गाड़ी थोड़ी-बहुत शंटिंग करके आमतौर पर आगे बढ़ जाती है। लेकिन जब यह मंडल कमीशन और आरक्षण की पटरियों पर आ जाए तो बड़ी तेज खड़खड़ाहट होने लगती है, डिब्बे एक-दूसरे से टकराने लगते हैं और कभी-कभी लगता है कि गाड़ी पटरी से उतर जाएगी।

उस दिन तिक्काजी ने बड़े जोर से कहा था—"हमारा संविधान सबको बराबरी का अधिकार देता है। वह ब्राह्मण और चांडाल में कोई अंतर नहीं मानता, फिर यह रिजर्वेशन क्यों? यह बात देश के संविधान की भावना के सरासर खिलाफ है।"

इक्काजी बड़ी शालीनता से बोले थे, "मैं ऊँच-नीच और छुआछूत नहीं मानता। मैं यह भी मानता हूँ कि दलितों और पिछड़े वर्गों को आगे बढ़ने का पूरा मौका दिया जाना चाहिए। पर आरक्षण की बात मेरी समझ में नहीं आती। आरक्षण एक बैसाखी है। इसके सहारे चलेंगे तो ये लोग सदा अपाहिज बने रहेंगे। मैं ऐसे लोगों से कहता हूँ, आरक्षण की बैसाखी फेंक दो, अपने पैरों पर खड़े हो जाओ, तुम्हें किसी से भीख माँगने की जरूरत नहीं है। अपने अंदर स्वाभिमान पैदा करो और आगे बढ़ो।"

इससे पहले कि और कोई कुछ कहता, पंजी ने जोर से ताली बजाई थी—"वाह इक्काजी, कमाल है! दलितों और पिछड़े वर्गों का इस देश में आप से बढ़कर कोई हितैषी नहीं। अच्छा, मैं आपसे एक बात पूछती हूँ।"

इक्काजी अंदर-ही-अंदर कुछ घबरा गए थे।

"पूछिए।"

"आपकी पत्नी, मेरा मतलब है इक्कीजी का भतीजा पोलियो का शिकार है, है न?"

इक्काजी की समझ में नहीं आया था कि पंजी पूछना क्या चाहती है। उन्होंने बड़ी संशय भरी और सतर्क आवाज में कहा था, "हाँ, तो फिर...?"

"आप उसे यह सलाह क्यों नहीं देते—बच्चे, अपनी बैसाखी दूर फेंक दे, अपने पैरों पर खड़ा हो जा। अपने साथ के दूसरे लड़कों की तरह तू भी दौड़, अपने अंदर स्वाभिमान पैदा कर।"

इक्काजी अंदर-ही-अंदर तिलमिला उठे थे—पंजी की बच्ची ऐसे ही किसी टेढ़े-मेढ़े दृष्टांत से उन्हें दबोचेगी।

दुक्काजी का खयाल था कि पंजी ने बड़ी मूर्खतापूर्ण बात कही है—"पंजीजी, भला यह भी कोई बात हुई? बात आरक्षण पर हो रही है। इसके दो पहलू हैं। पहला तो यह कि आप दलित या पिछड़ा हुआ किसे मानती हैं। देखा जाए तो इस देश में थोड़े से बिड़ला-

टाटा को छोड़कर सभी दलित और पिछड़े हुए हैं। दूसरी बात यह है कि जिनकी आप वकालत कर रही हैं, क्या उनके हाथ-पैर टूटे हुए हैं? क्या वे लूले-लँगड़े हैं?''

पंजी का स्वर तेज हो गया था—''हाँ, ये लोग लूले-लँगड़े हैं। आपके पूर्वजों ने इनके हाथ-पैर तोड़ दिए थे। अपाहिज बना दिया था। जिंदगी के सभी हक इनसे छीनकर इन्हें अंधे कुएँ में ढकेल दिया था। आज जब वे उससे बाहर निकलने की कोशिश कर रहे हैं, लड़खड़ाते कदमों से आपके साथ चलने की ताकत बटोर रहे हैं, आप उनसे रिजर्वेशन की छोटी सी बैसाखी भी छीन लेना चाहते हैं।''

चौकाजी की गरदन लगातार हिल रही थी। उन्हें इक्काजी की इस बात में वजन दिखाई दिया था कि आखिर रिजर्वेशन का सहारा ये लोग कितने दिन तक लेते रहेंगे। दुक्काजी की यह बात उन्हें नहीं जँची थी कि बिड़ला, टाटा को छोड़कर यहाँ सभी दलित और पिछड़े वर्ग के हैं। लीजिए, अब ये भी अपने आपको इस वर्ग में शामिल कर रहे हैं। उन्हें मालूम है कि दुक्काजी का नंबर दो का अच्छा-खासा कारोबार है और उससे ढेर सारी कमाई है। पंजी की बात सुनकर तो वे सचमुच उछल पड़े हैं।

''दुक्काजी, अपने पूर्वजों के पाप का प्रायश्चित्त तो हमें करना ही पड़ेगा।'' वे मंद-मंद मुसकराए थे।

इक्काजी ने बड़ी सहजता में कहा था, ''हमीं क्यों प्रायश्चित्त करेंगे, हमारे बेटे-बेटियाँ और पोते-पोतियाँ भी करेंगे।''

एकाएक उन्हें अपने बड़े बेटे का खयाल आ गया था—''इक्कू इस साल सीनियर सेकेंडरी की परीक्षा देगा। अगर उसके सत्तर प्रतिशत भी नंबर आए तो उसे किसी अच्छे कोर्स में एडमीशन नहीं मिलेगा और मिलखूराम का बेटा पचास प्रतिशत नंबर लेकर भी उस कोर्स में दाखिला पा जाएगा।''

यह महफिल पंजी के फ्लैट पर जमी हुई थी। घंटी बजी तो वह दरवाजा खोलने के लिए उठी। बंद मुट्ठी में सिमटी उसकी स्वस्थ और सुंदर काया सबकी आँखों में कौंध गई।

तिक्काजी बुदबुदाए—''इस धरती पर क्या कोई माई का लाल नहीं, जो इस बंद मुट्ठी को खोल सके।''

दुक्काजी बड़ी संजीदा मुद्रा बनाकर बोले, ''आप कोशिश क्यों नहीं करते?''

तिक्काजी को जैसे सौ बिच्छुओं ने एक साथ डंक मारा—''क्यों, क्या आपने हार मानकर हथियार डाल दिए हैं?''

पंजी वापस आई तो बेला उसके साथ थी। वह उसे डाँट रही थी—''यह भी कोई वक्त है आने का बेला? सुबह से सफाई नहीं हुई। मैंने तुझे कहा भी था कि आज शाम को मेहमान आएँगे।''

बेला ने सब की ओर नजर उठाकर देखा—ये तो आसपास के फ्लैटों में रहने वाले

ही लोग हैं। उसके चेहरे पर हलकी सी मुसकराहट आई और वह अपने काम में लग गई।

"इक्काजी, आप जानते हैं न बेला इस वर्ष दसवीं की परीक्षा देगी।"

इक्काजी ने कुछ देर पहले ही उसके बाप मिलखूराम का जिक्र किया था।

"आप इक्कू की पढ़ाई पर जो खर्च करते हैं, उसका सौवाँ हिस्सा भी बेला का बाप इसकी पढ़ाई पर खर्च नहीं करता और आपने अपने बेटे को जो सुविधाएँ दे रखी हैं, वह बेला सोच भी नहीं सकती। सारा दिन हाथ में झाड़ू लेकर यह लड़की आप लोगों के घरों की टट्टियाँ साफ करती है। क्यों तिक्काजी, आपकी बेटी भी तो दसवीं में पढ़ रही है। उसके मुकाबले में क्या यह लड़की आपको लंगड़ी-लूली नहीं दिखाई देती?"

सारी बिल्डिंग में यह बात चर्चा का विषय बन गई थी। चर्चा की बात यह नहीं थी कि बेला की शादी होने जा रही है। चर्चा की बात यह थी कि उसकी शादी के कॉर्ड छपे थे, उसकी माँ ने हर फ्लैट में जाकर कॉर्ड बाँटे थे और कहा था—"बीबीजी-बाबूजी! बेटी की शादी है, उसमें दर्शन दीजिए, आपकी बड़ी मेहरबानी होगी।"

हर फ्लैट की संभ्रांत गृहिणी अपने गाल में उँगली गड़ाती हुई अपने पति से कह रही थी—"लो···देखो अब ये लोग भी कॉर्ड छपवाने लग गए हैं—उसी तरह, जैसे हम लोग छपवाते हैं। और तो और, बेला की माँ सबको न्योता दे गई है। लड़की की शादी में जरूर आइए···देखना, अगले साल जब यह अपनी दूसरी लड़की की शादी करेगी तो कॉर्ड के साथ मिठाई का डिब्बा भी बाँटेगी।"

शनिवार समाज में यह बात पंजी ने उठाई थी—"सोमवार को बेला की शादी है। उसकी माँ सभी घरों में कॉर्ड दे गई है। मेरा खयाल है कि हम सबको उसमें शामिल होना चाहिए। बेला कितने सालों से हमारे घरों में काम करती आ रही है, ऐसा लगता है जैसे हमारी अपनी बच्ची है।" चौकाजी ने गरदन हिलाई और मुसकराए—"आप ठीक कहती हैं, हमें इस शादी में जरूर शामिल होना चाहिए।"

दुक्काजी बोले, "इस बात के दो पहलू हैं। एक—शादी में शामिल होना और जो बन पड़े मदद करना। दूसरे—इस बिल्डिंग के वे सभी लोग, जिनके घरों में बेला या उसकी माँ काम करती है, मिलकर कोई अच्छा सा उपहार खरीदें और बेला की शादी में दे दें।"

स्थिति कुछ असमंजस भरी थी। पंजी की बात भी ठीक थी कि हमें बेला की शादी में शामिल होना चाहिए, इससे छुआछूत की भावना हटेगी···समाज में सुधार होगा···अच्छी बात है। गांधीजी भी यही चाहते थे, पर दुक्काजी की बात भी ठीक है, सभी फ्लैट वाले मिलकर एक अच्छा सा उपहार दे दें। यह भी कुछ कम नहीं है, इससे इन लोगों के प्रति हमारी सद्भावना तो प्रकट होती ही है।

निदान इक्काजी ने निकाला—"पंजीजी, आपका सुझाव बिलकुल दुरुस्त है। जहाँ

तक कुछ देने-लेने का सवाल है, यह काम औरतों पर छोड़ दिया जाए। हम लोग तो सुबह-सुबह अपने काम-धंधों पर निकल जाते हैं। इन लोगों से वास्ता तो औरतों का ही पड़ता है।''

तिक्काजी कसमसा रहे थे—''मैं समझता हूँ, हम लोग ऐसे लोगों को कुछ ज्यादा ही सिर पर चढ़ा रहे हैं। एक तरफ तो राजनीति वाले वोटों की खातिर इनकी बेजरूरत ठकुरसुहाती करते हैं, दूसरी तरफ सरकार रिजर्वेशन के नाम पर ऊलजलूल लोगों की दफ्तरों में भरती किए जा रही है और आउट ऑफ टर्न प्रमोशन दे रही है। अब आप चाहते हैं कि हम इनके साथ खड़े होकर बारात का स्वागत करें? इट इज टू मच...रियली... इट इज टू मच।''

इक्कू पंजी का स्थायी साथी है। देर-सवेर कहीं आना-जाना हो तो वह उसे अपने साथ कर लेती है। वह शाम को कॉलेज से वापस आई तो उसने बुलावा भेजा—''इक्कू आज बेला की बारात आएगी। उसकी माँ ने सभी घरों में निमंत्रण दिया है। लेकिन मुझे पता है, वहाँ कोई नहीं जाएगा। तू चलेगा मेरे साथ?''

इक्कू के चेहरे पर हलका सा रंग आया। इससे पहले कि वह कुछ बोले, पंजी बोली, ''तुझे बेला अच्छी लगती है न?''

वह शरमाया भी और कुछ उदास भी हुआ, ''कैसी बात करती हैं आप आंटी!''

''मुझसे न तो शरमाने की जरूरत है, न घबराने की। जब भी तू उसे देखता है, तेरी आँखों की पुतलियाँ उछल-कूद मचाने लगती हैं। उस दिन सीढ़ियों में उसे रोककर तू क्या कहने की कोशिश कर रहा था?''

इक्कू सिर झुकाए उसकी बातें सुन रहा था। फिर वह धीरे से बोला, ''आप ठीक कहती हैं आंटी। बेला मुझे बहुत अच्छी लगती है। मेरा मन करता है, मैं उसकी बहुत मदद करूँ, उसे किताबें दूँ...वह बहुत पढ़-लिख जाए। मेरा मन गुस्से से भर जाता है जब मैं देखता हूँ कि मेरी मम्मी ने उसके लिए एक टूटा हुआ कप अलग रख छोड़ा है, जिसमें वह उसे चाय देती है। बेला भी यह जानती है। आंटी, एक दिन मैंने उससे कह दिया—बेला, जो लोग तुझे अछूत समझते हैं, तेरे लिए रसोई से बाहर एक टूटा-फूटा कप रखते हैं, तू उनकी दी हुई चाय मत पिया कर, उनकी दी हुई रोटी मत खाया कर।''

कच्चे-पक्के घरों और बदबूदार गलियों से निकलकर पंजी और इक्कू मिलखूराम के घर पहुँचे। घर के बाहर अशोक की पत्तियों का बंदनवार बँधा हुआ था। गली को कागज की नीली-पीली झंडियों से सजाया गया था। घर के बाहर एक खुला मैदान सा था। वहीं दरियाँ बिछी हुई थीं और बिरादरी के लोग उन पर बैठे हुए हुक्का गुड़गुड़ा रहे थे या गप्पें मार रहे थे। एक तरफ कुछ लोग बैठे मिट्टी के कुज्जों में देसी शराब ढाल रहे थे। उनसे कुछ दूर कूड़े के ढेर पर तीन-चार सूअर मुँह मार रहे थे।

इन्हें देखकर दरवाजे के बाहर खड़े बिरादरीवाले कुछ चकराए। इन जैसा वहाँ एक भी व्यक्ति नहीं था और न ही ऐसे किसी व्यक्ति के आने की उन्हें आशा थी। कुछ-एक के चेहरे पर ऐसे भाव भी उभरे जैसे उन्हें इनका वहाँ आना अच्छा नहीं लगा। खबर घर के अंदर पहुँची तो बेला के माँ-बाप बाहर निकल आए।

बेला की माँ बोली, "बीबीजी, मुझे पूरी आशा थी कि तुम आओगी।" फिर उसने इक्कू के गालों पर उँगलियाँ छुआते हुए कहा, "पर यह आशा नहीं थी कि इक्कू भैया भी साथ आएँगे। क्यों, तुम्हारे माँ-बाप ने तुम्हें आने की इजाजत दे दी?"

"आंटी, अब मैं इतना छोटा नहीं हूँ कि हर बात में मुझे माँ-बाप की इजाजत लेनी पड़े।"

बेला की माँ ने अपने लिए आज तक किसी के मुँह से आंटी शब्द नहीं सुना था। उसका चेहरा एकदम खिल गया—"बेटा, अब तुम आ ही गए हो तो खाना खिलाए बगैर मैं तुम्हें जाने नहीं दूँगी।"

इसका जवाब पंजी ने दिया—"देखो बेला की अम्मा, हम तो यह फैसला करके ही आए हैं कि खाना खाकर ही जाएँगे। अब जरा हमें बेला के पास ले चलो, अपनी बिटिया रानी से तो हम मिल लें।"

बेला की माँ दोनों को मकान के अंदर ले गई। बेला दुलहन बनी अपनी बहनों, सहेलियों से घिरी बैठी थी। इन्हें देखकर उसकी आँखों में कई रंग उभर आए। उसने इक्कू को बहुत सरल आँखों से देखा और पंजी से बोली, "आप आई हैं, इससे मुझे बड़ी खुशी हुई है।"

पंजी ने उसे कलावे में लेकर उसका माथा चूमा और दो जड़ाऊ कंगन उसके हाथ में थमा दिए।

इक्कू बोला, "शादी मुबारक हो बेला।"

बेला की आँखें उस पर टिक गईं, पर बोली कुछ नहीं।

"तुम्हारे लिए यह छोटी सी गिफ्ट लाया हूँ।" इक्कू ने जेब से केस में बंद घड़ी निकाली और उसे थमा दी।

बेला ने मुट्ठी भींच ली और आँखें झुका लीं।

बारात आई। दूल्हा बी.ए. पास और म्युनिसिपल कॉरपोरेशन में लोअर डिवीजन कलर्क था। बारात का स्वागत हुआ, मिलनी हुई, फिर खाना-पीना हुआ।

वापस लौटते हुए इक्कू ने कहा, "आंटी, खाना कितना स्वादिष्ट था। बड़ा मजा आया।"

पंजी हँसी—"मिर्च दिल खोलकर डाली गई थी।"

इस बार शनिवार-समाज तिक्काजी के घर में मिला था।

"सुना है, आप मिलखूराम की लौंडिया की शादी में शामिल हुई थीं।" तिक्काजी की आवाज में व्यंग्य, तिरस्कार और न जाने क्या-क्या मिला हुआ था।

"जिसका जिक्र आप कर रहे हैं, उसका नाम बेला है। उसे मैं अपनी बेटी की तरह मानती हूँ।" पंजी तिनककर बोली।

दुक्काजी बोले, "इस बात के दो पहलू हैं। आप उसमें शामिल हुईं, यह कोई एतराज की बात नहीं है। दरअसल, मैं भी वहाँ जाना चाहता था। यह बात अलग है कि मैं वहाँ कुछ खाता-पीता नहीं। दूसरा पहलू यह है कि आप अपने साथ इक्कू को भी ले गईं। क्या यह ठीक था?"

सभी लोग इक्काजी की तरफ देखने लगे। उनके रुख से यह भी आभास हो रहा था कि इस संबंध में उनमें पहले भी चर्चा हो चुकी है।

इक्काजी ने अपनी चिरपरिचित मुद्रा में बोलना शुरू किया--"इक्कू के जाने में वैसे तो मुझे कोई एतराज नहीं है। लेकिन ये उसकी पढ़ाई के दिन हैं, वहाँ उसकी पूरी एक शाम बरबाद हो गई। वैसे मैं इक्कू की माँ से कह गया था कि कोई-न-कोई अच्छा उपहार वह बेला के लिए जरूर भिजवा दे।"

चौकाजी ने उनकी बात को बीच में ही काट दिया—"मेरी पत्नी ने तो ग्यारह रुपए आठ-दस दिन पहले ही बेला की माँ को दे दिए थे शगुन के।"

"लेकिन इक्काजी, आपने तो इक्कू के हाथ बेला को सचमुच बड़ा खूबसूरत उपहार भिजवाया। एच.एम.टी. की लेडीज वाच चार-साढ़े सौ रुपए की जरूर रही होगी।"

पंजी के इस रहस्योद्‌घाटन से वहाँ एकदम सन्नाटा छा गया। इक्काजी के चेहरे का रंग ऐसा हो गया जैसे वे बहुत दिन से बीमार हों।

पंजी जानती थी कि इक्कू ने वह घड़ी अपने घरवालों से छिपाकर दी होगी। वह यह भी समझती थी कि यह बात बताकर उसने इक्कू के लिए मुसीबत खड़ी कर दी है। वह यह भी जानती थी कि वह यह रहस्य खोलेगी तो गहरे सन्नाटे की सीटी बड़ी तेजी से सभी के कानों में बजने लगेगी। लेकिन वह इस स्थिति का मजा लेना चाहती थी। ऐसा मौका वह कभी नहीं चूकती।

इक्काजी ने अपने आप को तुरंत सँभाल लिया—"मैंने इक्कू की माँ से कहा ही था। कोई अच्छा सा उपहार भिजवाना। ऐसे कामों में इक्कू तो मुझसे हमेशा ही दो कदम आगे रहता है। आई एम प्राउड ऑफ हिम।"

"यह तो मैं भी मानता हूँ।" तिक्काजी बोले, "गरीबों और बेसहारा लोगों की जितनी हो सके, उतनी मदद करनी चाहिए।"

चौकाजी के मन में आया—"यह बताकर मैंने बड़ी गलती की कि मैंने ग्यारह रुपए दिए हैं। एक सौ एक कह देता तो क्या कोई पूछने जाता।"

वे अपनी गरदन उसी तरह हिला रहे थे और पंजी बस मुसकराए जा रही थी।

दरवाजे की घंटी बजी, दरवाजा खुला और बहुत सकुचाती हुई दो-तीन शक्लें दरवाजे के पास ही खड़ी दिखाई दीं। उनमें से एक बोला, "हम लोग सफाई कर्मचारी हैं। आपकी गली और सड़कें साफ करते हैं।"

सुनकर पंजी खिलखिलाकर हँसी—"घबराइए मत, हम लोग भी वही हैं। हमारे चेहरे नहीं देखते? सफाई देते-देते कितने मटमैले हो गए हैं।"

आगंतुकों की समझ में कुछ नहीं आया।

"जी, हम लोग अपने देवता सुग्गा पीर का दिन मना रहे हैं। कल शाम को सुग्गा पीर महाराज की कथा होगी, फिर परसाद बँटेगा। हम आपको न्योता देने आए हैं। आप दो मिनट के लिए दरसन देंगे तो हमें बड़ी खुशी होगी।"

तिक्काजी तपाक से बोले, "क्यों नहीं, क्यों नहीं, तुम लोगों की खुशी में ही हमारी खुशी है…।"

दुक्काजी बोले, "पहले तो यह बताइए कि ये सुग्गा पीर कौन है? दूसरी बात यह बताइए कि इनकी कथा कौन सुनाता है?"

वही व्यक्ति बोला, "जैसे आप लोगों के बहुत से देवता हैं, वैसे ही हमारे भी कुछ देवता हैं। सुग्गा पीर भी उन्हीं में एक हैं। इनकी कथा हमारी बिरादरी के भगत पूरनमलजी सुनाते हैं। सुग्गा पीर सभी की मुरादें पूरी करते हैं।"

इक्काजी ने बड़ी संजीदगी से कहा, "यह तो धर्म का काम है। पुन्न का काम है। आप लोगों में भी यह भावना बढ़ रही है, यह देखकर मुझे बड़ी प्रसन्नता हो रही है।"

चौकाजी ने भी अपनी जानी-पहचानी मुद्रा में गरदन हिलाई और फुसफुसाए—"बहुत अच्छा काम है। सचमुच बहुत अच्छा काम है।"

चलते हुए उन्होंने एक बार फिर कहा, "आप लोग जरूर दरसन दीजिएगा।"

"क्यों नहीं।"

"ये तो बड़ी खुशी की बात है जो…।"

"भगवान् तो सभी के साझे होते हैं भाई! देवता देवता में कोई अंतर थोड़े ही होता है।" आखिरी बात इक्काजी ने कही।

उनके जाने के बाद कुछ देर तक कोई कुछ नहीं बोला। फिर पंजी इतने जोर से हँसी कि उसकी आवाज आसपास के फ्लैटों में रहनेवालों को भी सुनाई दी।

□

धुँधलका

उसे लगता है, उसके पास सबकुछ है। वह संसद् की सदस्य है। इस नाते पूरी कोठी, टेलीफोन, रेल और हवाई यात्रा सहित उसके पास अनगिनत सुविधाएँ हैं। उसकी पार्टी आज सत्ता में नहीं है। पर इससे क्या होता है? वर्षों तक उसकी पार्टी सत्ता में रही है। अगले चुनाव के बाद वह फिर सत्ता में आ सकती है। उस समय उसका मंत्री बन जाना कोई रोक नहीं सकता। आज उसे पार्टी के अध्यक्ष के बहुत निकट समझा जाता है। वह दो राज्यों में पार्टी के सभी कार्यकलापों की इंचार्ज है। वहाँ उसकी मरजी के बिना पत्ता भी नहीं हिलता।

पिछले दिनों इन दोनों राज्यों की विधानसभाओं के आम चुनाव हुए थे। उम्मीदवारों के चुनाव टिकटों के बँटवारे और चुनाव-प्रचार के लिए साधनों की सारी व्यवस्था उसकी आँखों के सामने से गुजरी थी। लाखों रुपए उसकी उँगलियों का स्पर्श लेते हुए निकल जाते थे। सभी उम्मीदवार चाहते थे कि पार्टी के अध्यक्ष एक बार उनके क्षेत्र का दौरा अवश्य करें। उनके नाम में ही ऐसा जादू था कि लोग उन्हें सुनने नहीं, मात्र उनका दर्शन करने के लिए उमड़ आते थे। सभी यह बात भी अच्छी तरह जानते थे कि यदि सविताजी चाहेंगी तो सुधाकर बाबू उनके क्षेत्र का दौरा करने का समय अवश्य निकाल लेंगे।

किंतु इन दोनों राज्यों में उनकी पार्टी की सरकार बनते-बनते रह गई। केंद्र में उनकी पार्टी की सरकार नहीं थी, हालाँकि देश के कुछ राज्यों में उनकी सरकारें थीं। सविता को आशा थी कि दोनों में न सही, कम-से-कम एक राज्य में तो उनकी सरकार बन ही जाएगी। उन्होंने जोड़-तोड़ की सारी तैयारी कर रखी थी। टूटकर आनेवाले विधायकों को कितना धन दिया जाएगा, कौन सा मंत्रि पद उन्हें मिलेगा, किस कॉरपोरेशन का अध्यक्ष पद किसे दिया जा सकता है, उसने पूरी सूची तैयार कर ली थी, पर ऐन मौके पर पासा पलट गया। एक राज्य में तो विरोधी दलों के गठबंधन को स्पष्ट बहुमत

मिल गया और दूसरे राज्य में विपक्ष के नेता ने अपना घोड़ा सीधी सड़क पर न दौड़ाकर उसे पहाड़ियों के शॉर्टकट से दौड़ाया और पूरे नतीजे आने से पहले ही जीत की ओर बढ़ते कदमों की आहट लेकर जर-जोरू-जमीन की सभी सुविधाओं के दरवाजों के द्वार उन संभावित विधायकों के लिए खोल दिए गए, जिन्हें मोहपाश में बाँधा जाना था।

वह पार्टी के अनेक साथियों की आँखें और होंठ परख रही थी। वह उस भाषा को अच्छी तरह पढ़ सकती थी जो उनकी आँखों और होंठों से बोली जा रही थी। पार्टी की हार का उन्हें मलाल था। लेकिन यह तो सविता की निजी हार मानी जा रही थी। बड़ी तेज फड़फड़ाने वाली कबूतरी के कुछ पंख जरूर टूट गए, यह बात कितने लोगों को सुख दे रही थी।

लेकिन सुधाकरजी ने उसे कलावे में लेते हुए कहा था—''सविता, सभी राज्यों में राजनीति के घोड़े तो दौड़ते ही रहते हैं, कभी किसी का घोड़ा आगे, कभी किसी का। इधर-उधर की बातें करने वालों की तुम चिंता न करना। ईर्ष्या-द्वेष मनुष्य के स्वभाव का अंग हैं। इसे तो देवता भी नहीं छोड़ पाए। मैं जल्दी ही पार्टी की कार्यकारिणी की मीटिंग बुला रहा हूँ। उसमें हम चुनाव परिणामों पर खुलकर विचार करेंगे। उस मीटिंग में अगर तुम्हारी कुछ आलोचना भी हो तो उससे घबराना नहीं। मैं हूँ न तुम्हारे साथ।''

यह कहते-कहते सुधाकरजी के कलावे की पकड़ में कसाव कुछ और बढ़ गया था।

शाम को अपनी कोठी के आगे के बड़े लॉन में वह अकेली चुपचाप बैठी हुई थी। आमतौर पर इस कोठी पर आने-जाने वालों की भीड़ लगी रहती थी। अपनी बैठक में वह एक-एक कर सबसे मिलती थी। फिर भी बहुत से लोग वहाँ घुस आते थे। सविता को बहुत झुँझलाहट होती थी। अपने बिलकुल पास बैठे हुए व्यक्ति से वह धीरे-धीरे बातें करती रहती थी। बिन बुलाए अंदर आनेवाले व्यक्ति अभिवादन करके सामने लगे सोफों पर बैठ जाते थे।

आज उसने गेट पर तैनात गार्ड से कह दिया था, आज मैं किसी से नहीं मिलूँगी। कोई भी आए, कह देना—मैं घर में नहीं हूँ। गेट के पास ही उनके निजी सचिव का छोटा सा कमरा था। उससे भी उसने कह दिया था—किसी का भी फोन आए, कह देना, मैं कहीं गई हूँ। मुझे डिस्टर्ब न करना। हाँ, अगर सुधाकरजी के पी.ए. का फोन आ जाए तो मेरी बात करा देना।

लॉन में थोड़ा-थोड़ा अँधेरा छाने लगा था। वहाँ उसने अधिक रोशनी करने से भी मना कर दिया था। अक्तूबर का महीना था। शाम को हल्की-हल्की ठंड महसूस होने लगी थी। नौकरानी से शॉल मँगवाकर उसने ओढ़ ली थी।

वह सोचने लगी, कभी-कभी ऐसी उदासी का दौर उस पर क्यों आ जाता है। ऐसी उदासी उसकी हड्डियों को मरोड़ने लगती है। सबकुछ बहुत व्यर्थ लगने लगता है,

बिलकुल बेमतलब। उस समय न किसी से बात करने का मन करता है, न कुछ करने का। उसे पढ़ने का शौक है। कितनी ही किताबें वह खरीदती रहती है। उसकी बैठक की बीच की मेज नई-नई पत्रिकाओं से भरी रहती है। पिछले दिनों उसने रॉबर्ट पेन के अंग्रेजी उपन्यास का हिंदी अनुवाद खरीदा था—'कत्लगाह'। यह उपन्यास सन् 1971 के भारत-पाक युद्ध और बँगलादेश के निर्माण पर था। उस समय पाकिस्तानी सैनिकों ने बंगालियों पर जो जुल्म किए थे, उसकी निर्मम गाथा इस उपन्यास में थी। यह उपन्यास वह लगभग आधा पढ़ चुकी थी। अत्याचारों, नरसंहारों, युद्धों की कथाएँ पढ़ने में उसका मन बहुत रमता था। चंगेज खाँ, हलाकू खाँ से लेकर हिटलर तक के नरसंहारों पर छपी हर पुस्तक उसके पास थी।

लेकिन आज उसका मन 'कत्लगाह' पढ़ने में नहीं लग रहा था। लॉन में बैठकर पढ़ने के लिए वह इसे बाहर ले आई थी। नौकर ने वहाँ रोशनी भी लगा दी थी। उसने दो-चार पृष्ठ पढ़े भी थे। फिर उसका मन उचट गया था। उसने पुस्तक बंद करके एक ओर रख दी थी और आँखें बंद कर ली थीं।

आज उसने अपने बेटे की तस्वीर किसी पत्रिका में देखी थी। उसके कॉलेज की क्रिकेट टीम ने किसी दूसरे कॉलेज की टीम को बुरी तरह हराया था। उसके बेटे ने सेंचुरी मारी थी। उसे मैन ऑफ द मैच घोषित किया गया था। वह अब यूनिवर्सिटी टीम का कैप्टन बन गया था।

वह उसके बारे में सोचने लगी।

राहुल से मिले, उसको देखे कई महीने गुजर गए। राज्यों में होने वाले चुनावों में वह इतनी व्यस्त रही थी कि सबकुछ भूल गई। पार्टी कार्यकर्ताओं से वह दिन-रात, घिरी रहती थी। उसकी व्यक्ति इकाई जैसे मिट गई थी। पार्टी, कार्यकर्ता, भीड़, नारे, दौरे, प्रचार ही उसमें रह गए थे। हर मिलने वाला चेहरा उसे भीड़ का एक चेहरा लगता था— सिर्फ एक चेहरे के बिना, सुधाकरजी का चेहरा। भीड़, चुनाव प्रचार, बड़ी सभाएँ, धुआँधार भाषण—इन सबके बीच, इन सबके ऊपर यही एक चेहरा उसके सम्मुख तिरता रहता था।

सुधाकर से उसकी मुलाकात पंद्रह वर्ष पहले हुई होगी। उस समय राहुल पाँच साल का होगा। जिस स्कूल में वह पढ़ाती थी, उसका वार्षिक दिवस समारोह था। सुधाकर उस समारोह का मुख्य अतिथि बनकर आया था। वह पार्टी के युवा मोर्चे का अध्यक्ष था। उसके बारे में यह कहा जाने लगा था कि वह पार्टी में बहुत आगे जाएगा, किसी दिन पार्टी का अध्यक्ष भी बन सकता है। पार्टी के अध्यक्ष पटवर्धनजी बूढ़े होते जा रहे थे। वे प्राय: कहा करते थे कि युवा पीढ़ी को आगे आकर नेतृत्व सँभालना चाहिए। जब वे ऐसा कहते थे, सबकी नजर अनायास सुधाकर की ओर उठ जाती थी।

छह फुट वाला सुधाकर सदा छोटी मोहरी का पाजामा और लंबा सफेद कुरता पहनता था। उसके पैरों में सदा पेशावरी सैंडल होते थे। सर्दियों के मौसम में वह कुरते के नीचे पूरी बाँह का सफेद स्वेटर पहनता था और शॉल उसके कंधों पर पड़ी होती थी।

स्कूल के समारोह का संचालन सविता कर रही थी। जब विद्यार्थियों के पुरस्कार वितरण का समय आया तो वह सुधाकर के बिलकुल साथ खड़ी थी। कोई अन्य अध्यापिका विद्यार्थी का नाम पुकारती थी और उसे दिया जाने वाला पुरस्कार सविता सुधाकर को पकड़ाती थी। विद्यार्थी आगे आकर पुरस्कार ग्रहण करता था। बीच-बीच में सविता उस विद्यार्थी के संबंध में बहुत धीरे-धीरे सुधाकर को कुछ बताती थी। वह बहुत मुसकराते हुए उसकी बात सुनता था। समारोह पूरा हुआ तो जलपान करते हुए सुधाकर ने कहा, 'सविताजी, आप मंच संचालन बहुत अच्छा करती हैं। आप के शब्दों का चुनाव तो अद्‌भुत है और वाणी में कितनी मिठास है।'

सविता के चेहरे पर चमक आ गई थी। कृतज्ञता भरे स्वर में उसने कहा था, ''यह मेरा सौभाग्य है कि आप जैसे लोकप्रिय नेता के मुँह से मैं ऐसे शब्द सुन रही हूँ।''

'मैं अतिशयोक्ति नहीं कर रहा हूँ, सविताजी।' सुधाकर की आँखों में सचमुच प्रशंसा का भाव था। ''आप जैसी प्रतिभा को तो फलने-फूलने के लिए एक बड़ी दुनिया मिलनी चाहिए।''

विदाई के समय स्कूल की प्रिंसिपल मिसेज मैथ्यू ने सुधाकर से हाथ मिलाया, फिर उसने सविता की तरफ हाथ बढ़ा दिया।

सुधाकर के हाथों का स्पर्श कई दिन तक उसके शरीर में झनझनाहट बनकर गूँजता रहा।

सुदर्शन की सरकारी अफसरी और सविता की स्कूल की टीचरी से जो मिलता था, उससे उनकी गिरहस्ती की गाड़ी दुपहिए स्कूटर की रफ्तार ठीक से पकड़ लेती थी। आमतौर पर सुदर्शन सविता को सुबह सात बजे स्कूल के दरवाजे पर उतार आता था। राहुल को लेकर उस समय तक कुछ परेशानी हुई जब तक वह तीन साल का नहीं हुआ। उसके बाद सविता उसे अपने साथ ही ले जाने लगी थी।

किसी स्थिर तालाब के किनारे बैठना कितना अच्छा लगता है। पानी में हल्की-हल्की लहरें आती रहती हैं। कभी-कभी कोई चिड़िया या कौवा आकर उसमें चोंच मारता है। पानी में हल्की सी हलचल होती है। किनारे बैठे लोग भी इतनी शांत स्थिरता देखकर कभी-कभी ऊबने लगते हैं। तब वे किनारे से छोटी सी कंकड़ी उठाकर उसमें फेंक देते हैं। पानी में छप सी होती है। लहरों में कुछ उछाल पैदा हो जाती है। किनारे बैठे व्यक्ति को अच्छा लगता है।

सविता की स्थिर जिंदगी के तालाब में सुधाकर एक कंकड़ी बनकर नहीं, पूरा

बड़ा पत्थर बनकर गिरा था।

वह पहले पार्टी के युवा मोर्चे की मेंबर बनी। फिर अपने मंडल की सचिव चुन ली गई। फिर वह पूरे नगर की सचिव बन गई।

कुछ सीढ़ियों की बनावट बहुत विचित्र होती है। उसमें ऊपर जाने वाली और नीचे उतरने वाली सीढ़ियाँ साथ-साथ काम करती हैं। जिन सीढ़ियों से व्यक्ति ऊपर चढ़ रहा होता है, पास की ही दूसरी सीढ़ियों से वह नीचे उतर रहा होता है। सविता के साथ भी ऐसा ही हुआ। वह राजनीति की सीढ़ियाँ चढ़ रही थी। सुधाकर युवा मोर्चे से निकलकर पार्टी की मुख्यधारा में आ गया था। जब वह पार्टी का महासचिव बना तो सविता पार्टी में शामिल कर ली गई और उसे महिला मोर्चे की जिम्मेदारी सौंप दी गई।

नीचे जाने वाली सीढ़ियों में उतनी रोशनी नहीं होती जितनी ऊपर चढ़ने वाली सीढ़ियों में होती है। ऊपर जाने वाली सीढ़ियों पर व्यक्ति मुँह ऊँचा करके चढ़ता है। महत्त्वाकांक्षाओं का संसार उसे सामने झिलमिलाता दिखाई देता है। नीचे जाने वाली सीढ़ियाँ उतरते समय व्यक्ति नीचे की तरफ देखता है और हर कदम पर फिसल जाने, चूक जाने का डर बना रहता है।

एक दिन सुदर्शन ने उससे कहा था, 'सविता, जिस रास्ते पर तुम चल पड़ी हो, वह कहीं थमने वाला रास्ता नहीं है। एक स्कूल टीचर ऊपर चढ़ता हुआ सीनियर टीचर बन जाता है। ज्यादा-से-ज्यादा प्रिंसिपल बनता है और रिटायर हो जाता है। मेरे जैसा सरकारी अफसर, जिसने जिंदगी एल.डी.सी. से शुरू की हो, कहाँ तक जाएगा···सेक्शन ऑफिसर तक, बहुत जोर मारेगा तो अंडर सेक्रेटरी तक। मैं तुमसे यह नहीं कह सकता कि तुम वापस आ जाओ। यह भी सच है कि तुम मुझे कितना भी खींचो, मैं तुम्हारा सहयात्री नहीं बन सकता···हमारे रास्ते भी अलग हो रहे हैं और दिशाएँ भी।''

सविता गुमसुम सी उसकी बातें सुन रही थी। पिछले कुछ वर्षों में उसके पारिवारिक जीवन में बहुत अंतर आ गया था। राहुल अपनी बढ़ती उम्र के साथ स्कूली पढ़ाई के अंतिम पड़ाव पर आ गया था। पहले उसने स्कूल से तीन वर्ष की छुट्टी ले ली थी। फिर सुधाकर ने उससे कहा था, 'यह टीचरी-फीचरी छोड़ो और सारा समय पार्टी को दो। चिंता न करो, पार्टी तुम्हारी जरूरतों का ध्यान रखेगी।'

सुधाकर ने अपनी बात पूरी की। वह उस प्रदेश से राज्यसभा के लिए चुन ली गई, जहाँ पार्टी के विधायकों की काफी गिनती थी।

जब लोधी एस्टेट में सविता को एक लंबी-चौड़ी कोठी एलॉट हो गई तो उसने सुदर्शन से कहा, ''अब हम लोग उस कोठी में शिफ्ट कर सकते हैं। अपना यह फ्लैट किराए पर उठा देते हैं। कम-से-कम छह वर्ष तो हमें यहाँ से कोई नहीं हिलाएगा।''

सुदर्शन के सामने एक दृश्य घूमने लगा, कोठी पर आने-जाने वालों का ताँता लगा

हुआ है। वहाँ लगातार एक शब्द गूँजता रहता है सविताजी···सविताजी···। वहाँ उसका एकमात्र परिचय है—सुदर्शन मेहरा—सविताजी के पति।

उसे एक बात और साल रही थी। उस कोठी के हर कोने में एक छाया व्यापी हुई होगी, जिसका चेहरा-मोहरा सुधाकर से कितना मिलता-जुलता होगा।

उसने कहा, ''सविता, मैं यह फ्लैट छोड़कर कहीं नहीं जाऊँगा। तुम कहाँ रहना चाहती हो, यह फैसला तुम कर लो।''

''आप मेरी बात समझते क्यों नहीं?'' सविता ने बड़े अधिकार भरे स्वर में कहा था, ''मैं संसद् सदस्या हूँ। पार्टी की सीनियर लीडर हूँ। मुझसे मिलने के लिए सैकड़ों लोग रोज आते हैं। पत्रकारों की भीड़ लगी रहती है। इस फ्लैट में तो यह नहीं हो सकता।''

जो हो सकता था, वही हुआ। सविता राहुल को अपने साथ रखना चाहती थी, किंतु सुदर्शन इसके लिए तैयार नहीं हुआ। राहुल भी अपने पिता के साथ रहना चाहता था। सविता अपनी पुरानी नौकरानी के साथ नई कोठी में आ गई।

वह पीछे कुछ छोड़ आई है, इसका कभी उसे एहसास नहीं हुआ। जिन ऊँचाइयों पर वह उड़ रही थी, वहाँ पीछे मुड़कर देखने का न ही समय था न कोई अकुलाहट, उड़ते-भागते क्षणों में जब कभी उसे लगता कि उसकी गाड़ी के चक्कों में कुछ चूँ-चूँ होने लगी है तो सुधाकर के कलावे को स्निग्धता उसमें तेल का काम कर देती थी।

लेकिन आज इस धुँधलाई शाम में अँधेरे में चुपचाप बैठी वह सोचने लगी, उसका एक अपना घर है, तीन कमरों वाला छोटा सा फ्लैट। उसका पति है, जो रोज उसे अपने स्कूटर पर बैठाकर स्कूल छोड़ने जाता था और मुड़ने से पहले मुसकराता था और उसका हाथ दबाता था। उसका एक बेटा है। वह कॉलेज में पहुँच गया है। क्रिकेट का अच्छा खिलाड़ी है। टीम का कप्तान बन गया है। उसे याद नहीं कि उसकी मसें कब फूटी थीं। पिछली बार जब उसने उसे देखा था, वह शेव किए हुए था।

एकाएक उसे कुछ चुभने लगा। उसके चारों ओर अँधेरा अधिक गहरा होने लगा। वह सोचने लगी, राहुल धीरे-धीरे कैसे बड़ा हुआ होगा, कब उसकी मसें फूटी होंगी, कब उसने पहली बार शेव किया होगा। उसके सामने सुदर्शन की तस्वीर भी घूमने लगी। उसके बालों में कितनी सफेदी आ गई है। पिछली बार जब वह उससे मिली थी, वह बता रहा था कि शायद वह प्रीमेच्योर रिटायरमेंट की स्कीम में रिटायरमेंट ले ले, पर वह सेवा मुक्त होने के बाद करेगा क्या?

वह अँधेरे में आँखें बंद किए बैठी थी। एकाएक उसे लगा, उसके पास कुछ भी नहीं है, वह बहुत अकेली है।

□

अंतराल

सोलह साल की उम्र में वह अपनी माँ के साथ इस देश में आया। माँ ने बताया था कि जब वह डेढ़-दो साल का था, वह उसे लेकर भारत आई थी। उसके बाद न माँ आई, न वह आया। सबकुछ न्यूजर्सी में ही हुआ, माँ एक बड़े 'मॉल' के कैश काउंटर पर काम करती थी। वह ऐसे स्कूल में पढ़ता था, जिसमें अमेरिकी गोरे लड़के-लड़कियाँ ही ज्यादा थे। थोड़े से काले और कुछ एशियायी।

स्कूल में प्रवेश के समय माँ ने अपने आप को तलाकशुदा लिखा था। वह उसकी संरक्षक थी। धीरे-धीरे उसे पता लगने लगा कि उसका बाप दिल्ली में है। कई साल तक वह आगरा के पागलखाने में रहा है। अब उसके भाई उसे वापस ले आए हैं। माँ को पता नहीं, उसका क्या हाल है।

जब वे दोनों अमेरिका से चले थे, उसने माँ से कहा था—'वहाँ मैं पापा से मिलूँगा।'

सरोज ने उसे बड़ी नम आँखों से देखा—'मनु, न तुम उन्हें पहचान सकोगे, न वे तुम्हें।'

'तो क्या हुआ? आखिर वो मेरे पापा हैं, मैं उनका बेटा हूँ।'

'मैंने तुम्हें पाला है···माँ की तरह भी, बाप की तरह भी।'

'माँ!' उसके स्वर में कुछ खीझ उभर आई थी—'इससे यह सच्चाई तो नहीं बदल गई!' कि मेरी एक मम्मी है, एक पापा भी। मुझे यह भी पता है कि उनकी दिमागी हालत ठीक नहीं है···बरसों तक वो पागलखाने में रहे हैं, फिर भी वो मेरे पापा हैं।'

सरोज ने उसके चेहरे को पढ़ने की कोशिश की—मनु बड़ा हो गया है, वह बहुत कुछ समझता है, उससे ज्यादा समझता है, जितना वह सोचती थी।

'गुड़गाँव में हम तुम्हारे मामाजी के पास ही रहेंगे।' वह बोली, 'उनसे भी सलाह कर लेंगे।'

'क्या तुम उनसे नहीं मिलना चाहोगी?'

'नहीं।' उसने अपना मुँह दूसरी तरफ मोड़ लिया।

जब उसको पता लगा था कि उसकी शादी की बात उस व्यक्ति से चल रही है जो अमेरिका में रहता है। वह बहुत पढ़ा-लिखा है। उसके पास बहुत अच्छी नौकरी है, न्यूजर्सी में उसका अपना फ्लैट है। उसने उसी वर्ष एम.ए. की परीक्षा दी थी। उसके माँ-बाप ने सोचा था, उसे बी.एड. करा देंगे। वह किसी स्कूल में टीचर लग जाएगी। शादी से पहले अगर वह दो-तीन साल नौकरी कर लेगी तो कुछ पैसा इकट्ठा हो जाएगा। सरकारी नौकर होने के कारण उसके पिता को क्वार्टर मिला हुआ था। अब रिटायरमेंट की तेज घंटियाँ उसके कानों में बजने लगी थीं। उसे पता था, जब ये घंटियाँ बजनी बंद हो जाएँगी तो सामने एक दोमुँहा साँप फुफकारता हुआ दिखाई देगा—सरकारी क्वार्टर छिन जाने के बाद सिर पर एक छत चाहिए और तीन लड़कियों के लिए वर।

विवाह करवाने वाली एक एजेंसी ने दीवान चंद को बताया, विनोद अमेरिका से आया हुआ है। तीन साल पहले ही उसकी शादी दिल्ली के एक वकील घराने में हुई थी। मीमांसा ने भी वकालत की डिग्री ले ली थी। शादी के बाद वह विनोद के साथ अमेरिका चली गई। वहाँ दोनों में पटी नहीं और मीमांसा ने कानूनी लड़ाई लड़कर विनोद से तलाक ले लिया।

एजेंसी मालिक ने एक बात बताई। मीमांसा किसी तरह अमेरिका जाना चाहती थी। किंतु उसे वीजा नहीं मिल रहा था। अमेरिका में बसे किसी व्यक्ति से शादी करने से वहाँ जाने का रास्ता खुल जाता था। उसने वही रास्ता अपनाया।

मीमांसा के साथ उसका विवाहित जीवन छह महीने से अधिक नहीं चला था। इन महीनों में उसने अपने और विनोद के बीच एक पारदर्शी दीवार खड़ी कर रखी थी। विनोद दीवार के उस पार झाँककर देखता था, लेकिन उसे छू नहीं सकता था। एक हिरणी की तरह कुलाचें भरती हुई मीमांसा उसे दिखाई देती थी। उस समय विनोद की स्थिति एक हिंसक पशु की तरह हो जाती थी। वह व्याकुल हो जाता था। कभी-कभी गुर्राता भी था।

ऐसे ही एक बार बहुत गुर्राते हुए जब उसने बीच की दीवार को तोड़कर हिरणी को दबोचने की कोशिश की थी। हिरणी ने अपने शरीर पर दो-चार जख्म हो जाने दिए थे। खून से रिसते हुए जख्मों को लेकर वह पुलिस के पास पहुँच गई थी। पति बहुत क्रूर है, अपनी पत्नी के साथ बहुत दुर्व्यवहार करता है, तलाक के लिए ये तर्क पर्याप्त थे।

एक अदद बीवी की तलाश में वह फिर दिल्ली आ गया। अपने लिए एक अच्छी लड़की ढूँढ़ने के लिए उसने मैरिज ब्यूरो के मालिक मिस्टर सूद को अच्छी-खासी रकम दे दी।

सूद कह रहा था—'दीवान चंदजी, आपकी लड़की के लिए विनोद बहुत अच्छा वर है। यह ठीक है कि जिस लड़की से पहले उसकी शादी हुई थी, अब वह उसकी जिंदगी में नहीं है। उससे उसका तलाक हो गया है। लेकिन यह बात अब किसी से छिपी नहीं है कि उस लड़की की अधिक रुचि अमेरिका की नागरिकता लेने में थी, न कि शादी करने में। अमेरिका में बसे किसी व्यक्ति से शादी करना उसके लिए वहाँ जाने का एक वसीला था, लेकिन आप की लड़की वहाँ बहुत सुखी रहेगी।'

दीवान चंद ने हिसाब लगाया—अपनी बिरादरी में सरोज के विवाह का अर्थ है कि कुछ लाख रुपए, फिर दूसरी···फिर तीसरी। उसकी पत्नी ने समझाया—लड़का दुहाजू है तो क्या हुआ। उसकी पहली शादी तो न होने के बराबर थी। एक लड़की अमेरिका चली गई तो न सिर्फ हमारा बोझ हलका होगा, वह अपनी छोटी बहनों की शादी में भी मददगार हो जाएगी।

सरोज ने माता-पिता की बात मान ली। जिस रास्ते पर उसे चलना था, उस पर झिलमिलाहट तो बहुत थी, पर बहुत अनताना था। जहाँ वह खड़ी थी वहाँ रोशनी बड़ी मद्धिम थी। उसमें सरकारी नौकरी से रिटायर होने वाले पिता के सफेद बाल नजर आते थे, तीन लड़कियों के नित बड़े होते जाने की चिंता ने माँ की आँखों की रोशनी कितनी कम कर दी थी। ऐसी मद्धिम रोशनी में रास्ते में पड़े तीन बड़े-बड़े पत्थरों से टकराकर लहूलुहान हो जाने का कितना डर था।

उसने झिलमिलाती दुनिया चुन ली और अमेरिका पहुँच गई।

विनोद के जीवन से मीमांसा चली गई थी। वह उसके जीवन में आई पहली औरत थी। अमेरिका में रहते उसे कई वर्ष गुजर गए थे। उसे लगता रहा कि वह किसी फिश-एक्वेरियम के बाहर खड़ा अनेक रंग-बिरंगी मछलियों को देख रहा है, जो बड़ी लुभावनी हैं किंतु जिन्हें वह छू नहीं सकता। बार-बार उसे लगता, वह बड़ा कुरूप व्यक्ति है। अपने चारों ओर बिखरी सुंदरता उसे बुरी तरह कचोटती थी। मीमांसा के साथ बिताए कुछ समय ने उसे मानसिक रूप से कितना विकृत कर दिया था। उसे वह बाकायदा शादी करके दिल्ली से लाया था। वह एक्वेरियम की मछली नहीं थी। उस पर उसका पूरा हक था। वह उसे पूरी तरह पा लेना चाहता था। किंतु मीमांसा ने बीच में एक ऐसी दीवार खड़ी कर दी थी, जिस पर वह एक खूँखार पशु की भाँति अपने पंजे मारता रहता था।

अब उसके जीवन में आ गई थी सरोज। वह कुलाँचें मारती हुई हिरणी नहीं थी, न हाथों से फिसलती हुई मछली थी। वह थी एक बकरी। सरकारी दफ्तर में काम करने वाले सामान्य गृहस्थ की तीन बेटियों में से एक, जिससे यह आशा की गई थी कि विदेश में काम करने वाला अच्छा कमाऊ पति पाकर वह अपनी दो छोटी बहनों की नैया पार लगाने में कुछ मदद करेगी।

शेर का शिकार करने वाले प्राय: एक ढंग अपनाते हैं। जिस ओर से शेर को आना होता है, वहाँ वे जाल बिछाकर एक बकरी बाँध देते हैं। वह अपने शिकार की ओर बढ़ता है और शिकारी के जाल में फँस जाता है।

विनोद के सामने भी एक बकरी थी, जिसे वह चबा-चबाकर खाना चाहता था। सरोज ने उसे कुछ समय तक मनमानी करने दी। फिर उसे महसूस होने लगा कि उसका वास्ता एक पुरुष से न होकर किसी व्याघ्र से आ पड़ा है। पुरुष सान्निध्य के संबंध में उसने जो कुछ सुना था, वह बड़ा मोहक था। रस से भरा हुआ था। इस संबंध में उसे मोह नहीं, पीड़ा मिलने लगी थी। उसे रस के स्थान पर रक्त दिखने लगा था।

उसमें माँ बनने के लक्षण दिखाई देने लगे। कुछ समय बाद उसने विनोद को इसका अहसास कराया था। पर उसके चेहरे पर उसे खुशी की कोई झलक नहीं दिखाई दी थी। सरोज को लगता था, प्रतिदिन उसकी भूख बढ़ती जा रही है। उसके चढ़ते हुए दिनों में भी उसका रवैया वैसा ही था।

एक दिन उसने पूछा, "आप मुझसे भी मीमांसा का बदला ले रहे हैं?"

उसने बहुत घूरते हुए उसे देखा, "बदला कैसा? तुम मेरी पत्नी हो, तुम्हारी देह पर मेरा पूरा हक है, उसे मैं जब चाहूँ...जिस तरह चाहूँ भोग सकता हूँ।"

सरोज ने बड़े ठंडे स्वर में पूछा, "सिर्फ देह पर? क्या आपको इस बात का अहसास है कि मैं एक जीवित इनसान हूँ। मेरी अपनी भी कुछ भावनाएँ हैं, कुछ इच्छाएँ हैं। मैं मात्र एक देह नहीं हूँ।"

वह एकदम खीझ उठा था—"यह सब बकवास है। मैंने एक स्त्री से विवाह किया है। विवाह क्या है? एक स्त्री देह से अपनी भूख को तृप्ति देने की कानूनी मान्यता। उसमें भावना का दखल कहाँ है। इसी तृप्ति के लिए जो लोग वेश्याओं के पास जाते हैं, क्या वे भावना जैसी किसी चीज का बोझ अपने कंधों पर उठाकर ले जाते हैं?"

"आपकी दृष्टि में पत्नी और वेश्या में कोई अंतर नहीं है?"

उसकी बात पर विनोद हँस पड़ा था—"सिर्फ इतना कि यहाँ मोल-भाव नहीं करना पड़ता, अपनी बारी की बाट नहीं जोहनी पड़ती।"

उस दिन विनोद बहुत बौखला उठा था, जब उसे पता लगा कि सरोज ने एक डिपार्टमेंटल स्टोर में नौकरी कर ली है।

"तुम्हें नौकरी की क्या जरूरत है? मैं तुम्हें खाना-पीना तो दे ही रहा हूँ।"

सरोज ने बड़े ठंडे स्वर में कहा, "मैं एक वेश्या बनकर नहीं, एक स्त्री बनकर जीवित रहना चाहती हूँ।"

"क्या वेश्या स्त्री नहीं होती?"

"किसी का दिया हुआ चारा खाकर जीने वाली वह एक बकरी होती है।"

"अच्छा, अब यह बकरी हमारा दिया चारा नहीं खाएगी?"

"इसीलिए मैंने नौकरी कर ली है।"

"इस शेर को बकरी का मांस खाने की जो आदत पड़ गई है, उसका क्या होगा?"

"शेर की जगह जंगल में होती है या पिंजरे में। वहीं उसे अपना भोजन भी मिल जाता है।" विनोद के सामने जैसे एक भयानक विस्फोट हो गया हो। वह अपने ऑफिस से अभी लौटा ही था। ऑफिस में आज उसके बॉस से उसकी खासी कहा-सुनी हुई थी। बॉस ने उससे शिकायत की थी कि आजकल काम में उसका मन नहीं लगता। जो प्रोजेक्ट उसे दिया जाता है, वह समय से पूरा नहीं होता। उसके साथी भी यह शिकायत करते कि वह सदा बौखलाया सा रहता है। उसके साथ काम करने वाली लड़कियाँ कहती हैं कि उसकी आँखें देखकर वह उससे डरने लगी हैं। वह उन्हें बड़ा 'खूँखार' व्यक्ति लगता है।

उस रात सरोज भी उससे बहुत पीड़ित हुई थी, जैसे सारी रात वह एक भूखे जानवर से लड़ती रही हो।

दूसरे दिन जब विनोद ऑफिस गया हुआ था, उसने उसका घर छोड़ दिया और कामकाजी स्त्रियों के लिए बने एक हॉस्टल में चली गई। पीछे वह उसके लिए एक पत्र लिखकर छोड़ गई—शेर और बकरी यदि एक साथ रहेंगे तो मांस केवल बकरी का नुचेगा।

सरोज ने अपनी माँ को पत्र लिखा—मैं माँ बनने वाली हूँ। कुछ समय के लिए आप यहाँ आ जाइए। अमेरिका की एंबेसी के लिए एक पत्र भेज रही हूँ। इसके आधार पर आपको वीजा मिल जाएगा। आपको आने-जाने का टिकट भी भेज रही हूँ।

माँ अमेरिका पहुँच गई। सरोज ने न्यूजर्सी के एक भारतीय परिवार में पेइंग गेस्ट के रूप में एक कमरा ले लिया। वहीं उसने बच्चे को जन्म दिया।

एक दिन विनोद के बॉस ने सरोज को अपने दफ्तर में बुलाकर पूछा, "मैडम, क्या आप अपने पति के साथ नहीं रहतीं?"

सरोज ने कहा, "नहीं।"

"आप दोनों में अलगाव क्यों हो गया है, यह जानने में मेरी कोई रुचि नहीं है। पर लगता है, मिस्टर विनोद किसी मानसिक विकृति के शिकार हो गए हैं।"

बॉस कहता जा रहा था—

"उसका व्यवहार प्रतिदिन बहुत अब्नॉर्मल होता जा रहा है। दफ्तर में उसके साथ काम करने वाली महिलाएँ उससे बहुत डरने लगी हैं। वह जिस तरह से उन्हें घूरता है,

बहुत अजीब ढंग से उनसे पेश आता है, वह बहुत दहलाने वाला होता है।''

वह कुछ क्षण रुककर बोला, ''आप मिस्टर विनोद को किसी मनोचिकित्सक को दिखाइए।''

वह बोली, ''आप जानते ही हैं, मैं विनोद के साथ नहीं रहती।''

''क्या आप में तलाक हो गया है?'' उसने पूछा

''औपचारिक ढंग से तो अभी नहीं हुआ।''

''इसका मतलब यह है कि कानूनी तौर पर आप अभी उनकी पत्नी हैं।''

''आप ठीक कहते हैं।'' सरोज बोली, ''जबसे उनसे मेरा विवाह हुआ है, मुझे वे हमेशा अब्नॉर्मल लगे हैं।''

''क्या आप इस बात का कोई कारण समझ सकीं?''

''मुझसे पहले उन्होंने एक भारतीय लड़की से विवाह किया था। लेकिन उस लड़की से छह महीने के अंदर ही उनका तलाक हो गया था।''

बॉस कुछ सोचने लगा। बोला, ''मिस्टर विनोद की जो हालत है, मुझे नहीं लगता कि वे इस दफ्तर में ज्यादा दिन टिकेंगे।''

सचमुच वह उस दफ्तर में ज्यादा दिन नहीं टिका। उसकी नौकरी छूट गई। अमेरिका में किसी की नौकरी छूट जाना बड़ी बात नहीं है। एक छूटती है तो दूसरी मिल जाती है। उसने दो-चार जगह कोशिश भी की। किंतु उसके पीछे उससे पहले रिकॉर्ड की लंबी काली लकीर उसके साथ-साथ चलती हुई वहाँ पहुँच जाती।

उसके दफ्तर में उसका एक भारतीय सहकर्मी था मेहरा। उसने एक दिन पूछा था—''विनोद तुम्हें क्या होता जा रहा है? तुम बहुत अब्नॉर्मल होते जा रहे हो। तुम्हारे लुक्स भी कितने बदले हुए लग रहे हैं, आखिर बात क्या है?''

विनोद ने उसके दोनों हाथ खींचकर पकड़ लिये थे—''मेहरा, तुम मेरे दोस्त हो ना?'' मेहरा ने अपने हाथ छुड़ाते हुए कहा, ''हाँ विनोद, मैं तुम्हारा दोस्त हूँ, सचमुच मुझे अपने दिल की बात बताओ।''

विनोद ने बहुत घूरते हुए कहा, ''मेरी शादी करा दो⋯।''

मेहरा को कुछ अहसास था। विनोद के मुँह की मांसपेशियाँ फड़फड़ा रही थीं और आँखों से कैसी भूख झर रही थी।

विनोद उसके हाथों को पलोसने लगा—''तुम्हें पता है ना, मैंने दो बार शादी की, पर दोनों ही मुझे छोड़ गईं।''

''किसी गोरी लड़की से शादी करोगे?''

''नहीं, मैं जानता हूँ, वह मेरा फ्लैट हथिया लेगी। मुझे सड़कों पर भीख माँगने के लिए छोड़ देगी।''

इस पर मेहरा हँस दिया। बोला, "अगले सप्ताह मैं दिल्ली जा रहा हूँ। तुम मेरे साथ चलो।"

वह दिल्ली आ गया। कानपुर से उसका बड़ा भाई उसे लेने के लिए आया हुआ था। उसके साथ वह कानपुर चला गया।

वहाँ एक भरापूरा परिवार था। बड़ा भाई प्रमोद, उसकी पत्नी शांता, उनके तीन बच्चे।

प्रमोद ने पूछा, "अब क्या करने का इरादा है?"

"आप मेरी शादी करवा दीजिए।"

फिर जो भी उससे मिलने के लिए आता, वह उससे कहता—मेरी शादी करवा दीजिए। कहते-कहते उसकी आँखों में से अजीब सा बौरायापन झलकने लगता।

उस दिन प्रमोद के घर में कुल देवता की पूजा का समारोह था। बहुत से संबंधी अपने परिवारों सहित आए हुए थे। विनोद उनके बीच ऐसे घूम रहा था, जैसे किसी खोई हुई चीज को ढूँढ़ रहा हो। फिर उसने एक सुंदर महिला का हाथ पकड़कर कहा, 'तुम बहुत सुंदर हो'''मुझसे शादी करोगी?'

डॉक्टरों ने कहा—उसे इलाज की जरूरत है।

बीच में कितने वर्ष किसी चौराहे पर लगी हुई हरी-पीली और लाल होती हुई बत्ती की तरह गुजर गए।

मनु ने जब घंटी दबाई तो दरवाजा ऐसे व्यक्ति ने खोला, जिसने बड़े मटमैले कपड़े पहने हुए थे और सिर के बालों में सफेदी के तार घुल-मिल गए थे।

वह बोला, "मैं मिस्टर विनोद शर्मा से मिलना चाहता हूँ।"

वह व्यक्ति उसे टकटकी लगाकर देखने लगा। उसकी आँखों में बड़ी नमी भरा बौरायापन झलकने लगा।

"मेरा नाम मनु शर्मा है। मैं अमेरिका से आया हूँ।"

"तुम अमेरिका से आए हो?" वह बहुत अटक-अटककर बोल रहा था, जैसे कुछ याद कर रहा हो। उसने उसका हाथ पकड़ लिया और उसे बहुत घूरकर देखने लगा—"तुम अमेरिका में रहते हो।" उसके चेहरे की मांसपेशियाँ फिरकने लगीं।

"मैं अपने पापा से मिलना चाहता हूँ।"

उसके हाथों की पकड़ कड़ी हो गई।

मनु ने देखा—आँसुओं से उसका हाथ गीला हो गया है।

□

आधी सदी का वक्त

मैं एकदम अचकचा गया था। वह मेरे पैरों पर झुककर कह रहा था—''मामाजी, पैरी पैना।''

मैंने उसकी ओर देखकर उसके चेहरे पर से कोई परिचित नक्श ढूँढ़ने चाहे। उसके चेहरे पर छोटी सी दाढ़ी थी। उसने सलवार के ऊपर लंबी कमीज पहन रखी थी। उसके गले में ताबीज भी था। सिर के खिचड़ी बाल पीछे की तरफ कढ़े हुए थे। उसमें कुछ भी अनोखा नहीं था। लाहौर की सड़कों पर ऐसे चेहरे किसी भी पाकिस्तानी की पहचान बताते हैं।

लाहौर में भारत और पाकिस्तान के लेखकों का तीन दिन का एक सम्मेलन था, जिसमें दोनों ओर के लेखक शामिल हुए थे। तीसरे दिन के सम्मेलन के समाप्त होने के बाद जब सभी लोग होटल की बड़ी लॉबी में गुटों में बँटकर गपशप कर रहे थे कि मुहम्मद हसन एकाएक मेरे सामने आ खड़ा हुआ था। मेरे आसपास तीन-चार पाकिस्तानी लेखक बैठे थे। उन्होंने भी जब उसे मेरे सामने झुकते और मुझे मामाजी कहते सुना तो उनके चेहरों पर भी कुछ अजीब सी रेखाएँ उभर आईं।

''मैं भगवंत कौर का बेटा हूँ।''

''भगवंत···?'' जीवन में ऐसा बहुत कुछ घटता है जो व्यक्ति को अवाक् कर देता है। किंतु हर अवाक् कर देनेवाली बात भी झटपट अपना रास्ता खोज लेती है। तब हम सारी स्थिति पर अपना ढेरों आश्चर्य उड़ेलते हुए एक लंबा सा अच्छा···आ···आ कहते हुए अपनी आँखें टिमटिमाने लगते हैं। किंतु यह बात तो ऐसी थी जैसे बरसों पहले मरा हुआ कोई व्यक्ति सामने आ खड़ा हुआ हो—देखो, मैं वही हूँ न।

वे कितने दहलाने वाले दिन थे। हम लोग जिस कैंप में आसरा लिये हुए थे, उस पर जब-तब दंगाइयों का हमला हो जाता था। उनकी नजर जवान औरतों पर होती थी। अपने को बचाने के लिए वे चीखती-चिल्लाती इधर-उधर भागती-फिरती थीं। सारे कैंप में हड़कंप मच जाता था। देखते-देखते दस-बीस लोग दंगाइयों की कुल्हाड़ियों,

तलवारों और लंबे छुरों का शिकार हो जाते थे। इस समय किसी को किसी की सुध नहीं रहती थी। जब दंगाई वापस चले जाते तो लोग रोते-चीखते अपने परिवार के लोगों की गिनती करते थे। ऐसे ही एक हमले के बाद जब हमने गिनती की तो देखा था कि भगवंत और सुखवंत दोनों ही नहीं हैं। दंगाई और बहुत सी औरतों के साथ उन्हें उठा ले गए थे।

किसी अगले हमले की आशंका से बुरी तरह डरे हुए जब हम अपनी एक-एक साँस की गिनती कर रहे थे, तभी सेना की कुछ गाड़ियाँ आ गई थीं और हमें भूसे की तरह भरकर सीमा के इस पार ले आई थीं। अठारह साल की भगवंत और सोलह साल की सुखवंत को मैंने और मेरे भाइयों ने उस तरह होनी मान लिया था, जिस तरह अपने माता-पिता और कितने ही निकट संबंधियों की खून से सनी लाशों को हमने अपनी सूनी आँखों में डुबो दिया था।

उन्हीं दिनों दोनों ओर की सरकारों ने जबरदस्ती अगवा की कई औरतों की खोज-पड़ताल शुरू की थी। भारतीय पंजाब से ऐसी अनेक औरतें उस तरफ भेजी गई थीं और उधर से बहुत सी औरतें इधर आई थीं। सुखवंत भी उनमें थी। उसी ने हमें बताया कि पास के ही एक गाँव के अमजद लोहार ने भगवंत को अपने घर में डाल लिया था। जब सेना की टुकड़ी उस गाँव में पहुँची तो उसने भगवंत को ऐसी अँधेरी कोठरी में छिपा दिया कि उसकी सिसकी का स्वर कोई सुन नहीं सका था।

मुहम्मद हसन कह रहा था—"कल अम्मी ने आपको टेलीविजन पर देखा। उसमें आपने अपने पुराने गाँव का नाम बताया था और नानाजी का नाम भी। सुनकर अम्मी चीख उठी थी—'अरे, ये तो प्रीतम है—मेरा सगा भाई।' उनके आँसू रुक नहीं रहे थे। मुझसे बोली—हसन, किसी तरह मुझे मेरे भाई से एक बार मिला दे, फिर उनसे कुछ बोला नहीं गया। उन्हें बार-बार गश आने लगे। मैंने पक्का इरादा कर लिया, मैं आपको उनके पास जरूर ले चलूँगा।"

"कहाँ रहते हो तुम लोग?"

"दस साल हुए, अब्बू का इंतकाल हो गया था। वो गाँव में लोहार का काम करते थे। वहीं मैंने दसवीं जमात पास कर ली थी। मुझे लाहौर की एक ट्रांसपोर्ट कंपनी में नौकरी मिल गई। तब से हम यहीं हैं।"

दूसरे दिन सुबह की फ्लाइट से हमें दिल्ली वापस आना था। मैंने पूछा, "हसन, अभी चलें?"

वह बोला, "मामाजी, मेरे पास मोटरसाइकिल है।"

"ठीक है।" मैं उठा तो मेरे पाकिस्तानी दोस्त असलम ने पूछा, "लाहौर में तुम्हारी बहन रहती है?"

मैं कुछ बोला नहीं। पता नहीं क्यों, मैं बहुत उखड़ सा गया था। इस सारी घटना ने मुझे बहुत व्याकुल और उदास कर दिया था। मुझे लग रहा था, हसन मुझसे न मिलता तो अच्छा होता। तीन दिन के सम्मेलन से मैं बहुत खुश था। पाकिस्तान के उर्दू और पंजाबी के कितने ही लेखकों से मेरा परिचय हुआ था। लाहौर के कॉफी हाउस में पिछली शाम को मैंने पाकिस्तानी लेखकों के साथ कितना हँसी-ठट्ठा किया था। वहाँ मैं खूब हँसा था। सभी लोग खूब हँसे थे। हमारे ठहाकों से पूरा कॉफी हाउस गूँज उठा था। आज का दिन भी बहुत अच्छा था। मैंने सुबह के सत्र की अध्यक्षता की थी। एक पाकिस्तानी प्रकाशक ने उर्दू में मेरी कहानियाँ छापने का मुझसे अनुबंध कर लिया था। शाम को जब मैं बहुत खुश सा होटल की लॉबी में गपशप कर रहा था, हसन ने आकर कहा था—मामाजी···।

अपनी मोटरसाइकिल की पिछली सीट पर बैठाए वह मुझे पुराने लाहौर की सँकरी सड़कों से घुमाता हुआ ले जा रहा था। भगवंत जब बिछुड़ी थी, वह अठारह साल की थी। अब वह सत्तर पार कर गई होगी···कैसी लगती होगी···? इतना लंबा अरसा—अमजद लोहार। मैं मन-ही-मन उसकी शक्ल बनाने की कोशिश कर रहा था।

हसन की मोटरसाइकिल एक पुराने, बिना पलस्तर के मटमैली ईंटों के मकान के सामने रुकी। उसने दरवाजा खटखटाया और वहीं से बोला, "अम्मी, देखो मैं किसे साथ लाया हूँ।

दरवाजा खुला तो देखा, सामने एक बूढ़ी कमजोर औरत खड़ी है। वह भगवंत थी।

मुझे देखते ही जैसे वह चीख पड़ी। दोनों हाथों से पकड़कर चौखट पार करते हुए वह लंबे स्वर में एक ही शब्द बोल रही थी—वीरा···वीरा···।

मैं इस दृश्य की कल्पना कर रहा था और अंदर-ही-अंदर डर रहा था। मेरे अंदर की घुमड़न एकदम तेज हो गई। कल शाम से ही मेरे अंदर बादल घुमड़ रहे थे। और उनकी गड़गड़ाहट भी सुनाई दे रही थी। मैं बहुत कमजोर इनसान हूँ। जरा सी कोई बात होती है तो मेरा गला भर आता है। मैं बड़े-बड़े संघातों का सामना करने से डरता हूँ। प्राय: मैं उनसे बचना चाहता हूँ, चुपचाप उनके पास से होकर निकल जाना चाहता हूँ।

भगवंत ने मुझे चादर बिछी चारपाई पर अपने साथ बैठा लिया था। उसने मेरे दोनों हाथ पकड़े हुए थे और रोए चली जा रही थी। मैं भी रो रहा था। हम दोनों चुप थे और सिर्फ रो रहे थे।

हसन पास खड़ा था। उसके साथ उसकी बीवी और दो छोटे-छोटे बच्चे हमें भौंचक्के देख रहे थे।

हसन ने आगे बढ़कर अपनी माँ के कंधे पर हाथ रखा—"अम्मी! मामू की कुछ

खैर-खैरियत भी पूछो। कुछ खातिर-तवज्जो भी करो।''

भगवंत ने मेरे हाथ छोड़ दिए और अपने दुपट्टे से आँखें पोछने लगी।

हसन ने अपनी बीवी की ओर देखा—''फातिमा!''

वह झटपट मुड़कर रसोई की ओर चली गई। मैंने दोनों बच्चों को अपनी ओर बुलाया। दोनों दूर सहमे खड़े थे। हसन उन्हें मेरे आसपास ले आया—''यह बिलावल है और यह अमीना है। बिलावल पाँचवीं जमात में पढ़ता है और अमीना तीसरी में है।''

मैंने दोनों को अपने पास बुलाने की कोशिश की, लेकिन दोनों अपने बाप की उँगलियाँ पकड़े खड़े मुझे टुकुर-टुकुर देखते रहे। मैं उनके लिए बहुत अजनबी चीज था।

फातिमा कई गिलासों में शरबत ले आई थी। बोली, ''आप अम्मीजी के भाई हैं। किसने सोचा था कि अल्लाह इतने लंबे अरसे बाद बहन-भाई को इस तरह मिला देगा।''

उसकी आँखों में जैसे समुद्र उमड़ आया—''मैं खाना पका रही हूँ।'' कहकर वह मुड़ने को हुई, फिर रुक गई—''मैं गोश्त नहीं पकाऊँगी···मुझे मालूम है सिख हलाल नहीं खाते हैं।''

''तुम्हें कैसे मालूम?'' मैं मुसकराया—''पाकिस्तान में तो सिख हैं नहीं।''

''ननकाना साहब में मेरा मायका है। वहाँ कुछ सिख परिवार हैं। कितनी ही सिख लड़कियाँ बचपन में मेरी सहेलियाँ थीं। वो हमारे घर सबकुछ खा लेती थीं, पर गोश्त नहीं खाती थीं।''

मुझे बँटवारे से पहले की बातें याद आने लगीं। हमारे गाँव में ज्यादातर घर मुसलमानों के थे। बहुत थोड़े से हिंदू-सिख परिवार उस गाँव में रहते थे। मुसलमान हमें झटका नहीं करने देते थे। हम लोग जब कभी पास के शहर में जाते थे, वहाँ से झटका किया मांस ले आते थे, वह भी चोरी-छिपे।

मैंने कहा, ''धीए, तुम जो भी पकाओगी, मैं खा लूँगा।''

मनुष्य को अपनी रसोई में लकीरें खींचना कितना अच्छा लगता है। यह खाना उनका है, जो प्याज-लहसुन नहीं खाते हैं। यह उनका है, जो प्याज-लहसुन तो खा लेते हैं पर मांस-मछली के नाम से जिन्हें उबकाई आ जाती है। यह उनका है जो मांस-मछली तो डटकर खाते हैं, लेकिन गो मांस का नाम सुनते ही उनकी रूह काँपने लगती है। ये वे लोग हैं जिनका मानना है कि 'मांस बिना सब घास रसाई', लेकिन रुकिए, होना चाहिए झटका, एक ही बार में बकरे का सिर धड़ से अलग। और ये वे लोग हैं जिनको किसी जानवर से कोई परहेज नहीं—बकरा, भेड़, ऊँट, गाय, बैल, भैंस सभी का मांस पकने पर बहुत जायका देता है—लेकिन होना चाहिए हलाल, कलमा पढ़कर पाक किया हुआ।

फातिमा जानती थी—सिख सिर्फ झटका किया हुआ मांस खाते हैं।

हसन बोला, ''मामाजी, आप अपनी बहन के साथ बैठकर बातें कीजिए, मैं थोड़ी देर के लिए दफ्तर हो आता हूँ। ट्रांसपोर्ट कंपनियों में शाम को काम बहुत बढ़ जाता है। मैं बहुत जल्दी आ जाऊँगा।''

मैं बोला, ''खयाल रखना, मुझे होटल पहुँचना है और बिलकुल सुबह हमारी फ्लाइट है।''

हसन ने मेरा हाथ थाम लिया—''आप बिलकुल फिक्र न करिए, यह मेरी जिम्मेदारी है।''

हसन चला गया। फातिमा रसोई के काम में लग गई। बच्चे अपना होमवर्क पूरा करने के लिए दूसरे कमरे में चले गए।

मैं बोला, ''भगतो...।'' मुझे ऐसा लगा, मैं कितने साल पीछे चला गया हूँ। दोनों बहनें मुझसे साल-दो साल छोटी थीं—भगतो और सुक्खो। यह संबोधन सुनकर वह फिर से छलक उठी—''मैंने उम्मीद नहीं की थी कि भगतो कहने वाला मेरा वीर कभी मेरे सामने बैठा होगा।''

''मैं जानता हूँ, तुम्हारे साथ कैसे-कैसे जुल्म हुए होंगे।''

वह सोच में पड़ गई। सोच के इस मंथन से मक्खन तो निकलना नहीं था।

''वीरा, मैंने हैवानियत भी देखी और इनसानियत भी। हमारे साथ जो और औरतें उठाई गई थीं, उन्हें तो धाड़वियों ने इस तरह आपस में बाँटा था जैसे वे बेरियों से बेर तोड़कर लाए हों। तुम्हें लाजो और रानो की याद होगी—लाला फकीरचंद की लड़कियाँ। मेरे देखते-देखते उन्होंने एक कुएँ में छलाँग लगाकर अपनी जान दे दी थी। मैं भी यही करना चाहती थी, पर सुक्खो के खयाल ने मुझे ऐसा नहीं करने दिया। धाड़वियों का एक गिरोह कुछ औरतों को लेकर किसी दूसरे गाँव की तरफ चला गया था। सुक्खो भी उनमें थी। मुझे पता नहीं, उसके साथ क्या हुआ था। पर कुछ दिन बाद मुझे यह पता लग गया था कि हिंदुस्तानी फौज उसे ढूँढ़कर बहुत सी अभागी औरतों के साथ सरहद के उस पार ले गई है।''

''क्या फौज के लोग तुझे नहीं ढूँढ़ पाए थे?''

''फौज हमारे गाँव में भी आई थी, पर मैं जान-बूझकर एक अँधेरी कोठरी में छिप गई थी।''

मेरी आँखें उस पर टिक गईं।

''वीरा, मेरे साथ कुछ कम अनहोनी नहीं हुई।'' भगवंत की आँखें एकदम गहरी हो गईं।

''धाड़वी मुझे लेकर जब गाँव में आए तो आपस में झगड़ने लग गए। यह बात

अमजद को पता लगी तो वह कुछ गाँववालों के साथ वहाँ आ गया। उनमें गाँव का मौलवी भी था। वह बोला—अल्लाह के लिए इस बच्ची पर जुल्म न करो, खुदा तुम्हें कभी माफ नहीं करेगा। तुम में से कोई एक इस लड़की से निकाह कर ले। वे मौलवी की बात सुनकर सोच में पड़ गए। तभी अमजद ने आगे बढ़कर कहा—मौलवी साहब, मैं इस लड़की से निकाह करने को तैयार हूँ। पिछले साल ही मेरी बीवी की मौत हो गई थी। मैं पूरी दयानतदारी से इसे बीवी का दर्जा दूँगा।''

गाँव के लोगों और मौलवी का रुख देखकर धाड़वी खून का घूँट पीकर रह गए। गाँव का बुजुर्ग लंबरदार मुझे बेटी बनाकर अपने घर ले गया। तीन-चार दिन बाद मुझे कलमा पढ़वाया गया और अमजद से मेरा निकाह कर दिया गया। जिस वक्त फौज हमारे गाँव में जबरन भगाई गई लड़कियों की खोज में आई थी, हसन मेरी कोख में आ चुका था। मैंने यह मान लिया था कि अब अमजद ही मेरा शौहर है, यही घर मेरा घर है।''

मेरे सामने से एक पूरी इनसानी दास्तान हल्के-हल्के कदम रखती हुई गुजर रही थी। इसमें कोई आहट नहीं थी, पदचाप भी नहीं सुनाई दे रही थी, हवा की सरसराहट भी नहीं थी…सबकुछ बहुत मूक होकर घट रहा था।

भगवंत अपने घुटनों पर हाथ रखती हुई धीरे-से चारपाई से उतरी। उसके मुँह से निकला—हे वाहेगुरु…।

वापस आकर जब वह फिर चारपाई पर बैठी, उसके मुँह से निकला—वाहेगुरु…।

''अमजद ने तेरे साथ किस तरह निभाया?''

''वह बहुत अच्छा इनसान था। पक्का नमाजी और खुदापरस्त। कलमा पढ़ने के बाद मेरा नाम मदीहा रख दिया गया था, लेकिन अमजद मुझे भगवंत कहकर ही बुलाता था। उसने मुझे कभी किसी बात के लिए मजबूर नहीं किया। एक बार तो मुझसे यह भी कहा था—अगर तुम्हारा मन पाठ करने में लगता हो तो मैं तुम्हें गुरबानी का एक गुटका ला दूँगा।''

कुछ देर में हसन आ गया। फातिमा ने खाना तैयार कर लिया था। हम सभी ने दस्तरखान पर बैठकर साथ-साथ खाना खाया। फातिमा ने मटर-पुलाव बनाया था। मसूर की दाल और आलू कोरमा की सब्जी भी बहुत जायकेदार थी। वह बोली, ''मामाजी, मैंने बाजरे की रोटी खास आपके लिए बनाई है। बाजरे का आटा मैंने दूध में गूँथा है। आप बाजरा खाते हैं न?''

मैं सिर्फ इतना बोल सका—''तुम जो खिलाओगी, मैं खा लूँगा।''

खाने के बाद पिस्ते-बादाम वाली खीर खाकर जब हम उठे तो रात के ग्यारह बज रहे थे।

भगवंत ने बड़ी डबडबाई नजरों से मुझे देखा और अपने दोनों हाथों से मेरा हाथ पकड़कर बोली, ''वीर, वायदा करो, जब भी लाहौर आओगे, अपनी इस बहन से जरूर मिलोगे।''

मैं कुछ बोला नहीं। गला और आँखें, दोनों ही मुझे बेबस किए दे रहे थे। कुछ ही घंटों में आधी सदी से ज्यादा मेरे आगे से निकल गई थी। अठारह साल की भगवंत का झुर्रियों भरा चेहरा मेरे सामने था।

□

पिता

पिताजी नहीं रहे। उनकी अंत्येष्टि हो गई, शांति-पाठ हो गया। माँ के साथ ही घर पर उनका चित्र भी लटक गया। माँ तीन महीने पहले चली गई थीं। पिछले कुछ समय से पिताजी का जैसा स्वास्थ्य चल रहा था, उसके देखते हमें ऐसा लगता था कि पिताजी अब हमारे बीच अधिक समय तक नहीं रहेंगे। माँ उनसे पहले चली जाएँगी, ऐसा किसी ने नहीं सोचा था।

पिताजी के बारे में सोचती हूँ। कैसा दबदबा था उनका। सूर्यभानु त्रिपाठी का नाम सुनकर कितनों की घिग्घी बँध जाती थी। कितने गाँवों को समेटे हुए उनकी जमींदारी थी। जमींदार तो बहुत होते हैं, किंतु उन जैसा तो विरला ही होता है। ज्योतिष में उनके ज्ञान के आगे बड़े-बड़े पंडित पानी भरने लगते थे। रामायण की व्याख्या करने लगते तो लोग मंत्रमुग्ध होकर उन्हें सुनते रहते। गाँव में उन्हें परशुरामी करवाने का बहुत शौक था। दूर-दूर से मंडलियाँ आती थीं प्रतियोगिता में भाग लेने के लिए। परशुराम का अभिनय करनेवाले पर उनकी खास नजर रहती थी। वही अभिनेता उन्हें पसंद आता था, जो अपने चेहरे, अपनी आँखों, अपनी आवाज और अपनी भंगिमा से परशुराम को सजीव बना देता था। कई बार तो वे गुस्से में आकर स्वयं मंच पर चढ़ जाते थे और बताते थे कि परशुराम का अभिनय कैसे करना चाहिए। उस समय वे साक्षात् परशुराम लगते थे।

इस समय हम उनकी तीन संतानें हैं—दो बहनें और एक भाई। उनकी इतनी ही संतानें और थीं। एक बहन और दो भाई बचपन में हमसे कब और कैसे बिछुड़ गए, मुझे याद नहीं। मुझे इतना याद है कि हम तीनों ही उनसे बहुत डरते थे। उनसे खुलकर बात करने का हममें साहस नहीं था। उन्हें देखते ही हम दुबक जाते थे। ऐसा सहम मेरे मन में सारे जीवन भर रहा।

जब जमींदारों का रोब-दाब कुछ कम होने लगा तो उनके चेहरे की तनी हुई नसें

कुछ और कस गईं। जिन लोगों को वे सदा अपनी रैयत समझते थे, जिन लोगों को उनके सामने जमीन पर बैठने की भी हिम्मत बटोरनी पड़ती थी, अब वे चुनाव लड़ते थे, अपनी जय-जयकार करवाते थे, गले में मालाएँ पहनते थे और उन्हीं के सामने कुरसी पर बैठते थे। उनके मुँह से अनायास निकलता था, साले···दो कौड़ी के लोग, जिन्हें उठने-बैठने का शऊर नहीं, अब ऊँट की तरह मुँह उठाए जुगाली करते फिरते हैं। 'दो कौड़ी का आदमी' सदा ही पिताजी का 'तकिया कलाम' रहा। जिस किसी पर उन्हें गुस्सा आता, वे उसे इन्हीं शब्दों से याद करते थे। उस समय उनके मुँह पर उसके लिए हिकारत भरी भंगिमा उभर आती थी और वे मुँह के अंदर कुछ बुदबुदाने लगते थे। एक दिन ऐसा ही एक आदमी उनके पास आया। परमेश्वरी लाल कई साल पहले उनका एक मामूली सा कारिंदा था। जब भी सामने आता था, खड़े-खड़े उनसे आदेश लेता था और चला जाता था। मैं उस समय दस-बारह बरस की रही हूँगी। पिताजी की बैठक में घुसने से पहले सभी अपने जूते उतार देते थे। आमतौर पर सभी कारिंदे उनके सामने नंगे सिर ही आते थे। उस दिन परमेश्वरी ने गांधी टोपी पहन रखी थी। आजादी की लड़ाई के दिन थे। उन दिनों गांधी टोपी पहनना फैशन भी था और यह भी दिखाता था कि मैं देशभक्त हूँ।

परमेश्वरी जब बाहर अपना चमरौंधा उतारकर पिताजी की बैठक में घुसा तो उन्होंने उसे घूरकर देखा। उनके नथुने फड़कने लगे थे।

'अच्छा···तुझे नेतागिरी का शौक चर्राया है?'

'नहीं पंडितजी' वह बहुत घबराई आवाज में बोला, 'लोग कहते हैं, यह गांधी बाबा का हुक्म है।'

'पहले मेरा हुक्म सुन। उतार यह टोपी, जा बैठक से बाहर खूँटी पर टाँग दे।' कहकर पिताजी भाँग वाली ठंडाई सुड़कने लगे थे।

परमेश्वरी ने उनके सामने टोपी नहीं उतारी और बैठक से बाहर आ गया।

फिर कई सालों तक उसका कुछ पता नहीं लगा था।

इस बार जब वह आया तो उसके शरीर पर लकलकाता सफेद कुरता था। नीचे सँकरी मोहरी का पाजामा था और सिर पर टोपी बड़ी नुकीली एवं माँड़ लगी थी।

उस दिन परमेश्वरी उनके पास कई घंटे बैठा रहा। उसे बैठक में ही चाय पिलाई गई। फिर वहीं उसे पूड़ी और आलू की सब्जी का भोजन कराया गया। शाम को पान चबाता हुआ जब वह गया तो पिताजी उसे दरवाजे तक छोड़ने गए थे।

पिताजी राजनीति में प्रवेश कर गए। जीवन की अंतिम साँस तक वे उसी क्षेत्र में जूझते रहे। पहले उन्होंने आजाद उम्मीदवार के रूप में विधानसभा का चुनाव लड़ा। लेकिन उसमें बुरी तरह हार गए। लाखों रुपए खर्च हो गए। परमेश्वरी उनका सबसे

बड़ा सहायक था। सारे चुनाव की व्यवस्था उसी के हाथ में थी। उनकी ड्योढ़ी पर महीनों तक जैसे सदाव्रत लगा रहा। सैकड़ों व्यक्ति दोनों समय हलवा-पूरी उड़ाते थे। प्रचार-कार्य पर बेहिसाब धन खर्च हुआ। उनके मुकाबले में एक स्कूल टीचर जीत गया, पिताजी की नजर में दो कौड़ी का आदमी। वे यह भी कहते, दो कौड़ी का परमेश्वरी उनके कंधे पर बंदूक रखकर चला गया और कई लाख रुपए डकार गया।

पीछे मुड़कर देखने का समय नहीं था। अब ड्योढ़ी पर जुहार करनेवालों की गिनती भी घटती जा रही थी। लोगों की नजरों में अब उन्हें अवज्ञा नहीं, उद्दंडता दिखाई देती थी।

इस हारे गए चुनाव से भी उन्हें एक लाभ हुआ। उनका परिचय कुछ पार्टियों के बड़े नेताओं से हो गया। उन्हें लगा, यदि राजनीति में रहना है तो इन नेताओं के संपर्क में रहना बहुत जरूरी है। उन्होंने लखनऊ में एक कोठी खरीद ली। हमारा सारा परिवार वहीं आ गया। लखनऊ आकर मैंने बी.ए. में एडमीशन ले लिया। छोटी बहन मीनू दसवीं पास करके ग्यारहवीं में आ गई और भाई उदय ने नौवीं में दाखिला ले लिया।

एक दिन पिताजी ने माँ के सामने ही हम तीनों को बैठाया और बोले, ''देखो, अपना कस्बा लालगंज छोड़कर हम बड़े शहर में आ गए हैं। वहाँ इंटरमीडिएट कॉलेज था। मैंने सोचा था, तुम सबको दसवीं-बारहवीं तक पढ़ा दूँगा। लड़कियों का इतना पढ़ जाना मुझे काफी लगता है। घर-गिरहस्ती करने के लिए इतना बहुत है। उदय के बारे में मैंने सोचा था कि इसे ग्रेजुएशन करा दूँगा। लेकिन अब तुम लोग यहाँ आ गए हो। अमिता बी.ए. करना चाहती है। मैंने इसकी अनुमति दे दी है। पर तुम लोगों को शहर की हवा लगे, ऐसा मैं बिलकुल नहीं चाहता। सीधे-सीधे पढ़ने के लिए जाओ और घर वापस आ जाओ। बेकार का घूमना-फिरना और मटरगश्ती मुझे बिलकुल पसंद नहीं। जिस दिन मुझे ऐसा महसूस होगा कि मेरी अवज्ञा हो रही है, उसी दिन तुम्हारी पढ़ाई-लिखाई खत्म हो जाएगी, इस बात को भूलना मत।''

पिताजी का यह आदेश हम सब लोग उस कड़वी दवा की तरह पी गए, जिसकी हमें आदत थी। वे इस प्रकार खुले शब्दों में न भी कहते तो भी हम वही करते जो वे चाहते थे। मैं बड़ी थी और सबसे ज्यादा सहमी हुई थी, पिताजी की आँखें सदा मेरी पड़ताल करती रहती हैं। वे देखती रहती हैं कि मैं दिन-पर-दिन कितनी बड़ी होती जा रही हूँ। मेरा बड़ा होते जाना जैसे मेरे चारों ओर किसी घने काँटेदार जंगल का बड़ा होते जाना है, जिसमें मुझे हर कदम को बहुत सँभाल-सँभालकर रखना है।

मैं देख रही थी, पिताजी की राजनीतिक व्यस्तताएँ बढ़ती जा रही हैं। लालगंज में सिर्फ एक परमेश्वरी था। लखनऊ में कितने ही परमेश्वरी पिताजी को घेरे रहते हैं। एक दिन वे प्रभुदयाल से बातें कर रहे थे। प्रभुदयाल कह रहा था—''त्रिपाठीजी, राजनीति

की सड़क बड़ी ऊबड़-खाबड़ है। यह तो गाँव की कच्ची सड़क से भी खराब होती है। कच्ची सड़क पर तो बरसात में कीचड़ हो जाता है, जो ज्यादा-से-ज्यादा हमारे कपड़े खराब करता है। लेकिन ऊबड़-खाबड़ सड़क पर नुकीले पत्थर होते हैं, जो चुभते हैं और कभी-कभी लहूलुहान भी कर देते हैं।''

पिताजी मुसकराए थे—''प्रभुदयाल, मैं गाँव की कच्ची कीचड़वाली सड़क छोड़ आया हूँ। अब मुझे इसी सड़क पर चलना है। यह कितनी भी ऊबड़-खाबड़ और नुकीले पत्थरों वाली क्यों न हो। तुम्हारा काम दोहरा है। मैं एक खानदानी जमींदार हूँ, नुकीले पत्थरों को ठोकर मारकर अपना रास्ता बनानेवाला। लेकिन मैं जानता हूँ, राजनीति की सड़क पर जमींदारों की ठसक नहीं चलती। यहाँ तो टके-टके के आदमी की भी बदतमीज़ी बरदाश्त करनी पड़ती है। तुम ऐसे लोगों को मेरे पास तो लाओ ही, लेकिन इनकी शोख आँखों में मेरे रोब का थोड़ा सा सुरमा डालकर लाओ। इस काम के लिए सोने की जितनी भी सुरमेदानियों और सलाइयों की जरूरत पड़ेगी, मैं प्रबंध कर दूँगा।''

प्रभुदयाल की आँखों की चमक बढ़ गई थी। वह बड़ी विनम्रता से बोला, ''दूसरा काम त्रिपाठीजी?''

''दूसरा काम इससे ज्यादा महत्त्वपूर्ण है।'' वे कहने लगे—''देखो, अब मुझमें इतना धीरज नहीं है कि मैं इस क्षेत्र में ए बी सी डी के पाठ के साथ प्रवेश करूँ। जमींदारी चले जाने के दुर्दिन मुझे न देखने पड़ते तो मैं इस रास्ते पर थूकता भी नहीं। लेकिन क्या करूँ। देश में आजादी क्या आई, हमारी तो बरबादी ले आई। मेरे बाप-दादा ने कैसा शानदार जीवन जिया था। सारे इलाके में हमारी तूती बोलती थी। बड़े-बड़े कलेक्टर और कमिश्नर हमारी हवेली में आकर ठहरते थे। राजमहलों जैसा वैभव दिखता था वहाँ। गरमी हो, सर्दी हो, बरसात हो, हमारी रैयत घंटों हमारी ड्योढ़ी पर खड़ी रहती थी और हमारी पलक के इशारे का इंतजार करती थी। अब वे दिन नहीं रहे। हम जानते हैं कि अब वैसे दिन वापस आने वाले नहीं हैं। अब अगर हमारा रोब-दाब थोड़ा-बहुत दोबारा कायम हो सकता है तो वह राजनीति के रास्ते पर चलकर ही हो सकता है। प्रभुदयाल, यह काम तुम्हें करना है। किसी पार्टी से मेरा रत्ती भर भी मोह नहीं है। सभी लोकतंत्र और आम जनता की सेवा तथा भलाई की बातें करती हैं। लोकतंत्र मतलब अनपढ़ों, गँवारों और मूर्खों का राज। मुझे इस शब्द से नफरत है। पर क्या करूँ? राजनीति में रहना है तो इन्हीं शब्दों की डोर पकड़कर चलना पड़ेगा।''

प्रभुदयाल टकटकी लगाए उन्हें देख रहा था। उनकी आँखों में सुर्खी और बेबसी किस तरह घुल-मिल गई होगी, मैं इसका अनुमान लगा सकती हूँ।

पिताजी प्रभुदयाल से कह रहे थे—''तुम्हारा तो सभी पार्टियों के नेताओं से संबंध है।''

उनके स्वर में व्यंग्य उभर आया—''तुम तो रोटी ही इसी बात की खाते हो। ऐसा करो कि मेरे बारे में इन पार्टियों के नेताओं से बात करो। लालगंज के जवार में मेरी बड़ी प्रतिष्ठा है। प्रतिष्ठा को लोकप्रियता में किस तरह बदलना चाहिए, इसका गुर मैं कुछ-कुछ सीख गया हूँ। मैंने उस इलाके में अपने कुछ लोग लगा दिए हैं। वे मेरी तरफ से गरीब-गुरबा की मदद कर रहे हैं। टूटी-फूटी झुग्गियों की वे मरम्मत करवा देते हैं। मैंने उन्हें आदेश दिया है कि जिस भी गरीब, हरिजन की बेटी का ब्याह हो, उसे मेरी तरफ से एक सौ इक्कीस रुपए का नेग दिया जाए।''

प्रभुदयाल थोड़ी देर सोचता रहा, फिर बोला, ''त्रिपाठीजी, यह तो आप बहुत नेक काम कर रहे हैं। अपने जवार के तो आप राजा हैं। मेरी समझ में नहीं आता कि आप अपना पिछला चुनाव क्यों हार गए थे, वह भी एक फटीचर टीचर के मुकाबले में।''

मैं देख रही थी, पिताजी के चेहरे पर बड़ी क्रोध भरी खिसियाहट उभर आई थी।

''मुझे तो उस धूर्त परमेश्वरी ने धोखा दिया था। मैं अपने इलाके का दौरा करना चाहता था। वह मुझसे कहता था—आपको इन कमीन लोगों में जाने की क्या जरूरत है। ये तो आपका नाम सुनते ही गरदन झुका देते हैं। आपके अलावा ये और किसी को अपना वोट देने की बात सोच भी नहीं सकते। मुझसे वह गरीब-गुरबों में बाँटने के लिए हजारों रुपए ले गया। किसी को उसने एक पैसा नहीं दिया, सब खुद हजम कर गया।''

''त्रिपाठीजी, आप आजाद उम्मीदवार के रूप में क्यों चुनाव लड़े थे? किसी पार्टी के टिकट पर चुनाव लड़ते तो अच्छा होता।''

''यह भी परमेश्वरी की ही करतूत थी। मैं कुछ जानता-समझता नहीं था। उसने कहा, आपका इस क्षेत्र में इतना रोबदाब है कि आपको किसी पार्टी के टिकट की जरूरत नहीं है।''

प्रभुदयाल ने खूब जाँच-पड़ताल की। प्रदेश की सभी पार्टियों के नेताओं की नब्ज टटोली। अंत में उसने उन्हें किसान-मजदूर लोक पार्टी के टिकट पर विधानसभा का चुनाव लड़वा दिया। एक खास जात-बिरादरी की इस क्षेत्र में बहुतायत थी। पार्टी का शीर्ष नेता भी इसी जाति का था। ऐसी पिछड़ी जाति के लोगों को पिताजी ने कभी अपने पास फटकने भी नहीं दिया था। इस बार वे उन्हीं लोगों के दरवाजे पर जाकर हाथ जोड़कर वोट देने के लिए विनती करते घूमे थे।

उस चुनाव में पिताजी जीत गए थे। उनके मुकाबले में उसी जाति का उम्मीदवार केवल पाँच सौ मतों के अंतर से हार गया था। हर लड़की के विवाह पर एक सौ इक्कीस रुपए नेग देने का गुर काम कर गया था।

राजनीति की ऊबड़-खाबड़ सड़क पर पिताजी की यह पहली सफलता थी। उनके पैर लहूलुहान जरूर हुए थे, किंतु चुनाव में जीत के संतोष ने उनके चेहरे पर जो

दमक भर दी थी, उसमें उनके पैरों के लहूलुहान होने का कोई दखल नहीं था।

विधानसभा में उस बार किसी एक पार्टी को स्पष्ट बहुमत नहीं मिला था। विधायकों की खरीद-फरोख्त का बाजार बहुत गरम था। प्रभुदयाल के माध्यम से चार निर्दलीय विधायकों को पिताजी ने अपनी पार्टी के लिए खरीद लिया था। वे अपनी पार्टी में अपना एक गुट बनाना चाहते थे। प्रदेश में मिली-जुली सरकार बनी थी। उनकी पार्टी के तीन सदस्यों को मंत्रिमंडल में लिया गया था। पिताजी को राज्य मंत्री बनने का अवसर मिल गया।

वे मंत्री बन गए। लोग उन्हें बधाइयाँ दे रहे थे। लेकिन एक बात पिताजी को अंदर-ही-अंदर मथ रही थी। उनके ऊपर कैबिनेट स्तर का जो मंत्री था, वह अनुसूचित जाति का था। मुझे···सूर्यभान त्रिपाठी को भगवानदीन के मातहत काम करना पड़ेगा। यह सोचकर उनके चौड़े माथे पर नीली नसें उभर आती थीं। उन्होंने बड़ी कोशिश की कि कैबिनेट स्तर मिल जाए, कम-से-कम किसी विभाग का स्वतंत्र प्रभार ही मिल जाए, किंतु ऐसा नहीं हुआ।

यह उनके अहं को बहुत बड़ी ठेस थी।

मुझे मालूम नहीं कि पिताजी को यह कैसे पता लग गया था कि मैं कविताएँ लिखने लगी हूँ। उन्होंने माँ से पूछा था—"सुना है, अमिता को कविता लिखने का शौक चर्राया है?"

"मैं क्या जानूँ?" माँ उनके किसी भी प्रश्न का सीधा उत्तर नहीं देती थीं।

"वह क्या करती है, इसकी जानकारी रखना क्या तुम्हारा काम नहीं है?"

मैं पास के कमरे में पढ़ रही थी। उनकी कड़कती आवाज वहाँ तक पहुँच गई थी। मैं सहमती हुई उनके सामने आ खड़ी हुई।

"सुना है, तुम कविताएँ लिखती हो?"

उनका स्वर ऐसा था कि मेरे पैर काँपने लगे।

"जी···बस ऐसे ही।"

"ऐसे ही क्या? लाओ···मुझे दिखाओ।"

"जी उसमें दिखलाने लायक कुछ भी नहीं है। बस ऐसे ही···मन में कुछ आया तो लिख दिया।"

"तुम्हें कविता लिखने का शौक है?"

मैं निर्णय नहीं कर पाई कि इसका उत्तर हाँ में दूँ या ना में। "जी, थोड़ा शौक तो है।"

"सुनो अमिता, कविता लिखने, साहित्य की रचना करने के शौक को मैं बुरा नहीं मानता, लेकिन हमारे देश में ये शौक बैठे-ठाले लोगों के हैं। जिसे कोई काम-धाम

नहीं, वो कविता लिखने लग जाता है। मुझे तो ऐसे लोगों को देखकर चिढ़ होती है। तुम कविता लिखोगी, ये तुम्हारे पास आएँगे, तुम इनकी संगत में उठो-बैठोगी। मुझे यह पसंद नहीं है। तुम अपनी पढ़ाई पूरी कर लो। मैं किसी अच्छे घराने में तुम्हारा ब्याह कर दूँगा। कविता लिखने-विखने का काम अपनी ससुराल जाकर करना, यदि उन्हें पसंद हो तो।''

एक फुहार थी, जो खिड़की खोलकर अंदर आ गई थी। मेरे भीगने से पहले ही वह बंद हो गई। जिस कॉपी में कुछ लिखा था, उसे मैंने सहेजकर रख दिया।

फिर समय-चक्र तेजी से घूमने लगा। पिताजी राजनीति में धँसते चले गए। एक-दो बार वे संसद् के सदस्य भी चुने गए। पर वे किसी भी पार्टी में ज्यादा समय तक टिकते नहीं थे। पार्टी के दूसरे नेताओं से उनका झगड़ा हो जाता था। वे उन्हें दो कौड़ी का कहते और दूसरी पार्टी में शामिल हो जाते थे। प्रभुदयाल उनसे कहता था—''पंडितजी, राजनीति में नुकीली टोपी वाला व्यक्ति तो चल जाता है, पर नुकीली मूँछों वाला व्यक्ति आँखों में चुभने लगता है।''

''तुम्हारा मतलब है कि अब मैं इन टटपूँजिए लोगों के सामने अपनी मूँछें नीची कर लूँ?''

''मैं मूँछें नीची करने के लिए नहीं कहता हूँ।'' प्रभुदयाल बड़े धीरज से बोला था—''कोशिश कीजिए कि ये किसी को चुभें नहीं। राजनीति का दूसरा नाम समझौता है। समझौते में अवसर आने पर…।''

वह अपना वाक्य पूरा नहीं कर पाया था कि पिताजी बोल पड़े—''गधे को भी बाप बनाना पड़ता है।''

बी.ए. पास करने के बाद पिताजी ने मेरे विवाह की तैयारी शुरू कर दी। मैंने कहा कि मैं एम.ए. करना चाहती हूँ। वे बोले, ससुराल जाकर करना।

पुनीत वाजपेयी के पिता पुराने आई.सी.एस. अफसर थे। मैंने जमींदारी वाले माहौल में आँखें खोली थीं, जहाँ हमारी ड्योढ़ी के आगे लोगों की भीड़ लगी रहती थी। दूसरी बार मेरी आँखें खुलीं तो देखा, मैं अफसरों के घर में हूँ। यहाँ बड़े करीने से खाने की मेज सजती है और छुरी-काँटे की खनक सुनाई देती है। जमींदारी में महाराजिन या महाराज खाना बनाते थे। बड़े से चौके में हम धरती पर बैठकर खाना खाते थे। परोसने का काम माँ करती थी। यहाँ रसोई नहीं, बावर्चीखाना है और खाने की मेज पर परोसने का काम खानसामे करते हैं।

जब मैंने पुनीत से कहा कि मैं एम.ए. करना चाहती हूँ तो उन्होंने बड़ी खुशी जाहिर की और सास-ससुर ने भी कोई एतराज नहीं किया।

मैंने इतिहास में एम.ए. कर लिया और एक कॉलेज में लेक्चरर हो गई। पुनीत का

तबादला होता रहता था। मैं उनके साथ जहाँ कहीं भी गई, मुझे नौकरी मिलने में कोई कठिनाई नहीं हुई।

एकाएक मुझे महसूस हुआ, बरसों पहले मुझे एक घुमावदार हवा के झोंके ने घेरा था। मुझे अपनी नस-नस में कुछ स्पंदन महसूस हुआ था। अपने आसपास मैंने कितने बिंब उभरते महसूस किए थे। एक सोंधी फुहार ने मुझे थोड़ा सा भिगोया था। वैसा ही कुछ फिर से लगने लगा। मैंने अपनी सहेजी हुई कॉपी निकाल ली। पुरानी चीजों को पढ़ा। ऐसा लगा, जैसे बरसों से बिछुड़ी सहेलियों ने मुझे घेर लिया है। बीच में चार-पाँच साल का अंतराल था। उस समय कॉलेज में पढ़ने वाली लड़की का कुँवारा अहसास था, इस समय मुझ में एक अफसर की पत्नी और एक वर्ष के शिशु की माँ होने की तृप्ति थी। किंतु एक बात मन को लगातार टीसती थी। कुछ है जो मेरे पास नहीं है। कुछ ऐसा है जो मुझे बार-बार अकेला कर देता है। कई बार मुझे ऐसा लगता, जैसे कोई शून्य मेरे सामने आ खड़ा हुआ है। कभी उसका आकार पसरकर बड़ा हो जाता है, कभी वह एकदम सिकुड़ जाता है।

उस समय मैं पिताजी के सामने सहमी रहती थी। अब मुझे अपने ससुर का रोब घेरे रहता था। वे अंग्रेजों के जमाने के अफसर थे। रिटायर हो जाने के बाद भी उनकी आँखों का गुरूर कुछ कम नहीं हुआ था। सारी उम्र उन्होंने अपने लिए 'सरकार' शब्द सुना था। आज भी वे यह उम्मीद करते थे कि उनसे मिलने आने वाला व्यक्ति उन्हें 'सरकार' कहकर अपनी आँखें नीची करके उनसे बात करेगा।

पुनीत में ऐसा तो कुछ नहीं था, किंतु उन्हें समझने में भी मुझे बहुत सारी उलझनों से गुजरना पड़ता था। पल में माशा पल में तोला वाली बात उन पर पूरी तरह लागू होती थी। शायद यह सबकुछ मुझे कविता के संसार में वापस ले जाने के लिए काफी था।

एक दिन मुझे पता लगा, प्रभुदयाल पिताजी को अच्छी-खासी चपत लगाकर उनसे दूर हो गया है। मैं पिताजी से मिलने गई तो उन्हें देखकर धक् से रह गई। वे एकदम बूढ़े लगने लगे थे। चेहरे पर वह रोबदाब भी नहीं था। प्रभुदयाल ने तो उन्हें पूरी तरह तोड़ दिया था।

"वह तो बहुत ही बदमाश निकला, एकदम हरामखोर···।"

मैंने पूछा, "वह तो आपका बड़ा खैरख्वाह था, बड़ा विश्वासपात्र···।"

"बिटिया, राजनीति बिलकुल कमीनों का खेल है। इसमें कोई किसी का न खैरख्वाह होता है, न विश्वासपात्र।" वे बड़ी थरथराती आवाज में बोल रहे थे—"इस दुनिया के लोगों की जाति बिच्छू की होती है। दस-बीस बिच्छू मिलकर यदि एक राजनीतिक दल बना लें तो बताओ, क्या होगा? सब साथ-साथ चलेंगे। लगेगा कि सब बड़े शरीफ हैं और एक-दूसरे से शंकित रहेंगे, अपने डंक निकाले रहेंगे और इस बात की ताक में

रहेंगे कि दूसरे का डंक उन्हें लगे, इससे पहले वही उसको डंक मार दें।''

फिर वे प्रभुदयाल की बात सुनाने लगे—''मुझसे बोला, मुझे जन कांग्रेस के पार्लियामेंटरी बोर्ड के चेयरमैन का संकेत मिला है। वे आपको लोकसभा का टिकट दे सकते हैं। मौका अच्छा है। यदि आप चुन लिये गए तो केंद्र में मंत्री बन जाना पक्का है।''

मैंने पूछा, ''लालगंज संसदीय क्षेत्र का टिकट मुझे दिलवा सकते हो?''

वह बोला, ''यह मेरे बाएँ हाथ का खेल है।''

मैंने पूछा, ''मुझे क्या करना होगा?''

वह बोला, ''कम-से-कम दस लाख पार्टी फंड के लिए और पाँच लाख चेयरमैन के अपने चुनाव फंड के लिए।''

मैंने प्रभुदयाल के जरिए ऐसे काम इससे पहले कई बार किए थे। वह तो इस क्षेत्र का दलाल है। मैं उसे दलाली भी देता था। पर इस बार तो वह पूरी रकम डकार गया। टिकट किसी ओर को मिल गया और मैं टापता रह गया।

मैंने क्षुब्ध होकर कहा, ''पिताजी, आप ऐसी राजनीति को छोड़ क्यों नहीं देते, जिसमें इतनी गंदगी भरी हुई है।''

वे बड़े उदास स्वर में बोले थे—''बिटिया, यही तो मुश्किल है। इस कीचड़ में जो एक बार फँस जाता है, वह लाख चाहने पर भी निकल नहीं पाता। उसकी नाक कीचड़ की दुर्गंध की आदी हो जाती है। अब तो जीना यहाँ, मरना यहाँ।''

पिताजी जीवन भर इसी कीचड़ में जीते-मरते रहे। जिए कम, मरे ज्यादा। इतना जरूर हुआ कि छोटी बहन की शादी उन्होंने धूमधाम से की। उसमें अनेक पार्टियों के नेता भी आए। भाई को उन्होंने मेडिसिन की पढ़ाई के लिए अमेरिका भेज दिया। माँ को गठिया ने पकड़ लिया और उन्हें हाई ब्लड-प्रेशर रहने लगा।

मेरी कविताओं की एक कॉपी पूरी भर गई थी। दूसरी कॉपी में भी मैं कुछ कविताएँ लिख चुकी थी। कविता लिखकर मुझे अच्छा लगता था, जिस दिन कोई कविता लिख देती, मन में बड़ा हलका-हलका महसूस करती, जैसे मैं पूरी तरह भारहीन हो गई हूँ। बहुत मन करता था कि ये कविताएँ किसी को सुनाऊँ। लेकिन सुनाऊँ किसे? मीनू का पति साड़ियों का व्यापारी था। उसने उसी बाजार में एक बुटीक खोल दिया था। सिर्फ अपनी साड़ियों और जेवरों की बात करती थी। उदय बहुत दूर था।

एक दिन सुमंगल से भेंट हो गई, किसी के विवाह के स्वागत-समारोह में। पता लगा, किसी दैनिक पत्र में उपसंपादक है। समारोह के हँसी-ठहाकों के बीच पुनीत ने कहा था—''मेरी बीवी को भी कविताएँ लिखने का शौक है। लेकिन लिख-लिखकर जमा करती जाती है। उन्हें हवा नहीं लगने देती।''

सुमंगल ने कहा था—"कविताएँ होती तो मासूम चिड़ियों की तरह हैं, पर उन्हें कैद करके नहीं रखना चाहिए। उन्हें थोड़ी सी हवा लगनी चाहिए। इन्हें खुला छोड़िए और देखिए, ये उड़-उड़कर किस तरह आपके पास वापस आती हैं।"

सुमंगल ने मुझे वह संसार दिखाया, जिससे एक बार पिताजी ने अपनी बड़ी चिढ़ जताई थी। कुछ लेखकों-लेखिकाओं के बीच मैंने भी अपनी कुछ कविताएँ सुनाईं और सराहना तथा मार का एक साथ ऐसा स्वाद लिया, जो मेरे लिए एकदम अछूता था।

पिताजी दो चुनावों में लगातार हारे और दो बार दिल के दौरे से जूझे। अगला चुनाव लड़ने से पहले उन्हें फिर से दौरा पड़ा था। उन्हीं दिनों मेरा पहला कविता-संग्रह प्रकाशित हुआ था। मैं उन्हें अस्पताल में देखने गई तो अपने साथ उसकी एक प्रति भी लेती गई। संग्रह मैंने उन्हें समर्पित किया था।

वह दृश्य मुझे नहीं भूलता, जब संग्रह मैंने उनके हाथ में दिया था। कवर पर मेरा नाम देखकर उन्होंने मेरी ओर देखा था। मैंने आज तक उनकी वैसी आँखें नहीं देखी थीं। क्या था उनमें? गुस्सा? असंतोष? स्नेह? करुणा? मैं कुछ नहीं समझ पाई थी। फिर वे पन्ने उलटने लगे। समर्पण पृष्ठ पर आकर वे रुक गए थे। आगे के पृष्ठ उन्होंने नहीं खोले थे। उनकी आँखों पर लगा चश्मा एकदम धुँधला गया था। खुली पुस्तक उनकी छाती पर रखी थी। वे चश्मा उतारकर अपनी आँखें पोंछ रहे थे और चश्मा भी।

☐

कितने सैलाब

पिछले दिनों उसके चेहरे पर लकवे ने हमला कर दिया था। उसका चेहरा बाईं ओर से कुछ टेढ़ा हो गया। चेहरे पर कुछ फर्क पड़ा है—इस बात का पता बहुत ध्यान से देखने पर ही लगता था। लेकिन उसे उसका अहसास बड़ी गहराई से हो रहा था। बात करते समय उसकी जुबान कुछ लड़खड़ाती थी। तब उसे लगता था कि देखनेवालों को इस बात का साफ पता लग जाता होगा।

उसके चेहरे पर कुछ झुर्रियाँ पड़ती जा रही हैं, कुछ समय से इसका खयाल होने लगा था। इन्हें छिपाने के लिए वह देसी-विदेशी क्रीमों का इस्तेमाल करती थी। उसने बरसों तक फिल्मों में सिर्फ हीरोइन का रोल किया था। बढ़ती उम्र के बावजूद निर्माताओं से उसका आग्रह यही रहता था कि उसे मुख्य हीरोइन के रूप में ही कास्ट किया जाए। फिल्म वितरकों के बीच उसका नाम बिकता था, किंतु वितरक भी चाहते थे कि नए और ताजा चेहरे दर्शकों के सामने आएँ। इसलिए निर्माता ऐसी कहानियाँ चुनने लगे थे, जिसमें लीडिंग रोल में दो या तीन हीरोइनों को लिया जा सके।

रोशन उस समय नीना के संपर्क में आया था, जब वह चालीस की गिनती पूरी कर चुकी थी और इंडस्ट्री में अभी भी उसे नंबर वन माना जाता था।

रोशन की कुशल मेकअप मैन के रूप में पूरी इंडस्ट्री में चर्चा थी। हर हीरोइन शॉट देने से पहले उससे मेकअप कराना चाहती थी। डायरेक्टर को यह समझौता करना पड़ता था। आमतौर पर सभी बड़ी हीरोइनों के अपने-अपने मेकअप मैन होते हैं। लेकिन अब तक रोशन किसी एक से नहीं बँधा था। जब वह पूरी तरह उससे बँध गया। उस समय उसकी उम्र तीस से कम थी। इंडस्ट्री में जब ऐसी बातें होने लगीं कि रोशन अब नीना के साथ रहने लगा है तो किसी को आश्चर्य नहीं हुआ। वहाँ की 'गॉसिप मार्केट' में कुछ वक्त के लिए यह अच्छा मसाला था। किसी ने इस बात की सिर-खपाई नहीं की कि दोनों ने बाकायदा शादी की है कि नहीं। नीना इससे पहले

कम-से-कम तीन शादियाँ रचा चुकी थी और अपने फिल्मी-गैर-फिल्मी पतियों को छोड़ चुकी थी। इस चर्चा में अगर लोगों की रुचि थी तो सिर्फ इतनी कि रोशन कुँवारा था। उसके किसी प्रेम-प्रसंग की बात भी नहीं सुनी गई थी। वह नीना से दस-बारह साल छोटा था और यह भी कि पिछले कुछ सालों से नीना ने सिर्फ उसी से अपना मेकअप कराया था। शूटिंग कहीं भी हो रही हो, देश में या विदेश में, रोशन के मेकअप के बिना नीना सेट पर नहीं जाती थी।

एक दिन रोशन ने उससे कह दिया था, ''एक दिन मेरा भी वही हाल होगा, जो उसका···उसका···उसका हुआ था।''

नीना ने उसकी तरफ चुभती आँखों से देखा था, ''वो···वो···वो···आए और चले गए। उनके लिए मैं एक दुधारू गाय थी···सोने के अंडे देनेवाली मुरगी थी। उनमें से एक-आध तो ऐसे थे, जो गाय को मारकर सारा दूध एक साथ पी जाना चाहते थे या मुरगी को जिब्ह करके सारे अंडे एक साथ पा लेना चाहते थे। मैं उन्हें न भी भेजती तो भी वे चले जाते।''

फिर वह उसकी ओर बड़ी गहरी आँखों से देखने लगी। उसकी आँखें रोशन के चेहरे पर एक खुफिया पुलिस अफसर की तरह दौड़ने लगीं, ''तुम तो अभी तीस के भी नहीं हो?''

''अगले साल हो जाऊँगा।''

''मैं चालीस की हो गई हूँ।''

''मुझे मालूम है।''

''जब मैं बूढ़ी हो जाऊँगी, तुम उस समय भी जवानी की मस्त तरंगों पर तैर रहे होगे।''

रोशन के जहन में नीना के ये शब्द उसके बिना कहे ही कई बार गूँजे, वह बहुत धीरे-धीरे बोला, ''देखो अदाकारा···मुझे इस बात का कतई भ्रम नहीं है कि अगर मैं तुम्हारे साथ रह रहा हूँ तो मैं तुम्हारा पति हूँ। तुम मेरे लिए सिर्फ एक औरत नहीं हो। औरतें तो मुझे बहुत सी मिल सकती थीं। मैं कॉलेज में पढ़ता था, जब मैंने तुम्हारी पहली फिल्म देखी थी। फिर जैसे यह मेरा पागलपन हो गया···ऑब्सेशन···तुम्हारी जो भी नई फिल्म लगती, मैं पहले दिन और पहला शो जरूर देखता। तुम्हारी कोई पुरानी फिल्म किसी थिएटर में लगती, उसे भी मैं देखने जाता। तुम्हारी कुछ फिल्में तो मैंने दस-दस बार देखीं।''

नीना ने उसका एक हाथ अपने दोनों हाथों में लिया हुआ था। वह उस पर बिल्कुल एक नवोढ़ा की तरह झुकी थी।

रोशन कह रहा था, ''मेरे लिए तुम्हारा अस्तित्व स्क्रीन पर था। पता नहीं कैसे मैं मेकअपमैन बन गया और तुम्हारे सजीव चेहरे का रेशा-रेशा अपने ब्रश से सँवारने लगा। सपने सभी देखते हैं। अनगिनत लोग उन्हें अपनी कल्पनाओं में जीते भी हैं। मेरे जितने किस्मतवाले कितने हैं, जो अपने सपने हकीकत में अपनी मुट्ठी में भर भी सकते हैं।''

उसने नीना के चेहरे को अपनी मुट्ठियों में ले लिया।

''रोशन, मेरे चेहरे पर आया यह फर्क साफ दिखता है?''

नीना यह बात कितनी बार पूछ चुकी थी।

''वैसे देखने से तो कुछ खास पता नहीं लगता। लेकिन कैमरा तो बहुत क्रूर होता है। वहाँ परदे के नीचे छिपी चीजें भी साफ नजर आने लगती हैं। मुझे नहीं लगता कि तुम एक-दो महीने सेट पर जा सकती हो।''

''लेकिन प्रोड्यूसर तो हमारी जान खा जाएँगे, उन्हें महीनों पहले से डेट्स दी हुई हैं।''

''तुम्हारी इस समय तीन फिल्में सेट पर हैं। मैंने तीनों डायरेक्टरों से बात कर ली है, कह दिया है कि तुम्हारी तबीयत ठीक नही है। डॉक्टरों ने तुम्हें विदेश जाने की सलाह दी है।''

''मेरे रोल का क्या होगा? एक फिल्म में मैं माँ हूँ, एक में सास हूँ, एक में बुआ का रोल कर रही हूँ। बुआवाला रोल तो मेरा यादगारी रोल है। जब मेरा शॉट आता है तो इस फिल्म में काम करनेवाली दोनों जवान छोकरियाँ फीकी पड़ जाती हैं। डायरेक्टर कहता है, नीनाजी यह पूरी फिल्म तो आपके कंधों पर खड़ी है। मैं कुछ दिन के लिए गायब हो गई तो कहीं ऐसा न हो कि मेरे रोल को काट-पीटकर छोटा कर दिया जाए।''

रोशन हँस पड़ा। ''देखिए मैडम, आजकल आप हीरोइन का रोल नहीं कर रही हैं, लेकिन हर प्रोड्यूसर और डायरेक्टर आपकी वकत जानता है। आज भी डिस्ट्रीब्यूटर आपका नाम देखकर फिल्म खरीदता है। ये तीनों फिल्में, जिन्हें मैं इस समय आप काम कर रही हैं, इनकी कहानी आपको केंद्र में रखकर लिखवाई गई है। लेकिन स्क्रीन पर आपके चेहरे पर हल्का सा भी दोष अगर लोगों की नजर में आ गया तो आपकी इमेज पर बहुत बुरा असर पड़ेगा।''

नीना सोच में पड़ गई।

''तुम्हीं बताओ, मैं क्या करूँ?''

''चिंता की कोई बात नहीं है, मैंने सभी प्रोड्यूसर से कह दिया है कि वे उन सभी सींस को फिल्मा लें, जिनमें आप नहीं हैं। जहाँ बहुत जरूरी हो, वहाँ डुप्लीकेट

से काम चला लें। दो महीनों के लिए हम सचमुच विदेश चले जाएँगे। तुम्हारा इलाज भी ठीक से हो जाएगा।''

एक बड़े समारोह में नीना को 'लाइफ टाइम एचीवमेंट' पुरस्कार दिया गया। हॉल पूरी तरह भरा हुआ था। पहली कतार में बैठा हुआ रोशन तालियों की गड़गड़ाहट सुन रहा था। राज्य के मुख्यमंत्री ने अवार्ड का मोमेंटो नीना को दिया था। हर वक्ता ने उसकी अभिनय कला पर दिल खोलकर बोला था। इंडस्ट्री में जिन ऊँचाइयों को उसने छुआ था, कितने ही वक्ताओं ने उसकी चर्चा की थी।

ला बेला में उसने उसके साथ कॉफी पी। कॉफी पीते-पीते वह पूछ बैठी, ''अगर मैं आपकी दोस्त बन जाऊँ तो नीनाजी को बुरा तो नहीं लगेगा?''

वह कुछ बोला नहीं।

उसने फिर पूछा, ''आपने मेरी बात का जवाब नहीं दिया।''

''संसार के सभी संबंधों का फैसला अगर इस बात पर निर्भर करता है कि किसे अच्छा लगता है, किसे बुरा लगता है तो कभी कोई संबंध नहीं बन सकता। मेरे-तुम्हारे बीच इतना ही काफी होना चाहिए कि हम दोस्त हैं...बस।''

बाहर बरसात शुरू हो गई थी। वे दोनों जहाँ बैठे थे, वहाँ से बरसता हुआ पानी साफ दिखता था।

''बारिश देखना मुझे अच्छा लगता है। मेरे फ्लैट के सामने खुला समंदर है। अपनी बालकनी में घंटों बैठकर बारिश देखती रहती हूँ।''

''बारिश में भी गना कैसा लगता है?''

''वह भी अच्छा लगता है। लेकिन भाग-दौड़ करते हुए नहीं। बारिश में खुलकर भीगने और नहाने का मौका भी नहीं मिलता।''

''आप नीनाजी के साथ उनकी हर शूटिंग पर जाते हैं?''

रोशन ने देखा, बात घूम-फिरकर नीना की तरफ मुड़ जाती है।

''उनकी शूटिंग का सारा शैडूल मैं ही बनाता हूँ। डायरेक्टर को डेट्स मैं ही देता हूँ। शूटिंग के वक्त उनका मेकअप भी मैं ही करता हूँ।''

नानी ने एक दिन उससे पूछा, ''रंजना कौन है?''

''एक फिल्म जर्नलिस्ट है। दो-चार बार तुम्हारा इंटरव्यू भी ले चुकी है।'' वह कुछ याद करने की कोशिश करने लगी।

''तुम्हें कैसे जानती है?''

वह हँस दिया, ''इतने बरसों से आपके साथ हूँ। इस नाते सारी दुनिया मुझे जानती है।''

"लगता है यह लड़की तुम्हें कुछ ज्यादा ही जानने लगी है।"

रोशन को लगा, नीना के चेहरे पर बड़ी उलझन उभर आई है। फिर उसे लगा, वह दिन-पर-दिन ज्यादा अकेली होती जा रही है। एक समय था, उसके घर के बाहर कितनी भारी भीड़ सिर्फ इसलिए खड़ी रहती थी कि जब वह निकलेगी, उसकी एक झलक देखने को मिल जाएगी। घर के अंदर प्रोड्यूसरों-डायरेक्टरों का ताँता लगा रहता था। समय बदल गया था। अब उसके पास गिने-चुने ऑफर ही आते थे। उसकी फिल्मी, गैर-फिल्मी सहेलियाँ भी अब अपने परिवारों में बहुत व्यस्त हो गई थीं। महीने में ऐसे अनेक दिन होते थे, जब उसकी शूटिंग नहीं होती थी। फिल्मी दुनिया में कुछ ऐसी एजेंसियाँ थीं, जो निर्माताओं के लिए जूनियर आर्टिस्टों का प्रबंध करती थीं। वे उन जाने-माने कलाकारों के लिए भी निर्माताओं से संपर्क करती थीं, जिनकी अब ज्यादा माँग नहीं रही थी। रोशन उन एजेंसियों के संपर्क में रहता था।

गैर-शूटिंगवाले दिनों में नीना अपने कमरे में टीवी देखती रहती, संगीत सुनती रहती या सोती रहती। रोशन अपने कमरे में कुछ पढ़ता रहता या टीवी देखता रहता या टेलीफोन पर कितने ही लोगों से बातें करता रहता।

नीना चाहती थी, वह उसके पास बैठे। रोशन को लगता था, उनके पास बातचीत करने का कोई विषय नहीं है। आखिर फिल्म संसार की नित्य उड़ती हुई अफवाहों पर कितनी देर बातचीत की जा सकती थी। राजनीति में क्या घट रहा है, इसमें नीना की अधिक रुचि नहीं थी।

केवल एक बात नीना को सुख देती थी। शाम को सज-धजकर किसी डिनर पर जाना उसे अच्छा लगता था। पहले रोशन सदा उसके साथ होता था। अब उसकी दुनिया में कुछ और लोग भी आ गए थे। ऐसे समय में नीना के चेहरे पर की लकीरें सारे मेकअप को लाँघकर बाहर निकल आती थीं।

नीना की एक ऐसी दुनिया भी थी, जिसमें रोशन का ज्यादा दखल नहीं था। पैडर रोड पर जिस डबल फ्लैट में वे रहते थे, वह नीना के नाम था। उसके बिजनेस पक्ष को उसका एक पुराना एकाउंटेंट मेहता सँभालता था। किस प्रोड्यूसर से कितना धन लेना है, किस बैंक में कितना रुपया है, किस लॉकर में क्या रखा है, इसे केवल नीना ही जानती थी।

नीना का स्थायी मेकअपमैन होने की हैसियत से मेहता रोशन को हर महीने एक बँधी रकम दे देता था, जैसे ड्राइवर तथा घर के दूसरे कर्मचारियों को दी जाती थी।

रंजना रोशन से कहती थी, "तुम्हारी उस घर में कानूनी हैसियत क्या है? तुम उसके पति का दरजा तो रखते नहीं। तुम्हारी स्थिति तो एक रखैल जैसी है—पुरुष रखैल।"

रोशन सोचने लगा, सचमुच, मेरी स्थिति क्या है? नीना की अपनी कोई संतान नहीं है। मैंने अपना घर बसाया नहीं। कल जब नीना नहीं रहेगी तो मेरा क्या होगा? उसके दूर-दराज के रिश्तेदार आकर उसकी जायदाद पर कब्जा कर लेंगे। तब मुझे कौन पूछेगा? एकाएक उसके मन में आया, मैं शादी क्यों न कर लूँ? रंजना ही इसके लिए तैयार हो सकती है। उसने अपने पति को कब का छोड़ा हुआ है। मेरे अपने बच्चे हो सकते हैं। लेकिन नीना···?

उसके सामने हथौड़े की तरह चोट करनेवाला एक बड़ा प्रश्न-चिह्न खड़ा हो गया। नीना के साथ रहते उसे पच्चीस साल हो गए थे। वह बड़े पूजा भाव से उसके साथ जिया था। उसे यह महसूस होता रहा था कि नीना उसे बहुत चाहती है, उस पर बहुत निर्भर करती है। वह जब कभी उसके पास बैठता था, वह अपने दोनों हाथों में उसका एक हाथ दबा लेती थी। कई बार जब वह उठने लगता, उसकी पकड़ और कड़ी हो जाती थी, चेहरे पर किसी चीज के छूट जाने का भाव गहरा जाता था।

एक दिन नीना की साँस बड़ी तेज चल रही थी। बोली, "रोशन, मैंने रात को बड़ा अजीब सपना देखा। एक बड़ी उमड़ी हुई नदी है। दूर-दूर तक सिर्फ पानी-ही-पानी दिखाई दे रहा है। बड़ी तेज लहरें आ रही हैं। नाव में मैं तुम्हारे साथ बैठी हूँ। तुम चप्पू चला रहे हो, पर लहरों के सामने तुम्हारा बस नहीं चल रहा है। मैं तुम्हें कसकर पकड़े हुए हूँ। एकाएक एक बड़ी तेज लहर आती है। नाव उलट जाती है। मैं पानी में गोते खाने लगती हूँ। तुमने मुझे पकड़ रखा है। मुझे लगता है कि मैं अब डूबी कि तब डूबी··· इतने में मेरी आँख खुल जाती है···मैं महसूस करती हूँ कि मेरी छाती जोर-जोर से धड़क रही है। ऐसा लगता है कि तुम न होते तो मैं सचमुच डूब जाती।"

मुंबई की बारिश··· उफ तौबा!। शुरू हो जाए तो रुकने का नाम नहीं लेती। सड़कों पर छतरियों और गम बूटों का भी सैलाब उमड़ पड़ता है। सड़क पर जमा पानी कमर को छूने लगता है।

जब नीना और रोशन अँधेरी के स्टूडियो से निकले थे, उस समय भी बड़ी तेज बारिश हो रही थी। बांद्रा पहुँचते-पहुँचते इस तरह फँस जाएँगे, यह किसी ने नहीं सोचा था। बीच सड़क में उनकी कार रुक गई और बहुत सी गाड़ियाँ रुकी हुई थीं। लहराता हुआ पानी खिड़की से अंदर आ रहा था।

ड्राइवर ने बड़ी कोशिश की, पर उसका कोई बस नहीं चला।

"जादव···कोई टैक्सी देखो···। पानी उतरने पर गाड़ी घर ले आना।" रोशन ने कहा।

"साहब, इस समय टैक्सी भी कहाँ मिलेगी?"

''नीना, बांद्रा स्टेशन पास में ही है।'' वह बोला, ''किसी तरह वहाँ तक चलते हैं। शायद कोई टैक्सी मिल जाए···नहीं तो लोकल ट्रेन से ग्रांट रोड तक चलते हैं।''

नीना घबराई आवाज में बोली, ''लोग मुझे देखेंगे तो परेशान नहीं करेंगे?''

''तुम इसकी चिंता न करो, मैं तुम्हारे साथ हूँ न···अपना चेहरा जरा ढककर रखना।''

नीना बोली, ''तुम मेरी छतरी हो। गरमी हो, सर्दी हो, धूप हो, बारिश हो, सदा मुझे अपनी छाया में लिये रहते हो।''

रोशन के मन में आया, वह कहे, 'तुमने कभी यह सोचा है कि छतरी पर भी गरमी, सर्दी, धूप, बारिश का कुछ असर होता है।'

एकाएक उसके चेहरे पर उदासी झलकने लगी। वह हँसकर नीना से बात करना चाहता था। उसे लगा, उससे हँसा नहीं जा रहा है। हँसने-मुसकराने की कोशिश में उसकी बाँछें फैलने को होती हैं तो उनमें खिंचाव आने लगता है।

नीना ने उसे आँखें गड़ाकर देखा।

''मैं देख रही हूँ कि कुछ समय से तुम कुछ बेचैन रहते हो।''

''नहीं···ऐसी तो कोई बात नहीं।'' रोशन ने उसका एक हाथ पकड़कर दबाया, ''तुम्हें ऐसा क्यों लग रहा है?''

नीना हँस दी, ''मैं एक अभिनेत्री हूँ। फिल्मों में मैंने सभी तरह के रोल किए हैं। किस समय चेहरे पर कैसा भाव लाना चाहिए, इसका मुझे अभ्यास है। यह सब करते-करते इस बात की भी कुछ समझ आ गई है कि चेहरे पर कौन सा रंग आ रहा है···वह कितना सही है, कितना बनावटी है।''

रोशन को लगा, सचमुच उसका चेहरा कुछ बोल रहा है।

''रोशन, मैं तुम्हारी बेचैनी, तुम्हारी परेशानी का राज समझती हूँ।''

''क्या समझती हो?'' वह चौंककर बोला।

वह आँखें गड़ाकर उसे देख रही थी। दोनों चुप थे। रोशन सामने पड़े पेन को उठाकर उसमें अपनी उँगलियाँ फँसा रहा था। नीना गोद में रखे तकिए को बार-बार अपने साथ दबा रही थी।

एकाएक वह बोल पड़ी, '' रोशन···तुम शादी कर लो, अपना घर बसा लो।''

वह कुछ चौंका और हँस पड़ा।

''तुम हँस इसलिए रहे हो कि तुम्हारी जिंदगी के कीमती बरस तो मैं खा गई। अब कह रही हूँ, शादी कर लो।''

''वे मेरी जिंदगी के सबसे अच्छे बरस थे···अनमोल और खूबसूरत।''

''रोशन, अब वह बात नहीं है। इसे तुम भी समझते हो, मैं भी समझती हूँ। ऐसी हालत में तुम्हारे अंदर बेचैनी पैदा हो जाए, परेशानी महसूस होने लगे, यह बहुत कुदरती बात है।''

उसकी आँखें डबडबा आईं।

''मैं जानती हूँ, मैं क्या कह रही हूँ।''

रोशन बिल्कुल उसके साथ सट गया। वह उसके दोनों हाथ अपने हाथों में लेकर पलोसने लगा।

''तुम नहीं जानती, तुम क्या कह रही हो।''

□

निगति

इस बार जब मैं उनसे मिलने गया तो देखा, चारपाई पर वह अकेले लेटे हुए हैं। भाभी अस्पताल में है, लखनऊ से आई बेटी अपनी माँ की तीमारदारी में उनके साथ है। नौकर उन्हें खाना देने गया हुआ है।

मैं उनके पास बैठ गया। वे कुछ देर टकटकी लगाए छत की ओर देखते रहे। बोले, ''तुमसे एक खास बात करना चाहता हूँ।''

''बोलिए।'' मैंने कुरसी उनकी चारपाई के पास खिसका ली।

''देखो, मेरी बात सुनकर न मेरी हँसी उड़ाना, न मुझे उपदेश देना।''

मैं कुछ समझा नहीं। केवल उन्हें देखता रहा। वे मेरी तरफ करवट बदलना चाहते थे। एक-दो बार उन्होंने कोशिश की, पर कुछ हुआ नहीं।

''जरा मुझे अपनी तरफ मोड़ दो।''

मैं उठा। उनकी पीठ को सहारा देकर मैंने उनकी करवट बदल दी।

''देखो, मैंने दोनों बेटों से कह दिया है। सबसे पहले वे तुम्हें दिल्ली फोन करके इस बात की खबर दे देंगे। हो सकता है, पुलिस उन्हें तंग करे। तुम्हारी यहाँ बहुत जान-पहचान है। तुम यहाँ आकर सारी स्थिति सँभाल लेना।''

मैं समझ गया था कि वे कहना क्या चाहते हैं। उनकी बात सुनकर हँसी भी आ रही थी और ख़ीझ भी हो रही थी।

''आपने आत्महत्या करने का निश्चय किया है?''

''मैं सोचता हूँ, मेरे लिए यही ठीक रहेगा।'' वह बहुत धीरे-धीरे बोल रहे थे—''मैं बहुत यातना भोग चुका हूँ। अब मुझसे सहा नहीं जाता। मैं इस जिंदगी से छुटकारा पाना चाहता हूँ।''

''और पीछे रह गए लोगों को जिंदगी भर का क्लेश और शरमिंदगी देकर जाना चाहते हैं।''

"क्लेश और शरमिंदगी दो-चार दिन रहेगी। बाद में सब नॉर्मल हो जाएगा।"

"आप चाहते हैं कि मैं आपको भरोसा दिलाऊँ कि आप बेफिक्र होकर आत्महत्या कर लीजिए। पुलिस कुछ गड़बड़ करेगी तो मैं सब सँभाल लूँगा।"

"चाहता तो मैं यही हूँ।"

हम दोनों चुप हो गए और गुमसुम भी। मैंने उन्हें अपने बचपन से ही यातना सहते हुए देखा है। वह मुझसे कई साल बड़े हैं। मुझे याद है, उन्हें सिरदर्द होता था। हमेशा होता रहता था। इलाज कराने के लिए उन्होंने क्या कुछ नहीं किया। कितनी बार नाक की हड्डी का ऑपरेशन कराया। डॉक्टर कहते थे कि सिरदर्द 'साइनिसिस' के कारण है, अंदर से नाक की हड्डी कुछ बड़ी हो गई है। वैद्यों और हकीमों से भी इलाज कराया, पर कोई लाभ नहीं हुआ। किसी ने कहा—किसी शरीक ने इन पर जादू-टोना कर दिया है। किसी ने हमें पंजाब के एक डेरे के बारे में बताया। वहाँ होली के अवसर पर बहुत बड़ा मेला लगता है, जिसमें हजारों लोग शामिल होते हैं। उस समय वहाँ झाड़-फूँक में माहिर बहुत से मसंद होते हैं। वे अपने हुनर से भूत को अपने वश में कर लेते हैं। ये लोग भूत से यह भी उगलवा लेते हैं कि टोना किसने किया है।

ऐसी बातें सुनकर वे हँस दिया करते थे।

"सारी दुनिया बहुत बेवकूफ है, जो बीमारियों का इलाज करने के लिए इतनी कोशिश करती रहती है। वैज्ञानिक रोज नई से नई खोज करने का दावा करते रहते हैं, नई से नई दवाएँ बाजार में आती रहती हैं। इन सबको इस देश में बुलाकर झाड़-फूँक करनेवाले ओझाओं की शार्गिदी में दे देना चाहिए। जब झाड़-फूँक से सारी बीमारियाँ दूर हो सकती हैं तो डॉक्टरों की इतनी बड़ी फौज खड़ी करने की क्या जरूरत है?"

उनकी बातें सुनकर हमारी माँ बहुत खीझ जाया करती थीं। हठ करके वह उन्हें उस डेरे पर ले गईं। मैं भी साथ गया। मसंदों ने बहुत जोर लगाया। झाड़-फूँक के सभी तरीके उन पर आजमाए गए। एक मसंद ने बहुत खीझकर कहा—तू बहुत जिद्दी आदमी है।

उन्होंने हँसकर कहा था—'आपसे मेरी जिद नहीं टूटती तो मेरे अंदर के भूत को आप कैसे निकालेंगे?'

'हम जैसा कहें, वैसा करो, फिर देखो हम भूत को कैसे निकालते हैं?'

'आप गुणी हैं। आपका दावा है कि आप इस विद्या को पूरी तरह जानते हैं।' वे उन्हें चिढ़ाते हुए बोले थे, 'आपको यह तो नहीं लगता कि मेरा रोग दूर करना आपके वश में नहीं है।'

डेरे से हम लोग वापस आ गए थे।

कितने ही वर्ष बीत गए। वे रोग से लड़ते रहे और जिंदगी से भी।

कभी-कभी मैं उनसे कहता था—'लड़ना अच्छी बात है। पर उसके लिए अपने आपको ही निशाना बना लेना अच्छी बात नहीं है। आप दूसरों से कम, अपने आपसे ज्यादा लड़ते हैं।'

आज वे मुझसे कह रहे थे—"लड़ते-लड़ते मैं हार गया हूँ। मेरा शरीर जर्जर हो गया है। मैं सब पर बोझ बन गया हूँ।"

मैंने उनका एक हाथ अपने दोनों हाथों में ले लिया और दबाने लगा। सांत्वना के कितने शब्द मैंने अपने अंदर समेट लिये थे। मैंने महसूस किया कि हर शब्द बाहर निकलने से कतरा रहा है।

लंबे समय तक किसी बीमारी से जूझनेवाला व्यक्ति कितना चिड़चिड़ा हो जाता है। वे भी ऐसे ही हो गए थे। बात-बातपर भाभी से लड़ने लगते थे। दोनों बेटों को वे हमेशा बुरा-भला कहा करते थे—'क्या बेटे ऐसे होते हैं? मैंने अपने जीवन भर की कमाई इन पर लुटा दी। दोनों को काम-धंधे से लगाया...इन्हें इस लायक बनाया कि अपना और अपने बच्चों का पेट पाल सकें। अगर मैं यह न करता तो अपने बीवी-बच्चों को लेकर इधर-उधर धक्के खाते फिरते। इनकी योग्यता ही क्या है? अपने तई तो ये दो वक्त की रोटी भी नहीं कमा सकते।'

मैं कहता—'भाई साहब, अच्छे-भले तो हैं आपके बेटे। दोनों की दुकानें भी अच्छी चल रही हैं। जहाँ तक मैं समझता हूँ, कमाई भी ठीक-ठाक है। आप व्यर्थ ही इन्हें कोसा करते हैं।'

वे बहुत झुँझलाकर कहते—'इन्हें इस योग्य किसने बनाया? बताओ अब मैं बीमार पड़ा हूँ। दोनों में से मुझे कोई नहीं पूछता। अपने बीवी-बच्चों में ही मस्त रहते हैं।'

भाभी भी बहुत बीमार रहती थीं। उनकी रीढ़ की हड्डी में सदा दर्द रहता था। हमेशा कमर में बेल्ट बाँधे रखतीं। वे भाई साहब से बहुत कम बोलतीं। लेकिन उनकी ऐसी बातें सुनकर उनसे रहा नहीं जाता था। वे मुझसे कहतीं—'भैया, तुम अपने भतीजों को अच्छी तरह जानते हो। हर रोज दुकानों पर जाने से पहले इनका हाल-चाल पूछने जरूर आते हैं। जिन दवाइयों की जरूरत होती है, शाम को लाकर देते हैं, किसी चीज की कोई कमी नहीं रहने देते, फिर भी ये उन्हें हमेशा कोसते रहते हैं।'

नौकर ने टी.वी. चला दिया था। उसे पता था कि भाई साहब कब खबरें सुनते हैं, कब कौन सा सीरियल देखते है। पति-पत्नी में ऐसी नोक-झोंक की बातें वह रोज सुनता था। भाई साहब ने अपने लिए एक खास कुरसी बनवा रखी थी, जिस पर बैठकर टी.वी. देखने में उन्हें आसानी होती थी। नौकर को पता था, उन्हें घंटे-दो घंटे बाद खाने को कुछ चाहिए। उसने पूछा, "आप कुछ खाएँगे?"

भाई साहब पास पड़े रूमाल से अपना मुँह पोंछने लगे। पास में ही उनके दाँत

शीशे की पानी से भरी परात में पड़े थे। वे उन्हें उठाकर मुँह में लगाते हुए बोले, ''हम लोगों के लिए थोड़ी-थोड़ी चाय ले आ, नमकीन बिस्कुट भी।

रसोई में जाने से पहले नौकर ने उनकी कुरसी को उस ऐंगल पर रख दिया, जहाँ से वे टी.वी. देखते हैं। फिर उन्हें हाथों का सहारा देकर कुरसी पर बैठा दिया। मुझे उनसे मिले कई-कई महीने गुजर जाते हैं। लेकिन वे मेरे ध्यान में हमेशा रहते हैं। उनका चेहरा एकदम पिचक गया है। जबड़े अंदर की ओर धँस गए हैं। सूनी-सूनी आँखें किसी गुफा में से झाँकती हुई लगती हैं। दो साल हुए उन्हें लकवा मार गया था, तब से शरीर का बायाँ भाग बहुत कम काम करता है। कई महीनों तक फिजियोथैरेपी देनेवाला व्यक्ति उनकी बाँहों-पैरों का व्यायाम कराता रहा है। उन्हें कुछ लाभ भी हुआ है। वे वाकर का सहारा लेकर बाथरूम तक चले जाते हैं।

जब कभी मैं यहाँ आता हूँ, मुझे अजीब सा सन्नाटा पसरा हुआ दिखाई देता है। मकान की पहली मंजिल पर भाई साहब और भाभी रहते हैं। छोटा बेटा नीचे रहता है। बड़े बेटे ने कुछ दूरी पर अपना मकान बना लिया है। नौकर खाना बना देता है, सफाई कर देता है और भाई साहब की छोटी-बड़ी जरूरत पूरी करने में लगा रहता है। भाभी कराहती हुई अपने कमरे में लेटी रहती हैं या कभी-कभी रसोई का चक्कर काट लेती हैं। दोनों के बीच कोई संवाद नहीं है। उन्हें देखते ही भाई साहब की त्योरियाँ चढ़ जाती हैं।

''तुम रसोई में जाकर इतना भी नहीं देख सकतीं कि रामू मेरे लिए क्या बना रहा है? वह जो कूड़ा-करकट पकाता है, मुझे खिला देता है। क्या तुम्हारा कोई फर्ज नहीं बनता?''

''अपना फर्ज निभाते मुझे साठ साल से ज्यादा हो गए हैं। मुझे ऐसा दिन भी याद नहीं आता जब मैंने आपसे कोई गाली न सुनी हो।''

उस दिन भाभी मुझे अपने पास बैठाकर सुनाने लगीं—''जिंदगी भर इनकी जली-कटी सुनती रही हूँ। अब तो तुम्हारे भाई ने बस हद कर दी है। कहते हैं, तुम मेरे टुकड़ों पर पल रही हो। मैं जब चाहूँ तुम्हें घर से बाहर निकाल सकता हूँ, तब तुम भीख माँगती फिरोगी।''

मैं सिर झुकाए सुनता रहा।

''मैंने कहा, मेरे दो बेटे हैं। क्या वे मुझे दो वक्त की रोटी भी नहीं देंगे।''

''जानते हो, उन्होंने क्या जवाब दिया?''

मैं भाभी की ओर देखने लगा।

''वे बोले—हाँ, तुम्हारे बेटे हैं, पर पता नहीं, उनकी रगों में किसका खून बह रहा है। मेरा खून होता तो मेरा भी कुछ खयाल करते।''

मुझमें हिम्मत नहीं हो रही थी कि मैं भाभी की ओर देखूँ।

वे बिलकुल रुआँसी हो आई थीं।

''आज मैं पोतों-पोतियों वाली हो गई हूँ। हमारी शादी को साठ साल से ऊपर हो गए हैं। हम दोनों के पैर कब्र में लटके हुए हैं। क्या ऐसी भद्दी और बेहूदा बात सुनने के लिए मैं जिंदा हूँ? भगवान् हम दोनों में से किसी को उठा क्यों नहीं लेता?''

मैं चौंक पड़ा। यह कैसी कामना है?

एक दिन उन्होंने मुझसे कहा, ''तुम, एक-दो दिन के लिए आते हो, ऐसा लगता है जैसे मैं रेगिस्तान से निकलकर किसी नखलिस्तान में आ गया हूँ। चारों तरफ घने पेड़ हैं और ठंडी हवाएँ चल रही हैं। कहते हैं, साँप के अंदर बहुत तेज जहर होता है, जिसके असर से वह सदा जलता रहता है। जलते-जलते उसकी चमड़ी पूरी तरह जल जाती है। एक दिन वह किसी पेड़ या चट्टान का सहारा लेकर अपनी केंचुल को उतार देता है। उस समय उसे बड़ी शांति मिलती है, वह बहुत शीतल अनुभव करता है। कुछ समय बाद वह अपने अंदर के जहर से फिर जलने लगता है और उसकी चमड़ी जलने लगती है। मेरा भी यही हाल है।''

उन्होंने एकाएक मुझसे पूछा, ''तुम भगवान् को मानते हो ना?''

''नहीं मानता हूँ, ऐसा मैंने कभी दावा नहीं किया।''

''तुम उसे कभी याद करते हो?''

''केवल उस समय, जब मैं किसी मुश्किल में पड़ जाता हूँ। वह भी इसलिए नहीं कि हे भगवान! तुम मुझे इस मुश्किल से उबार लो। मैं कहता हूँ, हे भगवान् यदि तुमने मुश्किल पैदा की है तो उसे सहन करने, उससे निबटने की शक्ति भी तुम्हीं दो।''

''कभी तुमने उससे कुछ माँगा है?''

मैंने कहा, ''देखिए भाई साहब, सभी के मन में कुछ कामनाएँ होती हैं, जिनकी वह पूर्ति चाहता है। मेरे मन में भी हैं। उनकी पूर्ति के लिए मैं प्रयास करता रहता हूँ। मुझे याद नहीं आता कि मैंने अपनी किसी कामना की पूर्ति के लिए भगवान् से प्रार्थना की हो।''

''मैं प्रार्थना करता रहता हूँ।''

''किस कामना की पूर्ति के लिए?'' मैंने पूछा; फिर मुझे याद आया—भाभी ने भगवान् से कुछ कामना की थी, जिसे सुनकर मैं चौंक पड़ा था।

□

दंश

इस बात का पता उसे फोन पर लगा। पड़ोसी मेहताजी का बेटा बोल रहा था—"अंकलजी, बलबीर बोल रहा हूँ...आंटीजी...आपकी माताजी नहीं रहीं।"

उसे धक्का लगा—"क्या हुआ था उन्हें?"

"उन्हें रात को दिल का दौरा पड़ा था। पिताजी को सुबह पता लगा। उन्होंने डॉक्टर को बुलाया, फिर उन्हें अस्पताल में भरती कराया गया। वहीं उन्हें दूसरा दौरा पड़ा और मृत्यु हो गई।"

"अंतिम क्रिया...?" उसने पूछा।

"कल हो गई।"

सहजीवन सोसाइटी की आठवीं बिल्डिंग की तीसरी मंजिल पर उनका फ्लैट था। कितने ही साल से वह अकेली रह रही थी।

कई साल पहले जवान होते हुए बेटे ने एक बार पूछा था—'मम्मी, क्या मैं आहूजा अंकल का बेटा हूँ?'

उसकी बात से वह बहुत चौंकी थी। फिर सहज हो गई थी।

'क्या तुम्हारे लिए इतना काफी नहीं कि तुम मेरे बेटे हो?'

'इतना काफी नहीं है।'

फिर वह बहुत गंभीर होकर बोला था, 'सभी जानते हैं कि मैं रामनाथ कोहली का बेटा हूँ, जो अब इस दुनिया में नहीं हैं। स्कूल सर्टिफिकेट में भी यही लिखा है, पर सच क्या है?'

वह भी गंभीर हो गई थी—'सच वही होता है जिसे हम मानते हैं।'

'मानने को जानना भी तो चाहिए।'

'देख निंदी, हर चीज को जानना जरूरी नहीं है। कुछ चीजों को बिना जाने ही यदि जीवन अपनी राह पर ठीक-ठाक चल रहा हो तो जानकर उसमें व्यवधान डालने से क्या लाभ?'

नरेंद्र ने अपनी आँखें उन पर गड़ा दी थीं।

'आप समझती हैं कि जो बात मैंने आप से पूछी है, उसे जानकर मेरे जीवन में व्यवधान पैदा हो जाएगा।'

वह कुछ क्षण मौन बैठी रही थी। उस दिन सुबह से ही मूसलधार बारिश हो रही थी। मुंबई में ऐसी बारिश कोई अनजानी बात नहीं है। बारिश कभी तेज तो कभी धीमी होती रहती है, बिलकुल जिंदगी की भाँति। इसी में इस नगर का जीवन चलता और थमता रहता है। पर आज तो बारिश पूरी एक ही गति से हो रही थी। उसके कुछ थमने या धीमे होने का कोई आसार नजर नहीं आ रहा था। काम-धंधों पर जाने वाले लोग गमबूट पहने और छतरियाँ थामे कोनों में दुबके खड़े थे।

उसने फैसला कर लिया था कि वह दफ्तर नहीं जाएगी।

वह भी मन-ही-मन मान बैठा था कि ऐसी बारिश में कॉलेज में कोई पीरियड नहीं लगेगा।

आज रीमा ने बड़े मन से उसके लिए नाश्ता बनाया था, वरना दोनों ही टोस्ट चबाते और दूध गटकते हुए जल्दी-जल्दी फ्लैट से बाहर निकलते थे।

उस दिन वह बात इसी बिंदु पर आकर लटक गई थी।

रीमा अपने कमरे में जाकर लेट गई थी।

नरेंद्र बड़े कमरे में आकर टी.वी. पर कोई मूवी देखने लगा था।

उसने अपनी माँ से यह सवाल दुबारा कभी नहीं पूछा।

उसने ग्रेजुएशन की, फिर पोस्ट ग्रेजुएशन की, फिर एम.बी.ए. किया। जब वह एम.बी.ए. कर ही रहा था, उसे एक मल्टीनेशनल कंपनी से ऑफर मिल गया था।

इस बीच अपनी माँ से उसका संवाद बहुत कम हो गया था। दोनों एक ही छत के नीचे थे, लेकिन दोनों के बीच एक शीशे की दीवार उभर आई थी।

तभी नरेंद्र ने रविवार की छुट्टी के दिन रीमा को बताया, 'माँ, प्रिंस्टन इंटरनेशनल ने मुझे चुन लिया है। एडवांस ट्रेनिंग के लिए कंपनी एक साल के लिए मुझे लंदन भेज रही है।'

आज बहुत दिन बाद वह माँ के पास बैठा था। वर्षों से दोनों के बीच दीवार पर लगी घड़ी की पैंडुलम की तरह वह बात दाएँ-बाएँ होती रहती थी। नरेंद्र को रह-रहकर याद आता था कि उसने अपनी माँ से एक बात पूछी थी। दीवार पर लगी घड़ी हर घंटे यह बात याद कराती है कि कुछ समय और बीत गया है। जब भी वह सामने पड़ता था, रीमा को उसकी बात घड़ी के घंटे की तरह याद आ जाती थी।

आज उसकी बात सुनकर रीमा का हाथ उसके एक गाल पर टिक गया।

''यह तो बहुत अच्छी खबर है। कब जाना होगा?''

"अगले महीने।"

"बहुत कम समय है। चेक लिख देती हूँ। बैंक से पैसे निकलवाकर कुछ सूट सिलवा लो और जरूरी चीजें खरीद लो।"

"पर आप?"

"मेरी चिंता न करो। मेरे रिटायर होने में अब कुछ महीने ही रह गए हैं।"

पता नहीं क्यों, उसे लगा, जैसे माँ ने कहा हो—आहूजा अंकल तो हैं ही।

नरेंद्र एक साल के लिए लंदन चला गया। वहाँ से उसने सिर्फ एक फोन किया—"माँ मैं पहुँच गया हूँ। कंपनी का गेस्ट हाउस बहुत अच्छा है। उसी की गाड़ी मुझे ऑफिस ले जाती है और छोड़ जाती है।"

उसने माँ से और कुछ नहीं पूछा। उसे अंदर तक हिचकोले देती एक बात उमड़ती महसूस होती। आहूजा अंकल उनका पूरा खयाल रखते होंगे, अब वे रोज आते होंगे।

कंपनी उसके काम से खुश थी। एक-एक साल करके उसे दो बार एक्सटेंशन मिला। एक दिन उसने रीमा को फोन किया—"माँ, मैंने लिंडा से शादी कर ली है। वह मेरे दफ्तर में ही काम करती है—बहुत अच्छी लड़की है।"

रीमा ने बहुत ठंडी साँस लेकर बुदबुदाया—निंदी ने शादी कर ली है। उसने सोचा था, एक दिन निंदी की शादी होगी, घर में बहू आएगी। उस समय भी उसे लगा था, वह अपनी पत्नी को लेकर अलग हो जाएगा...अपना अलग घर बसाएगा, उसके साथ नहीं रहेगा। लेकिन सबकुछ इस तरह हो जाएगा, यह उसने नहीं सोचा था।

उसने फोन पर ही कहा, "बेटे, बहुत-बहुत बधाई। ईश्वर से यही प्रार्थना है कि तुम दोनों बहुत खुश रहो। लिंडा की कोई तसवीर भेजना।"

रीमा ने उसे एक दिन फोन किया—"बेटे, मैं रिटायर हो गई हूँ। कल दफ्तर के सभी लोगों ने मुझे विदाई दी। पार्टी बहुत अच्छी थी। मैं सबको बहुत मिस करती हूँ, पर यह दिन तो आना ही था। दफ्तर जाती थी तो सारा दिन बहुत भरा-भरा सा लगता था। अब बहुत अकेली हो गई हूँ, दिन कटना मुश्किल हो जाएगा। तुम लंदन में हो, जैसी भगवान् की मरजी।"

नरेंद्र के अंदर एक घूमता, बल खाता हवा का गोला बन गया—वह अकेली कैसे हो गई—आहूजा अंकल तो हैं। वो भी रिटायर हो गए होंगे, सारा दिन माँ का अच्छा साथ रहता होगा।

उसके मन में यह भी उमड़ा—अब वह मुंबई वापस नहीं जाएगा, लंदन में ही रहेगा।

उसके मन में आहूजा अंकल की शक्ल उभर आई। लंबा-चौड़ा, एकदम पेशावरी रंग और मजबूत कद-काठी। रामनाथ कोहली की तस्वीर भी उभरी...उसका पिता। दोनों एक ही कॉलेज में पढ़ाते थे और अच्छे दोस्त थे। जब वह पैदा हुआ था, लोग कहते हैं

कि वह बहुत गोरा-चिट्टा था। उसका वजन और लंबाई भी आम बच्चों से ज्यादा थी। रीमा भी लंबी-चौड़ी और बहुत गोरी थी। रामनाथ कोहली साँवला था और कुछ ठिगना भी। लोग कहते थे, बच्चा अपनी माँ पर गया है। पर कुछ लोग फुसफुसाते हुए यह भी कहते थे—नैन-नक्श तो सारे आहूजा जैसे हैं।

ये बातें रीमा, कोहली और आहूजा के कानों में भी पड़ती थीं।

कोहली और आहूजा प्राय: शाम को इकट्ठे व्हिस्की पीते थे। दो पेग, कभी-कभी तीन पेग। रीमा उनके लिए सलाद काट देती थी। पता नहीं क्या हुआ, कोहली ज्यादा पीने लगा। उसके पेग भी बड़े होने लगे। आहूजा उससे पूछता, तुम्हें क्या होता जा रहा है? तुम इतनी तो नहीं पीते थे। रीमा कुछ कहती नहीं थी। बस उसे टुकुर-टुकुर देखती रहती थी। कभी-कभी वह ढक्कन लेकर बोतल बंद कर देती थी। उस समय कोहली उसे बड़े गुस्से से देखता था और उसके हाथ से बोतल लेकर गिलास में व्हिस्की उड़ेल लेता था।

फिर कोहली बीमार रहने लगा। उसे डॉक्टरों को दिखाया गया। उनकी समझ में भी कुछ नहीं आ रहा था। रीमा और आहूजा ने उसे बड़े-बड़े अस्पतालों में भी दिखाया। सभी ओर से उन्हें यह भरोसा मिला कि वह जल्दी ही ठीक हो जाएगा। एक रात सोते में ही उसके प्राण निकल गए।

नरेंद्र दो-तीन नौकरियाँ छोड़ने के बाद अब जिस कंपनी में था, उसका वह वाइस प्रेसिडेंट था। यह उस कंपनी का सबसे ऊँचा पद था, जिसे वह प्राप्त कर सका था। लिंडा दो सुंदर लड़कों को जन्म दे चुकी थी और उसने अपने दफ्तर से लंबी छुट्टी ले ली थी।

एक दिन वह नरेंद्र से बोली, "क्यों न हम लोग कुछ दिन के लिए मुंबई चलें। वहाँ तुम्हारी बूढ़ी माँ हैं। मैं समझती हूँ, वह वहाँ बिलकुल अकेली हैं। क्या उनसे मिलने को तुम्हारा मन नहीं करता?"

नरेंद्र कुछ देर पहले ही ऑफिस से लौटा था। लिंडा ने उसे कॉफी पिलाई थी। दोनों बच्चे दूसरे कमरे में बैठे अपना होमवर्क कर रहे थे। मुंबई छोड़े उसे दस वर्ष से अधिक हो गए थे। वह चाहता तो इस बीच कितनी ही बार मुंबई हो के आ सकता था। पर उसका मन ही नहीं किया। एक गाँठ थी जो खुल ही नहीं रही थी। इस गाँठ को लिये-लिये बरसों बीत गए थे। न यह गलती थी, न फोड़ा बनकर फूटती थी। यह उसकी हर साँस के साथ अंदर-ही-अंदर ऊपर-नीचे होती रहती थी।

रीमा इस बात को जानती थी। वह व्याकुल होती थी। कुछ उसके मन को बुरी तरह से कचोटता था। कभी-कभी उसे लगता था कि वह निंदी की गोद में सिर रखकर रोए, इतना रोए कि गाँठें घुलकर बह जाएँ। लेकिन ऐसा नहीं हुआ।

उस समय लिंडा के सामने उसके मुख से इतना ही निकला था—"चलेंगे, मौका मिलते ही मुंबई चलेंगे।"

फिर पड़ोसी मेहताजी के बेटे बलबीर का फोन आ गया। उससे यह भी पता लगा

कि उनका दाह-संस्कार हो गया है—उस समय दूर के दो-चार रिश्तेदार थे। यह भी पता लगा कि अगले रविवार को उनका उठाला है।

उसने लिंडा से कहा, ''इस समय तुम्हारा और बच्चों का वहाँ जाना ठीक नहीं है।''
फ्लैट माँ की यादों से भरा हुआ था। उसमें पहुँचते ही वह बहुत भावुक हो उठा। माँ का ड्रेसिंग गाउन उनके बाथरूम में लटक रहा था। टेबल पर उसकी तसवीर रखी हुई थी। उसके साफ-सुथरे कमरे में दरवाजे के पास ही उसकी चप्पलें रखी हुई थीं। उसका धुला कुरता-पाजामा उसके सिरहाने रखा हुआ था, जैसे उस कमरे को उसके आने का इंतजार था।

आर्यसमाज मंदिर में उठाले की रस्म हुई। कुछ लोग आए हुए थे। हवन हुआ। फिर पंडितजी ने आत्मा की अमरता और संसार की नश्वरता पर भाषण किया। बाद में किसी रिश्तेदार ने उसके सिर पर पगड़ी बाँधी। वह सभी से मिल रहा था। सभी अफसोस जता रहे थे। तभी सफेद साड़ी में एक महिला उसके सामने आ खड़ी हुई।

''तेरी माँ तो मेरी बहन की तरह थीं।'' उसकी आँखें भर आई थीं।

वह उसे पहचानने की कोशिश कर रहा था। सफेद बालों में दो-चार काले तार नजर आ रहे थे। चेहरे पर बुढ़ापा पूरी तरह उतर आया था। पर सफेद साड़ी में से तीखे नैन-नक्श और गोरा रंग पूरी तरह झाँक रहे थे।

''तेरे पिताजी और आहूजा साहब बहुत अच्छे मित्र थे। बिलकुल सगे भाइयों की तरह।''

उसे सबकुछ याद आ गया।

''क्षमा कीजिएगा आंटी, मैं पहचान नहीं पाया था। आहूजा अंकल…?''

''उनको गुजरे तो कितने साल हो गए?''

''अरे, क्या हुआ था उन्हें?''

''पता नहीं कौन सी बात उनके दिल को लग गई थी। तुम्हारे पिता को बहुत याद करते थे। तुम्हारे लंदन जाने के बाद तुम्हारी माँ का भी बहुत खयाल रखते थे।''

वह लगातार अपनी साड़ी के पल्लू से अपनी आँखें पोंछ रही थी—''एक दिन दिल का ऐसा दौरा पड़ा कि बिना कुछ कहे-सुने हमें छोड़ गए।''

जब-जब आहूजा अंकल का उसे स्मरण होता था, वह अशांत हो जाया करता था। उसके अंदर एक चुभन उठती थी और वह व्याकुल हो उठता था। वह जब लंदन से चला था, उसे लगा था उनसे भेंट अवश्य होगी। यह सोचकर उसे बड़ी अकुलाहट महसूस हुई थी।

आहूजा अंकल नहीं रहे, सुनकर उनकी बहुत सी तसवीरें उसकी आँखों के आगे से गुजर गईं।

वह समझ नहीं पा रहा था कि यह खबर उसे कैसी लगी है, वह बहुत उदास हो गया था।

□

माँ

शुचि ने माँ के बालों में कुछ सफेद तार देखे तो धक से रह गई। उसे लगा, माँ ने शायद यह स्वीकार कर लिया है कि वह विधवा हो गई है। डैडी को मरे कुछ ही दिन हुए हैं। कल उनका उठाला है। सारी बिरादरी इकट्ठी होगी। आज भी माँ ने सफेद साड़ी पहनी हुई है। शुचि जानती है, कल माँ की साड़ी बिलकुल लकलकाती सफेद होगी।

शुचि ने इसी वर्ष फिलॉसफी लेकर बी.ए. ऑनर्स में दाखिला लिया है। कोई नहीं जानता उसने फिलॉसफी पढ़ने का फैसला क्यों किया। एक बार बीमार डैडी ने यह पूछा भी था—"तुमने फिलॉसफी ऑनर्स करने की बात क्यों सोची? तुम्हारे नंबर तो इकोनॉमिक्स में भी बहुत अच्छे थे, हिस्टरी में भी। तुम पोलिटिकल साइंस भी ले सकती थी।"

शुचि बोली थी—"जीवन में जब रास्ते सीधे-सीधे, सुलझे-सुलझे दिखाई दें और भविष्य की योजनाओं के जुगनू आसपास चमकते नजर आएँ तो वे सारे विषय पढ़ने में अच्छे लगते हैं, जो आप बता रहे हैं। लेकिन जब जीवन की गुत्थी उलझी-उलझी नजर आए और उसका सिरा ढूँढ़ने में परेशानी महसूस होती हो तो फिलॉसफी से ज्यादा अच्छा विषय दूसरा नहीं है।"

डैडी उसकी बात सुनकर पहले तो मुसकराए, फिर गंभीर हो गए। शुचि ने उनका व्यंग्य भरा मुसकराना देखा, फिर गंभीर हो जाना भी। उसने दोनों बातों का अर्थ निकाल लिया। इस घर में बरसों से यही होता दिख रहा है—या तो विद्रूपता से मुसकराओ या कुछ सोचने लगो, ऊल-जलूल, बे सिर-पैर, उलझा-उलझा।

पहले डैडी और मम्मी दोनों ही डाई लगाते थे। डैडी कम उम्र में ही अपने बैंक में डिप्टी जनरल मैनेजर पद पर पहुँच गए थे। मम्मी ने एक मल्टीनेशनल कंपनी में पब्लिक रिलेशन असिस्टेंट के रूप में ज्वॉइन किया था, फिर पब्लिक रिलेशंस और पब्लिसिटी की चीफ मैनेजर बन गईं। बैंक में लोग मिस्टर सरीन का रोब खाते थे और कंपनी में मिसेज

सरीन की उँगलियाँ एक सधे हुए खिलाड़ी की तरह धीरे-धीरे उठती थीं।

एक दिन अचानक मिस्टर सरीन ने डाई लगाना छोड़ दिया। देखते-देखते पहले उनके बाल भूरे हुए, फिर सफेदी की खुली घोषणा करने लगे। बैंक में लोगों ने इसे जनरल मैनेजर बनने की योजना का हिस्सा समझा।

पर यह बात न पत्नी की समझ में आई, न बेटी की। शुचि ने बचपन से ही महसूस किया था कि उसके माता-पिता में कोई खास संवाद नहीं है। दोनों की दुनिया में भी ऐसी कोई साँझ नहीं है कि संवाद का रास्ता ठंडी सड़क बनकर सामने नजर आने लगे। भाई-बहन के नाम पर शुचि अकेली थी और यह बात एक उलझी हुई गुत्थी की तरह उसके हाथ में हमेशा बनी रही कि वह अकेली क्यों है, उसका कोई भाई-बहन क्यों नहीं है? सरीन साहब की अपनी एक भरी-पूरी दुनिया थी, जिसमें सिर्फ उनका बैंक था। एक क्लर्क आखिर कितना महत्त्वाकांक्षी हो सकता है। लेकिन उन्हें बैंक की नौकरी की शुरुआत करते ही एक बात का अहसास हो गया था कि यह बैंक ही वह किला है, जिसकी सीढ़ियाँ उन्हें जीवन भर चढ़नी हैं। इस चढ़ाई में उनकी नजर सबसे ऊपर बने दो-तीन गुंबदों पर ही रहनी चाहिए, महाभारत के उस अर्जुन की तरह जिसे पेड़ पर बैठी चिड़िया की सिर्फ आँख ही दिखाई देती थी और कुछ नहीं। चालीस की आयु पार करते ही वे सधे कदमों से बढ़ते हुए डिप्टी जनरल मैनेजर की पोजीशन पर पहुँच गए थे। अब जी.एम. बनना और ई.डी. की कुरसी पर नजर गड़ाए रखना पेड़ पर रखी चिड़िया की आँखें थीं।

सरिता सरीन शादी से पहले सिर्फ सरिता थी। उसके पिता भी कोई सरनेम लगाते होंगे, लेकिन उसे सरिता रहना ही अच्छा लगता था। सारी डिग्रियाँ उसने सरनेम के बिना ही प्राप्त कर ली थीं और नौकरी भी।

पर इस बात को कौन झुठला सकता था कि वह मिसेज सरीन है, यशवंत सरीन की पत्नी है।

इस बात ने पति-पत्नी के बीच कुछ कसैलापन पैदा कर दिया था। हर मौके पर यशवंत सरीन परिचय कराता—मेरी पत्नी, सरिता सरीन। हर मौके पर वह अपना परिचय देती—आय एम सरिता···मीट माई हस्बैंड मिस्टर यशवंत सरीन।

'तुम्हें अपने आपको सरीन कहने में झिझक क्यों होती है?' एक दिन उसने पूछा था।

उसका जवाब था—'मुझे सरिता बने रहना पसंद है। मैं कभी सूरज प्रकाश ढल की बेटी सरिता ढल नहीं बन सकी। न ही यहाँ यशवंत सरीन की बीवी सरिता सरीन बनकर जीना मुझे जरूरी लगता है।'

'तुम मेरी बीवी नहीं हो? यशवंत सरीन की बीवी···?' वह कुछ बड़बड़ाया था।

'इससे मुझे इनकार नहीं है। न ही मुझे किसी तरह का संकोच है। लेकिन सरिता

रहकर भी मैं आपकी बीवी हूँ। शुचि की माँ हूँ। क्या सरीन की मोहर लगाना इस रिश्ते के लिए जरूरी है?'

यशवंत सरीन की हड़बड़ाहट बौखलाइट में बदलने लगी—'सभी लड़कियाँ पति के घर जाकर उसका सरनेम ग्रहण कर लेती हैं। पहले तो यह भी होता था कि ससुराल आने पर लड़की का नाम भी बदल दिया जाता था।'

'यह बात बिलकुल ठीक है, उसी तरह जैसे हर नदी आगे चलकर किसी बड़ी नदी में मिल जाती है या समुद्र में गिरकर गुम हो जाती है। लेकिन मैं सरिता बनकर ही आप के साथ-साथ चलूँ, बिना जज्ब हुए तो आपको क्या एतराज है?'

यशवंत की समझ में नहीं आया कि वह क्या जवाब दे। थोड़ा खीझकर बोला था—'तुम्हें मालूम है, जो सरिताएँ किसी बड़ी नदी से नहीं मिलतीं या समुद्र में नहीं गिरतीं, वे सूख जाती हैं।'

सरिता एकदम सोच में डूब गई थी। ऐसा लगा था कि वह किसी गहरे ऊहापोह में आ गई है। फिर बड़ी आहिस्ता-आहिस्ता बोली थी—'अपनी पहचान लेकर बहने और फिर सूख जाने में क्या बुराई है। गंगा में मिलकर अपनी पहचान डुबो देने वाली यमुना को भी लोग याद करते हैं और उस सरस्वती को भी, जो लंबी राहों में पता नहीं कहाँ गुम हो गई थी।'

शुचि के लिए यह सबकुछ बहुत अनबूझ सा था। उसने हायर सेकेंडरी शुचि सरीन बनकर पास की थी और कॉलेज में भी इसी नाम से दाखिल हुई थी। इस स्थिति में उलझाव कहाँ है?

उलझाव सिर्फ इस बात में ही नहीं था। पता नहीं, और क्या-क्या एक-दूसरे में उलझ गया था।

शुचि को मूवी देखना अच्छा लगता था। बचपन में वह अपने मम्मी-डैडी के साथ जाती थी। यह देखकर उसके अंदर हुमक पैदा होती कि दोनों ही कितने स्मार्ट दिखते हैं। मम्मी तो सचमुच ऐसी लगती हैं जैसे कोई कुँआरी लड़की हो, ज्यादा-से-ज्यादा नवब्याहता हो। जब वह कुछ और बड़ी हुई तो उसकी सहेलियाँ समझती थीं वह उसकी बड़ी बहन है। जब वह मैट्रिक की परीक्षा पास कर गई तो उसे पता लगा, मम्मी और डैडी दोनों ही डाई लगाने लगे हैं।

एकाएक डैडी ने डाई लगाना बंद कर दिया। उनके बालों ने जब अपना असली रंग दिखाना शुरू किया तो माँ-बेटी दोनों ही चौंकी थीं। शुचि बहुत मजा लेकर बोली थी—'डैडी, मैं नहीं चाहती कि आप इतनी जल्दी बूढ़े लगने लगें। जब मेरी सहेलियाँ कहती है कि तुम्हारे डैडी तो तुम्हारे बड़े भाई जैसे दिखते हैं तो मुझे बहुत अच्छा लगता है।'

मम्मी अपने ऑफिस जाने को तैयार हो रही थीं। शुचि ने उनकी तरफ देखा—कौन

कह सकता है कि वे उन्नीस साल की लड़की की माँ हैं। उनकी साड़ी से उनका गोरा गदराया शरीर जैसे पिंजड़े में बंद गोरे-चिट्टे खरगोश की तरह बाहर निकलकर कुलाँचें भरने को आकुल हो रहा था।

शुचि की बात सुनकर वह चौंकी थी। उसने एक बार पूरी नजर भरकर पति की तरफ देखा था।

''डाई आपको कुछ तकलीफ देने लगी है?'' उसने पूछा था।

''नहीं, ऐसी कोई बात नहीं है।'' डैडी ने बड़े अनमने ढंग से उत्तर दिया था—''बस लगता है, ये बेकार का झंझट है। जो हो रहा है वह हो, उस पर मुलम्मा चढ़ाने की क्या जरूरत है?''

मम्मी ने अपनी साड़ी की सलवटों पर हाथ फेरते हुए कहा, ''ये जिंदगी क्या मुलम्मों के बगैर चलती है? इस्तिरी किए कपड़े पहनना भी तो मुलम्मा है।''

कहती हुई वह बाहर निकल गई थी।

शुचि सोचती रही, कहीं-न-कहीं कुछ गड़बड़ जरूर है। मम्मी-डैडी आपस में लड़ते होते तो बात समझ में आ जाती। सभी तरह की लड़ाइयाँ अपने साथ अनेक कारणों के बड़े-बड़े झंडे झुलाती हुई आती हैं। उसने कभी इन्हें ऊँचा बोल बोलते भी नहीं देखा था। कभी उन्हें आपस में बहुत जोर से हँसते, ठहाके लगाते भी नहीं देखा था। ऐसे विषय बहुत थोड़े थे जिन पर वे आपस में बहस करते या बातें करते थे। डैडी के बैंक में बहुत 'पॉलिटिक्स' थी। सभी अफसर एक-दूसरे को काटने में लगे रहते थे। सभी चेयरमैन के नूरेनजर होना चाहते थे। सभी उन्नति की सीढ़ी पर एक-दूसरे को धकियाकर आगे बढ़ना चाहते थे।

पहले शुचि देखती थी—डैडी मम्मी से अपने बैंक की राजनीति पर बात करते थे। मम्मी भी अपने ऑफिस की बातें डैडी से करती थीं। ऐसे ही बातों-बातों में एक बार मम्मी ने बताया था, उनकी कंपनी का नया मैनेजर इंग्लैंड से आया है। बिलकुल छोकरा सा है। वेरी हैंडसम⋯वेरी स्मार्ट।

फिर उसी कंपनी में मम्मी की तरक्की का सिलसिला शुरू हुआ। उसने पब्लिक रिलेशंस असिस्टेंट के रूप में नौकरी शुरू की थी। जल्दी ही वह असिस्टेंट मैनेजर बन गई। देखते-देखते इस सरपट दौड़ में उनका घोड़ा आगे दौड़ने वाले कितने ही घोड़ों को पछाड़ता हुआ आगे निकल गया। वह पब्लिक रिलेशंस और पब्लिसिटी डिपार्टमेंट की फुल फ्लैजेड मैनेजर बन गई।

उस दिन शुचि को अपने डैडी के चेहरे पर दो सफेद खूँटियाँ दिखाई दी थीं, जिनकी तरफ उसका पहले ध्यान नहीं गया था। मम्मी ने बताया था कि उनकी मल्टीनेशनल कंपनी अब उन्हें जितना वेतन दे रही है, वह डैडी के वेतन से कहीं ज्यादा है।

डैडी अकसर छह बजे तक घर आ जाते थे। उन्हें कभी-कभार देर होती थी या जब भी देर होने की संभावना होती, वे फोन करके सूचित कर दिया करते थे। लेकिन अब मम्मी तो हर दिन ही देर से आती थीं। नौ बजे आना तो आम बात थी। कभी-कभी कहती थीं—पब्लिसिटी और पब्लिक रिलेशंस की इंचार्ज होना बड़े झमेले का काम है। अपनी पार्टियों के बॉसेज को एंटरटेन करना उनकी ड्यूटी का हिस्सा है।

फिर पता नहीं क्या हुआ, डैडी का स्वास्थ्य गिरने लगा। उन्हें एक बड़ा सख्त झटका लगा था। जनरल मैनेजर के इंटरव्यू में उनका सलेक्शन नहीं हो पाया, जिसकी उन्हें पूरी उम्मीद थी। इस पद के लिए मेहता का चुन लिया जाना उन्हें बहुत खला था। क्योंकि सारे बैंक में यह चर्चा थी कि मेहता चेयरमैन का बहुत मुँह लगा है और उसकी बीवी भी बहुत खूबसूरत है।

पर ऐसा नहीं लगता था कि ऐसी अनहोनी इतनी जल्दी घट जाएगी। डैडी उस दिन दफ्तर से आए तो बड़े थके-थके लग रहे थे। शुचि ने उन्हें पानी पिलाया था, फिर चाय पिलाई थी और पूछा था, 'डैडी, आप बहुत थके-थके से लग रहे हैं। तबीयत ठीक है ना?'

डैडी ने इतना ही कहा था—'बेटा, मैं ठीक हूँ।'

यह कहकर वे अपने बैडरूम में जाकर लेट गए थे।

उस दिन मम्मी बहुत देर से आई थीं। विदेश से कोई डेलीगेशन आया हुआ था। उसके ठहरने वाले होटल, खाने-पीने की सारी व्यवस्था मम्मी को ही देखनी थी। आधी रात को जब वह लौटीं, डैडी सो रहे थे। शुचि भी अपने कमरे में चली गई थी। नौकरानी ने सिर्फ इतना बताया था कि साहब कुछ बीमार लग रहे थे। थोड़ा सा खाना खाकर जल्दी सो गए।

सुबह डैडी जागे ही नहीं।

बेड टी के समय पता लगा कि रात में ही किसी समय उनके प्राण निकल गए थे।

डैडी का उठाला हो गया। बिरादरी के लोग, मम्मी के दफ्तर के लोग बड़ी संख्या में आए थे। सभी अफसोस करते हुए वापस चले गए।

मम्मी को सप्ताह से अधिक हो गया था, दफ्तर नहीं गई थीं। उठाले के दूसरे दिन भी नहीं गईं तो शुचि को कुछ अटपटा लगा। वह तो डैडी की मृत्यु के तीसरे दिन से ही कॉलेज जाने लगी थी। आज वह कॉलेज से वापस आई तो देखा, मम्मी बड़ी गुमसुम अपने कमरे में लेटी हुई हैं। वह उनके पास जाकर बैठ गई। सबसे पहले उसकी नजर उनके बालों पर पड़ी। कितनी सफेदी झलक रही थी उनमें।

''मम्मी'', वह कुछ कहने ही जा रही थी कि उसने देखा, उनकी आँखें छलछला आई हैं। उसने उनके दोनों हाथ अपने हाथों में ले लिये। मम्मी एकदम फफक उठीं—''शुचि, तेरे डैडी की मौत की मैं जिम्मेदार हूँ।''

''क्या कहती हो मम्मी?'' वह ऐसे चौंकी जैसे बिच्छू ने डंक मार दिया हो—

"आप जिम्मेदार क्यूँ हैं?"

"मैं उन्हें पल-पल टूटता, पल-पल मरता देखती रही। मैंने कुछ नहीं किया।" उनकी आँखों से आँसू बहते चले जा रहे थे।

शुचि को लगा, जैसे मम्मी ठीक कह रही हैं। वह उनका हाथ थामे चुपचाप बैठी रही।

नौकरानी आकर चाय रख गई। कितनी ही देर तक दोनों बिना कुछ बोले धीरे-धीरे चाय पीती रहीं।

मम्मी दूसरे-तीसरे और चौथे दिन भी दफ्तर नहीं गईं। इन तीन दिनों में भी घर में माँ-बेटी में कोई संवाद नहीं हुआ। टी.वी. भी नहीं चलाया गया। मम्मी अपने कमरे में लेटी कबीर के कैसेट सुनती रहतीं और शुचि अपने कमरे में लेटी कोई पॉप म्यूजिक। नौकरानी रसोई में उलझी रहती, कभी घर की सफाई करती दिखाई देती। ऐसा लगता, जैसे सारे घर से शब्द गुम हो गए हैं। बोलने, बतियाने का सारा काम सिर्फ साँसें कर रही हैं।

मम्मी ने जब शुचि को देर तक सोते देखा तो झिंझोड़कर पूछा, "शुचि बेटा! कॉलेज नहीं जाना है क्या?"

वह उठकर बैठ गई—"नहीं।"

"क्यों? छुट्टी है क्या?"

"नहीं कोई छुट्टी नहीं है। पर आज मैं कॉलेज नहीं जाऊँगी।"

"क्यों?"

"इसीलिए कि आज आपके साथ मूवी देखने जाऊँगी। अप्सरा में ऐसी पिक्चर लगी है, जिसने इस बार नौ एकेडमी अवार्ड जीते हैं।"

मम्मी मुसकराईं—"तू अपनी किसी सहेली को बुला ले। उसके साथ चली जा।"

शुचि ने उनके गले में अपनी बाँहें डाल दीं—"तुमसे अच्छी मेरी कोई सहेली नहीं है, मम्मी।"

नाश्ता करने के बाद शुचि ने एक प्लेट में डाई घोली—"मम्मी, जरा इधर आना और हाँ, चुपचाप आकर यहाँ बैठ जाओ।"

वह जैसे बिलकुल अबोध बच्ची बन गई। ड्रेसिंग टेबल के सामने बैठती हुई कुछ लाड़ भरी खीझ से बोली, "ये क्या कर रही हो तुम?"

"आपके बाल ठीक कर रही हूँ और हाँ, कल से आप अपनी ड्यूटी ज्वॉइन करेंगी।"

□

वंशज

बड़ा चौकोर कमरा है। दीवारों के साथ सोफे लगे हुए हैं। कोनों में कुछ कुरसियाँ भी रखी हुई हैं। बीच में एक बड़ी मेज है। उस पर दो-तीन अखबार पड़े हुए हैं। मंत्रीजी से मिलने की प्रतीक्षा में लोग बैठे हुए हैं। बाहर के दरवाजे से जो भी आता है, वह कमरे में बैठे लोगों पर नजर दौड़ाता है और खाली जगह ढूँढ़ता है। फिर वह किसी के साथ सटकर बैठ जाता है।

बड़े कमरे के साथ ही लगा मंत्रीजी के निजी सहायकों का कमरा है। वहाँ कई टेलीफोन रखे हैं। उनकी घंटियाँ लगातार बजती रहती हैं। कमरे में छाए सन्नाटे को वे घंटियाँ तोड़ती तो हैं, लेकिन हलकी सी दहशत भी पैदा कर देती हैं। लोगों का यह अहसास एकदम बढ़ जाता है कि वे किसी बड़े आदमी से मुलाकात करने के लिए आए हुए हैं।

सभी लगभग चुप हैं। आपस में बात भी करते हैं तो बहुत धीरे-धीरे। जो दरवाजा मंत्रीजी के कमरे की ओर खुलता है, उस पर एक हट्टा-कट्टा आदमी खड़ा है, जो एक-एक करके मुलाकातियों को अंदर जाने का इशारा करता है।

सारे सन्नाटे में सिर्फ एक आदमी चहकता, मुसकराता, आँखें झपकाता और बतियाता दिखाई देता है। उसने एक ढीला मटमैला कुरता-पैजामा पहन रखा है। कुरते में पूरे बटन नहीं लगे हैं, इसलिए वह कभी बाईं तरफ और कभी दाईं तरफ कंधे से नीचे ढुलक जाता है। वह अपने साथ बैठे व्यक्ति से कहता है, ''मेरे परदादा ने इस देश की आजादी का झंडा उस समय उठाया था, जब अंग्रेजों के सामने मुँह खोलने की किसी में हिम्मत नहीं थी। उस वक्त गांधी बाबा दक्षिण अफ्रीका से आए ही थे। जलियाँवाला बाग का खूनी नजारा मेरे परदादा ने अपनी आँखों से देखा था। जब जनरल डायर ने गोलियाँ चलवाईं, वे बाग के साथ लगे एक मकान में छिपे हुए थे। गोलियाँ चल रही थीं तड़ातड़-तड़ातड़। लाशें गिर रही थीं। लोग बुरी तरह चीख-चिल्ला रहे थे, पर

उनकी सुननेवाला कोई नहीं था। जालिम डायर चीख रहा था—फायर···फायर और गोरखा सिपाही उसके हुक्म पर गोलियाँ बरसाते जा रहे थे। हे राम! क्या नजारा था वो। जैसे ही कत्लेआम करके वे लोग बाग से बाहर निकले, मेरे परदादा सबसे पहले उस जगह पहुँचे। लोग घरों में दुबके बैठे थे। उन्होंने ललकारकर कुछ लोगों को बाहर निकाला और जुट गए उन लोगों की सेवा में, जिनकी साँसें अभी चल रही थीं।''

वह बड़ी टिमटिमाती आँखों से आसपास बैठे लोगों को देखता है—जैसे कह रहा हो, मैं कोई मामूली आदमी नहीं हूँ।

लोग उसकी बातें सुनते हैं, मुसकराते हैं और कौतूहल भरी नजर से उसे देखते हैं।

एक व्यक्ति सामने के दरवाजे से अंदर आता है। उसकी आँखें जैसे उसे लपक लेती हैं। अपनी जगह पर बैठा-बैठा वह कहता है—''आइए-आइए! आप भी मंत्रीजी से मिलने आए हैं? क्या बात है? पिछले हफ्ते ही मैंने आपका लेख पढ़ा था। क्या खूब लिखते हैं आप?''

वह व्यक्ति मुसकराता है, लेकिन उसकी मुसकराहट से ऐसा नहीं लगता कि वह इसे जानता है। वह अपनी नजर कमरे में बैठे सभी लोगों पर दौड़ाता है, जैसे पूछ रहा हो--क्या तुम भी जानते हो कि मैं एक पत्रकार हूँ। पर किसी भी चेहरे पर ऐसी स्वीकृति का कोई चिह्न नहीं है। सभी अपनी-अपनी फाइलों या छुट-फुट कागजों को अपनी गोद में लिये बैठे हैं।

वह आदमी कुछ खिसकता है, ''आइए, यहाँ बैठिए।'' फिर वह पास बैठे व्यक्ति से कहता है, ''आप जरा सा उधर खिसकिए, आप जानते नहीं ये बहुत बड़े पत्रकार हैं। इनकी कलम में बड़ा जोर है, जिसे चाहें आसमान में चढ़ा दें, जिसे चाहें जमीन पर पटक दें।''

पासवाले व्यक्ति पर उसकी बात का कोई असर हुआ हो, ऐसा नहीं लगता। वह नजर उठाकर उस आए व्यक्ति को देखता है और खिसककर उसके बैठने की जगह बनाता है।

मेरा नाम शर्मा है···रघुनंदन शर्मा। मैं रामलुभाया शर्मा का परपोता हूँ, आपने उनका नाम जरूर सुना होगा। जलियाँवाला बाग का किस्सा उनकी आँखों के सामने हुआ था। मेरे परदादा जनरल डायर के सामने छाती खोलकर खड़े हो गए थे—'ले जालिम! इतने मजलूमों के खून से अगर तेरी प्यास अभी तक नहीं बुझी है तो मेरा भी खून ले ले।'

वह अपने कुरते को दोनों हाथों से हटाकर अपनी छाती दिखाता है। अंदर से गंदी बनियान के नीचे झाँकते हुए कुछ बाल दिखाई देते हैं।

तभी आसपास बैठे लोग देखते हैं, उसके दोनों हाथ बुरी तरह काँप रहे हैं। सारा कमरा जैसे किसी राक्षस का पंजा है। मंत्रीजी से मिलने के लिए आए सभी लोग जैसे उस पंजे में समाए हुए हैं। दरवाजे के पास खड़ा वह लंबा-चौड़ा आदमी जैसे उस पंजे की अँगूठे की साथ वाली उँगली है। जब वह हिलती है तो सारा पंजा हिल जाता है। फिर हथेली में समाया हुआ एक व्यक्ति उठता है और डरता-सिकुड़ता मंत्रीजी के कमरे में प्रवेश करता है। शेष सभी लोग हथेली के कंपन के साथ हिलते हुए अपनी जगह पर स्थिर होने लगते हैं।

वह व्यक्ति पास बैठे पत्रकार से मुखातिब होता है, ''मंत्रीजी मेरे बहुत पुराने जानने वाले हैं। पिछली बार इनके हलके से कांग्रेस का उम्मीदवार जीता था, उस समय मैं कांग्रेसी था। मेरे पिता, दादा, परदादा, सभी कट्टर कांग्रेसी थे। अपने परदादा की बात मैं आपको बता ही चुका हूँ। पिछले चुनाव में मैंने कांग्रेसी उम्मीदवार का साथ दिया था, डटकर दिया था। यही मेरी खास बात है। मैं जिसका साथ देता हूँ, बस उसके लिए अपनी जान लड़ा देता हूँ। सारे इलाके में ऐसा कौन है, जो हमारे खानदान को नहीं जानता? अगर मैं कहूँ कि गधे को अपनी वोट दे दो तो उसकी पीठ पर अपना वोट चिपकाकर आ जाएँगे, ऐसा दबदबा है हमारे खानदान का।''

वह अपनी बात सुना तो पत्रकार को रहा है, पर इस तरह कि कमरे में बैठे काफी लोग उसे सुन लें। अपनी बात कहकर वह एक विजेता की नजर से इधर-उधर देखता और यह परखने की कोशिश करता है कि क्या असर हुआ है। कुछ चेहरों पर उसे कुछ हँसी, कुछ कौतूहल और कुछ प्रभावित हो जाने के आसार दिखाई देते हैं। उसकी आँखें खिल जाती हैं।

''इस बार मैंने इनका साथ देने का फैसला किया। मुझे पक्का यकीन था कि इस बार इनकी पार्टी सरकार बनाएगी। मुझे यह भी यकीन था कि अगर सरकार इनकी पार्टी की बनी तो ये मंत्री जरूर बनेंगे।''

वह खिली हुई धूप की तरह मुसकराता है। अपनी छोटी-छोटी मूँछों पर हाथ फेरते हुए कहता है, ''राजनीति तो हमारे खानदान के छोटे-से-छोटे बच्चे की साँसों में बसी हुई है जी। हमें यह अंदाजा लगाते देर नहीं लगती कि इस बार कौन जीतेगा और हमारा अंदाजा कभी गलत नहीं निकलता। इस मामले में हमसे कभी चूक नहीं होती। परमेश्वर की बड़ी दया है हम पर।''

इस बार पंजे की उँगली कई बार हिली है और कुछ लोग मंत्रीजी से मिलने में सफल हो गए हैं। उसका नंबर अभी तक नहीं आया, इस बात की हलकी सी उलझन उसके चेहरे पर झलकती है, किंतु वह दूसरे क्षण ही संयत हो जाता है।

''आप क्या समझते हैं, क्या मंत्री की कुरसी इन्हें मिल जाती, अगर मैं इनका साथ न देता? ये तो अकसर कहते हैं, अपने साथियों के बीच भी मानते हैं कि मेरी जीत का

सेहरा तो रघुनंदन शर्मा के सिर बँधता है। इलेक्शन लड़ना कोई बच्चों का खेल है क्या? इस खेल में तो रघुनंदन शर्मा जैसा खिलाड़ी साथ होना चाहिए।''

वह फिर गरवीली मुसकराहट से चारों तरफ देखता है।

एकाएक उसकी आँखें चमक उठती हैं। सामने दरवाजे से एक बड़ी कद्दावर शख्सियत कमरे में प्रवेश करती है। उसकी चाल-ढाल और कपड़ों से ऐसा लगता है कि वह भी कोई ऊँची हस्ती है। उसके साथ दो और व्यक्ति हैं, जो अपनी शक्ल-सूरत से ही उसके सहायक दिखते हैं।

पहले वह अपनी जगह पर बैठा-बैठा कसमसाता है, जैसे किसी खिलौने में चाबी भरी जा रही है। फिर वह एकदम उछलता है और बाहरी दरवाजे के पास पहुँच जाता है।

''आइए-आइए, राणा साहब।'' वह अपने दोनों हिलते हाथों से उनका हाथ थाम लेता है—''पिछले असेंबली चुनाव के बाद आज आपके दर्शन हुए।''

वह आदमी कुछ इस ढंग से देखता है जैसे पूछ रहा हो—तुम कौन हो भाई?

वह कहता है, ''आपके चुनाव में मैंने घर-घर जाकर आपका प्रचार किया था। लोगों को घरों से निकालकर पोलिंग बूथों तक पहुँचाया था।''

वह आदमी मुसकराया है, ''कैसे हैं आप?'' कहकर वह कुछ सोचने लगता है, जैसे कुछ याद कर रहा हो।

''मैं रघुनंदन शर्मा, पंडित रामलुभाया शर्मा का परपोता।''

वह आदमी एकदम सहज हो जाता है। वह रघुनंदन शर्मा के दोनों हाथों को अच्छी तरह दबाता है और धीरे-धीरे पी.ए. के कमरे की ओर बढ़ने लगता है। फिर वहीं मेज से कागज का एक टुकड़ा उठाता है, उस पर कुछ लिखता है और पी.ए. को दे देता है। पी.ए. कागज पर नजर दौड़ाता है और एकदम सीधा खड़ा हो जाता है, जैसे किसी सिपाही को उसके अफसर ने अचानक अटेंशन में कर दिया हो।

''मंत्रीजी को मेरा नाम बताइए और कहिए कि मैं तुरंत मिलना चाहता हूँ।''

''जी सर···।'' कहता हुआ पी.ए. मंत्री के कमरे में सीधे घुस जाता है। रघुनंदन शर्मा उसके पास खड़ा सबकुछ देखता रहता है।

दूसरे ही क्षण पी.ए. मंत्रीजी के कमरे से निकलता है, ''साहब, आपको अंदर याद कर रहे हैं।''

वह आदमी भारी कदमों से धीरे-धीरे इस तरह आगे बढ़ता है जैसे वह हाथी हो, और कमरे में मंत्रीजी से मिलने की प्रतीक्षा में बैठे सभी लोग मिमियाती हुई बकरियाँ हों।

पंडित रामलुभाया का परपोता आकर अपनी जगह बैठ जाता है।

''आप जानते हैं यह आदमी कौन है, जो अभी-अभी मंत्रीजी के कमरे में गया

है?'' वह साथ बैठे पत्रकार से पूछता है।

पत्रकार गरदन हिलाता है, ''जानता हूँ।''

''अपने प्रदेश में इनकी तूती बोलती है। ये मुख्यमंत्री नहीं हैं, लेकिन गृह विभाग इनके पास है। इनके काम में दखलअंदाजी करने की हिम्मत मुख्यमंत्री भी नहीं करता।''

पत्रकार गरदन हिलाकर हामी भर देता है। फिर वह पी.ए. को इशारा करता है, ''मंत्रीजी से मेरा सिर्फ दो मिनट का काम है।''

पी.ए. पत्रकार को जानता है। यह भी जानता है कि मंत्रीजी उसे बहुत मानते हैं। ''मैंने आपका कार्ड अंदर भेज दिया है। जरा सा खाली होते ही वे आपको बुला लेंगे।''

रामलुभाया का परपोता कहता है, ''किसी का काम हो या न हो, मेरा तो होना ही है। मंत्रीजी मुझे नजरअंदाज नहीं कर सकते। आखिर उन्हें अगला चुनाव भी तो लड़ना है।''

वह हँसता है, ''अब वे जमाने लद गए जब सरकार चुनी जाती थी और पूरे पाँच साल काम करती रहती थी। अब तो सरकारें दस-दस, बारह-बारह खपच्चियों पर खड़ी रहती हैं। एक खपच्ची खिसकी, सरकार भरभराकर गिरी। मंत्री लोग तो बस अपने दिन गिनते रहते हैं, अब गए कि तब गए।'' वह जोर से हँसता है। सब उसकी तरफ देखकर हँसने लगते हैं।

इसी बीच पत्रकार का नंबर भी आ गया है। उससे पहले तीन-चार लोग और निपट जाते हैं। पत्रकार मंत्रीजी के कमरे से बाहर आकर अपना ब्रीफकेस ठीक करने लगता है। इतने में मंत्रीजी का दरवाजा खुलता है और वे बड़ी तेजी से बाहर निकलते हैं, कमरे में बैठे प्रतीक्षा करते लोग हड़बड़ाकर खड़े हो जाते हैं। मंत्रीजी जिस ढंग से बाहर निकलते हैं, उससे लगता है उनकी मेज पर कहीं से दो-चार साँप आकर गिर गए होंगे। मंत्रीजी बड़ी हड़बड़ी से बाहर जा रहे हैं। उनके पीछे-पीछे पी.ए. दौड़ रहा है। दरवाजे पर पहरा देनेवाला हट्टा-कट्टा आदमी कह रहा है, ''मंत्रीजी, आज अब किसी से नहीं मिलेंगे। प्रधानमंत्री का बुलावा आ गया है। कैबिनेट की अर्जेंट मीटिंग है।'' कहता हुआ वह भी कमरे से बाहर निकल जाता है।

पूरे कमरे में सन्नाटा छा जाता है। प्रतीक्षारत लोगों में कुछ लोग दूर-दूर के शहरों से भी आए हुए हैं। कुछ लोग कई घंटे से वहाँ बैठे हुए हैं। किसी की समझ में कुछ नहीं आ रहा है कि अब वे क्या करें? वे ऐसे स्टेशन पर खड़े हैं, जहाँ से एक गाड़ी धड़धड़ाती हुई चली गई है और दूसरी कब आएगी, यह किसी को भी पता नहीं है।

इस गुमगुमी में पंडित रामलुभाया का परपोता उसी तरह चहक रहा है—''मैं कहता था ना, खपच्चियों पर खड़ी सरकार का क्या भरोसा? अजी साहब सियासत के

खेल में हमारी कई पीढ़ियाँ निकल गई हैं। भूकंप के झटके लोग तब महसूस करते हैं जब सचमुच भूकंप आ जाता है। लेकिन हमें तो उसका अनुमान पहले ही हो जाता है। आखिर चार पीढ़ियों से हम झख तो नहीं मार रहे हैं।''

वह खूब जोर से हँसता है।

सभी उसे देखने लगते हैं और मुसकराने लगते हैं।

□

बेटी

यह शब्द उसके हाथ से छिटक के बहुत दूर जा गिरा था। बहुत सहेजा था उसने इस शब्द को। आमतौर पर बेटियों को यह शब्द सहेजना नहीं पड़ता। यह शब्द उन्हें जन्म लेते ही मिल जाता है और सारा जीवन उनके साथ चिपका रहता है।

शब्द उसे भी मिला। लेकिन अपनी जगह बदल ली। जिस स्त्री के गर्भ से उसने जन्म लिया था, वहाँ पहले से ही चार बेटियाँ मौजूद थीं। संसार में उसका आना अंगूर न बनकर नीम की निबोलियों जैसा था। उस कडुवाहट और बेस्वादगी में जब पाँचवीं बेटी की माँ को पता लगा कि उसकी मौसेरी बहन उसे गोद लेने को तैयार है तो उसे लगा था, नई जनमी बेटी के मुँह में उसके सूखे स्तनों की बजाय चाँदी की चम्मच आ गई है।

इस घर में वह ऐसी माँ की बेटी बन गई, जो पिछले दस साल से सारी पाठ-पूजा और मनौतियों के बावजूद अपनी कोख में कोई फूल नहीं खिला सकी थी। उसे उस पिता की गोद मिल गई थी, जिसमें चटाई का रत्ती भर भी खुरदुरापन नहीं था, बस मखमल थी। बड़ी मुलायम, गदीली मखमल।

उस पर बेटी शब्द की बौछार हो रही थी। इस बौछार में भीगते-भीगते वह बड़ी हो गई। उसे पता नहीं लगा कि कब वह स्कूल से निकलकर कॉलेज पहुँच गई। कब उसके माता-पिता को लगने लगा, वह विवाह के योग्य हो गई है।

उन्हीं दिनों उसे यह भी पता लगा कि कई सौ किलोमीटर दूर एक स्त्री है, जिसने उसे जन्म दिया था। उसकी चार बड़ी बहनें और एक भाई भी है। एक ऐसा व्यक्ति भी है, जो उसका पिता कहलाने की सीमा से बहुत दूर चला गया है।

चलिए, इनके कुछ नाम भी रख लेते हैं। लड़की को नवनीत मान लेते हैं। जिस स्त्री ने उसे जन्म दिया था, वह लाजवंती है और जिसने उसे बेटी बनाया है, उसे भागवंती कह लेते हैं। दोनों बापों के पूरे-पूरे नामों को जानने की जरूरत नहीं है। हमारे

यहाँ जाति सूचक नाम ही पूरे नामों को दरशा देते हैं। इसलिए जन्म देने वाले पुरुष को चावला मान लेते हैं और पिता की मखमली गोद देने वाले को गुलाटी कह लेते हैं। इतने नामों से अभी कहानी का काम चल जाएगा। आगे जरूरत पड़ी तो कुछ नाम और गढ़ लेंगे।

सबकुछ कितना ठीक लग रहा था। चावला और लाजवंती के मन में एक कसक है कि उनकी जायी एक बेटी उनसे बहुत दूर है। उन्होंने अपनी चारों बेटियों को थोड़ा-बहुत पढ़ा-लिखाकर और फिर ब्याह का जोड़ा पहनाकर विदा कर दिया है। अब आगे उनका भाग्य। पति-पत्नी दोनों ही कहते हैं कि हम बच्चों को जन्म तो दे सकते हैं, लेकिन भाग्य की रेखाएँ तो ऊपरवाला अपनी कलम से लिखता है। उसने चार बेटियों का भाग्य आम नीली स्याही से लिख दिया, लेकिन अनचाही नवनीत का भाग्य लिखते समय उसके हाथ में सोने की कलम थी और दावात में सुनहरी स्याही।

कितने बरसों तक गुलाटी और भागवंती अपनी दुलारी नवनीत पर अपना दुलार लुटाते रहे। वे दोनों उसका नाम नहीं लेते थे, सिर्फ बेटी, बिटिया, बचड़ी कहकर ही पुकारते थे। गुलाटी कहता था, इसके आते ही हम यह भूल गए हैं कि अमावस भी होती है। ऐसी चाँदनी खिली है कि घर तो जगमग हो ही गया है, काम-धंधा भी ऐसा चमका है कि उसके सगे-संबंधियों को यह चिंता सताने लगी है कि ब्याह करके नवनीत तो अपने घर चली जाएगी, गुलाटी की इतनी धन-दौलत का वारिस कौन होगा?

एक दिन गुलाटी को भी ऐसा महसूस हुआ। उस दिन भागवंती को उसने कुछ ज्यादा ध्यान से देखा। उसे लगा, यह औरत तो एकदम बूढ़ी हो गई है। इसके बालों में कितनी सफेदी आ गई है। आगे के दो दाँत भी टूट गए हैं। आँखों पर चढ़ा चश्मा जब देखो नाक के नीचे खिसकता रहता है।

गुलाटी को पिछले साल अपने बालों में कुछ सफेद तार नजर आए थे। उसे बड़ा झटका लगा था। पैंतालीस पार करते ही वह बूढ़ा तो नहीं हो गया। उसने डाई लगानी शुरू कर दी थी।

चंचल उसकी फैक्टरी में पैकिंग डिपार्टमेंट में थी। उसके मैनेजर मेहता ने बताया था—बिचारी मुसीबतों की मारी है। शादी के तीन साल बाद ही पति चल बसा था। फिर वह हँसते हुए पंजाबी में बोला था—विचारियाँ रंडियाँ तो रंडेपा कट लैण पर रंडे नहीं कट्टण दिंदे (बिचारी विधवाएँ तो अपना वैधव्य काट लें, पर रंडुए नहीं काटने देते)।

गुलाटी की उस पर नजर टिक गई। बूढ़े मेहताजी ने इस नजर को भाँप लिया।

"चंचल, कौन-कौन है तेरे परिवार में?"

वह बहुत कम बोलती थी। फैक्टरी में कारों-स्कूटरों में लगने वाले रबड़ पार्ट्स बनते थे। और भी कितनी औरतें वहाँ काम करती थीं। वे सब हँसी-ठट्टा भी करती

थीं और चुटकियाँ भी लेती थीं।

"तू कैसी चंचल है? न हँसती है, न बोलती है, बस सारा दिन काम में लगी रहती है।"

उसने मेहताजी की तरफ देखा—"बूढ़े माँ-बाप हैं। दो बड़ी बहनें अपने घरों में हैं। एक भाई गोवा में नौकरी करता है।"

"घर का सारा खर्च तुम चलाती हो?"

वह मुसकराई। मेहता ने देखा, इसे अगर ठीक ढंग की देखभाल मिल जाए तो यह बड़ी साधारण सी दिखने वाली लड़की एक खूबसूरत औरत में बदल सकती है।

"और कोई कमानेवाला नहीं।"

"भाई कुछ मदद करता है?" मेहता ने पूछा।

"उसका अपना ही पूरा नहीं पड़ता। बीवी और तीन बच्चों को लेकर परदेस में रहना क्या आसान है?"

"तुम चिंता न करो।" मेहता बहुत हमदर्दी दिखाते हुए बोला, "मैं गुलाटी साहब से कहूँगा। वह तुम्हारी जरूर मदद करेंगे। तुम जानती हो...वो बहुत अच्छे इनसान हैं।"

चंचल के नेत्रों में कृतज्ञता झलक आई—"यह उन्हीं की मेहरबानी है कि मुझे नौकरी मिल गई। कम-से-कम दो वक्त की रोटी तो नसीब हो जाती है।"

कुछ दिन बाद मेहता ने उसे बुलाकर उसके हाथ में एक लिफाफा थमा दिया।

"इसमें कुछ रुपए हैं। गुलाटी साहब ने कहा है, जब भी कोई जरूरत हो, निस्संकोच बता देना। वो पूरी मदद करेंगे।"

मेहता ने एक स्वामिभक्त सेवक की भूमिका निभा दी। आगे के रास्ते पर ज्यादा कंकड़-पत्थर भी नहीं थे, न उलटे-सीधे मोड़ थे। सबकुछ उसी तरह हुआ जैसे होता है। गुलाटी ने एक फ्लैट खरीद लिया। चंचल के चेहरे पर आए परिवर्तन को सबसे पहले उसके साथ काम करने वाली औरतों ने देखा। फिर उसके माँ-बाप भी महसूस करने लगे।

लेकिन मेहता को कुछ बेचैनी सी रहने लगी। उसे महसूस हो रहा था, उसने गुलाटी के लिए कितना बड़ा काम करवा दिया है, लेकिन इतना बड़ा काम करने के लिए गुलाटी को उसका जिस तरह शुक्रगुजार होना चाहिए, वह नहीं है। फैक्टरी का काम तो वह बरसों से सँभाल रहा है। इसी काम का उसे वेतन मिलता है। यह ठीक है कि इस उम्र में उसके कितने ही साथी रिटायर होकर सुबह-शाम अपने हमउम्रों के साथ पार्क में बैठकर पुराने दिनों की जुगाली करते हैं या किसी नुक्कड़ में बैठकर ताश खेलते हैं। गुलाटी ने उसे अपनी सारी फैक्टरी के प्रोडक्शन का इंचार्ज बना रखा है और अच्छी-खासी तनख्वाह भी देता है।

यह ऐसा ही है जैसे किसी को दोनों वक्त भरपेट अच्छा भोजन मिलता हो। किंतु भोजन करने मात्र से ही तो पूरी तृप्ति नहीं मिलती। भोजन के बाद दो-चार अच्छे डकार न आएँ तो बहुत से लोगों को भोजन का पूरा स्वाद नहीं मिलता।

मेहता ने गुलाटी का बढ़िया काम कर दिया था, इसकी उसे तृप्ति तो थी। लेकिन यह तृप्ति ही उसे बेचैन कर रही थी। दो-चार डकार आ जाएँ तो बेचैनी दूर हो।

पहला डकार उसने अपने स्टॉफ में ही लिया—महिला कर्मचारियों के बीच। किसी ने पूछ लिया—"मेहताजी, आजकल चंचल बहुत छुट्टियाँ लेने लग गई है। आती भी है तो अपनी मन मरजी से, उसके रंग-ढंग भी बहुत बदले हुए लगते हैं।"

उसने कहा, "देखो, तुम लोग अपने काम से काम रखा करो। चंचल अब पुरानी चंचल नहीं है। गुलाटी साहब ने उसे कुछ अहम जिम्मेदारियाँ सौंप दी हैं। सेल्स प्रमोशन के लिए वे चंचल की पूरी मदद लेते हैं।"

यह सब कहते-कहते वह बहुत मधुर-मधुर मुसकराता था और एक-दो बार उसकी बाईं आँख अपने आप ही दब गई थी।

इस डकार की अनुगूँज सारी फैक्टरी में सुनाई दी और देखा-देखी सभी कर्मचारी डकार लेने लगे।

दूसरी डकार उसने भागवंती के सामने ली। दोपहर के बाद गुलाटी साहब फैक्टरी नहीं आए थे। वह फैक्टरी बंद करवाकर चाभियाँ देने घर चला आया।

चाभियाँ लेते हुए भागवंती ने पूछा, "क्यों मेहताजी, गुलाटीजी फैक्टरी में नहीं थे?"

मेहता का चेहरा बड़ा मासूम बन गया—"मैं क्या बोलूँ बीबीजी, आजकल गुलाटीजी फैक्टरी की तरफ बहुत कम ध्यान देते हैं। कितने ही ऑर्डर पेंडिंग पड़े रहते हैं। कच्चा माल नहीं होगा तो प्रोडक्शन कैसे होगा। कई बार तो कर्मचारियों के पास कोई काम नहीं होता। वो सारा दिन हाथ पर हाथ धरे बैठे रहते हैं।"

भागवंती के चेहरे पर चिंता की रेखाएँ उभर आईं—"क्यों? गुलाटीजी कहाँ रहते हैं?"

"अब मैं क्या बताऊँ, जितने मुँह उतनी बातें। हमारी फैक्टरी में ही एक औरत काम करती है। विधवा है, सुना है सारा दिन उसी के साथ गुजारते हैं। भगवान् जाने कितनी सच्चाई है इस बात में।" उदासी के बोझ में मेहता का सिर झुक गया।

भागवंती किसी सोच में डूब गई थी। उसका पति कुछ बदला-बदला सा लगता है, इसका अहसास उसे भी हुआ था। किंतु ऐसा कुछ होगा, उसने नहीं सोचा था।

मेहता ने सिर उठाकर भागवंती की ओर देखा—"बीबीजी, एक बात बताइए। इस मकान के अलावा भी आपका इस शहर में कोई और मकान या फ्लैट है?"

''नहीं तो।'' वह कुछ चौंककर बोली, ''यही एक मकान है?''

''याद कीजिए, गुलाटी साहब ने क्या कभी आपको यह नहीं बताया कि जमुनापार में उनका एक फ्लैट है?''

''मुझे तो नहीं बताया। हाँ, यह आपको कैसे मालूम हुआ?''

''यह बात तो फैक्टरी में सभी को पता है। लोगों को यह भी पता है कि चंचल को लेकर गुलाटी साहब अपना ज्यादा वक्त वहीं गुजारते हैं।''

मेहता घर से बाहर निकला तो उसे लगा कि इस लंबे डकार के बाद उसके अंदर की भरी हुई गैस बाहर निकल गई है और बहुत हद तक उसकी बेचैनी दूर हो गई है।

अब भागवंती की बेचैनी अपने चरम पर थी। वह भी किसी के सामने उबल पड़ना चाहती थी। किसके सामने उबले? नवनीत अपने कमरे में पढ़ रही थी। उसके पैर उस तरफ बढ़ गए। नवनीत ने देखा, माँ बहुत बेचैन है। उसकी आँखें लाल हैं और मुँह से झाग फूट रही है।

रात के दस बजने वाले थे।

''क्यों मम्मी, पापा अभी तक नहीं आए? आजकल वो बहुत देर से आने लग गए हैं।''

''आजकल वो बहुत से गुल भी खिलाने लग गए हैं।'' फिर उसे लगा, वह बेटी को क्या बताए?

''आज आने दे उन्हें?'' कहती हुई वह वापस चली गई।

आधी रात को जब गुलाटी आया, नवनीत सो गई थी और भागवंती अंगारों पर लेटी हुई करवटें बदल रही थी।

सारी बातें रात को ही हो गईं।

''आपने जमुनापार एक फ्लैट ले रखा है?''

''हाँ।''

''वहाँ किसी औरत के साथ रंगरलियाँ मनाते हो?''

गुलाटी ने सभी स्थितियों के लिए अपने आपको पूरी तरह तैयार कर रखा था।

''हाँ।''

''वह औरत आपकी फैक्टरी में काम करती है?''

गुलाटी ने मानते हुए गरदन हिला दी—''हाँ...।''

भागवंती के नथुने फूल गए।

''शर्म नहीं आती?''

गुलाटी ने उसे घूरकर देखा।

''तुम मुझे एक बेटा दे सकती हो?''

भागवंती को कुछ सूझा नहीं, क्या जवाब दे।

"अगर मैं बेटा नहीं दे सकती तो आप इधर-उधर मुँह मारते फिरेंगे?"

"सुनो भागवंती, मुझे बेटा चाहिए। मैंने इतना बड़ा कारोबार खड़ा किया है; उसे देखने-सँभालने वाला कोई चाहिए। मुझे अपना वारिस चाहिए।"

"हमारी बेटी है...दामाद आएगा, उसके बच्चे होंगे। क्या वे हमारे वारिस नहीं होंगे।"

गुलाटी ने उसे बड़ी पैनी नजर से देखा—"किसी दूसरे के बगीचे से तोड़कर तुमने एक पौधा अपने आँगन में रोपा है। कल वह पौधा भी तुम्हारा नहीं रहेगा। किसी पराये आँगन में उसमें जो फूल आएँगे, मैं उन पर भरोसा नहीं करता। मुझे अपने आँगन में अपने फूल चाहिए।"

"आप क्या करेंगे। उस विधवा से शादी करेंगे?"

"यूँ समझो कि मैंने उससे शादी कर ली है।"

"मैं यह बरदाश्त नहीं करूँगी। आप मेरे सिर पर सौतन लाकर बैठाना चाहते हैं?"

गुलाटी बड़ी मिन्नत भरे स्वर में बोला, "देखो, भागवंती, मैं तुम्हें दुःख नहीं पहुँचाना चाहता, न ही तुम्हारे साथ अन्याय करना चाहता हूँ। मेरी भावना को भी समझने की कोशिश करो। हमारा अपना कोई बेटा होता तो मुझे यह सब करने की जरूरत नहीं थी।"

"आप मेरी बेबसी का फायदा उठाना चाहते हैं? मैं यह सब नहीं होने दूँगी।"

यह कोहराम रात भर चलता रहा।

नवनीत सुबह कॉलेज चली गई। किंतु उसे इस बात का अहसास हो गया था कि रात भर आँधी चलती रही थी और घर की खिड़कियाँ-दरवाजे तेजी से खड़खड़ाते रहे थे। कुछ दिन पहले नवनीत की शादी की बात चली थी। इंतजार केवल इस बात का था कि उसकी परीक्षाएँ हो जाएँ। परीक्षाएँ हो गईं तो सबकुछ पक्का हो गया। गुलाटी ने बड़ी धूमधाम से अपनी बेटी की शादी की।

उन्हीं दिनों चंचल ने एक बेटे को जन्म दिया। गुलाटी को यह अहसास अंदर तक छू गया कि वह अब एक बेटे का बाप है।

अब वह ज्यादा समय अपने जमुनापार वाले फ्लैट में ही गुजारता था। उसके सभी रिश्तेदारों और नए बने समधियों को भी सारी बात का पता लग गया था। भागवंती बिलकुल अकेली हो गई थी। बेटी और दामाद कभी-कभी आते थे। उन्हें देखकर उदासी और बढ़ जाती थी।

एक दिन गुलाटी ने उससे कहा, "भागवंती, बेटी भी अपने घर चली गई है। तुम

एकदम अकेली हो गई हो। कहो तो चंचल को यहाँ ले आऊँ। इतना बड़ा मकान है। फर्स्ट फ्लोर पर वह रह लेगी। घर की मालकिन तो तुम्हीं हो। तुम्हारा यह हक तुमसे कोई नहीं छीनेगा। अब तो वह मेरे बेटे की माँ भी है। वह तुम्हारा भी बेटा है। उसके यहाँ होने से कितनी रौनक आ जाएगी। बच्चे के साथ तुम्हारा मन भी बदला रहेगा।''

भागवंती की आँखें एकदम लाल हो गईं, ''मैं जानती थी कि आप यही कहेंगे। मैं अपने जीते-जी उस चुड़ैल को यहाँ कदम नहीं रखने दूँगी, मेरे मरने के बाद उसे यहाँ ले आना।''

अपनी बिरादरी में, अपने बाजार में, अपने मिलने-जुलने वालों में गुलाटी की पहले ही काफी बदनामी हो चुकी थी। वह उसे अब और बढ़ाना नहीं चाहता था।

पहले उसका इस घर में आना कम हुआ, फिर एकदम बंद हो गया। मकान के ऊपर के दो भाग किराए पर उठे हुए थे। भागवंती के गुजर-बसर के लिए उतना काफी था।

देखते-देखते कई बरस गुजर गए। चंचल ने एक और बेटे को जन्म दिया। इन बरसों में नवनीत भी दो बच्चों की माँ बन गई। बेटी, दामाद, नाती, नातिन हर दूसरे-चौथे दिन आ जाते थे। लगता था, ऐसे भी चलता रहे तो भी ठीक ही है। आखिर यह जिंदगी है क्या? न भागती है, न पूरी तरह ठहरती है। यह तो बस कटती है, घसीटती है। एक पूरी कतार है जो घसीटते-घसीटते आगे बढ़ती है और किसी अंधे कुएँ में गिरती जाती है।

किंतु उस घसीटती हुई जिंदगी में भी कभी कुछ ऐसा हो जाता है, जो अनहोना सा लगता है। यह अनहोना ही यह अहसास कराता है कि जिंदगी सिर्फ घसीटती ही नहीं, वह कभी-कभी लड़खड़ाती भी है और अपने होने का ऐलान करती है।

बरसों बाद ऐसा ही कुछ भागवंती के साथ हो गया। नाती का जन्मदिन था। वह बेटी के घर गई हुई थी। गुलाटी दल-बल सहित उस घर पर जा धमका, जहाँ वह पिछले कई सालों से नहीं आया था। उसके साथ ट्रक भरकर उसकी फैक्टरी के लोग थे। अदालत का ऑर्डर था। अदालत का कर्मचारी भी साथ था। उसके जवान होते हुए दोनों बेटे साथ थे। अदालत ने लंबी सुनवाई के बाद एकतरफा यह फैसला दे दिया था कि गुलाटी की तलाकशुदा बीवी भागवंती उसके मकान पर जबरन कब्जा किए हुए है। अदालत ने आदेश दे दिया था कि कानूनी रूप से गुलाटी उस जायदाद का मालिक है। इसीलिए भागवंती को वहाँ से बेदखल करके उसे उस मकान पर कब्जा करने का हक है।

फैक्टरी के कर्मचारियों ने दरवाजे पर लगा ताला तोड़ दिया और भागवंती का सामान बाहर निकालकर फेंकने लगे।

गली के बहुत से लोग उस मकान के सामने इकट्ठे हो गए। पुलिस को भी खबर हो गई। भागवंती को भी सूचना भेज दी गई। उसका दामाद, बेटी और समधियाने के कितने लोग भी आ गए।

गुलाटी को भी कुछ लोग समझाने लगे—"गुलाटी साहब, आप यह क्या कर रहे हैं? आखिर भागवंती आपकी पत्नी है।"

"यह मेरी पत्नी नहीं है। कई साल पहले ही मैं उसे तलाक दे चुका हूँ।"

उसने अदालत का वह फैसला भी दिखा दिया, जिसमें एकतरफा तलाक मंजूर कर लिया गया था।

"आपको अपनी बेटी का भी खयाल नहीं आया? वह तो आपका अपना खून है।"

"वह मेरा खून नहीं है। मेरा खून मेरे ये दो बेटे हैं।"

पुलिस के हस्तक्षेप और गली के बहुत से लोगों के जमा हो जाने से अदालती काररवाई कुछ देर के लिए रुक गई थी। गुलाटी भी स्थिति को अधिक बिगाड़ना नहीं चाहता था। ड्राइंगरूम में पुलिस इंस्पेक्टर, गुलाटी के कुछ रिश्तेदार, भागवंती, नवनीत, उसका पति और ससुर बैठे हुए थे। कॉलोनी की वेलफेयर सोसाइटी के कुछ पदाधिकारी भी आ गए थे। वे समझौते का कोई रास्ता निकालने की कोशिश कर रहे थे।

गुलाटी और नवनीत आमने-सामने बैठे थे। दोनों ने एक-दूसरे को कनखियों से देखा था, पर कोई बात नहीं की थी। नवनीत की गोद में उसका एक वर्ष का बच्चा खेल रहा था।

दोनों के बीच एक मूक संवाद चल रहा था।

"आप मेरे पापा हैं, आपकी गोद में पलकर मैं बड़ी हुई हूँ। आज आप मेरी बूढ़ी माँ को घर से निकालने के लिए पूरी फौज लेकर आ गए हैं? इनका क्या बनेगा, यह आपने बिलकुल नहीं सोचा?"

"तुम्हें हमेशा मैंने अपनी बेटी माना। बेटे के लालच में मैंने एक और शादी कर ली। क्या बुरा किया? जिस फ्लैट में हम इतने बरसों से रह रहे हैं, अब वो हमें पूरा नहीं पड़ता। तेरी माँ को समझाने की मैंने बड़ी कोशिश की, पर वह जिद्दी औरत अपनी जिद पर अड़ी रही। मेरे सामने और कोई रास्ता नहीं था।"

"इतने बरसों में आपने अपनी बेटी को कभी याद नहीं किया। आप नाना बन गए हैं।"

"तुमने मेरे बेटों को देखा? ये तेरे भाई हैं।"

नवनीत की गोद का बच्चा कुछ कसमसाया और रोने लगा। नवनीत उसे पुचकारने लगी। गुलाटी का मन किया कि वह आगे बढ़कर बच्चे को अपनी गोद में ले ले। उसने

नवनीत की ओर देखा। उसने बच्चे को अपनी गोद में कसकर भींच लिया। उसका चेहरा एकदम सख्त था।

गुलाटी के बेटे बार-बार उसके पास आते थे और फिर बाहर चले जाते थे। नवनीत ने एक बार उन्हें नजर भरकर देखा—कितने सुंदर हैं, कितने स्मार्ट, उसका चेहरा कुछ तरल हो गया।

एक समझौते पर सभी की सहमति हो गई। गुलाटी के पास तीन सौ गज का एक प्लॉट है। उसे वह भागवंती को दे देगा। साथ में पाँच लाख रुपए भी देगा।

सभी लोग उठकर एक-दूसरे से बातचीत करने लगे। बड़े तनाव से भरे हुए वातावरण में कुछ सहजता आ गई।

नवनीत अपने सोफे से उठी। सामने खड़ा गुलाटी दो-तीन लोगों से बातचीत कर रहा था। नवनीत को उठते हुए देखा तो आगे बढ़कर उसने नवनीत के बच्चे को चूमा और नवनीत के सिर पर हाथ रखते हुए बोला, ''तुम भी मेरी बेटी जैसी हो।''

नवनीत के सारे शरीर में जैसे बिजली की तरंगें फैल गईं। अपने सिर पर रखा हुआ हाथ उसे आग के गोले जैसा लगा। उसने गुलाटी का हाथ बुरी तरह झटक दिया। फिर एकदम उसकी चीख निकल गई। उसके रोने की आवाज से कुछ देर के लिए सबकुछ थम गया।

□□□